THE FIRST DAY ON THE SOMME

MARTIN MIDDLEBROOK

Martin Middlebrook

Pen & Sword
MILITARY

First published in Great Britain in 1971 by Allen Lane.

Reprinted in 2003 by Leo Cooper.

Published in this format in 2006 by
Pen & Sword Military
An imprint of
Pen & Sword Books Ltd
47 Church Street
Barnsley
South Yorkshire
S70 2AS

ISBN 1 84415 465 3
ISBN 978 1 84415 465 4

A CIP catalogue record for this book is
available from the British Library

Printed and bound in England
By CPI UK

Pen & Sword Books Ltd incorporates the Imprints of
Pen & Sword Aviation, Pen & Sword Maritime, Pen & Sword Military, Wharncliffe Local History, Pen & Sword Select, Pen & Sword Military Classics and Leo Cooper.

For a complete list of Pen & Sword titles please contact
PEN & SWORD BOOKS LIMITED
47 Church Street, Barnsley, South Yorkshire, S70 2AS, England
E-mail: enquiries@pen-and-sword.co.uk
Website: www.pen-and-sword.co.uK

This book is dedicated to the front-line soldiers of all nations, 1914-1918

Contents

List of Maps

Maps drawn by Leo Vernon

List of Plates

Abbreviations

General	Gen.
Lieutenant-General	Lieut-Gen.
Major-General	Maj.-Gen.
Brigadier-General	Brig.-Gen.
Lieutenant-Colonel	Lieut-Col.
Major	Maj.
Captain	Capt.
Lieutenant	Lieut
Second-Lieutenant	2nd Lieut
Regimental Sergeant Major	R.S.M.
Company Sergeant Major	C.S.M.
Battery Sergeant Major	B.S.M.
Quartermaster Sergeant	Q.M.S.
Sergeant	Sgt
Lance Sergeant	L/Sgt
Corporal	Cpl
Bombardier	Bdr
Lance Corporal	L/Cpl
Private	Pte
Rifleman	Rfmn
Drummer	Drmr
Bugler	Bglr
Driver	Dvr
Trooper	Tpr
Gunner	Gnr
Sapper	Spr
Royal Horse Artillery	R.H.A.
Royal Field Artillery	R.F.A.
Royal Garrison Artillery	R.G.A.
Royal Engineers	R.E.
Royal Army Medical Corps	R.A.M.C.
Royal Flying Corps	R.F.C.

The Men

Company Sergeant Major Percy Chappell
1st Somerset Light Infantry
4th Division

Lieutenant-Colonel Reginald Bastard, D.S.O.
2nd Lincolns
8th Division

Private 'Paddy' Kennedy
18th Manchesters (3rd Manchester Pals)
30th Division

Private Billy McFadzean
14th Royal Irish Rifles (Belfast Young Citizens)
36th (Ulster) Division

Private Dick King
10th King's Own Yorkshire Light Infantry
21st Division

Lieutenant Philip Howe
10th West Yorks
17th (Northern) Division

Bugler Bill Soar
1/7th Sherwood Foresters (Robin Hood Rifles)
46th (North Midland) Division

Lance Corporal Charles Matthews
6th Northamptons
18th (Eastern) Division

Private Albert McMillan
16th Middlesex (Public Schools Battalion)
29th Division

Lieutenant Henry Webber
7th South Lancs
19th (Western) Division

These ten soldiers have been chosen as the principal representatives in the story of the Army of 1916. They are listed in their order of appearance in the book and with the ranks they held and their units on the day of the battle.

Author's Preface to Replica Edition

The First Day on the Somme was the result of a visit to the Western Front four years earlier from which I had returned emotionally moved, not just by the large numbers of British cemeteries and graves, but by the frequency of the date '1st July 1916' on the headstones. I decided that, were I to write a book about the fateful opening day of the Battle of the Somme, it would not only give me access to original sources but an excuse to talk to those who had taken part. As I had written nothing longer than a business letter since leaving school and becoming a poultry farmer, the prospect of my book being published was at best remote.

Initially my plan proceeded favourably. The official wartime documents had just been released to the Public Record Office and the men, mostly retired but still young enough to remember reliably, were willing to help someone who had taken the trouble to carry out the research into their unit's part in the battle. I decided that I needed a minimum of a hundred men to get a reasonable cross section of experiences; to my surprise 535 British and 20 Germans eventually responded to my appeals.

I pressed on and wrote ten chapters. I stumbled on the technique of allowing the participants to describe their experiences on that day directly to the reader by including many quotations *verbatim* in my text. My agent submitted those first chapters, together with a synopsis of the remainder, to Allen Lane, the hardback imprint of Penguin Books where my chief editor, James Price, had shown an interest. He sent my offering to a recognised military historian for his expert advice. A long thirteen weeks later came the reply. The historian was not impressed: 'mugged-up knowledge by an outsider', 'familiar and elementary stuff', 'all the old bromides', 'his account of the army's organisation and the trench system... rather like a child's guide', 'flat and wooden in the narrative' are a few of the comments. If James Price had taken the advice he had paid for, my book would have been rejected. He sent for me and showed me the letter with the name and address removed. But James thought that my efforts 'had something new' – the direct use of the memories of the ordinary soldiers. A contract was offered and, after a good deal of further work, the book was published in 1971.

While never a 'best-seller', *The First Day on the Somme* more than met my expectations, remaining in print up to the present day and becoming, so I am told, a 'cult book'. However, it has not been available in hardback for over twenty years, unless purchased second-hand and, in response to numerous requests, I recently determined to rectify this. My thanks therefore to Charles Hewitt of Pen & Sword Books, who have published my work before, for agreeing to reprint.

What is more, we have set out to produce a replica edition as similar in as many respects as modern techniques permit, even down to being printed in the now out-of-date quaintly named 'bastard' page size. As there are no revisions, I should here highlight the only two known minor errors in the 1971 edition; namely Major J.K. Dunlop was in the 53rd, not the 43rd, Machine Gun Company (page 186), and the photograph of troops of 29th Division 'advancing into No Man's Land' is very probably an enactment. Since 1971, *A Tour of the Somme Battlefield* described on pages 332-341 has undergone some changes. There is no longer the concrete roof of a German machine-gun post in front of Serre on page 333; the cottage at Thiepval on page 337 no longer sells souvenirs; the Y Sap and Kasino Point mine craters on pages 338 and 340 have been filled in; the Brickworks chimney on page 340 has gone. Also, probably all of the contributors acknowledged on pages 342-352 have now died, rather than the handful marked as dying between the time they helped me and the first edition being published.

Martin Middlebrook,
Boston, Lincolnshire, November 2002

Introduction

The First World War, or the Great War as it was called until 1939, started for Britain on 4 August 1914, when she declared war on Germany. Britain's stated war aim was to secure the neutrality of Belgium, but in reality she wished to curb the power of Germany, whom she regarded as a growing rival to her trade, maritime and imperial interests. It was for Britain a very popular declaration of war. The entire country, and beyond it, the Empire, entered wholeheartedly into the conflict. For most of the men who wished to fight there was only one anxiety: that the war would end before they could get into action. The popular forecast was 'all over before Christmas'.

Britain had no formal treaty with France but the two governments had long had an understanding that, in the event of a war with Germany, a British Expeditionary Force (which became known more simply as the B.E.F.) would cross to France and take up a position alongside the French Army. Britain had earmarked six infantry divisions and a cavalry division for this purpose and these duly crossed to France, safely escorted by the Royal Navy. The B.E.F. was superbly trained but, by Continental standards, it was a minute force; the Germans described it as 'a contemptible little army' – a phrase adopted with great pride by the perverse British, the members of the original B.E.F. from that time calling themselves the 'Old Contemptibles'.

In the autumn of 1914, Belgium and northern France was the scene of a massive war of movement. The Germans, who held the initiative from the start and showed the greater ability, had the best of the fighting; they reached the Channel coast in Belgium and advanced deep into France. They were frustrated, however, in the main aim – to take Paris and gain a swift and complete victory over the French.

Consequent upon this German failure to take the French capital, there developed attempts by both sides to turn the other's northern flank. The result was a campaign known as the Race to the Sea. Neither side was able to outflank the other and gradually the war of movement ceased with all parties exhausted: the Belgians, their army nearly destroyed and all but a small corner of their country occupied by the Germans; the French, whose large professional army had fought with more courage and audacity than skill, badly mauled; the Germans, baffled in their failure to get a decisive victory and uncertain what to do next. Russia had come in with France and Britain, and Germany was facing something that she had wanted to avoid – a prolonged war on two fronts.

In all this the B.E.F. had played its small part. Actions – they could hardly be classed as battles – at Mons, Le Cateau and on the Marne had enabled it to show its skill and gain more respect from the Germans. In the final desperate fighting, during the Race to the Sea, they had helped in the successful defence of the Belgian town of Ypres. The B.E.F.'s casualties had reached 86,000 by the end of the year and, although this was small compared with those of the other armies, it represented a large proportion of Britain's Regular Army.*

With the end of the war of movement came the beginning of trench warfare. The exhausted armies dug themselves into the ground wherever they happened to be until a continuous line of trenches stretched from neutral Switzerland to the Belgian coast; after that there were no more flanks to turn. The soldiers of all countries, unprepared for this type of warfare, passed a miserable winter. Troops from Britain's Empire arrived to enlarge her force, Indians and Canadians being the first, the former suffering particularly severely in the winter conditions.†

In 1915 the British were the first to attack, in March, at Neuve Chapelle. The Germans followed this, in April, with a series of heavy attacks on Ypres (these becoming known as the Second Battle of Ypres). Again the British played an honourable part in the defence of the town. The attacks were

* During the same period the approximate losses of other armies on the Western Front had been: France 850,000 and Germany 650,000. Throughout this book, the terms 'losses' and 'lost' include all casualties: killed, died of wounds, missing, prisoners and wounded.

After the war there was much controversy over casualty figures. It was suggested that the British system of making casualty returns tended to magnify the real figures, while the German system concealed the true extent of their losses. I do not wish to comment on these theories and, apart from casualties suffered on 1 July 1916, only give approximate figures.

† Subsequent mention of 'British' troops and the B.E.F. will include the Empire troops which, by 1918, represented about twenty per cent of the B.E.F.'s strength.

repulsed, and this proved to be the only German offensive of the year in the West. The Allies persisted with fresh attacks throughout the summer and autumn, the British adding the names of Aubers Ridge, Festubert and, finally, Loos to their battle honours.*

Each fresh effort was more demanding than the last; the scale, of troop involvement, artillery preparation and eventual failure, went remorselessly up. The more ambitious an attack, the heavier the cost. 1915 was a year of complete victory for defence; a combination of machine-guns, barbed wire and artillery defied all offensive moves.

Meanwhile further countries had entered the war. Turkey joining the Germans and Italy the Allies. In an attempt to use their superior naval power, a combined French and British force of warships and troops was dispatched to the Mediterranean in an endeavour to capture the Turkish peninsula of Gallipoli. The operation, if successful, would have opened up the sea route to Russia, protected the Suez Canal from attack and might even have forced Turkey out of the war.

This imaginative effort aroused much controversy inside the British military and political establishments, there being a strong faction who thought victory could only be gained by fighting the Germans in France.† The expedition failed partly through strong Turkish opposition, partly through disease and partly through military incompetence on the Allied part. Casualties were heavy – the British and French losing 250,000 men between them – and the troops were withdrawn, mainly for service in France, to the satisfaction of those who had not wanted them to be diverted to the East in the first place.

Once again the armies settled down for the winter. While the soldiers made the best of their miserable conditions, the politicians and generals made their plans for 1916. The main Allies – France, Britain, Russia and Italy – planned to make simultaneous offensives on three separate fronts; the British

* Losses on the Western Front during 1915 were: Britain, nearly 300,000; France, over 1,000,000, and Germany, nearly 700,000.

† The B.E.F. was fighting in both France and Belgium on what became known as the Western Front. The term 'France' will often be used in this book instead of the more technically correct 'Western Front' for several reasons: the book is concerned mainly with France, the length of front held in Belgium was very short and the term 'France' itself was much used in similar circumstances at the time. It is hoped that the reader will excuse this expedient.

and French efforts were to be side-by-side in France. But the Germans struck first. Their attack at Verdun, in February, gained striking early successes but the battle soon settled down to the normal situation of the defence holding the attack. The Germans persisted, determined to break at least one of the Allies. The French, having already lost much territory in 1914, were equally determined to hold them and a terrible battle of attrition ensued.

So hard did the Germans press their attacks that it was feared the French would not be able to hold on at Verdun. The Allied plans for their own simultaneous offensives were thrown into disarray as the French cried out for help.

The British were in a difficult position. Their old Regular Army had been nearly wiped out and a large new one had been raised and was in France, but it had not been fully trained and was intended to fight in 1916 only as part of a combined Franco-British offensive. After Verdun the French share in this was reduced drastically and it fell to the British to assume the greater burden. The British were not even to be allowed time to complete their training and gain experience, for the battle would have to be fought before mid-summer as the French insisted that they could not hold out at Verdun after June. The Allies were in danger of losing the war. In these desperate straits lay the origins of the Battle of the Somme.

At 7.30 A.M. on Saturday, 1 July 1916, the opening British and French attack was launched astride the River Somme in northern France. For Britain it was the biggest battle her army had ever fought, or probably ever would fight, in a single day. As events were to prove, it was fought on the middle day of the middle year of the war. This book tells the story of the battle fought on that day and of the men who fought it – what I call the Army of 1916.

In writing this book I freely admit the advantage of hindsight and have some sympathy for the politicians and generals who had to make the decisions in 1916.

I realize that the French role in the battle is given little space but make no apology for a deliberate omission; the French effort is not the subject of this book. I would also like to point out that I have chosen to describe the British Army of 1916 through the men and the units who were present on the Somme on 1 July of that year. Many others equally brave fought in 1916 but, once again, this is not their story.

1

The Men

Soon after the B.E.F. landed in France in 1914 it fought its first action at the Belgian town of Mons. Just over four years later, when the war ended, it was back, after many adversities, in exactly the same place. During this time the B.E.F. had changed in nearly every respect: in size, in equipment and certainly in character. This process of change was continuous; each year of the war brought forth an army different in character from that of the year before. What sort of men were the soldiers of 1916?

Within a few days of the outbreak of war, Field-Marshal Lord Kitchener was offered, and accepted, the political appointment of Minister of War. The British Army for which he became responsible had two distinct components – the professional, full-time Regulars and the part-time Territorials.

Britain was the only major European country whose army was not based on conscription but relied upon voluntary enlistment. She had never been disposed to a large standing army on the Continental scale, preferring in her island position to make the fleet the first line of defence. Sufficient volunteers could be found to keep the army strong enough to fulfil its twin commitments – the provision of an Expeditionary Force for the French *entente* and the policing of the Empire.

The fighting part of the army was composed of the cavalry, the artillery and the infantry, these last being destined to bear the brunt of the action in the coming war. The standard infantry unit was the battalion, which contained about 1,000 men when at full strength. A small number of battalions were provided by such *élite* organizations as the Brigade of Guards and the Rifle Brigade, but the main infantry strength came from the county regiments.

In the British Army, unlike most others, the infantry regiment is not an operational unit but is the parent body of several battalions. In 1914, each regiment had its own strictly defined recruiting areas and a depot which housed its headquarters and trained the recruits. Large counties had several regiments; very small counties had to combine, one with another, to form a single regiment.

Most regiments had at least two Regular battalions (numbered 1st and 2nd); one battalion would be stationed abroad and the other somewhere in the United Kingdom. The overseas battalion would remain abroad for many years, its soldiers being replaced from time to time by fresh men sent out from England.

The agreement with the French, which dated from 1906, was not a binding treaty, merely a plan for common action if the two countries were engaged against Germany. On the outbreak of war the units of the B.E.F. filled up with Reservists to their full strength and were soon across the Channel and in action alongside the French.

The first of the ten men whose fortunes will be followed to the Somme was one of these pre-war soldiers. Percy Chappell was a native of Bath and was serving in the 1st Somerset Light Infantry, a typical county regiment. Chappell was twenty-eight years old in 1914 and had been a soldier for ten years, always with the Somersets. In 1914 he was a staff sergeant living with his wife at Colchester Barracks. In four hectic days the battalion took in 400 Reservists, clothed and equipped them and was ready for duty. During the next few days the Reservists were put through an intensive training course including many route marches to break in soft feet and new boots. While this was going on all the battalion trophies, silver and records were packed away for safekeeping until the end of the war. Seventeen days after the outbreak of war the Somersets had sailed from Southampton, and Percy Chappell was in France.

That part of the army not with the B.E.F. was mostly at its overseas stations. This was the heyday of the British Empire and battalions were stationed in every corner of the world. After the outbreak of war most were rushed home, as the Germans were making great strides across Belgium and France and the tiny B.E.F. was in danger of extinction. On their return these battalions were hastily formed into divisions and sent off to France.

Stationed in the lovely islands of Bermuda were the 2nd Lincolns. Compared with the hot, dusty stations of Africa and Asia, Bermuda was a perfect posting. One of the Lincolns officers was thirty-four-year-old Reginald Bastard. A Regular officer, he had been educated at Eton and joined the army just in time for the Boer War in which he had seen much action. A lieutenant at the end of that war, peace-time promotion had been slow and he was still, in 1914, only one rank higher – a captain. He was a good regimental officer, still unmarried, who took his career very seriously. On their arrival in England the Lincolns were included in a new division, the 8th, and were in France by Christmas.

As the fighting in France died down with the onset of winter, the last battalions of all were returning to Europe from the farthest outposts of the Empire. Some even saw a little action before they were brought home. The 2nd South Wales Borderers, stationed at the International Settlement at Tientsin, had been in barracks next to a German unit there and had formed many friendships. When war appeared to be imminent the Germans moved to protect their own settlement at Tsingtao and a few days later the Welshmen were ordered to join Britain's new Allies, the Japanese, in attacking their former friends. The siege of Tsingtao was short but bitter; the weather was wet and cold and the Germans were well dug in behind barbed-wire defences. The Welshmen's hardships were partly relieved by presents sent specially to them by the Mikado of Japan – cigarettes and little chrysanthemum-shaped cakes. The South Wales Borderers lost fourteen dead and thirty-six wounded before Tsingtao fell.

Another battalion, the 1st Royal Dublin Fusiliers, had been at Madras when the German raiding cruiser *Emden* bombarded the port, but there were no casualties amongst the Dubliners.

These last arrivals were made up into the 29th Division but the division was one battalion short. An Edinburgh Territorial battalion was added to complete the division, a rare distinction for a Territorial unit as the Regulars were jealous of their position in the army. The 29th Division stood by ready for duty – the last of the Regular Army.*

After the B.E.F. had sailed for France on the outbreak of war the only effective troops remaining in England were the

* The title of this division is misleading. There were only eleven Regular divisions at this time, numbered 1 to 8 and 27 to 29; those numbered 9 to 26 were the first of the New Army divisions.

Territorial Force – the part-time soldiers. The Territorials had been born at the time of the Haldane Reforms in 1908 which had completely reorganized the army in face of growing and aggressive German power. Provision had been made for fourteen infantry divisions, fourteen cavalry brigades (the Yeomanry) and all the supporting arms. In every respect it was a completely separate army, designed primarily to replace the B.E.F. in time of war and to guard the Homeland but also to reinforce the B.E.F. in the event of a prolonged war.

Like the battalions of the Regular Army, the Territorials recruited on a regional basis; in fact their local ties were even stronger than those of the Regulars. Each town had its drill hall where men would report for training in the evenings and at week-ends, and each summer they would all go off to the annual camp where they would meet the rest of the county unit for training as complete units.

Recruiting for the new force was brisk and by 1910 over a quarter of a million men had joined. The first officers and non-commissioned officers came from the old Militia and the Volunteers, the Reserve bodies which had been disbanded by the reforms, but it was not long before suitable new men were promoted to supplement these veterans and eventually take their places completely.

Territorial soldiers had certain legal rights. They could not be sent abroad, even in time of war, unless they volunteered by signing a 'General Service Obligation', nor could they be forcibly transferred from one unit to another until a special Act of Parliament was passed in 1916.

The recruits were of a very high standard and were, of course, all volunteers. Units soon developed their own *esprit de corps*, some of the city units becoming very selective. A London battalion, the London Rifle Brigade, whose drill hall was at Bunhill Row, actually charged an entrance fee of 25*s*. per man and restricted its membership to those from the commercial classes.

By 1914 the Territorial Force was well up to strength and, when it was 'called out' for full-time service on the outbreak of war, was well fitted to perform its role of Home Defence. In the event of their being required for overseas service, the Territorials had been promised a six-month training period, but the critical situation of the B.E.F. in the early months of the war called for swift help. The Territorial Force was asked to waive its six months' training and volunteer for immediate overseas duty. All over the country the Force made its decision, almost a universal 'Yes'; only a few individuals within the units refused and were left behind. By Christmas 1914, twenty-two Territorial battalions had joined the B.E.F. in France and, by February 1915, twenty-six more had joined them.

When Kitchener became Minister of War the popular opinion was that it would be a short war. The new minister did not agree and his forecast of a conflict lasting at least three years caused surprise and some dismay. If he were right there would need to be a much bigger army. Kitchener was faced with a difficulty that became greater as the days passed: he had no army on which to build. The Regulars had either gone to France or were being sent there as fast as they could be recalled from overseas; the Territorials were following them.

Kitchener decided on his own bold expedient to meet the crisis: he would build a completely new army. He would use the county regiment system and their depots but that would be all. The officers, staffs and non-commissioned officers he would get from where he could; the private soldiers would come from a direct appeal to the civilian population. The Regulars and the Territorials would have to hold the enemy in France until this new force could be raised and trained for active service.

This unorthodox plan met with some opposition but it had the advantage of being swift and simple. Parliament promptly passed the necessary Bill sanctioning the raising of 500,000 men to be formed into eighteen new divisions and, by the end of August, Kitchener made his famous appeal for the 'First Hundred Thousand'. This was the birth of what officially became known as the 'New Army' – many called it 'Kitchener's Army' and those who served it in were always proud to refer to themselves as 'Kitchener's Men'. All this was freely reported in the press and, when Kitchener's plan became known in Germany, the newspapers there scoffed and forecast that the men would become '*Kannonenfutter*' – cannon fodder.

This one appeal by Kitchener immediately caught the country's imagination. Spurred on by the bad news of the B.E.F., now in headlong retreat and in danger of being cut off, a wave of enthusiasm swept the country. There were several reasons for this. Many of the more mature men felt a genuine patriotism. There was an intense pride in Britain and the Empire and a general dislike of the Germans. It was seriously felt by many that the future of the British Empire was at risk and that it was their duty to enlist. The younger men were almost certainly more inspired by the thoughts of adventure and travel at a time when few people had been farther than their own city or the nearest seaside resort. The miners, industrial workers and the unemployed often saw the call as a means of escape from their dismal conditions. In the years preceding the outbreak of war, the decline in the value of wages led to strikes in the mines, the docks, the railways and among the cotton-workers and boiler-makers. This was an England where a boy left school at thirteen and, if he could get work at all, went into the local factory, mill or pit to work between fifty and sixty hours a week for 5*s*. or less. The average wage for a man was under £2 per week and for this he had to work from 6.0 A.M. to 6.0 P.M. with thirty minutes for breakfast and an hour for lunch. Tea-breaks and the five-day week were concessions unheard of and not due to appear for nearly half a century. Although money values have changed, the lot of most labouring families was one of constant poverty.

It is not surprising that the mining and industrial areas produced the most men, even more than their actual population warranted. It was almost as if those doing the dirtiest and most depressing jobs couldn't wait to get out into the open air and this was a heaven-sent opportunity; away from factories, mines or the street corner; away from slums and large families and into a new life, where there was fresh air, good companionship, regular meals and all the glamour of Kitchener's Army.

This massive exodus from the factories and mines was to leave Britain's industry short of skilled men and was a factor in the critical shortages of guns and shells in 1915 and 1916. The places of the 1914 volunteers were taken by men who had no intention of going to war and by women – a major step on the road to female emancipation.

In the country areas, men were sometimes given little choice in the matter. The local land-owner often selected men from his domestic staff or farm labourers and took them to the nearest recruiting office. The men involved accepted with few qualms.

Thousands of recruits did not fit into any of these categories; their only reason for joining was that everyone else was doing it. They scarcely stopped to ask themselves why; they simply followed their friends.

Many local authorities and prominent people took the initiative in sponsoring units of their own, even recruiting, paying and clothing the men out of their own pockets, confident that the War Office would eventually take over the new units and refund their expenses. Recruiting offices were opened at barracks, police stations and town halls, and were soon overwhelmed with crowds of men of all ages and from every class, clamouring to be accepted, many truly afraid that the war would be over before they could reach 'The Front'.

Many men enlisted on the spur of the moment, walking out of their factories in the middle of shifts or leaving their offices before the day's work had ended: 'I worked for the County Council and, one morning, I left home to go to work; we were repairing the roads in Windsor Park at the time, but on the way I met a friend who was going to enlist. Instead of going on to work, I went back home, changed into my best clothes and went with him to the Recruiting Office at Reading.' (Pte J. H. Harwood, 6th Royal Berks)*

Once the would-be soldier had managed to get inside the recruiting office his next obstacle was a medical inspection. This was usually very strict; with such an abundance of human material there was no point in accepting anything but the best. There were many rejects, the standard of physical health being very low, especially in the industrial areas. Even so, well-meaning and overworked doctors passed many who should have been failed.

'I tried to enlist but, after waiting for two hours with crowds of others, I was examined by a doctor and was rejected. My chest only measured twenty-eight inches. I went

* When quoting survivors of the battle, their rank, unit and decorations, if any, of 1 July 1916 will be given.

across the Tyne on the ferry and tried the recruiting office at North Shields. I found the doctor there more easily suited and he marked my chest as thirty-eight inches. I went home and told my mother but she cried, saying I was only a boy. I was eighteen!' (Pte B. Richardson, Newcastle Commercials)

'I never thought of joining up but I had an old school mate, Walter, who was a very ardent patriot and, when he heard of the so-called atrocities committed in Belgium, he was so incensed that he decided to enlist and dragged me in with him. I was a big lad for my age, 16½, but Walter was of slighter build and while I passed as suitable, he was turned down because he was an inch too short. He was furious and I was staggered. He had shanghai'd me into the army, while he, who was a more willing candidate, had been turned down.

'Then I had a brainwave. I had noticed that there were so many recruits that, when our height was measured, they just did it with our boots on, then subtracted an inch in lieu of the boots. My boots were bigger than his, so I packed them up with paper and told Walter to put them on. In he went again and this time he passed with no bother.' (Pte G. Brownbridge, 13th Northumberland Fusiliers)

Thousands of boys below the minimum age of nineteen succeeded in joining up, often aided by unscrupulous recruiting sergeants who collected a bonus for every man they enlisted. 'I was a member of the village cricket and football teams (the village was Mattishall) and nearly every one of their members enlisted. I was only sixteen but I tried to join up, too. The recruiting sergeant asked me my age and when I told him he said, "You had better go out, come in again, and tell me different." I came back, told him I was nineteen and I was in.' (Cpl J. Norton, 8th Norfolks)

'I was only fifteen and every time I tried to join up in London it was no good, they wouldn't have me. So I went by rail to Birmingham, on a penny platform ticket. I went into a recruiting office there and told them I was seventeen. The sergeant said, "Why don't you go out and have something to eat? When you come back you might be a bit older." I told him that I had no money and he gave me two bob. When I came back he spoke to me as though he had never seen me before. I said I was eighteen and, this time, I got in all right.' (Pte A. E. Hollingshead, 2nd Middlesex)

Once accepted, the new recruits found that there was even a

choice of units. Most wanted the infantry – the main fighting arm – but some settled for the cavalry or artillery, particularly city-dwellers who wished to work with horses. The unglamorous administrative units found great difficulty in attracting recruits. Nearly all chose the local battalions with their friends but some decided, for a variety of reasons, to go farther afield: 'Both my parents were dead, I was very poor and had never had a holiday in my life. When I joined up at Nottingham, I refused the local units and asked which other battalions were open. I chose the Northumberland Fusiliers because it gave me the longest train ride' (L/Cpl H. Fellows, 12th Northumberland Fusiliers). By such fickle choices men decided their destiny.

Some men enlisted under false names, usually to avoid being traced by their families, but one man had another reason: 'I had run away from home when I was fifteen and joined up in Birmingham. I was very worried about my surname; I thought it sounded German. Anyway I didn't want my family to find me as I was only fifteen. I told the sergeant I was nearly twenty and gave a false name. My first name was Charles and I had a pal whose surname was Dickens. I thought Charles Dickens sounded quite decent and I served under that name for two years.' (Pte C. G. Barff, 1/8th Royal Warwicks)

The first rush of recruits were formed into units containing men of all types, but soon, as so many men came forward, the unofficial 'raisers' saw that there was an opportunity for men from a particular district or walk of life to serve together in one battalion. These battalions were formed so quickly that they had named themselves before the War Office could adopt them and give them a proper title. These informal titles were retained even after the official ones were allocated, so that some battalions went through the war with two names, their own and the army one.*

The big cities were the first to get themselves organized and produced their famous 'City Battalions', often known in the industrial areas of the north of England as 'Pals Battalions'. Sometimes the Pals would all be men of a particular occupation. A typical example was the 3rd Manchester Pals, recruited from the 'Clerks and Warehousemen of Manchester'

* Wherever possible, the informal battalion titles will be used to retain the atmosphere of the period.

– a subsidiary title they were proud to bear. One of their recruits was twenty-one-year-old Paddy Kennedy, a clerk in a cotton export office (wages 25*s*. for a forty-four-hour week). Paddy had a military background, his father and two uncles were Irishmen serving as Regular soldiers in Irish regiments and Paddy had been born at Dover Barracks. A Catholic, young Kennedy was a member of the Manchester Company of the Irish Volunteers, a body of armed men prepared to fight against any partition of Ireland by the Home Rule Bill then being introduced. During his summer holidays in Ireland, Paddy Kennedy had actually been involved in a clash with English troops soon after rifles and ammunition from Belgium had been landed for the Irish Volunteers at Howth near Dublin. When the war with Germany broke out Kennedy would have liked to join his father's old regiment but it was now recruiting in Protestant Ulster, so, with many of his Manchester friends, he joined the Clerks' and Warehousemen's Battalion.

Hull raised four battalions which were destined to serve together as the city's own brigade. One, the Commercials, was recruited entirely from men of the business offices; a second was the Tradesmen's Battalion and another the Sportsmen's Battalion. For want of a better name, the last battalion became 'T'Others'.

Glasgow raised three battalions very quickly. The first was raised by the City Tramways Department; their recruiting office opened at the Tram Depot and within sixteen hours the battalion was complete. The second was raised by the Boys' Brigade and was composed entirely of former members. The third, the Glasgow Commercials, was the work of the city's Chamber of Commerce.

Some towns tried to compete with the cities and succeeded in forming their Pals battalions. Accrington, the Lancashire cotton town, was one of these. The mayor, a retired army officer, formed a committee and recruiting started at a little office in the town. Within ten days there were enough men. Accrington could only supply half of these, the remainder coming in from the surrounding towns of Burnley, Chorley and Blackburn; but the battalion was always to be known as the Accrington Pals.

In Grimsby it was the headmaster of a local grammar school who took the initiative. He decided to raise a company of 250 men, all old boys of his school, and offer it to one of the local Territorial battalions. When other men from the town asked to be included, it became obvious that the 250 mark would soon be passed. The headmaster handed his company over to the town council, which decided to try for a complete battalion for the New Army. More men came in from the surrounding villages and from other Lincolnshire towns – Boston, Scunthorpe and Louth – and finally, with the help of a group of men sent from Wakefield, another battalion was ready for Kitchener – the Grimsby Chums.

The less populated country areas frequently had difficulty filling their units and often had to ask the cities for men to make up the shortage. Thus, a London recruit was persuaded to join a West Country battalion, the 9th Devons. He found that it contained so many Londoners and Lancashire men that it had been jokingly re-named the 9th London and Lancs.

In 1914 the political situation in Ireland, still part of the United Kingdom, was delicate. The larger part of the country, the Catholic South, wished to see an independent state composed of the whole country. It was this movement that Paddy Kennedy and his Irish Volunteers supported. But there was bitter resistance to this prospect from the northern province of Ulster, composed of nine counties and largely Protestant. The Irish question had bedevilled British politics for some time. There existed, in Northern Ireland, the Ulster Volunteer Force (U.V.F.), composed of 80,000 men, properly armed and organized on military lines. Its members were prepared to fight anyone, English or Southern Irish, to avoid being forced into a union with the Catholics. The U.V.F. was, in theory, illegal but was so strong that the London Government had made no attempt to disarm it.

In his search for men, Kitchener asked Sir Edward Carson, the M.P. for Dublin University but leader of the Ulster politicians, if he would hand over the Force to his New Army. At first there was hesitation but, as the news from France worsened, Carson and his fellow Ulster M.P.s agreed, provided the Home Rule Bill was not implemented while the U.V.F. was away in France. Kitchener was hoping for a brigade; Carson offered him a division and the U.V.F. units became battalions of the British Army.* Another Ulster

* A brigade contained four battalions and a division contained three brigades. The Ulster Division's artillery was eventually raised in London.

M.P., Capt. Charles Craig, immediately ordered 10,000 uniforms and his fellow M.P.s promised that Ulster money would be raised to meet the bill.

Back in Ulster, there were many who had misgivings about the action their representatives in London had taken. The U.V.F. had no direct quarrel with Germany, who had supplied the rifles for their illegal army. Moreover, it was feared that the London Government would force Ulster into the hated Home Rule with the South while their menfolk were away fighting the Germans. But the people of Ulster soon became caught up in the all-pervading enthusiasm for the new war and thousands of U.V.F. men volunteered for the new division.

One recruit was a young Belfast man, William McFadzean, known to his friends as Billy. He lived in one of the city suburbs, Cregagh, and was the eldest boy in the family. His father was a J.P. and the family were all members of the Presbyterian Church. Billy was an apprentice to a Belfast linen firm (£100 for a full five-year apprenticeship), and in his spare time he had two occupations; he was a junior player for the Collegians Rugby Club and a member of the 1st Belfast Regiment of the U.V.F. When recruiting started for the Ulster Division, Billy McFadzean immediately joined the Belfast Young Citizens' battalion, sometimes known as the 'Chocolate Soldiers' because most of its men had a commercial background and came from 'good' families.

Those living in England who had Irish or Scottish connexions could sometimes find a place in battalions formed specially for them. The Territorials already had such units in London and Liverpool; other cities tried to form New Army battalions to copy them. In Manchester some Scots businessmen started recruiting for the Manchester Scottish, hoping that the War Office would adopt the new unit. Over 300 men enlisted but, when official recognition was refused, the disappointed men were given a choice: stay and join one of the Manchester Pals battalions or go to Edinburgh and become part of a proper Scots unit. Most of them chose Edinburgh and went there by train to be incorporated into the 1st Edinburgh City Battalion.

Tyneside was luckier. Here the raisers attempted to form both Tyneside Scottish and Tyneside Irish battalions. Recruiting was brisk and the two battalions were soon complete. The raisers then decided to go further and recruit for a brigade each. There was intense competition and the whole of Tyneside waited to see which side could find the required number of men first. It is uncertain who won; both sides claimed victory by a narrow margin.

When the recruits for the two brigades were examined more closely, it was found that both had accepted men with no Scottish or Irish connexions. Although the Tyneside Irish contained many of their large immigrant community in the North-East, at least seventy-five per cent of the Tyneside Scottish were pure Geordies who had joined for the glamour of the name. They were even hoping to be given full kilted uniform, but they were to be disappointed; they were, however, given a glengarry hat and a special cap badge.

The four counties of the Industrial North between them produced 134 New Army battalions, just over one-third of the thirty divisions eventually raised by Lord Kitchener in the whole of the United Kingdom.* Cities vied with each other to raise their Pals; Manchester appears to have held the record with fifteen battalions. There were some surprises; little Barnsley raised two, proudly named the 1st and 2nd Barnsley Pals, while nearby Sheffield – nine times her size – only raised one, named, more sedately, the Sheffield City Battalion. Sheffield preferred to support the local Territorials, the famous Hallamshires.

A typical mining recruit was Richard Richardson King, Dick to his friends. He was a Nottinghamshire man who had married a local girl, Emma, and then moved to south Yorkshire because the thicker coal seams there offered better prospects of pay. He settled in the village of Tickhill, near Doncaster, and raised his family there. In 1914 he was thirty years old with three daughters and a son. One day he was late home from work and when he did arrive, walked in with 'Here comes Kitchener's Army'. He had enlisted without consulting his family. Within a few days he was Pte King of the 10th King's Own Yorkshire Light Infantry (the K.O.Y.L.I.), a new battalion forming at Pontefract.

The miners made good soldiers; they were used to hard work and dangerous conditions and they made light of digging and maintaining their trenches when they reached the Front. One south Yorkshire battalion contained so

* Lancashire, fifty-six; Yorkshire, forty-eight; Northumberland, nineteen; Durham, eleven.

many miners that they were hard put to it to find orderly room clerks, while others, the Commercials, for example, had over 900 men sufficiently qualified for the position. A Newcastle unit contained only railwaymen and served as the Railway Pals Battalion.

At the other end of the social scale a group of raisers decided they would form a battalion so that former public schoolboys could serve together. An advertisement was placed in leading newspapers and some 1,500 applications were received. Among the volunteers were two men who came from Turkey specially to join and two retired cavalry officers (Queen's Bays and 19th Hussars) who both joined as private soldiers. There were enough former international players in the battalion to field two full rugger teams and one soccer team.

Eventually the formation of so many units, which had taken the War Office by surprise, was formally ratified and they were taken over and given places in the county regiments. Sometimes ceremonial parades were held to mark the formal taking over of these latest additions to the British Army. The new units had no background or tradition of any kind other than that of the county regiment which took them over. The informal titles they took to themselves were never forgotten and men frequently thought of themselves as, say, a Leeds Pal or a Bradford Pal first and a West Yorkshire Regiment man second.*

Billy McFadzean's Belfast Young Citizens became the 14th Royal Irish Rifles, the Public Schools Battalion became the 16th Middlesex and the Tyneside Scottish and Irish were taken over by the Northumberland Fusiliers. The Grimsby Chums were accepted by their county regiment and became the 10th Lincolns. Not all went smoothly; in Glasgow the Boys' Brigade had difficulty in getting official recognition for their special battalion and threatened to offer it to the Cameronians, not traditionally a Glasgow regiment. Eventually, all was smoothed over and the three Glasgow units were taken over by the Highland Light Infantry.

* The New Army battalions were numbered after the Territorials. For example, the 2nd Royal Berks were Regulars, the 1/4th were Territorials and the 6th was a New Army battalion. The Territorials are easily identified, for all their battalions have a prefix. The 1/6th Royal Warwicks (from Birmingham) was a pre-war battalion; the 2/6th and 3/6th were raised during the war.

In Edinburgh, the 1st City Battalion, which contained 300 Mancunians, became the 15th Royal Scots. This famous regiment had been the old First of Foot before county regiments had been formed and its long history was impressed upon the recruits, a history which went back so far that the regiment was nicknamed 'Pontius Pilate's Bodyguard'.

Densely populated Lancashire and Yorkshire had no less than thirteen regiments between them, and battalions from every one of these were to be present on the Somme on 1 July 1916. The Manchester Pals and Liverpool Pals became battalions in the Manchester Regiment and the King's (Liverpool) Regiment and Accrington's Pals the 11th East Lancs. The Sheffield City Battalion and the neighbouring Barnsley Pals went into the Yorks and Lancs, a regiment that, despite its name, only recruited in south Yorkshire, and, at Hull, the 'T'Others' became more formal as the 13th East Yorks.

What were the Regulars and Territorials doing about getting their recruits while this huge flood of men was enlisting for Kitchener's New Army? The Regulars had no trouble, although their battalions in France were suffering heavy casualties. The Kitchener units may have been exciting but there was still an extra aura to the Regular Army; to many men it was the real army, and they felt it was an honour to serve in it. If this was not enough, the promise that they could be at the Front more quickly with the Regulars was often sufficient to persuade recruits to join. It was quite possible to have been a civilian in September 1914 and in France with the Regulars before Christmas of the same year.

The Territorials had greater difficulty. They had to compete with the Regulars and the New Army for recruits and sometimes found themselves a poor third to their more glamorous rivals. Those units with a severe shortage solved it by unofficially lowering their medical and other standards. Many men, finding themselves too young, too short or medically unsound elsewhere, were welcomed by the Territorials; their persistence and enthusiasm usually made them good soldiers in spite of nature's minor imperfections.*

* Later, in March 1915, the army accepted men between five foot and five foot three in height (five foot three had previously been the minimum) for the unique Bantam Division. The Bantams had a certain advantage when holding

'My four brothers had all joined up but I was too short and felt very ashamed not to be in the army. So I went to the Territorial Drill Hall in Derby Road, Nottingham, and offered the recruiting sergeant there a 2*s.* postal order if he would accept me. He did so and, when it was over, we both went along to the Sir Borlace Warren [a local pub], cashed the postal order and drank the proceeds. My wife was working in the shell factory at the time and, when she came home, I told her I had joined up.' (Pte J. Singleton, 1/7th Sherwood Foresters) *

The New Army had no such problems. Within three weeks, by the end of September, over 500,000 men had joined. Kitchener's wildest hopes had been fulfilled; he had his men. But half a million civilians don't become an army overnight. Where was he to get his officers and his non-commissioned officers? Who was going to train his eager battalions?

Kitchener tackled the problem of providing officers in the same direct manner that he had used when forming the New Army itself. It was discovered that some 500 British officers from the Indian Army were at home on routine leave. He arbitrarily directed them to report for duty with the new battalions. To provide junior officers, the War Office had prepared a list of 2,000 'young gentlemen' (who had recently left public schools or universities) and immediate invitations were sent to these men, encouraging them to apply for commissions. One of these was twenty-one-year-old Philip Howe, a Sheffield man who had gained a law degree at Sheffield University that summer. He received a letter from the War Office on the day war was declared. His father thought that the war would be a long one and advised the young solicitor to apply early for a commission. Howe was bored with living at home and, seeing adventure in this war, rather than out of patriotism, he took his father's advice and was directed to report for a short course at the Officers' Training Corps at his old university. When Philip Howe arrived at the O.T.C. he was surprised to find many of his old undergraduate friends there; but after a month, he became very impatient and, hoping

trenches in France; tall men were always in extra danger from German snipers. The division did not take part in the battle on 1 July 1916, but, as the 35th Division, it did well in later stages of the Somme Battle. It became an ordinary division in 1917 due to lack of suitable reinforcements.

* Known in 1914 as the Notts and Derby Regiment.

to see action more quickly, he and several others left the O.T.C. and joined the Sheffield City Battalion as privates.

Kitchener's 500 Indian Army officers and 2,000 young gentlemen did not go far. The former were supplemented by many retired officers, men who had seen active service in long-forgotten wars and who were far too old for this one, but who at least had some experience and were delighted to get back into the army.

The first Kitchener battalions were the luckiest; they had the pick of the few experienced officers available. But as more and more units were formed, the supply ran out and battalions were reduced to getting their officers as best they could. When the Pals began to form they were lucky if they could get one Regular serving officer and possibly one retired officer. The remainder (and a battalion needed over thirty officers) were simply appointed from among the professional and business men who had joined.

Philip Howe found that there was no immediate prospect of action with the Sheffield City Battalion so he tried again for a commission. This time it was granted immediately and, without any training at all, he found himself a second-lieutenant in the 10th West Yorks, a battalion raised in the Leeds and Harrogate areas. The commanding officer was a retired officer who had fought in the Ashanti War of 1873, forty-one years earlier, and the adjutant, the only Regular, was in a bad temper because sickness had prevented him going to France with his own battalion.

In the Public Schools Battalion every man was a potential officer but most preferred to serve in the ranks. The officers eventually appointed to this battalion give some indication as to how wide Kitchener had cast his net, for they included representatives from the following regiments: Natal Mounted Rifles, Bombay Light Horse, Rangoon Volunteer Rifles, the Sikhs and the Westminster Dragoons.

To give some overall idea of the inexperience of the officers of Kitchener's Army let us look at a complete division, the 21st, part of his Third Hundred Thousand. Every one of the battalion commanders had been retired on the outbreak of war; of the other officers, only fourteen had had any experience of the army at all. The remainder, over 400, were newly commissioned and mostly without any officer training.

The shortage of non-commissioned officers was even more

acute. Mobilization on the outbreak of war had brought most of the Reservists back into the Regular units, which were now in France. There were so few left for Kitchener's New Army that battalions were lucky to get more than half a dozen each. To make up the number, there was no alternative to promoting likely looking men in the ranks. But many resisted such offers. Men had joined up in a holiday mood and their patriotism did not always prove so strong that they were prepared to accept responsibility for their friends' lives by becoming junior N.C.O.'s. Groups of pals had joined together and made solemn pacts that they would never accept promotion or allow themselves to be split up. There was a perverse pride in being a private in Kitchener's Army.

There were some remarkable scenes as the new battalions were formed, as witness this new arrival at Newcastle Barracks: 'There was absolute chaos there and on the first day I was issued with one blanket, nothing else. Tea was served in a zinc bath and, as no cups were available, I went behind the cook house to find an empty tin. That evening stew was served in the same bath and we had to kneel down and scoop it out with our hands. On the first night no billets were available so we went down to the railway station and slept in some empty carriages.' (L/Cpl H. Fellows, 12th Northumberland Fusiliers)

Some battalions were formed in a matter of minutes, or almost as an afterthought. At Lincoln, so many men had volunteered that they were lined up in fours on the parade ground and a sergeant walked down the ranks and counted out 1,000 men. When he had enough he stopped, put his hand out and said, 'Every man this side of me turn right. You are now the 8th Lincolns.'

So quickly had the New Army been formed that the necessary uniforms, equipment and arms were not immediately available. Some of the Pals battalions even lived at home until camps were ready for them. Each day they assembled and marched off for training in the local parks and sports grounds, clad in civilian clothes and carrying dummy rifles. When uniforms did arrive, they were usually of blue serge; the New Army was last in the queue for scarce khaki.

Small wonder that many were kept at home. 'Nobody who had anything to do with the raising of "Kitchener's Army" will ever forget August and September, 1914, when vast hosts of men, without officers, without N.C.O.'s, without uniforms, arms, camp equipment, rations, tents, or anything except the clothes that they stood in, were assembled in open spaces called camps, and there embodied as units of the British Army.' (Lieut-Col. R. Fife, 7th Green Howards) *

The following account is typical of the birth of a New Army battalion:

'I was a junior lieutenant in the Regular Army and was sent to be adjutant of a new battalion, the 8th East Surreys. I stood in the station yard at Purfleet and waited for the men to arrive. All I had for battalion headquarters was in my haversack. Three trains arrived during the day, bringing 1,000 men who had been wished upon us before any attempt had been made to provide accommodation.

'We only had two elderly retired officers and a quarter-master, and a very good sergeant major was the only N.C.O. We were given a dozen old Reservists, who we promptly made lance-corporals, much to their horror and indignation. Then the whole battalion was paraded and an appeal was made for anybody who had ever been in charge of anyone else, or who wanted to be. About forty men stepped forward; we tied white tape around their arms and made them lance-corporals too. A rough and ready system, but it worked out well and nearly all of them made good.' (Lieut-Col. A. P. B. Irwin, 8th East Surreys)

When the 1st Manchester Pals went to camp groups of men were allotted to each tent and the likeliest looking of each group, often a former Boy Scout, was detailed as the soldier in charge of each tent. An officer was approached by an ancient private (afterwards known as 'Father') who made the following complaint: 'If you please, sir, you have placed us in a bit of a predicament. We all come from the same warehouse, and him as has been made the head of the tent is the office boy, sir, and I'm the head of the department.'†

As the arms and equipment arrived, the battalions settled down to serious training but, as there were few instructors who had been to France, most of it was for open warfare.

* This passage is taken from *History of the 7th Battalion, Green Howards*, a narrative extract from the *Green Howards Gazette*. In 1914 this regiment was known as the Yorkshire Regiment.

† From *The History of the 16th, 17th, 18th and 19th Manchesters*.

There was plenty of parade ground drill, route marching, bayonet fighting and musketry (when sufficient rifles became available). Many men were selected for training as signallers, machine-gunners or scouts. Practice attacks were made on 'enemy-held positions' using fire and movement tactics whereby a body of men approached to within 200 yards of the enemy in short rushes before making a general assault. Before the war the Regulars had practised these tactics *ad infinitum*, as one soldier records, and the New Army men endeavoured to learn in a few months what the Regulars had taken as many years to assimilate. Little was known, in England, of the nature of trench warfare. After their offices, factories and mines the men really enjoyed this new open-air life, which, together with the marvellous spirit of companionship, made this, for some, the happiest time of their lives.

Not all were satisfied, however. 'I was approached by one of my men, a little Welshman, who asked to speak to the Colonel. I asked him what he wanted and he said, quite seriously, "Well, sir, I don't think my trade union would permit me to work the number of hours we are working now." I advised him to leave the Colonel alone.' (Capt. C. F. Ashdown, 8th Norfolks)*

One battalion met action and danger sooner than they expected. The Durham Pals were in camp at West Hartlepool when the German fleet bombarded the town in December, 1914, causing much damage and heavy casualties, 119 civilians being killed. The Durhams were alerted in case there was a German landing. Their losses, five killed and eleven wounded, were almost certainly the New Army's first casualties through enemy action.

Gradually the battalions were formed into brigades and then divisions. The Tyneside Scottish and Irish Brigades were allowed to serve together in the 34th Division. Paddy Kennedy found his battalion was part of the 30th Division; formed by Lord Derby and called 'Lord Derby's Own', it contained two Manchester Brigades and a Liverpool Brigade, a real collection of Pals.

The Ulster Division was given a number but allowed to retain its own name as part of the official title – the 36th (Ulster) Division – but known to many English troops as

* Battalion commanders were known to their men as 'the c.o.' or 'the Colonel' although the rank held was that of lieutenant-colonel.

'Carson's Army'. When this division moved to England to complete its training, the Tyrone Volunteers had to be left behind; they were in quarantine with measles but soon caught up with the rest.

When war broke out the larger members of the British Empire immediately offered their troops; whole divisions came from such countries as Australia, New Zealand, Canada and India, proud and eager to fight with the mother country. Ironically, the only Empire troops destined to take part in the fighting on 1 July 1916 were not from these large countries but from two island colonies, Newfoundland and Bermuda.

In 1914 Newfoundland, nearly as large as England but thinly populated, had no army at all. On the outbreak of war, the Governor organized a committee with twenty-five members to recruit a force of 500 men for service with the British Army; so great was the enthusiasm that the committee became fifty strong and the force over 1,000, sufficient for a complete battalion. Recruits came in from all over the island and from every occupation: fishermen, sailors, schoolteachers, lumbermen, office workers and many others. Some came from remote villages and had never even attended a school.

As in England, there were no uniforms and no rifles. Some men wore khaki drill, but most had to wear their civilian clothes. There were plenty of puttees, however, and every man was issued with a blue pair, the battalion immediately becoming known as the 'Blue Puttee Boys'. 500 rifles had been ordered privately from Canada at $28 each but delivery was slow and the battalion had to leave without them. After a very sketchy training, the battalion was named the 1st Newfoundland Regiment and declared itself ready to sail to England. The time taken to raise and organize it – one month.

The battalion sailed from St Johns to a great send-off from the islanders. A small steamer, the S.S. *Florizel*, had been chartered by the Newfoundland Government for the trip, the charge being $56 for each officer and $36 for each man. The 500 rifles arrived soon after the battalion had sailed and were sent on after them. 'We sailed from St Johns on October 4th. The *Florizel* had been out to the seal fishery that spring and she stank like hell. We joined the convoy bringing the first contingent of Canadian troops overseas. The ship we sailed on was only about 2,000 tons and looked like a row-boat compared to the ships the Canadians were on. While waiting to disembark, our quartermaster went aboard one of the Canadian ships and managed to scrounge enough service caps and greatcoats for us all.' (Pte J. F. Hibbs, 1st Newfoundland Regiment)

On arrival at Devonport the Newfoundlanders were kept a further week on their ship before being disembarked. One suspects that the War Office had not really expected them and were hard put to it to find them a camp. They eventually established a depot in Scotland, at Ayr race-course, which served them all through the war. The Newfoundlanders soon made friends with the English and Scots civilians and were popular because of their quiet manner. They were very anxious that they should not be known as Canadians, who sometimes got a bad name for rowdiness.

It has already been told how Reginald Bastard had been stationed at tiny Bermuda with the 2nd Lincolns. The European community there and the battalion had got on very well together, and when the Lincolns were called home on the outbreak of war the Bermudans raised a force of eighty men, the Bermuda Volunteer Rifle Corps, and sent it to England with the request that it should serve with the 2nd Lincolns. The War Office decided that the 1st Lincolns were more in need of men than the 2nd Battalion, so the Bermudans were sent out to join the 1st in France. The contingent was always kept at full strength, the island sending fresh men out to replace casualties.*

Back at home the flood of men gradually slackened off and more vigorous recruiting methods were used. The B.E.F. had suffered heavy casualties in the First Battle of Ypres and more men were still needed. The realization had come to all that the war would not be over by Christmas. A violent and unscrupulous propaganda campaign accused the Germans of terrible atrocities in the occupied areas of Belgium and France. Women were blamed for keeping their menfolk at home while other husbands were fighting. Young men

* During the war, seventy-five per cent of the Bermudan Rifles became casualties; forty men were killed or died of wounds. Some remained with the 1st Lincolns after the war and one became its c.o. in 1930.

walking in London streets without uniforms were stopped by society women and given white feathers – the traditional mark of cowardice.

It became very difficult for men to stay out of the army: 'I hated war and the thought of killing anyone but I lived in a small village and, when all the others had gone, people started asking me when I would be going. I got fed up with this and joined up but was determined to be a non-combatant. I tried the R.A.M.C. but could not get in so I finished up as a stretcher-bearer in the infantry.' (Pte F. S. Martin, Rangers)

As time passed, those who had been too young before became old enough to enlist. Bill Soar was an apprentice joiner living in the Meadows district of Nottingham who wanted to see more of the world. At the beginning of December he was only seventeen but was accepted together with two friends by the Territorials, always looking for men. The three joined the 2/7th Sherwood Foresters, known as the 'Robin Hood Rifles'. Soar did not have to go far away from home for his training which was done at Wollaton Park, on the Trent Rifle Ranges and at Belton Park near Grantham. He was trained as a stretcher-bearer and bandsman and given the rank of Bugler, a rank only found in certain regiments.

Charles Matthews had also been too young. He was a clerk from Bletchley, in Buckinghamshire, working in the offices of a brewery at Northampton. He knew that the 8th Northamptons were training men for other battalions and that they were stationed at Penzance, being known as the 'Riviera Boys'. He decided to enlist in May 1915, and, instead of joining a Buckinghamshire battalion, chose the 8th Northamptons; if he was going to spend the summer training he preferred to do it at Penzance. After he had enlisted he was surprised not to be sent off to Cornwall but kept at the depot at Northampton, even being allowed home in his uniform – an army tunic, a policeman's overcoat but no cap; there was none to spare.

Two weeks later he was sent to the 8th, but not to Penzance; it had been moved to Colchester. Matthews was not to get his summer by the sea. He spent three months training under some ancient N.C.O.'s, doing much 'square bashing', open field training and bayonet practice, but, like so many, nothing at all to prepare him for trench warfare.

Another late joiner was Albert McMillan, who lived at

Islington and worked for the Great Central Railway at Marylebone Goods Yard (14*s.* per week). A real Cockney, McMillan had never even seen the sea. Rejected in 1914 with 'Get a couple more inches on your chest, Joe', by the recruiting sergeant at the Metropolitan Music Hall in Edgware Road, and sacked by the Railway for trying to join without permission, he took a job as a carter delivering salt in London. In 1915, Albert tried again to enlist and this time was accepted by the Middlesex Regiment. McMillan seemed doomed to trouble. At the end of his training at Chatham he and a friend decided to go to London although neither had a pass. Sure enough, he was picked up by the police while chatting to some girls on a street corner, returned to camp and sentenced to twenty-one days' detention. When this was over he asked to see his C.O. and begged to be sent to France. His request was granted and he was sent out as a reinforcement.

One of the most remarkable members of the Army of 1916 must have been Henry Webber. In 1914, Webber was sixty-six years old, over twenty years past the army's normal age limit, and his family of four sons and four daughters were all grown up. He had already lived a very full life, having been a member of the London Stock Exchange for forty-two years. He lived at Horley in Surrey and was prominent in a great variety of local affairs: a Justice of the Peace, a County Councillor since the formation of Surrey County Council, a churchwarden and president of the local Boy Scouts Association. He took part in many of the fashionable sports: cricket, shooting, hunting (as Master of the Old Surrey and Burstow Hunt). Three of his sons were army officers serving in France, and he longed to join them.

First, Webber applied to the War Office, offering to serve 'in any capacity', but his offer was rejected. Next, he recruited a company of 'Roughriders' – fellow-horsemen like himself – and offered this unit complete to the army, but again he was rejected. He never gave up and, possibly to rid themselves of this persistent old gentleman, the War Office eventually gave him a commission. After a very short training period, Henry Webber went out to France as a battalion transport officer at the ripe old age of sixty-eight, a remarkable achievement of perseverance.

As the end of their training periods approached, the battalions made their final adjustments and filled any gaps in their ranks. There were some odd moves; an Essex man, a professional musician at the Ilford Hippodrome, answered an advertisement in a theatrical magazine and became a bandsman in the 2nd Bradford Pals. A sailor in the 4th Battle Squadron, bored with lack of action, took himself off and enlisted in a Dublin battalion. This self-organized transfer took several years to sort out but, thanks to the intervention of his M.P., the ex-sailor suffered no penalty. He was to see plenty of action with the Dublin Fusiliers.

Dick King's young brother, Frank, had joined the Yeomanry and Dick asked his own c.o. if Frank could join him in the K.O.Y.L.I. Permission was granted and the two served together, Dick as a machine-gunner and Frank as an officer's servant. A third brother served in another unit of the same division.

Some two million men had volunteered for the army and the Territorial Force but, towards the end of 1915, the numbers of new enlistments had slowed to a trickle. Lord Derby, who had sponsored the New Army's 30th Division in Lancashire, became Director General of Recruiting in October 1915. He immediately produced his 'Derby Scheme' which mentioned a word never used before in Britain – conscription. Before this was brought in (for single men to start with), in the same month a last chance to volunteer was offered and, by the end of 1915, over 200,000 took advantage of it.* Thereafter no more voluntary enlistment was allowed; men were called up as required and directed where needed. For political reasons the scheme was not applied to any part of Ireland. It was the end of the 'Kitchener Men' and the beginning of the 'Derby Men', but none of the conscripts was out in France when the Somme Battle opened. They were to become the Armies of 1917 and 1918.

As the year 1915 grew older, the New Army divisions finished their training and prepared to go to France. This was a very emotional time for them. They were desperately anxious to get to the war and prove themselves, but the

* One effect of this was a rush to the altar as reluctant men tried to avoid conscription by getting married. There was an increase of twenty-five per cent in the number of marriages in 1915. New Zealand was the only Dominion country to follow Britain's lead in introducing conscription.

casualty lists from the battles of that year and the stories of the wounded made it clear that the war was no picnic. They were leaving their families in the knowledge that some of them would never return, but the soldiers' spirits were high nevertheless.

Among the first to go was the 21st Division. The three King brothers were, of course, all given leave and Dick took the opportunity to have his photograph taken with his wife and four children. He told Emma, his wife, that he did not expect to return and took a sad farewell of his family.

Early in 1916 it was the turn of the Tyneside Scottish to go. Two of the four battalions went on leave first, with pay and ration money for six days. When these returned the other two battalions went home but, to their anger, they were only allowed four days. As the trains took them north, the word was spread around: 'We're all taking six days like the others.'

Sure enough, after four days, the special leave trains left Newcastle nearly empty; only a few N.C.O.'s returned on time. Two days later the rest, nearly 2,000 of them, turned up at Newcastle Central Station looking for means of getting back to their camp near Southampton. There was utter confusion; a few of the Tynesiders had been drinking heavily and were quite incapable; wives, children and sweethearts were seeing their men off and some were in tears. There were no special trains and the men milled around in confusion. At that time, Stephenson's original steam engine, the Rocket, was displayed at the station and a young bugler climbed up on to it and played, of all tunes, the Last Post. Every woman on the station not already crying burst into tears.

Eventually the men got back to camp, were paraded and given strong lectures by various officers, but all except a few regular troublemakers escaped punishment.

Some divisions were destined not to go directly to France. The 29th Division, containing the last of the Regulars, was standing by to go to France, but was sent to Gallipoli instead. The Edinburgh Territorial Battalion had no organization in the area to supply them with reinforcements and its numbers fell so low during the campaign that they were only at one quarter of their proper strength. The remnants were withdrawn from the division and their place taken by the Newfoundlanders. These were not well received by the 29th Division who, as Regular soldiers, objected to having another batch of 'civilians'.

The 29th Division was away for nearly a year and earned a high reputation, becoming known as the 'Incomparable Division'. The Newfoundlanders did not see the worst of the fighting but twice were last off the beaches when parts of the peninsula were evacuated; in fact they were the last troops of all to get away when the campaign finally closed in January 1916.

The 29th Division went next to Egypt for a few weeks. 'At a Sunday morning drumhead service in Alexandria we heard that we would be going to France. The Padre spoke of "fresh fields and pastures new" but by the time we got there it was "pastures old".' (Pte H. Parker, 1st Essex)

Another division to find itself in the Middle East (or Near East as it was then known) was the 31st, containing all North Country battalions. It had been feared that Turkish troops might reach the Suez Canal and the division was sent to Egypt in great haste to defend the vital waterway. The Accrington Pals, part of this division, had a narrow escape when their troopship, which also carried sixty tons of lyddite explosive, was narrowly missed by a torpedo in the Mediterranean. The threat to the Suez Canal was averted; the 31st Division saw no action there and, like the 29th, was sent to France ready for the Somme.

Some men did not go to France with their unit. These were the late joiners who went out as reinforcements. Bill Soar was sent from the 2/7th Sherwood Foresters to the 1/7th, the pre-war Nottingham battalion, serving with the 46th (North Midland) Division, after it had lost very heavily during the storming of the Hohenzollern Redoubt at Loos in October 1915.

Charles Matthews of the Northamptons was posted to a draft for France just three months after he had enlisted. Some heartless army authority refused home leave to Matthews and the other men due for France; they were even confined to their barracks at Colchester. His mother and small sister made the tedious journey from Bletchley to say farewell to the eighteen-year-old boy but their meetings had to take place through the railings of the camp gate. This was so distressing that Matthews persuaded his mother to return home. He duly crossed to France as a reinforcement to the

6th Northamptons which was with a New Army division, the 18th (Eastern).

The veteran Lieut Henry Webber was sent to join the 7th South Lancs, another New Army battalion, in the 19th (Western) Division. He was accepted quite normally by the young officers of the battalion; he performed his duties well and not many knew his true age, although the c.o. found that his own father and Webber had rowed together at Oxford in the same year, over half a century earlier. Webber hoped that he might meet and salute his three sons who all held ranks higher than his.

Albert McMillan was released from detention and sent out to none other than the Public Schools Battalion, the 16th Middlesex. The need for officers was so great that the army could not allow this battalion to keep so many potential officers and over 1,400 were eventually persuaded to accept commissions; the gaps were being made good by ordinary recruits such as McMillan. The battalion was never to lose its distinctive title, however. It was always known as the Public Schools Battalion.

It was from such men as these, of every age from fifteen to Henry Webber's sixty-eight, but all with the same spirit of patriotism and adventure, that the Army of 1916 was formed and went off to a destiny that was eventually to place it on the Somme on 1 July 1916.

This extract, written in the language of the period by Billy McFadzean, shows the spirit of the men at this time. 'You people at home make me feel quite proud when you tell me "I am the Soldier Boy of the McFadzeans". I hope to play the game and if I don't add much lustre to it I will certainly not tarnish it.'

2

The Western Front

When the soldiers landed in France they found a harsh contrast between their new living conditions and those they had left behind in England. They were to lead a spartan existence that made the small privations of their training camps seem very mild. The inexperienced, newly arrived units suffered many hardships but they quickly learned the art of making the best of it from the 'old hands'.

The men found they had landed in a poor, inhospitable region. There were no fit young Frenchmen, only a few war-disabled, and all the work in the countryside had to be done by the women and by men too old for the war. As the 3rd Manchester Pals marched away from the coast, Paddy Kennedy noted that fallen fruit was going rotten and that crops had not been harvested. Just before they had left England they had been issued with many last-minute items of equipment. The authorities at home had fixed ideas of what would be needed in France and were determined that every man should go out fully equipped. The Pals marched along, bowed down under the heaviest loads they had ever carried.

At one of their halts in a very poor French village, one of the 'old sweats' in the battalion promptly started sorting out his equipment. Everything he considered superfluous he gave away to an eager villager. Soon the whole battalion followed suit and when it marched off a few minutes later under lighter loads, both soldiers and civilians were delighted by the transaction.

When the B.E.F. crossed to France in 1914 they were rushed up to the front and were in action within a few days of landing. The other Regular divisions, and most of the Territorials which followed, had the same experience.

When the later Territorials and the first of the New Army arrived in 1915, they had a more gradual introduction to the war. As these battalions only contained a handful of men who had seen any of the war in France, before returning to England wounded, they were unready for service in the trenches. There was more training to be done, but this time more realistic than the Boer War methods used at home. They were also introduced to that feature of life in France which was to be such a torment to them – fatigues.

The nature of trench warfare and the needs of an army which was largely unmechanized resulted in a vast amount of manual labour, mostly digging and carrying. Although special labour units were brought in later in the war, some from as far away as China, there were never sufficient, and an infantry battalion, out of the line at rest or training, could all too easily be called upon to fill the gap. It was unskilled, physical labour of the hardest kind; for the pre-war labourer it was something he had done all his life, but for the professional or commercial men – shop-keepers, clerks and the like – and for the young boys who had enlisted in the ranks (officers and senior N.C.O.'s were excused) it was pure drudgery.

'Another man and myself were detailed to fill sand-bags for the whole of one night. As dawn broke, after a wet, cold night, the rain ceased and a beautiful sunrise spread a bright light over the fair land of France. I straightened up and said to my pal, "Look Charlie, isn't that a wonderful view?" Charlie didn't unbend or look round but replied, "We're making a bloody mess of it putting it all away in sand-bags then!" ' (Pte R. Love, Glasgow Commercials) *

The time arrived for the battalion to be introduced to trench warfare. Firstly, selected groups of fifty or so men, mainly officers and N.C.O.'s, and then larger parties, would go into the line for instruction with an experienced battalion.

Billy McFadzean and his fellow Belfast men were attached to a battalion of the Royal Warwicks. One night a party of bombers drawn from both battalions was sent out to patrol No Man's Land. One young Belfast man was handed three grenades with no instruction at all. Although supposed to be a trained bomber, he had never handled live grenades before. Later, lying in No Man's Land with a Warwick, he started to examine them, not very carefully. Angrily the Warwick took them from him. 'Leave them alone. You'll blow us all up!' Fortunately they all got back safely.

Others weren't so lucky. A Sheffield City Battalion man was killed during his instruction period and his belongings were sent back to where the rest of the battalion was billeted. A

*Love had been an architect before the war.

stretcher-bearer was given the job of sorting out his kit and found, with horror, that the hat still contained his comrade's brains.

'Our first experience of trench warfare took place on 27 January 1915, the Kaiser's birthday, and, believe me, this proved a very nerve-racking experience, with the Germans celebrating the occasion by a heavy bombardment all the day long on our front line.' (Pte W. B. Corbett, 1st Edinburgh City Battalion)

Kitchener's New Army had reached the war.

The reader might imagine that life for the soldier in France was full of violent action, either of furious attack or desperate defence. There were such moments but they took up no more than two or three days a year for the average soldier. The remainder of his time was spent in the dull routine of trench warfare.

The normal trench system had three lines of trenches: the front line, the support and the reserve. All were built in a right-angled zig-zag pattern, to minimize the effect of shells bursting in the trench, each short straight stretch being known as a bay. The three lines of trenches were joined to each other by communication trenches, and the whole system was entered from the rear by an access trench which started in ground invisible to an enemy.

The trenches contained only the crudest living accommodation; small holes dug into the ground, dug-outs, housed only the officers and the senior N.C.O.'s, and other ranks had to find shelter in smaller holes scraped into the side of the trench or often simply under a waterproof sheet. The floor of the trench was covered with slatted timber sections known as duckboards and on the side facing the enemy a fire-step was built so that the men could repel any attack.

The opposing trench systems were separated from each other by No Man's Land, which could vary in width from half a mile in very open country to a few yards where neither side was prepared to concede a vital position to the other. Each side protected its front-line trench and sometimes its support and reserve lines with thick belts of barbed wire.

Daily routine in the trenches followed a set pattern. Before dawn all men were roused for 'stand to', when they would man the fire-step in case of a German attack at first light. Sometimes 'stand to' was accompanied by 'morning hate', when both sides nervously fired off large quantities of rifle and machine-gun ammunition at each other.* As both sides were also careful to keep their heads down, there were few casualties.

After 'stand to' it was hoped that a quiet day would follow. Breakfast was cooked over little fires; men would shave and get washed although water, which had to be carried to the trenches, was always short. Food was plentiful but mostly tinned and always monotonous; fresh food was eagerly sought. In quiet sectors, both sides observed a truce in this morning domestic period. Any friendly artillery which did not observe it was roundly abused because it only encouraged prompt retaliation from the enemy.

Men tried to use the remainder of the day to relax or catch up on sleep, but it was never possible to enjoy an unbroken period of rest. Other men walked by, kicking the sleeper's legs; officers inspected the trenches; jobs were found; an odd shell arrived.

At dusk, the 'stand to' and 'hate' of the morning might be repeated. Then followed the best part of the day. In some units rum was issued and hot food brought up from the rear. In theory every soldier was entitled to a carefully measured tot of thick, strong rum each day but some commanders refused to accept the issue, partly on religious grounds but mostly because they thought it would befuddle their men in a crisis. There were some sectors where the German trenches were near and, if occupied by an easy-going enemy, an evening sing-song might take place. Each side would take turns, and as darkness fell applause and encores would sound out across No Man's Land. But for the most part the two sides neither saw nor heard their opponents for long periods.

When the night had properly fallen, both sides set to work; rations and stores had to be fetched from the battalion transport who had come up as far as the trenches, and repairs were made to the day's damage in the trenches.

Only at night was it safe to appear above ground level. Even then, however, men were vulnerable to random fire.

* Rifle cartridges were cheap enough at just over 1*d*. each (£4 13*s*. per 1,000).

Parties went out to repair the wire and scouts or patrols would cross No Man's Land, inspecting the German wire and defences or trying to hear their sentries talking. Some men liked this solitary type of warfare; it was one of the few occasions a man could use his initiative. The Germans, suspecting activity, fired occasional bursts of machine-gun fire or sent up flares or rockets. Those caught in the open by the flares had to 'freeze' immediately and hope to escape unseen.

Back in the trenches sentries were posted for the night to guard against an enemy raid. A man's turn for this duty lasted up to two hours and he had to struggle to keep awake; the penalty for being found asleep on sentry duty could be severe. So the long night hours would pass until gradually the horizon over the German trenches grew light again. Another routine day had dawned on the Western Front.

Although the enemy could not be seen, spasmodic warfare was waged between the combatants. As the armies had retired below ground level, direct small-arms fire was no more than a gesture. Of all wars ever fought, in none was the artillery more dominant than in this static encounter. Given good observation and plenty of shells, the gunner had his enemy at his mercy. Soldiers in the line could never free their minds from the fear of instant death or mutilation from shell fire at any time in the war. The sudden hurricane bombardments that could start at any moment were almost certainly the ultimate terror for the infantryman. There was nothing he could do to retaliate or protect himself, except cower and hope for survival.

The British soldiers soon learnt to distinguish between the different shells fired at them. Shells from the German 15-cm. guns, bursting with a violent explosion and clouds of black smoke, were called 'Coal Boxes' or 'Jack Johnsons' (after the American boxer who was world heavyweight champion at the time). A lighter gun, which the Germans could bring right up into their trenches, was much feared by the British. Unlike a normal shell, which heralded its approach with a long shriek, the flat trajectory and high velocity resulted in the shell from this gun arriving unannounced and it was known to the British as a 'Whizz Bang'.

A German mortar, the *Minnenwerfer*, fired a large metal

canister which was reputed to be filled with pieces of scrap metal. Wounds from this weapon would sometimes leave fragments from old clocks and other domestic instruments in the body.

If the opposing trenches were close the two sides might bombard each other with grenades. One battalion had its own original method. 'The bombers made a grenade launcher with a plank of wood, 6-in. nails and some strong elastic. As soon as this started firing, the Jerries naturally took cover.* One day our bombing sergeant decided to have some fun. Instead of grenades, he sent the Germans a succession of tinned stuff: jam, pork and beans, bully beef. After a bit he said, "Now I'll make the Germans blow their bugle for their stretcher-bearers", and he sent over a live grenade. Sure enough, we could hear the German bugle blowing.' (Pte T. Easton, 2nd Tyneside Scottish)

Those sectors of the front where the soil was suitable and No Man's Land narrow became mining sectors. Sappers tunnelled their way under the opposing trenches and laid explosive there. The explosion when these were blown destroyed the trenches, killing or burying those men who happened to be occupying them, and leaving a large crater. The debris blown skywards would fall around the crater causing a 'lip' which, being a few feet above the surrounding ground, constituted a minor defence in any open fighting. Sometimes mines were blown for nuisance value. But whenever they were part of an attack, troops would rush forward to occupy the crater and thus to establish a foothold in the opposing line.

Soon after Bill Soar had joined his battalion he went into the line on a mining sector. One night he was detailed to help some French tunnellers by removing the spoil from the mine shaft. Suddenly, there was a huge explosion and the Frenchmen came up shouting '*Allez, allez!*'; the Germans had blown their own mine. Soar rushed off into the dark but unfortunately he lost his way and stumbled into the newly blown crater, only to find it already occupied by the Germans. Poor Bill Soar, just out from England and only eighteen, was terrified but, keeping his head, he crawled out of the

* The British had many nicknames for the Germans: Gerry or Jerry, Fritz, the Hun or the Boche.

crater undetected and made off in what he thought a safe direction. Suddenly, in the pitch dark, he was stopped by a revolver pressed to his head. Thinking the worst, he kept still but found, to his great relief, that one of his own officers had come to look for him.

Even in the so-called 'quiet' times, a battalion could expect to lose about thirty men each month through death and wounds and a similar number through sickness. Lightly wounded or sick cases were mostly treated in France but more serious cases were evacuated to England, or 'Blighty' as it was known to the soldiers; a wound that needed prolonged treatment was therefore known as a 'Blighty wound'.

So the dull months of trench warfare passed. Battalions did their tour of four to eight days' duty in the trenches and then went back to their billets in the rear for a rest, although within a few hours they were soon drilling, training or back on the endless labouring fatigues. Very often they stayed on the same sector for month after month until their trenches became home to them. In summer the life could be tolerated; in winter, especially in wet sectors, it was pure misery.

Being so close to England, the army received many prominent visitors. After the 2nd Lincolns had arrived in France from Bermuda a party from Capt. Reginald Bastard's company was selected for special drill. After many rehearsals, they were turned out, with Bastard himself in charge, as a guard of honour for a party of important visitors. These were King George V, the French President Poincaré and the French Commander-in-Chief, General Joffre (known as 'Papa' Joffre from his fatherly appearance).

One member of the Royal Family who made himself very popular with the men was the young Prince of Wales (later King Edward VIII) who was attached, as a serving officer, to one of the headquarters. The men admired him because, unlike most visitors, he insisted on seeing the troops as informally as possible, often in the front-line trenches. Many a soldier was surprised to find the Prince appearing in his trench, chatting to the men and handing out cigarettes (usually Abdullahs, much better than the routine issue).

An infantryman's home was his battalion, a unit nominally composed of thirty-six officers and 1,000 men although, after some time in France, rarely at full strength.

There was a small headquarters with a lieutenant-colonel as C.O.; a major who acted as second-in-command; the adjutant, a captain who was the C.O.'s administrative officer, and the regimental sergeant major, the senior N.C.O. in the battalion.

The majority of the men in the battalion were in the four rifle companies, which were nominally commanded by majors; but, by 1916, casualties or promotion had taken so many of these that most companies were under the command of captains.

The company of 1916 was a very big sub-unit with 240 men on its strength. These were formed into four platoons of sixty men, each commanded by a lieutenant or a second-lieutenant. Like the majors, most of the lieutenants had gone and platoon commanders were usually newly commissioned second-lieutenants. The platoon in turn was subdivided into four sections each under a junior N.C.O.

The platoon rarely saw some of its members, for these were the specialists whose work kept them elsewhere: signallers, much envied because they heard important news before anyone else; bandsmen, who became stretcher-bearers in battle; cooks, sanitary men, transport men, clerks, pioneers and many more. The actual fighting strength of the platoon was fifty men and of the battalion about 800.

Many of the specialists never went into the trenches or took part in attacks but remained at a village in the rear which was the battalion's home when out of the line and was known loosely as the 'transport lines'. It was this part of the battalion that was the permanent core of the unit. As the original fighting men faded away and were replaced by the reinforcements, it was the 'transport' who passed the spirit of the battalion on to the newcomers. This was particularly so when a battalion had lost heavily in a big battle.

The reader may be interested to know what the various ranks were paid for their responsibilities or the dangers they faced (see table on next page).

These basic daily rates could be supplemented in various ways; the officers received field allowances of 2*s.* 6*d.* a day and the men could earn proficiency pay for various skills. But no one in the army was paid less than the infantryman.

The Guards were paid more than the county regiments; all Empire troops were paid several times more than those from the Homeland. The Newfoundlanders were frequently involved in arguments with jealous English troops, who called them the 'Fucking Five Bobbers'. Many men from poor families sent half of their pay home, leaving them less than 4*s*. a week. The soldiers drew their pay in francs and spent it in military canteens or in *estaminets* when out of the line.

Rank	*Responsibility*	*Daily pay*
Lieutenant-colonel	a battalion of 35 officers and 1,000 men	23*s*.
Captain	a company of 5 officers and 240 men	12*s*. 6*d*.
Second-lieutenant	a platoon of 60 men	7*s*. 6*d*.
Lance corporal	a section of 14 men	1*s*. 3*d*.
Private	himself	1*s*.

Every infantryman had his own weapon even if only eighty per cent of them went into battle. The officers had revolvers or swords, both of which were useless at other than short range and only made their owners conspicuous to German marksmen.

The N.C.O.'s and men were armed with the .303 Lee Enfield rifle, to which could be attached a long sword-like bayonet which was useful for chopping wood and other domestic work. The Lee Enfield was accurate up to 1,000 yards in the hands of a good shot, but seldom did the soldier of 1916 have the chance to use it. Some carried their rifles through several years of war but never had the opportunity to fire a single shot aimed at an enemy.

Two specialist infantry weapons were the Lewis machine-gun and the hand grenade (called a Mills bomb after its inventor). The Lewis was effective when all went well but it frequently jammed and took six men to operate it in an attack: the firer, one man carrying spare parts and four more carrying ammunition.

The Mills bomb was ideal for trench fighting and clearing dug-outs, its explosion being more lethal than that of its German counterpart. But the German hand grenade was mounted on a short stick and the leverage obtained from this gave it a slight, but important, advantage in range.

Grenadiers, or 'bombers' as they were called, were specially trained men (Billy McFadzean was one), who wore a small grenade on their sleeve as the mark of their trade. It was rumoured, almost certainly untruly, that the Germans had crucified captured bombers in retaliation for the damage caused by grenades in night raids on their trenches. But, because of the rumour, bombers often removed their grenade badge before they went on such raids.

Various items of clothing were issued to the men as protection from winter conditions. In the winter of 1915 Billy MacFadzean's company of Belfast men were paraded one day while they were out of the line and issued with fur jackets ready for their next tour of duty in the trenches. The jackets had been made from a variety of furs of different colours and shapes and some smelt strongly. The company paraded in new jackets and was inspected by a major mounted on horseback. After a long, silent look he said, 'Well, C Company, you look just like a lot of London prostitutes. Dismiss.'

Another novelty, only issued as late as the spring of 1916, was the steel helmet, intended to reduce the number of head wounds. Until then the men had nothing better than their soft service caps. The helmets were so effective that such wounds were reduced by seventy-five per cent, but one divisional commander, who also forbade the issue of rum, refused at first to permit the use of steel helmets. He considered that it would encourage the men to get soft.

If a soldier's first loyalty was to his battalion, then his second was to his division.* This was the largest formation to hold the same units permanently and its function was to operate the fighting infantry and the immediate supporting arms. The divisional commander held the rank of major-general. His infantry was divided into three brigades (of four battalions each) under brigadier-generals. In 1915 when

* This section refers to infantry divisions only. There were five cavalry divisions in the B.E.F. at the time.

the nature of trench warfare became apparent, a thirteenth infantry battalion, the divisional Pioneers, was added to help with labouring and construction work.

Where possible, divisions contained battalions of the same type, so that the Regular, Territorial and New Army spirit was reflected in complete divisions. The Territorials always kept their divisions exclusive but, after the Battle of Loos when the first New Army divisions in action had made a shaky start, some Regular and New Army battalions were exchanged to stiffen the inexperienced New Army men.

Of the units supporting the infantry, the most immediate were the brigade Machine Gun Companies and light Trench Mortar Batteries. Both were manned by infantrymen and both operated infantry weapons. As these new weapons had developed and multiplied, the heavier models of the machine-guns, the Vickers, and all the mortars had been withdrawn from the battalions and were operated under brigade control in specially formed units. The machine-gunners and mortar-gunners worked very closely with the battalions and occupied the same trenches.

Immediately behind the infantry stood the divisional artillery, whose weapons were the 4.5-in. howitzers, the 18-pounder field-guns and the heavy mortars. All these were manned by the Royal Field Artillery. The R.F.A. worked very closely with the infantry and a battalion in the trenches normally had a Forward Observation Officer and his signallers attached to it to give immediate artillery support.

Within the division the Royal Engineers had two responsibilities. The R.E. Signal Company was responsible for communications between the units in the division, although the infantry and artillery provided their own internal signals. The Field Companies supervised the construction and maintenance of trenches and dug-outs and the storage of ammunition in the trench system, although most of the actual work was done by the infantry, which led the men of one battalion to make up the following rhyme:

'God made the world,
Bees make honey.
The Essex do the work,
The R.E.s get the money.'

(L/Cpl W. G. Sanders, 10th Essex)

The medical services were operated by the Royal Army Medical Corps. Its most forward element was the battalion Medical Officer, who, with a handful of R.A.M.C. orderlies, occupied a dug-out in the trenches which was his first-aid post. It was his duty to give elementary treatment only; all but the lightest cases were evacuated to the next R.A.M.C. units. These were the Field Ambulances, a confusing term, since they were operational units and not the motor ambulance vehicles themselves. Field Ambulances had no facilities for major surgery or for holding large numbers of patients. Their function was simply to get sick and wounded men back as quickly as possible to the next R.A.M.C. units, the Casualty Clearing Stations, which were outside the battle area, beyond the range of enemy guns.

In 1916 the major-general had in his division a powerful and well balanced force. It lived and moved as an entity and fought as a team. His infantry and artillery could produce fire from 10,000 rifles, 204 machine-guns (compared with only twenty-four in 1914), forty trench-mortars and sixty-four guns.

It might interest the present-day reader to know that, to serve the 19,372 men in the division, there were over 5,000 horses but only sixty-one motor vehicles, of which three only were lorries.

The divisional commander was in a unique position. He held general's rank and at the same time he commanded a permanent infantry unit. Many became well known to their men and frequently shared their dangers. The commander of the 34th Division, which contained the Tyneside Irish and Scottish Brigades, was Maj.-Gen. Ingouville-Williams – 'Inky Bill' to his men. One day three wagons, loaded with trench-mortar bombs, were shelled on an exposed stretch of road. Two escaped safely but the driver of the third took cover, leaving his load in the open. 'Inky Bill', who had watched the episode, left the safety of a nearby trench, mounted the wagon himself and drove it to safety.

The majority of the actual fighting was done by the infantry divisions, but the B.E.F. also contained a miscellany of other units all necessary to command, feed, administer and support the divisions. The direction of the B.E.F. was in the hands of the Commander-in-Chief at General Headquarters;* between him and the divisions were two intermediate formations – 'army' and 'corps'. These performed two operational functions. First, they were the means whereby the c.-in-c.'s orders were passed down to the fifty-odd infantry divisions, and secondly, they operated the specialist units which supported the infantry but did not fit into their divisions.

There were four British armies on the Western Front by the spring of 1916 and they each comprised, on an average, four infantry corps which, in turn, contained an average of three divisions each. The big difference between armies and corps on the one hand and divisions on the other, is that the former did not hold infantry units on a permanent basis whereas the divisions did. Subject to major reorganization, a division contained the same brigades and battalions permanently, but the divisions themselves were frequently transferred from the control of one corps, or army, to another. Army and corps were merely headquarters units and formed part of the chain of command linking the c.-in-c. with the front-line troops. The ordinary soldier rarely knew or cared to which corps his division was attached at any given time.

The overall direction of the war, as far as the British Army was concerned, was in the hands of the War Committee (later re-named the War Cabinet) in London. This was a body of civilians, politicians from the Liberal Government of the time, strengthened by representatives from the leading Empire countries. The War Committee was responsible to the Cabinet and eventually to Parliament, and attempted to direct the war effort of the British Empire throughout the world. The Western Front, although the greatest, was only one of their responsibilities. As it had to rely heavily upon the advice of the military and consult frequently with its allies, the War Committee's orders all too often represented a consensus of opinion or vague guidelines rather than firm direction.

The War Committee expressed its wishes (one hesitates to use a firmer word) to the Minister of War, who passed them on to the Chief of the Imperial General Staff whose

* c.-in-c. and G.H.Q. are the abbreviations for Commander-in-Chief and General Headquarters.

responsibility it was to translate them into action. But, as with the War Committee, his interests too were world-wide.

The next link in the chain of command was the C.-in-C. of the B.E.F. He received only general instructions from London on what was expected of him and was then left to choose his own course of action. Communication between G.H.Q. and London on detailed matters was virtually non-existent. The C.-in-C. sent Despatches to the Government every few months but these only told of what had happened in his command since the last Despatch.* Of his future plans, he would give few details.

If the C.-in-C. was able to plan free of close control from London, he did have to consider his Allies. There was no combined command between the British, French and Belgian Armies but there was a close liaison between them. The British had started the war as a small contingent almost lost among the huge French Army and the British C.-in-C. had to conform to the moves of his ally. As his own army grew in size, the British commander's position became stronger but he was still the junior partner in 1916 and felt obliged to be guided in his strategy by the French C.-in-C.

Militarily, too, he was forced into this position. The B.E.F. was in a foreign country, cut off from its homeland by the sea. Any attempt to act independently could have led to its isolation and destruction by the Germans. The position in mid-1916, then, was that the British C.-in-C. was influenced as much by the French as by his own government.

In his relations with his subordinate commanders the C.-in-C. had no difficulty and strict obedience was ruthlessly enforced at all levels in the chain of command. So in 1916, the C.-in-C. sat at his G.H.Q. in France; behind him only weak political direction; alongside him the French from whom he was in theory independent but whom he could ignore only at his peril; in front of him the biggest army Britain had ever put into the field, completely compliant to his wishes.

When the C.-in-C.'s orders eventually reached the private soldiers they had been passed down through eight intermediate commanders. One of the tragedies of the First

* At the end of each Despatch the C.-in-C. would give a list of officers and men who had given good service, although they had not been awarded decorations, hence the expression 'Mentioned in Despatches'.

World War was the gulf between leaders and led. Of the commanders in the chain of command, only those below brigade level actually lived in the trenches. Brigade commanders would visit the trenches often, divisional commanders sometimes; above that level visits were rare. Corps and army commanders had no direct interest in the transient

The Chain of Command

THE WAR COMMITTEE
|
CHIEF OF THE IMPERIAL GENERAL STAFF
|
COMMANDER-IN-CHIEF, B.E.F.
(Usually a Field-Marshal)
|
ARMY COMMANDER (General)
|
CORPS COMMANDER (Lieutenant-General)
|
DIVISIONAL COMMANDER (Major-General)
|
BRIGADE COMMANDER (Brigadier-General)
|
BATTALION COMMANDER (Lieutenant-Colonel)
|
COMPANY COMMANDER (Captain)
|
PLATOON COMMANDER (Second-Lieutenant)
|
SECTION COMMANDER (Corporal)
|
THE SOLDIER

units passing through their commands. The trenches on their sectors were numerous, intricate and difficult of access from their H.Q.'s. With a few exceptions, they satisfied themselves with visits to the battalions out of the line, training or resting, to Casualty Clearing Stations to see the wounded and to divisional H.Q.'s.

The result was that corps and army commanders and the C.-in-C. himself had never experienced trench warfare, had no direct knowledge of the living conditions of the men at the front and had not been involved personally in the abortive attacks of 1915. At a time when aerial bombing was rare, the zone of danger in France was limited to the range of the heaviest German guns. Beyond this the senior generals and their staffs could live in absolute safety and, due to the habit of setting up their H.Q.'s in the best châteaux, in some luxury.

One might imagine from the size of the British Expeditionary Force that it was responsible for defending a large and vital part of France and Belgium, but this was not so. Its zone was of a rectangular shape bounded on the west by the sea, on the east by the front line and on the north and south by the Belgian and French zones. This rectangle measured a mere sixty miles, by fifty miles and was the same size and shape as the county of Lincolnshire. The junction with the Belgians would be on the River Humber and with the French at the Wash.

Because the front line was anything but straight the total length held by the British was eighty-five miles (in mid-1916); this compared with the French front of about 300 miles and the Belgian of only fifteen. A comparison between the Allies on the lengths of front held, however, is not a fair one. Much of the French line in the south was quiet for the whole of the war; for neither side was the territory there vital. On one sector near Switzerland the French even sat just inside Germany for the whole of the war and were hardly disturbed. On the B.E.F.'s northern flank the Belgian Army was never strong enough to mount an offensive, but remained defending the last corner of its country not occupied by the Germans. The sectors held by the British were, on the average, fought over harder than any others.

The British-held trenches started just north of Ypres ('Wipers' to the soldiers) in Belgium, wound past the frontier into northern France, through the mining area near Lens, past Vimy Ridge, over the River Scarpe near Arras and finally down through the Somme region to the junction with the French.

When the war of movement had ceased in 1914 it was found that the Allies, for this was mostly a French Army area in 1914, had held a series of small towns usually in ground lower than the surrounding countryside. The Germans had pressed forward on either side of the towns so that they

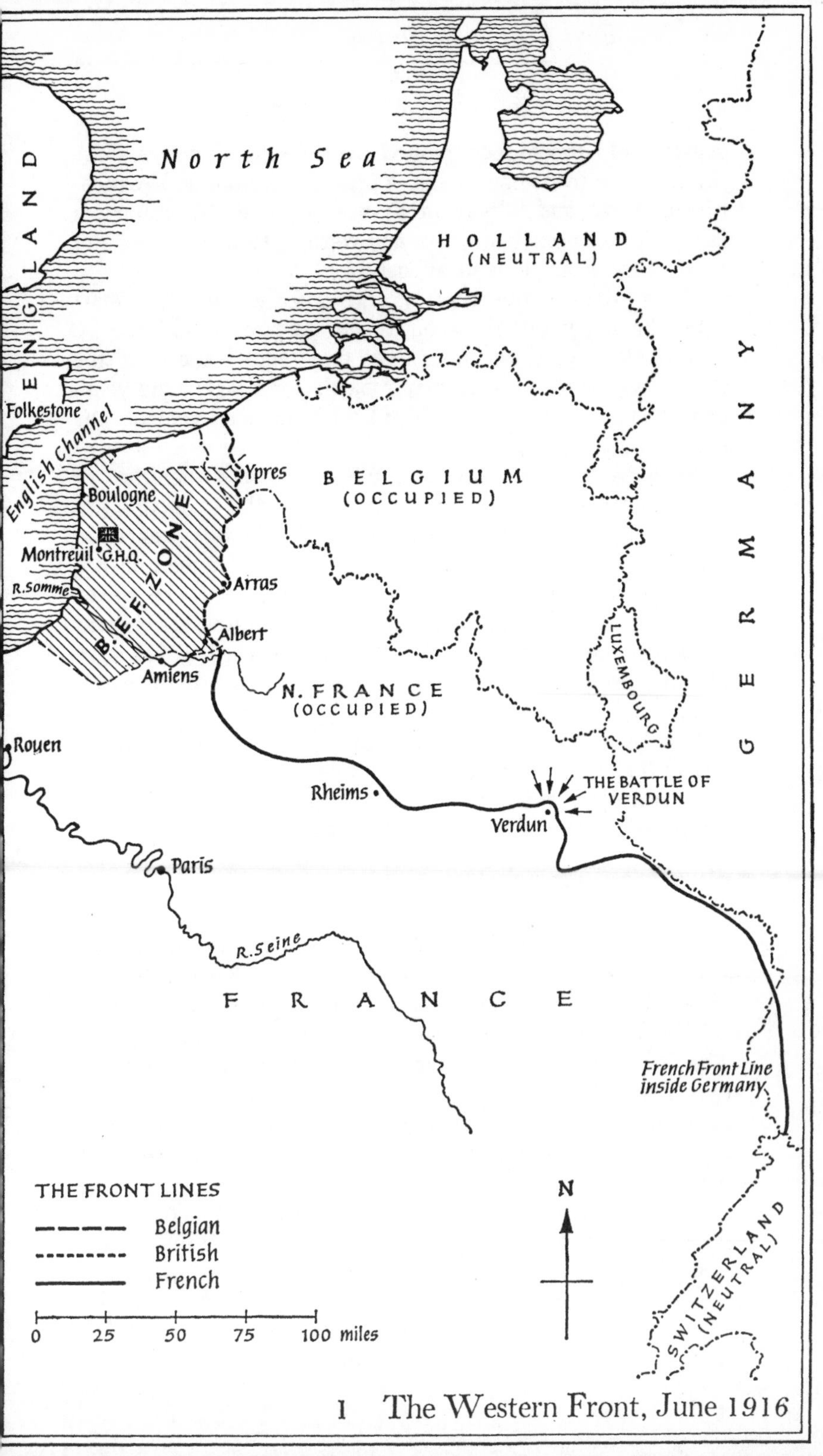

1 The Western Front, June 1916

usually held the higher ground overlooking them on three sides. These front-line towns, Ypres in Belgium and Armentières, Arras and Albert in France, were to be important factors in the next four years and were to be at the centre of most of the great British offensives.

Other parts of the front became quiet sectors and, apart from the petty bickering of trench warfare, would see no large-scale action for years. On one sector, south of the River Lys, there was no major battle for nearly four years and the lines did not move until the war of movement was resumed late in 1918.

Between the front line and the coast were the lines of communications. It was in this region, at the little town of Montreuil, that G.H.Q. was situated; also in this area were the five divisions of cavalry, patiently waiting for their chance of open warfare and mounted action. They were never allowed near the front with their horses unless action was probable; they needed so much fodder that they would have placed an intolerable strain on transport resources in the battle area.

Finally, on the coast, were the great bases – Étaples ('Heel Taps' or 'Eat Apples'), Le Havre and Rouen – with their hospitals and infantry reinforcement camps close to the ports connecting the B.E.F. to England.

After the big battles of 1914 the armies had become bogged down in a type of warfare that was almost a replica of the siege warfare of the Middle Ages, but with this difference – the position of neither side could be out-flanked. It is interesting to see how the combatants reacted to the stalemate.

The attitude of the French and Belgians was quite simple. They had both lost much territory and were determined on two things. Firstly, the Germans were not to be allowed to take another metre of ground and, secondly, they were to be driven off that which they had already taken as soon as possible.

The British position was not quite as simple. There was some moral obligation upon them to adopt the same policy as their Allies, although as they were not fighting upon their own soil they did not adopt the policy as passionately. In the British mind there were at least two other factors which counted as much as inter-allied loyalty.

CSM Percy Chappell, 1st Somerset LI. This photograph was taken in 1909 when the British Army used, for a short time, the German-type peakless cap.

Δ Lieutenant-Colonel Reginald Bastard, 2nd Lincolns.

∇ Private Billy McFadzean of the Belfast Young Citizens Volunteers, later the 14th Royal Irish Rifles.

Δ Bugler Bill Soar, 1/7th Sherwood Foresters. Soar has removed the wire from the rim of his hat to achieve the 'active service' effect.

∇ Henry Webber, the 68 year old stockbroker, who became a subaltern in a New Army infantry battalion.

The terms of service for the 'First Hundred Thousand'. Half a million men answered this appeal in less than three weeks.

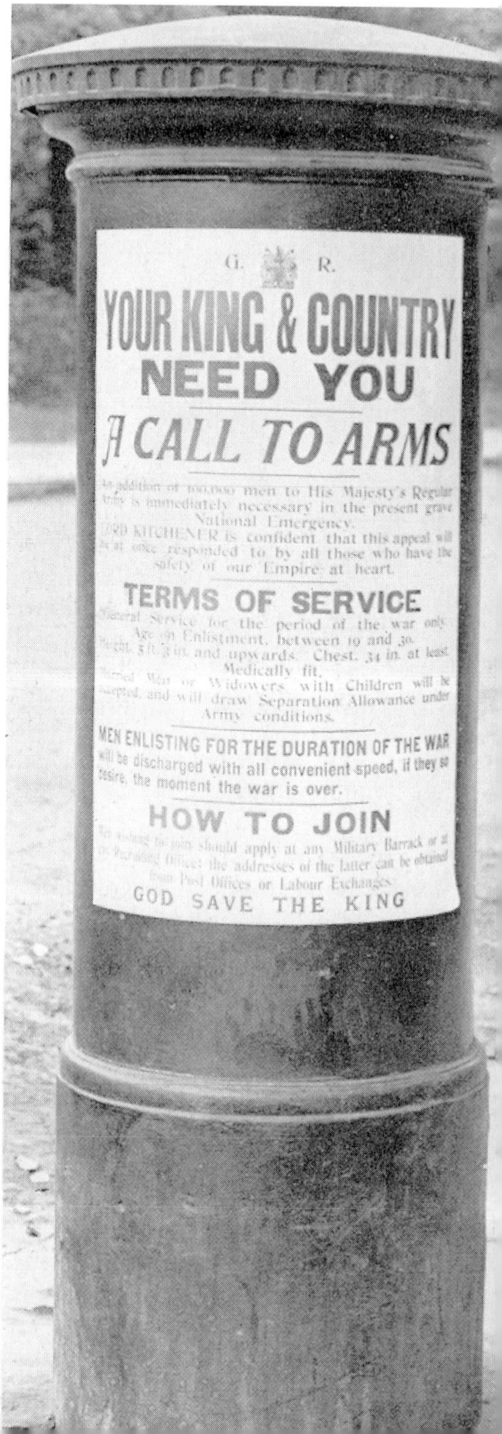

Δ Private Dick King, 10th King's Own Yorkshire Light Infantry. This family photograph was taken just before the 21st Division sailed for France in 1915.

∇ Private Albert McMillan who was posted to the Public Schools Battalion just in time for the battle.

Volunteers taking the oath in a Recruiting Office at the White City, London, 1915. The men in this group obviously came from a great variety of backgrounds.

∆ The Clerks and Warehousemen of Manchester, later the 3rd Manchester Pals and, later still, the 18th Battalion, the Manchester Regiment. Private Paddy Kennedy is the only man with a rifle.

∇ Men of the Sheffield City Battalion drilling at Bramall Lane Cricket Ground; no uniforms or rifles have yet been issued. The obvious fitness and intelligence of these men typifies the high standard of the first recruits for the New Army.

Δ Recruits of the Lincolnshire Regiment at rifle drill, September 1914. There appears to be plenty of rifles for these men but few uniforms.

∇ Men of the Northamptonshire Regiment. Note the obvious youth of the soldier on the right; there were thousands of such boys in the New Army. Charles Matthews (extreme left) later went out to the 6th Northamptons and became a lance corporal.

'When the Golden Virgin falls the war will end.' The basilica of Albert, 1916, showing the famous statue.

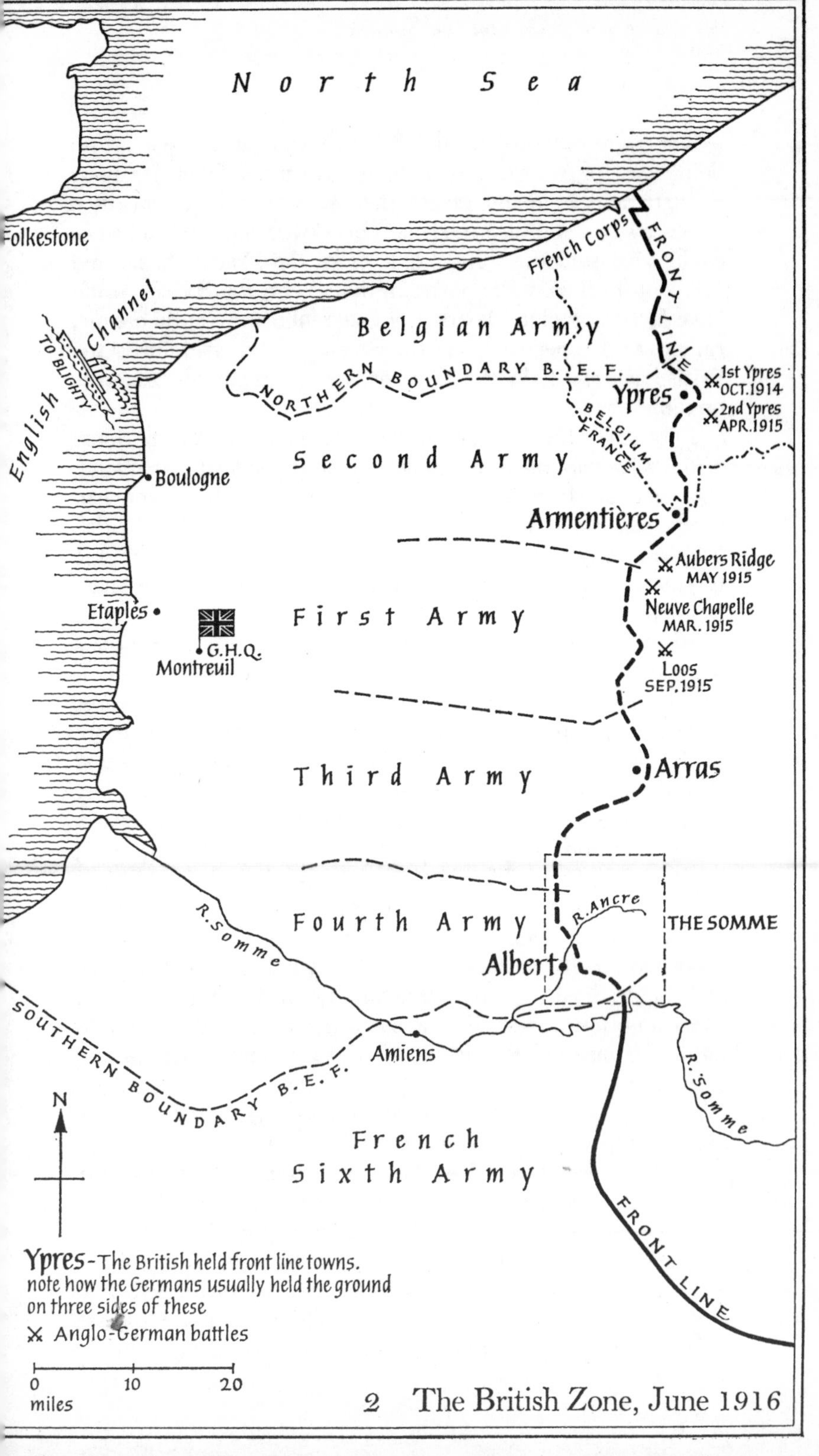

2 The British Zone, June 1916

The zone occupied by the B.E.F. was near the sea; at no point was its front line more than fifty miles from the coast in 1916 and in many places the sea was only twenty-five miles away. Another German breakthrough and advance could have separated the B.E.F. from the French Army and even cut it off from the ports. In that event, the B.E.F. would have faced complete destruction, surrender or frantic escape, rather as happened in 1940. Strategically, therefore, the British had to hold the Germans as far from the coast as possible.

Another factor influencing the British attitude was national pride. German pre-war industrial and imperial expansion, and particularly their decision to rival the British fleet, had been seen as a direct threat to the future of the British Empire. Anything other than complete victory over the Germans would have been politically and emotionally unacceptable.

So for different reasons the British, French and Belgians were all committed to the same policy – to hold their present positions and, eventually, to attack and defeat the Germans.

The Germans were in a completely different position. In the autumn of 1914 they had made breathtaking advances without gaining the complete and rapid victory that they considered essential if they were not to be trapped into a war of attrition. After one last effort at Ypres in spring 1915, Germany recognized that stalemate existed on their Western Front. They therefore decided to assume a basically defensive attitude for the time being and were easily able to defeat all French and British attacks. In 1915 they held every advantage and could afford to remain indefinitely on the defensive until some solution appeared – a collapse of the Allied will to fight, a compromise peace or a sudden chance to attack and gain victory.

So deep were they into their enemies' territory that the exact siting of their defensive positions was flexible. They were prepared to sacrifice a few kilometres in exchange for commanding positions. Once these were occupied, the Germans proceeded methodically to construct intensive defences of great strength – and therein lies the tragedy. Because the British were unwilling to fall back, they were compelled to accept, and to launch their attacks from, inferior positions at nearly every point of the line. In a war when the side having the best artillery observation could dominate every daylight move and a few metres in height were worth thousands of men's lives, the British soldiers found themselves under the German guns.

The British generals were aware early in 1916 that the victory that they considered inevitable would not be an easy one. The rebuffs of 1915 had convinced them that they would have to wait many months until the strength of their army was such that they could smash through the German trenches and then, in a renewed war of movement, use their greater numbers and particularly their cavalry to gain victory.

In the interval before all this became possible, they could not afford to allow their fighting troops to lose their offensive spirit in the stagnation of trench warfare. We have already seen how far the nature of trench warfare tended to promote tacit inactivity. Whereas the Germans were allowed to strengthen their defensive system, the construction of good, sound defences was discouraged in the British lines and little effort was made to provide adequate building materials. The generals feared that, once the soldiers had made themselves safe and comfortable in their trenches, they would never be made to leave them and get on with the war.

The generals hated trench warfare. It was a denial of every precept they had of war and of their own tactical initiative. In order to keep their troops offensively minded and to keep themselves occupied, they ordered a positive policy of limited offensive action. The slightest action from the Germans was to be met with instant and added retaliation; the slogan was 'Give them three for every one'. The fact that in any action the better defences and artillery of the Germans meant that the British lost more men didn't alter the policy; it is possible that the generals didn't even realize this fact but, if they did, they had plenty of men available. So the orders were issued but, by the time they had been passed down the lengthy chain of command, something the generals had not expected had happened.

The British soldier had gone to war full of patriotism and enthusiasm. He had been led to believe that the German was a barbarian who had trampled over half of Europe, raped women, murdered babies and committed every possible atrocity. He believed, also, that Britain had the most capable generals and the government and people at home were solidly behind him. To many it was more like a crusade than a political war. But after his arrival at the front the soldier's feelings changed. Although he didn't see many Germans he came to realize that his opponent was an honest fighter, a patriotic man, who loved his Fatherland as much as the British soldier his country, and that it was the ordinary soldiers who shared the danger and misery of the trenches. This change of attitude by the British soldiers was not immediate, nor was it universal, but it was very widespread.

As the British soldier softened his attitude towards the enemy in their trenches a few yards away, his feelings towards those behind him hardened. One of the controversies of the First World War was the extent to which the ordinary soldier lost faith in his generals. Having been in contact with over 500 men of 1916, I have come to this opinion. Initially, the British generals held the complete trust of their men. By their *apparent* inability to solve the stalemate and their *apparent* indifference to the sufferings of their men they gradually lost this trust. By 1916 the process had only just started; even by 1918 it was still not complete, for some had faith in the generals to the end. The real bitterness and hatred did not show itself until after the war was over and the men realized the full extent of the tragedy. Even then, a few remained loyal to their old leaders.

Disillusionment with those at home came much quicker. The factor causing this more than any other was the strikes which were occurring in factories. In 1915 and 1916 there were 1,200 stoppages and over five million working days were lost. Many of these were in ammunition factories although a special Act of Parliament forbade such strikes. There had been a steep rise in the cost of living, and the workers were anxious to recover this and to take the opportunity of bettering their conditions generally while they were in an ideal position to force their demands. The strikes were called by the workers' unofficial leaders or their shop stewards rather than by the trade unions. Some of the reasons for the strikes were ludicrous: two female workers would not join in the boycott of a factory canteen; a favourite engineer's release from the army was held up. To the volunteer soldier in the trenches earning 1*s.* a day it was unbelievable, for, if he deserted his post or downed his arms, he was liable to be put before a firing squad. It seemed unforgivable, therefore, that the politicians were unable to stop these strikes. The stoppages were freely reported in the press and the Germans were amazed. Enemy prisoners told the British that if such a thing happened in their factories the strikers would be sent to the front and replaced by soldiers.

It was against this background of disappearing hatred for the Germans and growing disillusionment with his own people behind him that the British soldier received orders to adopt an offensive attitude in quiet times. The result was an effort to adopt a 'live and let live' attitude; something the French generals had done between their big battles from the beginning of the war.

The British soldiers would have liked to have adopted the same policy, but their generals would not allow it. At Christmas, 1914, the British and Germans had held a spontaneous, unofficial and completely successful truce for a full week. Men had met in No Man's Land, exchanged cigarettes and cap badges, taken photographs of each other, and provided neither tried to go into the other's trenches, there was no firing at all. On New Year's Day the truce ended and strict orders were issued by the British generals that it was never to be repeated.

When General Sir Douglas Haig became C.-in-C. in December, 1915, he confirmed this order and one of the first problems he was faced with, after Christmas, was what disciplinary action to take over two officers of the Scots Guards who had immediately broken the order, and been court-martialled. Capt. Miles Barne, an acting battalion commander, was acquitted but Capt. Sir Iain Colquhoun reprimanded. Haig confirmed the sentence.* Opportunities for fraternization in 1914-style were rare, although in one village on a quiet sector near Lens, both sides used the same village pump quite amicably for several months.

The 'live and let live' attitude in normal times took a more subtle form; both sides simply refrained from provoking the other and settled down to live as comfortably as they could together. The British soldier was not afraid to fight and die when there was a chance of a successful attack

* Miles Barne became a major but was killed in 1917 when a damaged British aeroplane accidentally released a bomb on the British lines. Sir Iain Colquhoun became a brigade commander and survived the war.

and he would certainly defend his trench against an enemy assault, but he could not understand the belligerent policy forced upon him during quiet times which always brought him more loss than the enemy. There was, therefore, a conflict between the policy adopted by the generals and the attitude of the men in the trenches. The result was that the generals' orders were not always fully carried out.

It is difficult to pinpoint exactly where in the chain of command the first resistance was met. Army and corps commanders mostly passed orders on enthusiastically; the troops under their command were not permanently theirs and so the losses did not affect them directly; furthermore they were under the immediate eye of the c.-in-c.

The resistance probably started at the level of divisional commander. Most major-generals loved their divisions and wished to preserve them for the big attacks which would give them and their men a chance of glory. On the other hand, they were in a difficult position. The worst thing that could happen to a general in France was to be relieved of his command and returned to England (the two expressions used were 'stellenbosched', after a town in the Boer War, and 'degommered', from the French word meaning 'to become unstuck'). A career general would never get another field command; he would lose the temporary rank which most of them held; even death was preferable to the disgrace. To avoid this, any general whose position was threatened by the 'stickiness' of a junior would certainly get rid of that junior. This process was repeated in lessening degrees through the remainder of the chain of command, although at lower levels the penalty was a court martial rather than to be sent home. Most lance corporals would have happily gone home and the resulting loss of one stripe would not have bothered them.

3

The Somme and the Germans

That part of France finally chosen by the Allies for their summer offensive of 1916 was known as the Somme Front and was named after both a river and a department of that name. The British sector lay in the extreme north-east corner of the department and part of their battle front actually lay in the next, the Pas de Calais. Although the British rear areas lay astride the River Somme, it was through the French sector that the river actually flowed from German-held territory on its way to the sea.

Most British people thought of the Somme mainly as a river, and the use of that name to describe the battle was a slight misnomer since no British troops were to fight on the River Somme all that summer. But, as the French were to take part in the battle and as it was mostly to be fought in the department of the Somme, the choice of that name was as good as any other. The whole region had formed part of the old French province of Picardy and between the front and the sea could be found the ancient battlefields of Crécy and Agincourt.

The capital of the Somme department was the cathedral city of Amiens but only two, much smaller, towns were to play any part in the coming battle. North-east of Amiens was Albert, a dull little town of 7,000 pre-war inhabitants, little different from many others in this part of France. Albert had one outstanding feature: a large basilica dedicated to the Virgin Mary had been built there and it had been hoped at one time that the town would become a pilgrimage centre to rival Lourdes; but this had not happened. The basilica had a tall tower on the top of which was a statue of the Virgin offering her infant Son to His Father in Heaven. This gilded statue, known as the 'Golden Virgin', stood high above the little town and could be seen for some distance from the surrounding countryside.

Further north-east still lay the smaller town of Bapaume,

which had been the site of a battle during the Franco-Prussian War of 1870–71. The importance of all these towns lay only in their position as road and rail centres. The most important of the roads was one built by the Romans which ran perfectly straight from Amiens through Albert and on to Bapaume.

If the towns were dull, the countryside was not. A pleasant, open, chalk downland was covered with rich soil which grew mainly wheat and sugar beet. The main feature of the countryside was the woods. Whether extensive, dense woods of mature trees covering many acres, or small copses, they were to be dominant factors in the coming battle. Between the woods and the numerous villages the countryside was particularly open. There were no hedges; the chalk soil meant that no ditches were needed and there were hardly any trees. In these places natural cover was non-existent.

The region was crossed by two rivers. The larger, the Somme, ran due west to the sea. The original river ran in lazy loops in a valley it had cut for itself in the chalk uplands; but parts had been deepened and straightened to make a canal, leaving the original course as a wide marshy area. The river was lined with willow trees and the riverside villages were in pleasant contrast to their plainer upland sisters. The second river, the much smaller Ancre, ran south-west through Albert, where it flowed through a tunnel underneath the basilica, and on into the Somme half-way between Albert and Amiens. The Ancre was really no more than a small stream but it had the same characteristics as the Somme, the wide marshy valley cut into the chalk and the tree-lined banks.

The region had seen the limit of the German advance in 1914 when it was a completely French sector. The town of Albert had been taken and briefly held by the Germans but the French managed to push them out. The front line settled down about two miles outside the town, with the Germans, as so often, holding the higher ground. Bapaume was nine miles behind the German line and Amiens sixteen miles behind the French. Amiens was safe from long-range artillery but Bapaume not quite. Albert became a front-line town and most of its people left.

On 15 January 1915, a German shell struck the tower of the basilica. The statue of the Golden Virgin nearly fell and was

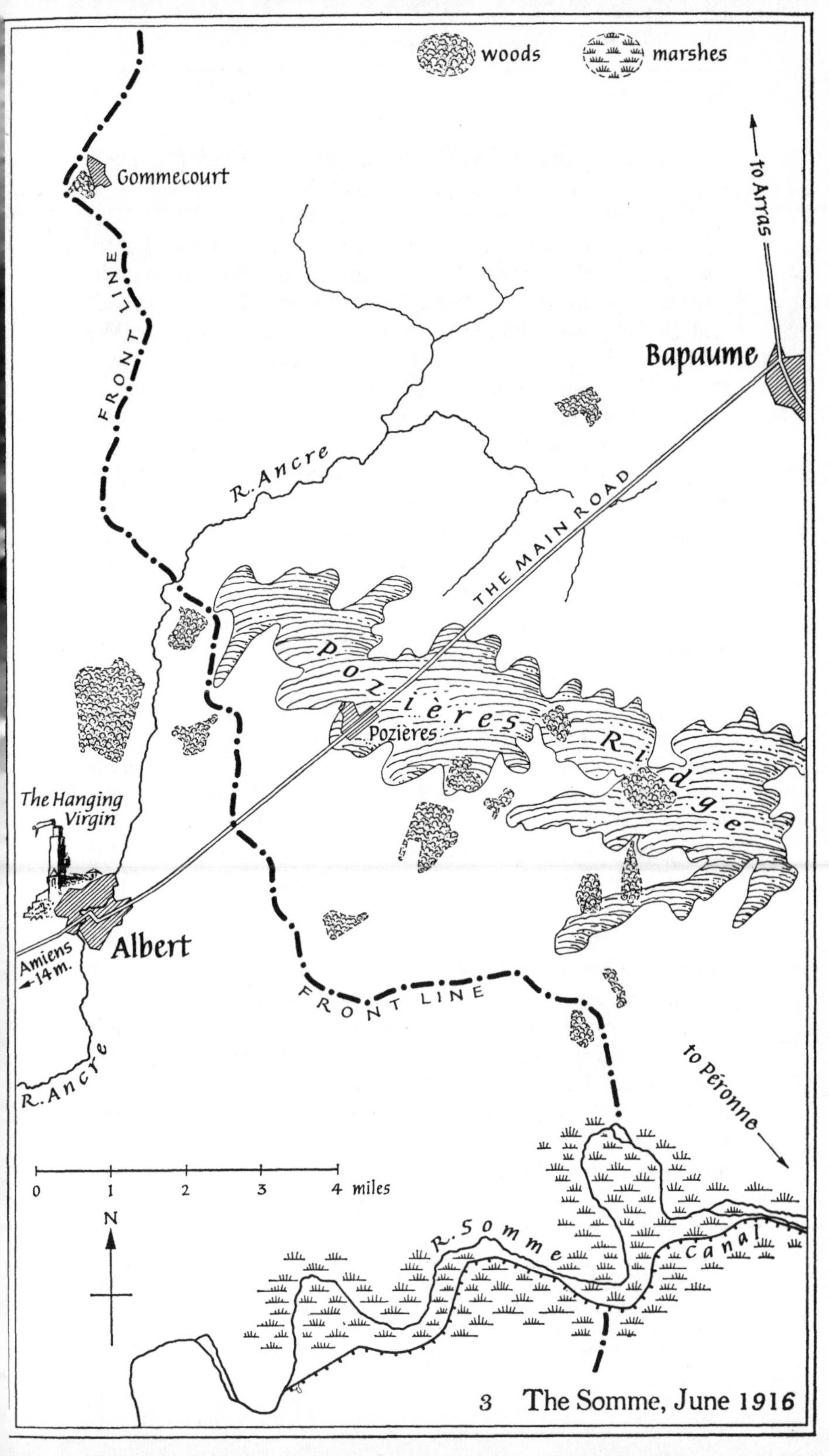

3 The Somme, June 1916

left leaning right out over the square below. French engineers secured the statue in this precarious position by a chain.

A legend arose among the French troops, and was later adopted by the British, that the war would not finish until the statue fell. From their positions around Albert, the Germans could see the damaged statue and, like the French and British, their soldiers too had their superstitions: 'We said that, if we could shoot down the statue, we would win the war and our artillery tried hard to hit it.' (Unteroffizier Karl Goll, 109th Reserve Regiment) But the Germans were not consistent in their legends, for an artillery observer in another division had a different version. 'We could clearly see the tower of the cathedral in Albert, with the Virgin's statue hanging over. Through our telescopes we could even see British observers at work there, their binoculars gleaming in the sun. But we refused to fire on the tower; we had a superstition that the nation which shot down the Virgin would be vanquished.' (Feldwebel Felix Kircher, 26th Field Artillery Regiment)

As the B.E.F. expanded, it had taken over the Somme sectors from the French during late 1915 and early 1916.* They found many differences between the Somme and their old sectors in the north. Because of the chalk just under the surface soil, the positions of their new trenches could be seen quite easily from the white spoil thrown out on either side; from the air, the trenches could be seen stretching like white ribbons into the distance. The chalk made it an ideal sector for mining and the R.E. tunnellers took over many mines from the French. The galleries did not need pumping out or shoring up, and there was little danger of collapse.

But the main difference for the British soldiers was their inheritance from the French of a sector with a well-established 'live and let live' routine. 'It was a "quiet" sector, i.e. no large attack had taken place for some time. Shells outside the trench system were hardly known. Neither side shelled the transport and shelling never began before 8 A.M., so that we could all have breakfast comfortably before settling down to the day's work.'†

* The French had had to leave behind them on the Somme and Arras fronts sixty-eight guns in permanent positions when they handed over to the British. Gen. Joffre asked the British for 2,000 soldiers and 1,000 labourers to be attached to his army in exchange. Papa Joffre was disappointed – Haig gave him neither.

† *History of the 55th Infantry Brigade*, author unknown.

Coming from the damp, dangerous north, the British found dry trenches, pleasant open countryside and accommodating Germans. They were well satisfied with the quiet Somme.

Let us look, now, at the men on the other side of No Man's Land on the Somme Front.

On the outbreak of war Kitchener's German counterpart may have had problems but these did not include that which troubled Kitchener most, the shortage of trained soldiers. The German system of conscription, which was a century old, had called up every fit young man at the age of twenty and given him two years' military service (one year only for students), a service under iron-hard discipline and training under dedicated professional officers and N.C.O.'s. After release the man was recalled for up to eight weeks' training at least twice every five years until he reached the age of forty. As this system had been in operation for over a century, nearly every adult male in Germany was a trained soldier when war broke out in 1914. A carefully prepared mobilization plan had called these men into their Reserve units which, together with the Regulars, provided Germany with an army of over 4,000,000 ready for immediate action.

While the basis of the British Army was the battalion, that of the German was the regiment. This, unlike the British regiment, was an operational unit composed of three battalions, with three regiments normally making a division. The regiments were raised on a local basis and, like some British units, often had two names, their official title and an older, traditional one, sometimes going back to before the creation of the modern German state; so that the 119th Reserve Regiment, for instance, was also known as Queen Olga's 1st Württemberg Regiment.

The German units were lower in strength than the British; the German battalions when at full strength had 750–800 men and, with only nine battalions, the total fighting strength of the division was just over half that of a British division. The lower number of infantrymen in the German units was compensated for by their higher fire-power. They were particularly strong in machine-guns and even British machine-gun officers acknowledged that, in 1916, the German army was well ahead of their own in the development of machine-gun tactics. The German machine-gunners were specially chosen and trained and could be relied upon to man their weapons to the last.

The German divisions on the Somme were a mixture of Regular and Reserve regiments, and the German policy of leaving a division in the same area indefinitely meant that most had been there since 1914, although some had fought in Russia in 1915. The same policy had spared them from the bitter fighting at Verdun, so that before the Somme battle opened they contained a high proportion of their original pre-war soldiers and certainly all their officers and N.C.O.'s were experienced men. They had occupied the same sectors for months and knew every feature of the ground intimately.

The British troops soon came to differentiate between the various German troops who held the trenches opposite them. The Prussians were recognized as the most aggressive of their opponents, the Silesians were reputed to be lazy and the Bavarians fairly easy-going. 'Once, in 1915, some Bavarians shouted across to us "Hold your fire. The Prussians will be here next week!" There was no love lost between the Bavarians and the Prussians.' (Maj. C. J. Low, D.S.O., 1st London Scottish)

The best liked of all the Germans, however, were the Saxons, who were found to be gentle soldiers who liked a quiet life. 'Whenever we held the line against Saxon troops we had an easy time. Sometimes they would advertise their presence by showing a placard from their trenches with the word "SAXON" painted on it. They would allow a quiet time and hoped for the same in return. The Prussians were a hard lot, they were always at it.' (Pte F. W. A. Turner, 11th Sherwood Foresters)

For their part, the German soldiers do not seem to have differentiated much between the various British troops. They were, however, amazed that the Scots should go into the trenches wearing kilts and, like many others before and since, were very curious as to what the Scotsman wore under his kilt. The Germans did not like the fierce Scots, calling them the 'Ladies from Hell'.

Knowing the political situation in Ireland, the Germans tried hard, but with little success, to subvert Southern Irish troops. 'During the Easter Rising in Dublin (1916), the Germans were shouting out with loud-hailers, "The English are murdering your people in Dublin. Come over to us." We gave them a heavy raid that night at platoon strength with bombs and coshes.' (Pte W. Durham, 2nd Royal Dublin Fusiliers)

At this stage of the war it was the more experienced French for whom the Germans had the most respect. 'The first days when the English arrived on the Somme, we had a good time. Their artillery wasn't in position and we could get out of our trenches and walk around. We were amazed at the great calm. We feared the French more than the English. The French were far more experienced and their artillery was accurate. But the English were more phlegmatic.' (Feldwebel Felix Kircher, 26th Field Artillery Regiment) The Germans particularly feared the French colonial troops who were reputed to be particularly averse to taking prisoners.

The German soldier may have disliked his enemies in general but this did not extend to the individual soldiers he occasionally saw or met. 'Before the bombardment started and while everything was peaceful, I could see through my periscope a young Englishman playing his trumpet every evening. We used to wait for this hour but suddenly there was nothing to be heard and we all hoped that nothing had happened to him.' (Feldwebel Karl Stumpf, 169th Regiment)

The ordinary British soldier was little different. 'Another man and myself went down to the River Ancre to get water and found two Germans there doing the same thing. One of them spoke good English, he had been a miner in Durham. He said, "This war's no bloody good." We had our rifles; they didn't. We could have taken them prisoner but we let them go.' (Pte A. V. Wilson, West Belfast Volunteers)

The German soldiers may have been bored with duty on the Somme but they realized they were lucky not to be fighting at Verdun. As with all front-line troops they longed for the war to be over and to be back at home. Their thoughts were almost identical to those of the British soldiers; extracts from letters found on German dead reflect all the familiar sentiments. From a girl friend to her soldier: 'Oh, sweetheart, we are still so young, life has so much to offer us yet. Let us hope that life will be better in the future than now. The two days we were together were real "rosy days", weren't they?'

From a grumbling wife: 'You write that things are not too good for you. We are no better off. The people here have nothing to laugh about, for everything is so expensive.'

From Ernst, a soldier, to his girl: 'The days are long here and lonely, I am hoping there will be an end soon. Dear, I shall marry you when I get my leave again, for sure; you must not mistrust me.' Whatever troubles his girl had, Ernst could not help – he was killed while out on patrol near Thiepval in June, 1916, before he could post the letter.

Many of the Germans, having been in the trenches since 1914, had reached the conclusion that neither side could achieve complete victory unless it was prepared to sacrifice limitless numbers of men. One colonel talked to a captured German officer earlier in the war and asked him when the war would end. The German replied, 'I do not know that, but I know where, and that is here. You cannot drive us back, nor can we drive you back.' (Lieut-Col. G. R. V. Steward, D.S.O., 4th Tyneside Irish)

After the British had completed their takeover of the line on the Somme, the nature of the war there changed. The front-line men of both sides would have been happy to let this remain a quiet sector but the attitude of the British generals soon made itself felt; raids, sniping, artillery fire and all the other means whereby the offensive spirit could be imposed upon trench warfare became more commonplace Naturally the Germans knew that the British had arrived. They expected that the British would attack some time that summer and they suspected that it might be on the Somme. This suspicion, added to the increased British activity, set the Germans to improving their defences even further. Their positions in this area were already strong and they were to have another six months, uninterrupted, to complete the work before the battle started. The German was a very thorough and industrious soldier; supplied by his leaders with the necessary tools and materials, he proceeded to make his fortifications on the Somme as strong as any on the Western Front.

The Germans assiduously sought out the higher ground and, if their front line crossed a valley, they would pull back their foremost trench to follow the contours around the valley. Their lines were anything but straight; out they went to take advantage of spurs in No Man's Land and then back again along the slopes overlooking the valleys.

The Germans put great faith in their machine-guns and protected them in very carefully sited and constructed posts, some made of concrete or steel plating. A well-trained machine-gunner could hit targets up to a mile away. There were approximately 1,000 of these machine-gun posts in the German positions that the British were to attack on 1 July.

Because they held higher ground and the region was naturally well drained, there was no limit to the depth to which defences could be dug. The Germans took advantage of this; their trenches were up to ten feet deep, but where they really profited was in their dug-out construction. These could be forty feet below ground, with several alternative entrances and even tunnels running right back to the next trench. Many were large enough to hold a platoon of men. The officers' dug-outs were panelled in wood or had cloth hangings to cover the rough chalk walls, and were furnished with tables, chairs and even pianos taken from nearby villages. Their men lived in miniature underground barrack rooms with rows of bunk beds and special alcoves or cupboards for each man's equipment. The whole system was lit by electricity, had forced air ventilation and was often supplied with piped water.

In 1915 the French had captured, intact, a perfect example of a typical German dug-out on the Touvent Farm sector, opposite Serre. When the sector was handed over to the British, this dug-out was used as a company H.Q. An officer of the South Antrim Volunteers, sent to this sector for his instruction in trench warfare, found the dug-out so unlike any other that he had seen, that he recorded careful notes of it in his diary. It was twenty feet underground, twenty yards long, seven feet wide and divided into separate sections for signallers, the officers' mess and servants' quarters. Cut into the wall of the officers' mess were recesses for beds to accommodate six officers. There were five entrances. It would seem that the existence of this model of a German-type dug-out was not noted by anyone concerned in the planning of the coming attack.

The Germans believed in defence in depth and had built the usual support and reserve trenches. They had gone further than this, however, and built three, and in some cases four, complete trench systems making a total of anything up to twelve trenches to be crossed before an attacker could reach open country. Not all of these systems, or 'Lines' as they were known to the British, were as strong as the front line, but many were replicas of it, complete with dug-outs, machine-gun posts and thick belts of barbed wire.

The Germans had tied the villages that lay within their positions into this strong trench system. They liked to place their front line just forward of these villages and then to fortify the ruins. The cellars, covered by the rubble from collapsed houses, made perfect machine-gun posts and, as in the trench system, they were linked to each other and to nearby dug-outs by tunnels. These villages became miniature forts with defences proof against most shell fire and, as they did not have the distinctive chalk diggings to give away their positions, they were more than usually difficult to detect.

The sector about to be attacked by the British contained nine of these fortified villages on an eighteen-mile front, all either in or just behind the front line. Their names were to become part of the history of the British Army. Reading from south to north, they were: Montauban, Mametz, Fricourt, La Boisselle, Ovillers, Thiepval, Beaumont Hamel, Serre and Gommecourt.

Where there was a part of their defences not covered by a village, the Germans constructed even more miniature forts. These were in open country, on sites chosen for their dominance of surrounding ground, and became known as redoubts. They were well fortified positions built especially for all-round defence and containing more than the usual number of underground dug-outs and passages. These passages were so intricate that an attacking force gaining a foothold could be counter-attacked from an unexpected direction. A typical German redoubt has been described as covering the same area as Piccadilly Circus.

Where possible, each side made use of the woods as places of concealment or even as part of their front line if available. None of the woods lay in disputed territory – No Man's Land was open ground along the whole of the sector.

That part of the front that was due to be the scene of the opening attack was shaped like a huge letter L. There was an oversize vertical arm running north and south for eleven

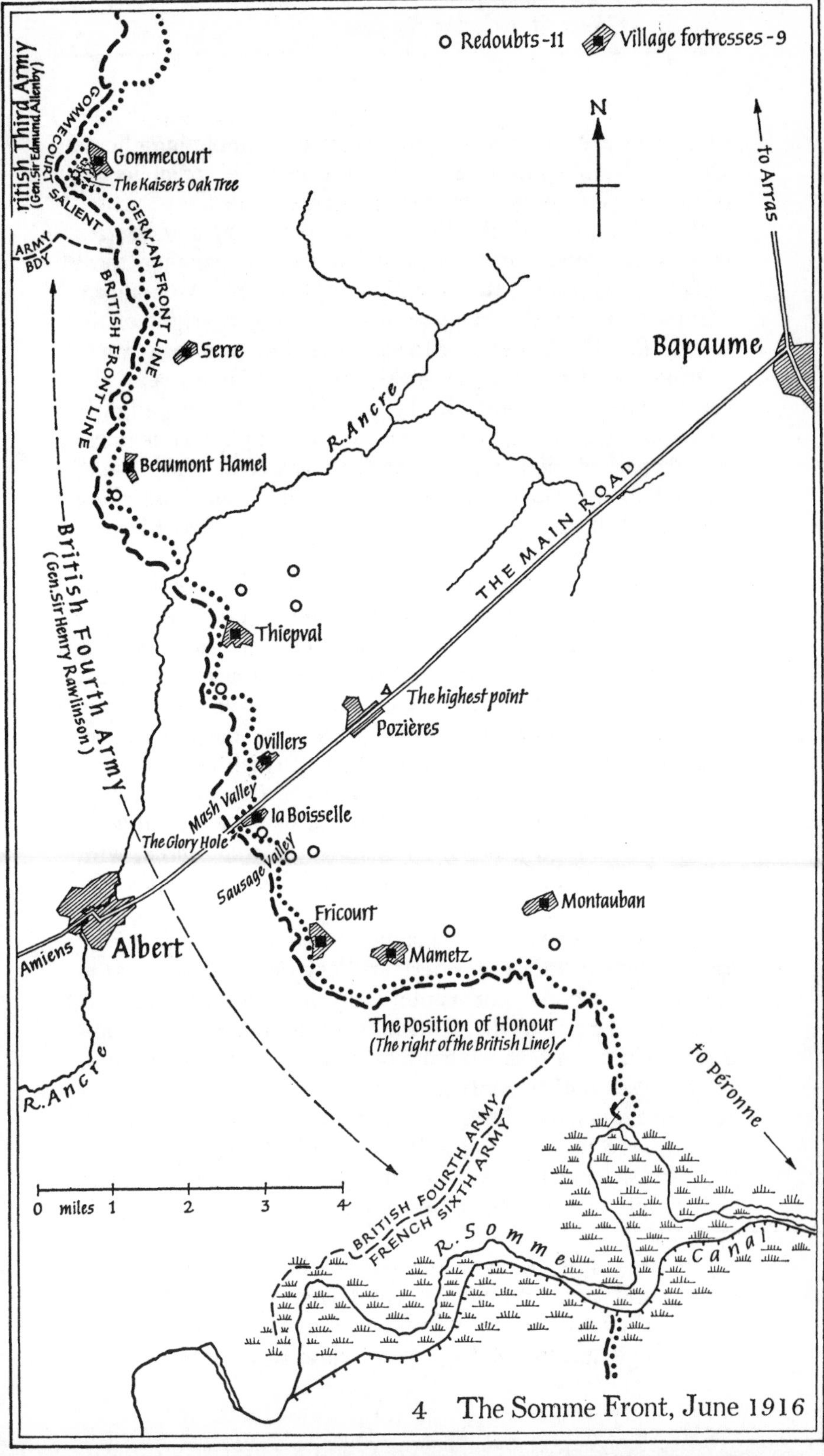

4 The Somme Front, June 1916

miles and a horizontal one of five miles completing the L. Due to the irregularities of the trenches the actual length of the attack front was more like eighteen miles.

The junction with the French was at the extreme eastern end of the lower arm; the British troops manning these trenches, opposite the fortified village of Montauban, occupied the traditional place of honour on the right of the whole British Army in France. The line ran westwards passing two more German-held villages, Mametz and Fricourt, to the corner of the L, the ground always rising slightly to the German lines. There were no marked physical features on this part of the front that the Germans could make use of when building their defences, but behind their lines there were no less than eight woods, with the ground between them quite bare.

Turning the corner of the L the line ran northwards, culminating at the point where the River Ancre flowed from the German lines into the British. This five-mile sector, which was to be the centre of the British attack, is of great interest and contained three elements that were to be very important to the battle. First of these was the old Roman road running north-eastwards from British-held Albert, through the German lines at La Boisselle and on through Pozières to the town of Bapaume. Second was a ridge of German-held high ground dominating the whole area, with Pozières again demanding attention as the highest point of all.

Here were two reasons making this an important sector for the British. In a war where artillery observation was the key to all success, the capture of the high ground was essential. Again, if the British were to make any break-through into the open country behind the German trenches, the possession of the only good road in the area provided an attractive axis for the advance. So there was Pozières, a little village just five miles behind the front, the vital point the British must have and, knowing this, the Germans had covered this five miles with four complete trench systems.

Nor was this all, for a third factor here was a series of valleys and spurs running at right angles to the front. In every valley the German trenches ran right back keeping to the high ground and on every spur there was either a fortified village or a redoubt. An attacker faced a dreadful dilemma: he could make a short, but dangerous and uphill, direct assault on the spurs or a longer approach along the naked floors of the valleys, being overlooked on two sides and with an enemy trench waiting at the far end of the valley. Typical of these valleys were Sausage and Mash on either side of the main road, with La Boisselle village on the spur between them. No Man's Land was 700 yards wide in Mash Valley and nearly as much in Sausage. Between them, where the spur pushed right up to the British trenches, the adversaries were only fifty yards apart.*

On the other side of the marshy Ancre valley the line continued mainly northwards past two more German village fortresses, Beaumont Hamel and Serre, then over a broad plateau before coming to a large bulge into the British line known as the Gommecourt Salient. The village itself formed the core of the salient but Gommecourt Park, part of the grounds of a château, covered the point of it. The German front-line trench actually lined the edge of the park. The German soldiers who manned the trench at the point of the salient had the distinction of being the most westerly members of a German Army that stretched all the way back to Russia in the east and Italy in the south. Before the battle there stood at this point a distinctive oak tree, undamaged by shell fire; it was known to the Germans as the *Kaisereiche* – the Kaiser's Oak.

This, then, is a quick tour of the area where the battle was to be fought and where the Germans had gouged for themselves, in the pleasant land of the Somme, defences which John Masefield, writing in 1917, was to describe in the following terms:

> They [the Germans] took up their lines when they were strong and our side weak and in no place in all the old Somme position is our line better sited than theirs, though in one or two places the sites are nearly equal. Almost in every part of this old front our men had to go uphill to attack.

* The Germans sometimes flew an observation or 'sausage' balloon at the head of the valley south of La Boisselle so the British soldiers christened it 'Sausage Valley'. Logically, to them, the other valley became 'Mash'. The sector in between, where No Man's Land was so narrow, became the 'Glory Hole' on account of its high casualty rate.

. . . the enemy had the lookout posts, with the fine views over France and the sense of domination. Our men were down below with no view of anything but of stronghold after stronghold, just up above, being made stronger daily.*

* From *The Old Front Line,* page 13.

4

The Plan

The year 1916 opened hopefully for the Allies. The major military powers of the Alliance – France, Russia, Italy and Great Britain – were hoping to launch simultaneous offensives from three sides in an effort to gain victory in that year. The planning for these had already started and the attacks were to be launched as early in the summer as possible. The British and French assaults were to be made side by side on the Somme.

For Britain, there was every indication that 1916 was to be her year of triumph. After the frustrations of 1914 and 1915, there were high hopes of the army of civilian soldiers which was only now coming to full strength and of a new military leadership. In December 1915 fresh men had come to the two vital positions of Chief of the Imperial General Staff and c.-in-c. of the B.E.F. Gen. Sir William Robertson ('Wully' to his friends) had taken over in London and Gen. Sir Douglas Haig was the new commander in France.

The British entered into the plan for a joint offensive with enthusiasm. The Dardanelles expedition was closed down and many of the troops involved there were directed to France. Haig felt very strongly that it was on the Western Front that the major British effort should be made and that all troops sent to other theatres were being wasted.

The Allied plans were rudely shattered when the Germans launched a heavy attack on the French at Verdun in February 1916. The Germans made some early gains and nearly took the town. The French, true to their policy of 'not another metre', held stubbornly and refused to give more ground; their defiant call, '*Ils ne passeront pas*' ('They shall not pass'), found a place in French history.

Steadily the French losses mounted, until it began to look as though they might collapse if the Germans were not diverted. The means for doing this were at hand, for the growing number of British divisions in France were not involved, at this time, in any major action. Anxious calls went out from the French that the British should attack and

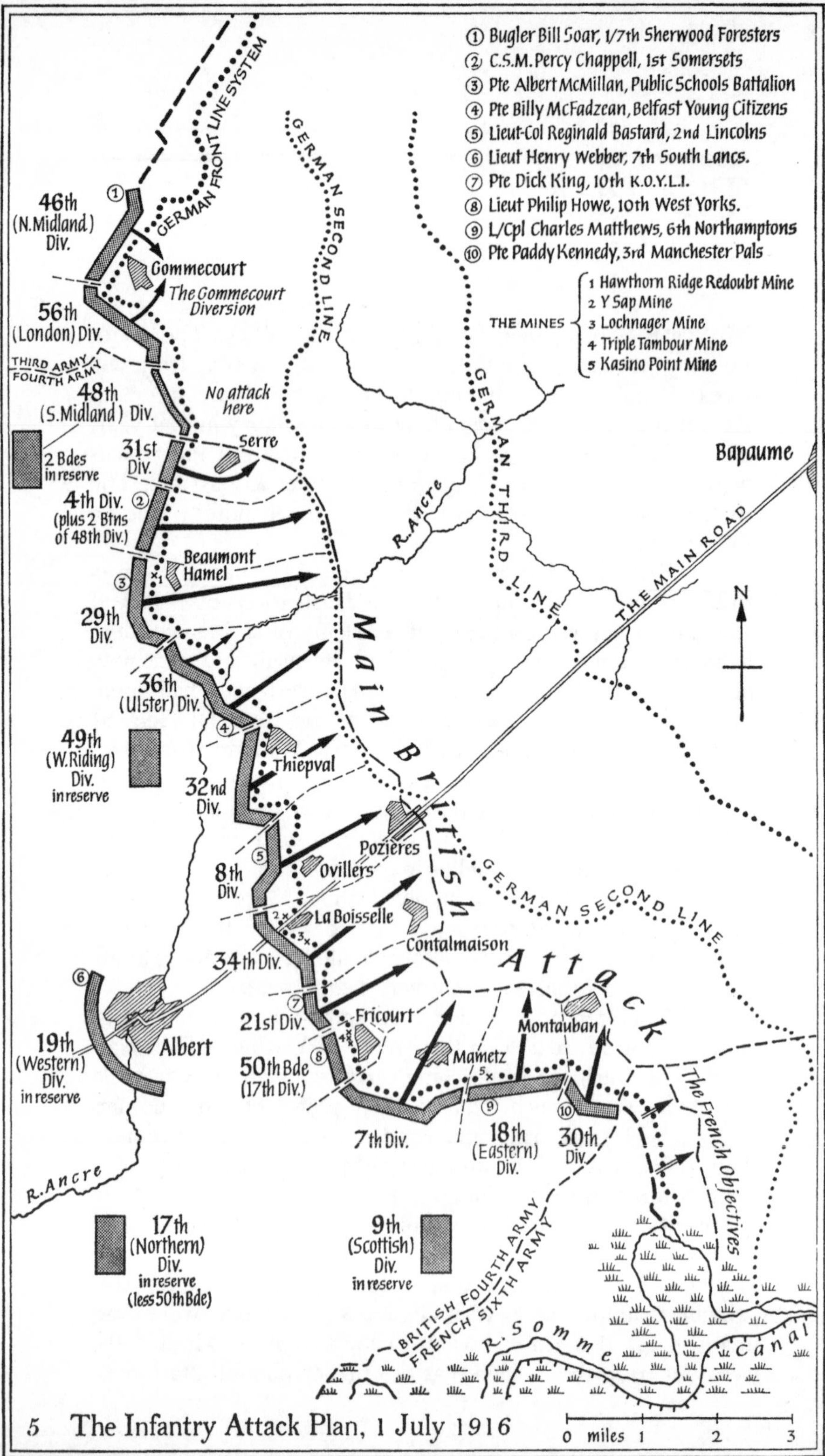

5 The Infantry Attack Plan, 1 July 1916

relieve them at Verdun. The British could not ignore this call and her government sent instructions to Haig to prepare his army for battle.

Sir Douglas Haig, the new C.-in-C., was to become the most controversial character of the war. By 1915 he had had a distinguished army career and there was no doubt about his personal bravery. He had spent many years with the cavalry (7th Hussars and 17th Lancers) and had commanded a group of mobile columns in the Boer War. In 1914 he was an infantry corps commander with the B.E.F. and became an army commander before the end of the year. Involved in the Battle of Loos, he had been severely critical of the handling of that battle by the former C.-in-C., Sir John French.

Haig had married one of the Queen's ladies-in-waiting and was a confidant of the king. After Loos, he was in London on leave and was called to Buckingham Palace where the king asked him about the battle. Haig repeated his criticisms of his superior. In December, Sir John French was recalled to England; Sir Douglas Haig was offered the position of C.-in-C. and he accepted. So Haig moved to G.H.Q. and became the commander of the whole of the British Army in France and Belgium. He was not, however, promoted immediately to the rank of field-marshal, but remained a full general, the same rank as his army commanders.

Haig, a dour, determined Lowland Scot of fifty-five and an ardent member of the Church of Scotland, firmly believed that God was on his side and received great satisfaction from the weekly sermons of his chaplain. His apparent disloyalty in openly criticizing Sir John French can only be excused by saying that Haig was firmly convinced that he was doing the right thing for the army; there is no evidence that he was seeking French's position, although he must have known that he was the most likely candidate. It remained to be seen whether he could do better.

Not an effusive man, he was given respect and loyalty by his subordinates and they credited him with the ability and determination to command the B.E.F. In his turn he was able to delegate powers easily to his generals, and if things went wrong he stood by them, frequently protecting them from the wrath of the government.

Douglas Haig was not a happy man in the spring of 1916. The original plan for a joint attack with the French on the Somme had suited him. The participation of the veteran French Army on his right would have made up for the inexperience of his own troops. Instead, because of Verdun, the French could only attack on an eight-mile front in the coming joint offensive instead of one of twenty-five miles as previously promised. In addition, the French were demanding more and more urgently that the British should open their attack and gave 1 July as the latest they could hold on at Verdun without some action to divert the Germans. This was earlier than Haig would have liked to get his still inexperienced army ready for what was becoming a predominantly British effort rather than a joint offensive.

Douglas Haig may have had faults, but disloyalty to his allies was not one of them. He accepted the French plea and prepared for an attack in June. He had no illusions about the task before him. In the original plan for a combined Allied offensive he had hoped to see the end of the war in 1916. He had dreamed of seeing the infantry break through the hated lines of trenches so that he could push his beloved cavalry divisions through into open country. He was certain that, in the resulting war of movement, he could beat the Germans. But, in the changed circumstances following Verdun, he felt that his army could not do this virtually alone. In May he told his army commanders that it was unsound to expect a victory in 1916 and that the summer attack had three objects: to relieve the French at Verdun; to inflict losses upon the Germans; and to place the British Army in positions favourable for the final victory that would now come in 1917.

He placed the main part of the attack in the hands of the newly formed Fourth Army, under Gen. Sir Henry Rawlinson who held the Somme front with the French on his right. He directed Rawlinson to mount an infantry attack and to seize the Pozières Ridge on a ten-mile front from Montauban, his most southerly point, to the River Ancre. North of this little river, one corps was to seize the German trenches on a further three-mile front and there form a flank guard to protect the main attack.

Basically the plan was for a simple infantry attack but Haig's optimism, which was to affect so many plans during the war, elaborated on this. There were five cavalry divisions in France which Haig could not bear to leave out of the battle. This might be the cavalry's last chance. It was being suggested in London that, because of the expense of maintaining the idle cavalry in France, they should be disbanded. If Rawlinson's infantry were able to break clear through the German lines, Haig could pass his cavalry through the gap and achieve his war of movement. If all went well he might even force the collapse of the Germans in 1916 after all.

Haig ordered the formation of a strong force of three cavalry divisions under Lieut-Gen. Sir Hubert Gough. These were to stand immediately behind the attacking infantry in case there was a breakthrough. If that event occurred, Gough was to be given some infantry divisions of his own and, with these supporting the cavalry, he would exploit the success independent of Fourth Army control. This force was to be known as the Reserve Army. Gough was given the necessary staff to create an army H.Q., but not the rank of full general to put him on a par with the Fourth Army Commander, Gen. Rawlinson.

Gough's orders from Haig were to wait for Rawlinson's infantry to attack and, if a break occurred, to push through that gap and seize Bapaume. He was to leave a covering force there, facing the German rear, and turn his main force northwards into the open country behind the lines towards Arras. At the same time, Rawlinson's infantry was to turn north and roll up the trench lines alongside Gough. The French, meantime, were to hold the right flank of the breakthrough and prevent German interference from the south.

If Haig had been a racing man it would be said that he had placed bets on two horses. He wanted to capture the German trench system on a wide frontage in conjunction with the French and, at the same time, he wanted a breakthrough so that his cavalry could get out into open country. One suspects that his reason led him to the former but his instinct to the latter. It is easy to sympathize with Haig in his planning for his first battle as C.-in-C. Deep down he felt that the B.E.F. had been ill-directed in 1915; he believed that he had the ability and, with his reinforcements, the troops to do better.

To give the attack an even better chance of success, Haig ordered the commanders of his First, Second and Third Armies to carry out constant threatening moves on their

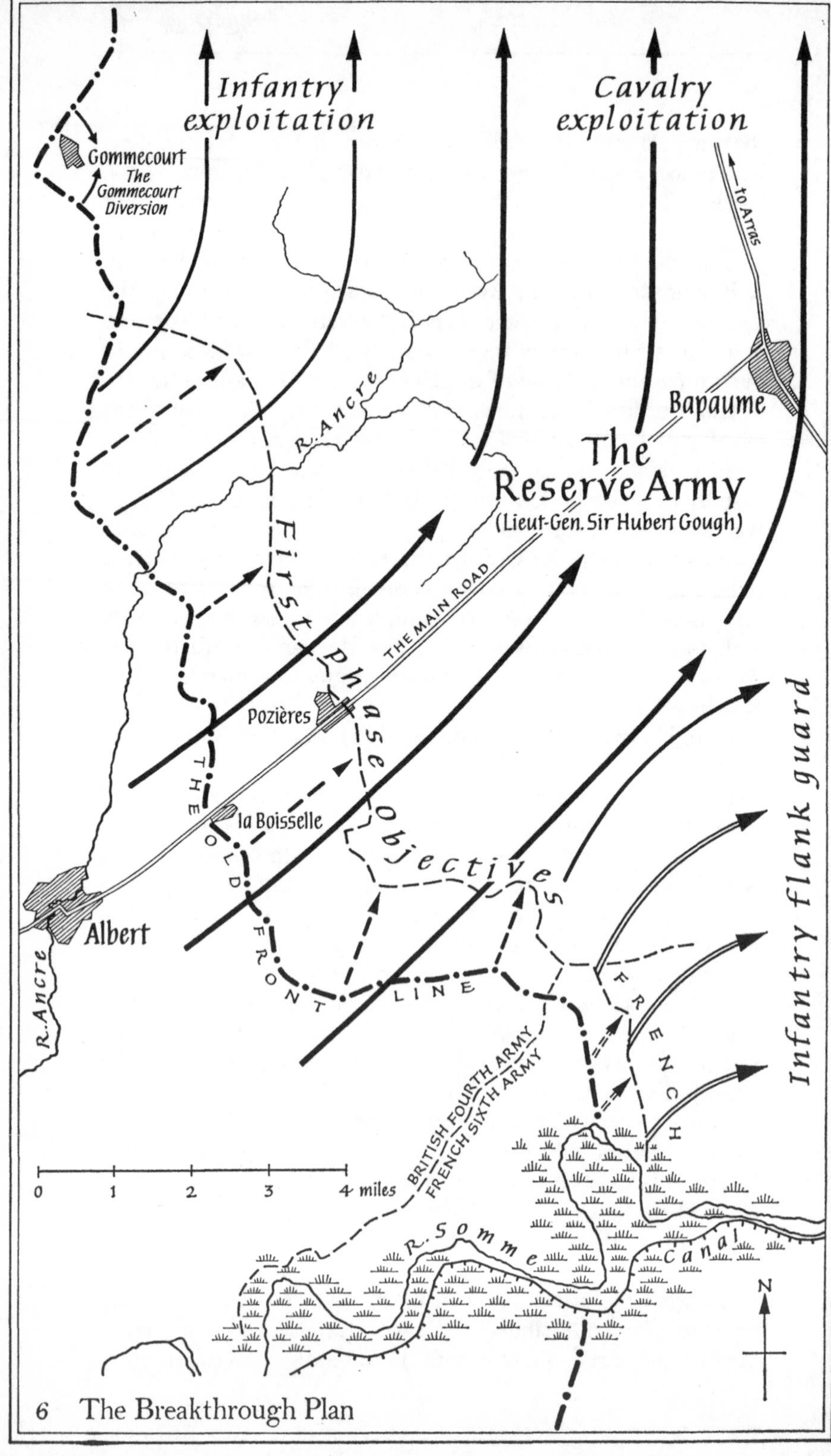

6 The Breakthrough Plan

fronts to keep the Germans guessing and to tie down their reserves. To the Third Army, which held the line north of Rawlinson's Fourth, he gave an even bigger task. On the opening day of the battle it was to mount a full-scale attack on the German-held salient at Gommecourt. Once again Haig was going to kill two birds with one stone. He wanted to eliminate the awkward salient and, at the same time, provide a worthwhile diversionary effort to assist the main attack of Rawlinson's Fourth Army.

Having decided upon his broad plan, Haig issued the necessary orders to his army commanders for their more detailed planning. He gave the first target date for the opening attack – 25 June.

In theory, three army commanders – those of the Third, Fourth and the Reserve Armies – were directly involved in the further development and detailed planning of the c.-in-c.'s plan of attack. In effect, two of them had little to do.

Gen. Sir Edmund Allenby (the 'Bull'), the commander of the Third Army, was responsible for the diversionary attack on the Gommecourt salient. He did not like the plan. There was to be a one-mile gap between his attack at Gommecourt and the northern flank of that of the Fourth Army. To Allenby there should have been no gap at all so that his troops at Gommecourt could have the protection on one flank at least of other troops advancing at the same time. If this was not possible then the diversion, to be successful, should be well away from the main attack. But Allenby was not personally on good terms with Haig; he did not press his objections too hard but left his corps commander on the spot, Lieut-Gen. Snow, to make the detailed preparations.

Certain decisions had already been made for Snow. His diversionary attack had to conform with the main one in the length of its preliminary bombardment and the timing of the attack itself. Two divisions were to be used and no extra troops were allotted for preparing the attack or for a reserve.

With his modest resources Snow decided not to attack the salient frontally; instead, each division would attack one shoulder of it with a proportion of their battalions. If both were successful, they were to push on, link up behind the village and cut off the salient. Neither Allenby nor Snow had much heart for this task. Not only would they be drawing upon their troops the fire of German artillery and infantry from three sides; in addition, to add to the effect of diversion, they had been ordered to make their preparations as obvious as possible.

After he had given his two divisional commanders their orders, Snow offered them some advice. He pointed out that their diversionary role was a strictly limited one, that there were no reserves behind them, and he stressed that they were only to advance when the German defences had been destroyed by the artillery. This advice was to have important repercussions.

Haig had chosen as the commander of the Reserve Army Sir Hubert Gough ('Goughy'), who came from a famous army family; his uncle, father and brother had all won the Victoria Cross. As a brigade commander in 1914, it was Gough who had ordered the first shots to be fired by the B.E.F. in the war. (German artillery were firing on his men and Gough ordered his own guns into action but, since they were outranged by the heavier German battery, they did no damage.) Thereafter his rise had been meteoric: April 1915, a divisional commander; July 1915, a corps commander; and, now, in the spring of 1916, he was commanding an army, although he was not immediately given the rank of full general. He was, at forty-five years old, by far the youngest of the senior generals in France, being seven years younger than Rawlinson and ten years junior to Haig.

As commander of the Reserve Army, Gough had little to do. He had been allocated three cavalry divisions, but they were still well to the rear and he had no responsibility for holding any of the line. Gough formed his army H.Q. and, although their roles depended upon Rawlinson's infantry creating a gap, began to plan for the coming battle with the cavalry staff. He was much heartened when, in mid-June, Haig allocated him further troops – a full corps of three infantry divisions; now he had the makings of a proper army.

If Allenby was despondent and Gough excited, the commander of the Fourth Army was calm. Unlike the other three generals involved, who were all cavalrymen, Gen. Sir Henry Rawlinson ('Rawly') had always been an infantryman (King's Royal Rifle Corps and the Guards). He had seen action in Burma, Sudan and the Boer War, where he had commanded a battalion at the Siege of Ladysmith. Between the end of the Boer War and 1914 he had travelled extensively, having visited India, Canada, the United States, Belgium, Germany, Russia, China, Japan, Algeria and Morocco. He had watched the armies of three great powers on manoeuvres: those of Germany, Japan and Russia.

In 1914 he had been Director of Recruiting at the War Office and directly concerned with the raising of the New Army. In France he had commanded successively the 4th Division, IV Corps and Fourth Army, the last of which he had formed himself. After Neuve Chapelle, some of the men under his command had named him the 'Arch Bitcher', following the vigorous handling of his corps in that battle. Unlike Allenby, Rawlinson was on easy terms with Haig who had personally selected him for his present position. As the commander of the army making the main attack, he was to be the key man in the coming battle.

Rawlinson did not share the cavalry generals' enthusiasm for the breakthrough. In his opinion it was going to be difficult enough to take the German lines one by one, without having to breach the trench systems completely for the cavalry to pass through. He accepted Haig's dual plan but only prepared for the first part of it.

Rawlinson had been impressed with the successful German opening attack at Verdun. A heavy artillery preparation had completely destroyed the French front-line trenches which had then been occupied by the German infantry. This process had been repeated several times and Rawlinson planned to employ it on the Somme. He had great faith in his own artillery and proposed to use the heaviest and longest bombardment of the war to destroy the German line. Every available gun was to be used for five days and nights before the infantry attacked. The infantry themselves were relegated to the role of mopping up and occupying defences that had already been destroyed for them by the artillery. He hoped the Germans would then counter-attack their lost positions so that he could exact a further toll of their infantry under conditions favourable to his own men.

Rawlinson planned to take one enemy line, or trench system, at a time. Having taken the first and allowed the counter-attacks to break themselves against it, he would bombard the second until it too was ready for capture. Given time and enough artillery ammunition, he would eventually break through the German defences and then the cavalry could have their chance. So confident was he in the power of the artillery that he was convinced there would be little resistance from the Germans when his infantry attacked. Rawlinson, therefore, ordered an infantry attack plan which provided for a slow, rigid, methodical advance over No Man's Land, in place of the standard assault tactics.

Rawlinson's Fourth Army had been given five strong corps; he spread four of these corps evenly along the front of the main attack between the Somme and the Ancre and the last of them north of the Ancre to form the flank guard to the main attack. The artillery too were spread evenly along the line.

The original date chosen for the attack could not be met and a new one had been chosen – 29 June. The time of the infantry attack had also been fixed – 7.30 A.M. The French would have liked it even later but Rawlinson said that this was the latest he could manage. The established principle of the infantry attacking at dawn, which was over three hours earlier, was to be sacrificed for the better artillery observation of full daylight.

It is interesting to examine the relationship between the three generals involved in the main attack. Douglas Haig, the newly appointed C.-in-C., was doing a field marshal's job but only held the rank of general. Henry Rawlinson was in theory his subordinate but held the same rank and was nearly the same age; in addition, he was the only one of the three who was an infantryman. Hubert Gough was supposed to hold a position equivalent to Rawlinson's but was a rank lower and nearly a decade younger. The result was that, instead of Haig exercising command over two equal subordinates, Haig and Rawlinson seemed to be more in partnership and the unfortunate Gough was beneath both of them.

The first result of this relationship was seen when Rawlinson's deliberate plan was submitted to the C.-in-C. Haig could not see in it the making of a breakthrough and a rolling up of the German lines to Arras. He urged Rawlinson to shorten the bombardment so that the Germans would have less warning of the attack. He advised, also, that the German trenches should be rushed as soon as the barrage lifted on the day of the attack and, finally, he asked Rawlinson to take at least two of the German lines on the first day and not one as Rawlinson had planned.

The first two were sensible suggestions and standard army practice but Rawlinson would agree to neither. His shortage of heavy artillery could only be overcome by increasing the length of the bombardment and he considered his infantry insufficiently trained to adopt more sophisticated tactics. If Haig had had the courage of his convictions he would have ordered Rawlinson to adopt these two tactics but, possibly in deference to Rawlinson's long infantry experience and seniority, he did not press his objections.

On the third point, that of the taking of more than one line, there was a compromise. North of the main road to Bapaume the German second line lay close behind their first and, on that section at least, Rawlinson agreed to take both lines on the first day. This would bring the high ground at Pozières into that day's objectives. South of the road the German second line lay farther back and, as the French on his right were only planning a small advance on the first day, to push on too far would leave Rawlinson's right flank open. Here only the first line was to be taken on the first day.

As the generals drew up their plans the divisions were gathering on the Somme for the battle. Some had been there ever since this front had been taken over from the French and these had got to know their sectors well, but for most it was a case of leaving old familiar trenches in the north. Reginald Bastard, now a lieutenant-colonel and commanding his battalion, the 2nd Lincolns, led it in a seven-day march by easy stages through pleasant Picardy before taking over part of the line opposite Ovillers.

The 30th Division, a New Army formation composed mostly of Liverpool and Manchester men, found themselves on the extreme right of the line next to the French. The Lancashire men were soon on good terms with the French soldiers whom they often met. At this stage of the war the French were considered to be veterans and the raw Lancashire troops were pleased to be alongside them.

From Gallipoli, the 29th Division arrived and went into the line opposite Beaumont Hamel. They were greeted at once by a large placard displayed by the Germans: 'Welcome to the 29th Division.' The division formed part of VIII Corps, north of the Ancre, which was to provide the flank guard to the main attack. The corps commander, Lieut-Gen. Hunter-Weston, a jovial Scot, had been the 29th Division's commander in Gallipoli, when the division had earned its 'Incomparable' reputation. Hunter-Weston was delighted to have his old division in his corps but the senior officers of his other divisions soon tired of hearing how good it was. The 29th Division had still to prove itself in France.

The divisions continued to arrive until the whole area was thick with troops. Nothing like it had ever been seen before; there were to be three times as many men as at Loos, the B.E.F.'s previous biggest effort. Eighteen divisions would be available for the first day of the attack; the reader should remember that these contained thirteen battalions each and were equivalent to twenty-six Second World War divisions. The superiority over the Germans was seven to one. Even the old-timers who had known the bad battles of 1915 were impressed; surely this huge force must succeed.

On the eve of the battle, Rawlinson was to examine the ration strength of his Fourth Army. It contained 519,324 men and prompted him to comment, 'It is not the lot of many to command an army of over half a million men.'*

Although strong in numbers, the army was very short of experience. The four Regular divisions were only shadows of their former selves; three had been 'diluted' in the exchange of battalions with New Army divisions and the Regular element was composed mainly of war-time volunteers with a few old hands like Reginald Bastard and Percy Chappell, now a company sergeant major in his old battalion, the 1st Somersets.

The Territorials, too, had changed. Their losses had been harder to replace, the rush of recruits in 1914 and early 1915 having sometimes passed them by. Many of their battalions were below strength and some of their reinforcements had only received the sketchiest of training. In the Third Army, Allenby had to provide two divisions for a

* From Rawlinson's Papers (attached to his Diary). There are two Rawlinson Diaries. The more commonly known one is available at the National Army Museum. It is a typed script, probably compiled after 1918. The other is kept at Churchill College, Cambridge, and is Rawlinson's original diary, written up daily in his own handwriting. All quotations in this book are taken from the original. As far as is known, this has only recently become available.

diversionary attack in which he had little faith and in which the divisions concerned might well be badly cut up. He chose to keep his other divisions intact and allocated two Territorial ones for Gommecourt, the 46th (North Midland) and 56th (London).

If the battle was anyone's it was to be the New Army's; some sixty per cent of the battalions due to attack on the first day belonged to it. Physically and intellectually they were the cream of the nation, but they were completely inexperienced in battle, except for the 21st Division which had seen a few chaotic hours at Loos. What the Kitchener Men lacked in experience they might make up in enthusiasm; of this they had plenty.

A close look at the composition of the army preparing for the battle will reveal that it was composed almost entirely of the county regiments of the British Army.* There were no Guards; no Australians, Canadians, Indians, New Zealanders or South Africans. An even closer look will show that, of those units due to see action on the first day, some parts of the United Kingdom provided very strong contingents; the Industrial North and Midlands, Ulster and London were to have a particularly large stake in the battle to come.†

There were two small exceptions to this all-United Kingdom rule. The Newfoundlanders were still attached to the 29th Division on its return from Gallipoli and the Bermuda Volunteer Rifle Corps had been found a place in the 1st Lincolns. It is true that there were other Empire troops, but only in the side lines: a complete brigade of South Africans held in reserve, Indian and Canadian cavalry regiments and a Canadian heavy artillery battery. Some men from the Empire could be found serving in the English units and even a few Americans, although it was not yet their war.

And so the Army of 1916 assembled for the battle – every man a willing soldier, either a pre-war Regular or a volunteer. There was not a conscript in the line.

* The Order of Battle of British divisions attacking on 1 July is given in Appendix 1 and of German divisions facing them in Appendix 2.

† In action, on 1 July, were the following battalions: Yorkshire 29; Lancashire 22; Ireland 20 (mostly Ulster); Tyneside 17; Midlands 14; London 13.

5

The Preparations

While the generals and their staff officers worked on the plans for the coming battle, their soldiers also prepared for it. There were so many divisions in the area that it was possible to withdraw them in turn from the line, so that each could rehearse its part in the attack. This was done on a tract of land chosen for its similarity to the sector to be attacked. Tapes marked the position of German trenches and notices indicated the sites of their redoubts and villages. Over and over again the sweating troops formed up, advanced, 'captured' German positions and consolidated, all under the watchful eye of staff officers and sometimes generals. 'We had been out in a little village near Amiens, practising for 1 July. We were inspected by a little, grey old man on a great black horse, with a glittering escort of Lancers, pennants fluttering in the wind.' (Pte A. V. Conn, 8th Devons) This was an eighteen-year-old boy's view of the great Haig – 'a little, grey old man'.

'We had been rehearsing all day and were resting in our tents, hot and tired. Blow me if Rawlinson didn't poke his head in and tell us we ought to be outside doing something or another.' (L/Cpl F. Lobel, M.M., 2nd Middlesex)

For the soldiers it was an exciting time; it was the first definite indication that they were to be in the 'Big Push', as it was being called. They were impressed by the concentration of troops, especially of artillery, who were moving into the area with their guns in large numbers ready for the opening of the five-day bombardment. They had mixed feelings but generally looked forward to the battle after the long months of trench warfare; they realized there would be casualties but again there was a feeling that the battle would get the war over before Christmas and avoid another winter in the trenches. Some were even more optimistic: 'I was very pleased when I heard that my battalion would be in the attack. I thought this would be the last battle of the war and I didn't want to miss it. I remember writing to my mother, telling her I would be home for the August Bank Holiday.' (Pte E. C. Stanley, 1/8th Royal Warwicks)

It was at about this time that two important items of news reached the troops. The first was reports of a big naval battle at Jutland, in which the British Navy had lost fourteen warships without managing to inflict a real defeat on the Germans. Three days later, on 6 June, news arrived that Lord Kitchener had been drowned when the cruiser, *Hampshire*, on which he was going to Russia, struck a mine and sank within hours of leaving Scapa Flow. A wave of gloom swept through the men on the Somme; to one soldier 'It was as bad as having lost a battle'. Kitchener, the founder of the New Army, was not to see it fight its first big battle. The Germans were quick to hear this news. 'We were in the front line, when all of a sudden a shout from the Jerry trenches told us that Kitchener was drowned and he would go to Hell.' (Pte J. Sutherland, 1st Edinburgh City Battalion)

Now that so many troops were in the area, the infantry could spend more time out of the trenches. After the rehearsals and training, there were still the usual labouring duties, but there was some time for relaxation. At a football match between two Glasgow battalions, the Commercials and the Boys' Brigade, a chance long-range German shell landed by the Boys' Brigade goal and the goalkeeper was killed.

Even Gen. Rawlinson found time to relax, attending an Old Etonian Dinner at Amiens with 167 other Old Boys, among them Lieut-Col. Reginald Bastard. The evening passed very pleasantly, Rawly first making a short speech and then entertaining the company with a song from *Carmen*.

In addition to the planning and training, there was a vast amount of extra labouring work to be done in preparation for the battle. On the morning of the attack many times the normal number of men would be packed into the trenches and special assembly trenches were needed for them just behind the front line. Each night these were dug and the chalk and soil had to be bagged up and carried to the rear to be dumped away from German eyes. But too much digging in a war area could lead to disturbing discoveries of what a battle meant. One party of diggers was ordered to restore an old trench that had been filled in, only to discover that it was packed with the bodies of French Moroccan troops.

Another problem concerned how the attackers were to cross No Man's Land where it was particularly wide. The current General Staff instructions were that no attack should start more than 200 yards from the enemy. No special orders were issued, and it was left to individual corps to decide whether the distance was a problem. One that decided to do something about it was VII Corps at Gommecourt, where No Man's Land was up to 800 yards wide. The 56th (London) Division there solved its problem in fine style. A brigadier-general was given the task of digging a completely new trench half-way across No Man's Land. In a carefully planned operation, 3,000 infantrymen protected by patrols went out and, after three nights, had dug 2,900 yards of new front-line trench and 1,500 yards of communication trench joining it to the old front line. This operation was completed at a cost of only eight dead and fifty-five wounded. Of course, the Germans could see what had been done but this was all part of the plan to make the preparations at Gommecourt as obvious as possible to draw German attention to the diversion.

Deep down under the ground more digging was in progress. Gen. Rawlinson had decided to use the mines that he had inherited from the French and work was carried out feverishly on the preparation of seven large mines and many smaller ones. These were to be exploded under vital German strong-points just before the infantry attack. The Germans must have been aware of the mining activity but do not appear to have done much counter-mining during this period of preparation. One Tunnelling Company did suspect that Germans were working near their own gallery, so they prepared a small counter-charge: 'To make the Germans think we were still digging, we tied a hammer to the end of a long rope. We hung the hammer over a bar in the roof and one man kept pulling the rope so that the hammer kept banging on the wall. Our officer was a parson's son. He took off his cap and knelt down and said, "Please God, help the poor devils down there." Then he pressed the plunger.' (Spr C. Nixon, 178th Tunnelling Company)

The tunnellers digging one mine (under a German post known as Kasino Point) had a dangerous moment when they penetrated an enemy dug-out. They were able to conceal the tunnel from the Germans but the incident shows how deep the German dug-outs were.

Behind the trenches, the whole area was a scene of seething activity as this one-time backwater of the war prepared for a major battle. Huge stocks of ammunition, food and fodder for horses were brought up and dumped as near to the front as possible. Water was very scarce, so that wells had to be sunk and miles of water pipe laid. A major problem was lack of communications; the region had only been served by one railway, one main road and a few country lanes.

One of the greatest needs was for stone for the extra roads, railways and railway sidings which had to be built. The local chalk was too soft and suitable material had to be fetched from as far away as Jersey and Cornwall. So precious was the stone that one Casualty Clearing Station, ordered to move to a new location in preparation for the battle, dug up all its pathways and took the stone with it to the new site, all twenty lorry-loads.

Every possible result of the battle was being anticipated: each corps built a large barbed-wire enclosure for the expected enemy prisoners; all the medical services were enlarging their accommodation; and sadly, but logically, mass graves were dug.

The organization for dealing with wounded men was based upon a systematic process of evacuation through various medical units, each of which had a particular service to offer the wounded man before passing him back to the next unit. This process started with the stretcher-bearers bringing in wounded from the battlefield and extended all the way back to the large military and civilian hospitals in England. The farther back a wounded soldier could get, the more considered and skilled the treatment he could expect.

The methods used to evacuate men from one unit to another varied. Motor ambulances were used from divisional units to the Casualty Clearing Stations, a distance of a few miles only, but from there to the base was a greater distance and the normal method used was the Ambulance Train. Properly equipped and staffed with doctors and nurses, these could take a load of 400 wounded men in comfort to the base hospitals. There was an alternative method of evacuation from the Somme Front whereby ambulance barges took the wounded down the River Somme. This was a particularly restful method but, as each barge only carried forty wounded, not of much use in times of stress.

When a major battle was being fought it was essential that this evacuation process ran smoothly. If any stage of it broke down, all those units forward of the failure would fill up and be unable to accept fresh cases or treat properly those they already held. Gen. Rawlinson had seen the effect of just such a breakdown in the evacuation of the wounded to the base at Loos, and was determined that there should be no repetition in his army. He took a close interest in the plans made by his Director of Medical Services, who had estimated that he would need seven Ambulance Trains and three Temporary Ambulance Trains daily.* Rawlinson believed that this was not enough and to ensure that his requirements would be met he wrote himself, on 14 June, to G.H.Q.:

To Q.M.G., British Armies in France

With reference to evacuation of wounded from Fourth Army area during active operations; I consider it essential that means of evacuation by trains should be provided for at least 10,000 wounded per day, in order to avoid undue overcrowding and discomfort for the wounded in the Casualty Clearing Stations and other medical units.

In order to evacuate this number, 12 ambulance trains and 6 improvised ambulance trains will be required daily by this Army.

I should like to be assured that this number of trains will be available, as I am informed that the total number of ambulance trains in this country is only 30, of which 6 are employed solely at the bases, and that the total number of improvised trains is only 6.

It appears to be necessary that the number of trains available for the Fourth Army should be considerably increased if the delays which I understand occurred during the Loos fighting in September last are to be avoided.

H. Rawlinson

Ambulance Trains and the evacuation of wounded to the base were the responsibility of the Quartermaster General's department at G.H.Q. In June 1916 the officer occupying this position was Lieut-Gen. R. C. Maxwell, a sixty-four-year-old officer, who had been within five months of retirement when

* A Temporary Ambulance Train was one brought specially into service to cope with large numbers of lightly wounded men. It could carry 1,000 sitting patients.

the war had started in 1914. Rawlinson's letter had been addressed personally to Lieut-Gen. Maxwell (technically of junior rank but twelve years his senior in age), who replied four days later:

(1) It is not anticipated that there will be any difficulty in meeting the needs of the Fourth Army during active operations.
(2) The distribution of the regular ambulance trains during times of pressure is regulated from General Headquarters according to the needs of the moment, and it is not considered advisable to allot them to Armies beforehand.
(3) No limit has been placed on the number of improvised ambulance trains. The number required will be brought into use as and when necessary.

And finally what must have been intended as a snub to Rawlinson:

(4) No reports of any delay in the evacuation of the wounded during the fighting round Loos can be traced in this office.

R. C. Maxwell*

His letter to G.H.Q. had had some effect however, for, on 20 June, the Quartermaster General issued two detailed memoranda giving extensive instructions 'Relating to the Regulating of Ambulance Trains in Time of Pressure' and copies were distributed to all railway and medical units. Rawlinson was more satisfied with this action and his staff made final preparations, secure in the knowledge that there should be no delay in the evacuation of the wounded from the battle area to the base and thence to England.

For once, the see-saw balance of power in the air was in the British favour. The R.F.C. had gathered a force of ten squadrons, 185 planes, against the German strength of 129 on this front. The British pilots were kept busy helping the artillery register their targets ready for the bombardment and keeping German scouting planes away from the British lines. Thanks to the superiority of the R.F.C., no German aircraft was able to observe the British preparations or shoot down their artillery observation balloons. Eventually there were to be fourteen of these, flying in a great arc round Albert, one for each infantry division in the line.

* Both letters are from Public Record Office, WO 95/447.

At this time, when the army was in need of every shell it could get, there were difficulties back at home. A shortage of shells had been blamed as one of the reasons for the failures of 1915 but now production was under the vigorous Lloyd George, Minister for Munitions, and output was booming. At the end of May, the government had considered postponing the Whitsun Holiday, so that work in the munition factories should not be interrupted. This idea had met with a hostile reception from some workers but, after Lloyd George had met trade-union leaders in London on 30 May, the Prime Minister, Mr Asquith ('Squiff'), was able to announce that the Whit Monday Holiday would be postponed and added on to the August Bank Holiday.

On the same day, Mr Arthur Henderson, M.P., an assistant to Lloyd George, addressing a meeting of munitions workers in Leeds, was asked why it was necessary to postpone the holiday. He replied, as evasively as he could, that the government had only asked for a postponement until the end of July, 'and that that fact should speak volumes'. The official censor allowed his reply to be printed in full in newspapers which were on sale in Holland the next day, so that the Germans were able to pick up the hint that a British offensive was imminent.

A few soldiers were still able to come home on leave, among them a Capt. D. L. Martin, a company commander in the 9th Devons. He took with him a large-scale map of the area his company was to attack: some German trenches in front of Mametz. While on leave, Capt. Martin, an artist, amused himself by making a plasticine model of the battlefield. The longer he looked at the model, the stronger his feeling grew that if and when his company advanced over a small rise by some trees called Mansel Copse, they would come under fire from a German machine-gun position built into the base of a wayside shrine in Mametz. On his return to France he showed the model to his brother officers and told them of his forecast.

Another company commander was Capt. W. P. Nevill of the 8th East Surreys. Nevill was a young officer who liked to stand on the fire-step each evening and shout insults at the Germans. His men were to be in the first wave of the assault near Montauban and he was concerned as to how they would behave, for they had never taken part in an attack before.

While he was on leave, Nevill bought four footballs, one for each of his platoons. Back in the trenches, he offered a prize to the first platoon to kick its football up to the German trenches on the day of the attack. One platoon painted the following inscription on its ball:

The Great European Cup
The Final
East Surreys v Bavarians
Kick Off at Zero

Many of the battalion commanders from the 32nd Division were given a week's leave in June. The c.o. of the 2nd K.O.Y.L.I. was none too pleased to be asked many times when the 'Big Push' was going to start. If everyone in London knew of the attack, what hope was there of keeping it a secret from the enemy?

Probably the busiest soldiers during this period were the artillerymen who were preparing for the five-day bombardment. Lloyd George had promised that, for this battle, the army should have guns standing wheel to wheel and, by the time the bombardment opened, his promise was almost literally fulfilled. There was a gun, howitzer or mortar for every seventeen yards of the enemy front line to be attacked. Compared with the previous best effort, at Loos, there were twice as many guns and six times as many shells. More shells were destined to be fired in one week than in the first twelve months of the war.

All through the first three weeks in June, fresh batteries came up at night into carefully prepared positions. After they had settled in, they registered their targets, helped by their own officers observing from the front-line trench, or by R.F.C. observers in balloons or aeroplanes. Once satisfied that this had been done properly, the batteries lapsed into silence and waited.

The bombardment opened on 24 June, for the infantry attack was still planned for the 29th, and the gunners settled down to a daily routine. Each morning they fired a concentrated barrage for eighty minutes, using every available gun. This was to be cut to sixty-five minutes on the morning of the attack, so that the infantry could 'go over' with the Germans still expecting another fifteen minutes' barrage. For the remainder of the day a continuous, but steadier, barrage was fired. At night half of the guns rested but the barrage was supplemented by heavy machine-guns, which put down specially harrassing fire on the enemy's rear, hoping to cut off the garrisons in the trenches from supplies and relief.

Despite the extent of the bombardment, there were some imperfections and deficiencies. The task of cutting the barbed wire had been given to the 18-pounders but nearly all the ammunition they were using was shrapnel shells. These descendants of the old grape-shot had a small charge which exploded the shell in the air, scattering steel balls on to the ground below, shot-gun fashion. If the fuse was set a fraction of a second too early, the shrapnel balls missed the wires; if too late, the shell exploded harmlessly in the ground. It required a very high level of skill by the artillery officers to cut wire with shrapnel, but it could be done.

Another drawback was the shortage of both heavy guns and ammunition, vital for the destruction of the deep dug-outs. There were only thirty-four artillery pieces above 9.2-in. calibre and half of these had been loaned by the French.

The final disappointment was that the mass production of shells, and especially of their delicate fuses, had led to a lowering of the quality and many shells failed to explode. One estimate put the proportion of duds as high as one third. This may have been an exaggeration but a soldier, captured by the Germans on a night raid towards the end of the bombardment, has described his journey to the rear: 'I was told to leave the dug-out and run after the German in front of me whilst another followed behind. I was running for a long time and climbing over huge shells that had not exploded, I must have seen hundreds of them. Duds.' (Pte F. McLaughlin, 1st Royal Dublin Fusiliers) These drawbacks were not all obvious at the time and the bombardment was on such a scale, compared with previous efforts, that they would not necessarily have been decisive.

After months of suffering from German shell fire, the British troops were tremendously encouraged by the display of their own artillery. In most places the Germans were so quiet that the infantry could walk about above ground for the first time and gaze in wonder on the German positions. 'The enemy's trenches look very pretty sometimes in the sunlight, our shells bursting over them in yellow, black or white puffs, many of the trenches covered with a bright yellow weed; while between the heavy white lines of chalk marking the principal trenches, there are frequently large fields of brilliant scarlet poppies.' (Maj. W. A. Vignoles, Grimsby Chums)*

The scene at night was spectacular. 'It was a real sight to see for miles to left and right, all the guns flash as they fired, and with the Very lights, machine-guns and all the other activity, it was something to remember.' (Gnr H. W. Beaumont, 170th (County Palatine) Brigade R.F.A.)

The firing of the heavy 15-in. howitzers, of which there were a handful manned by the Royal Marine Artillery, was a special treat for the infantry. All day long, there would be a gang of fascinated spectators to watch the elaborate loading of the howitzers. When one of the huge shells was fired, it could be followed in flight for some time, until it dipped at the top of its trajectory. A few seconds later a distant 'boom' would tell of its arrival in the German lines.

The sound of the bombardment could be heard quite plainly in England. Some people living on the South Coast thought that a naval battle was being fought; others realized that it foretold the beginning of the Big Push.

To the background of the rumbling of the bombardment, the generals were making their final plans but small strains began to appear under the great pressure of the impending attack. These were particularly apparent in the relationships between the three generals involved in the main attack – Haig, the C.-in-C., and Rawlinson and Gough, the commanders of his Fourth and Reserve Armies. Haig again wrote to Rawlinson just before the bombardment opened, urging him to reduce it from five to three days to give the Germans less warning of the attack, but Rawlinson was still certain he was right and again Haig declined to give a direct order.

Meanwhile, Lieut-Gen. Gough's command was crumbling away. It began to disintegrate on 21 June, when the infantry corps allotted to him by the C.-in-C. was taken away and placed in G.H.Q. reserve. Then, on the following day, his cavalry divisions were placed under Fourth Army control. Although he continued to call himself the commander of the Reserve

* From the diary of the late Maj. Vignoles, kindly lent by Maj. C. H. Emmerson, M.C., of Grimsby.

Army, Gough had, in fact, been relegated to the status of a corps commander under Rawlinson, and the only troops he had under his command were the cavalry that Haig was hoping would be used but that Rawlinson was convinced would not.

As late as 27 June, two days before the proposed attack, Gough complained to Haig that he was certain of neither his position, nor his objectives, under Rawlinson. Haig simply reiterated the plan: Gough was to push through any gap that might be made, seize Bapaume and turn northwards towards Arras. Gough explained that he had no infantry to work with his cavalry and that his advance would depend upon Rawlinson's goodwill, Gough not being in a position to demand the foot soldiers. Haig sent his Chief of Staff round the various H.Q.'s trying to establish an acceptable procedure and, eventually, a loose plan was worked out depending upon the progress of the battle. It was hardly satisfactory that, two days before their Big Push, the generals had still not settled their command system.

To the uncertainties and doubts of his subordinate infantry commanders, Rawlinson showed an attitude of absolute confidence. It is interesting that the two objections put to him by Haig, those of the long artillery preparation and the absence of any rushing tactics, were again raised. The recommended tactic at this stage of the war was that attacking infantry should approach to within 100 yards of enemy trenches, ready to rush in when the barrage lifted. At a Fourth Army corps commanders' conference it was suggested to Rawlinson that the infantry might go in even closer, to within forty yards in fact. Rawlinson refused to approve this, saying that nothing would exist at the conclusion of the bombardment. So dogmatic was he in his optimism and so thoroughly did it spread to his corps and divisional commanders that objections coming back from the men at the front were met with confident assertions at all levels.

To Gen. Sir Henry Rawlinson, more than to any other, this battle would belong. It was his plan that had been adopted, it was his will that had been imposed upon all those around him.

If the generals' work was nearly done, that of the infantry was growing apace. One of their tasks, as soon as the bombardment had opened, was the continuous raiding of German trenches. These raids were meant to see how much damage was being done by the bombardment; to identify German units; and to ensure that the Germans kept their front-line trenches manned during the bombardment. Each night the artillery fire would lift off the German trenches for a short time and every division in the line would make at least one raid. It was dangerous work, hated by the soldiers: 'It was a frightening experience, a matter of dodging from one shell hole to the next and, very often, finding that your companion in the shell hole was a partially decomposed body of a German or British soldier. I took part in a number of these excursions and I remember that our reward for the ones who came back was an extra tot of rum.' (Pte J. S. Kidd, 1st Edinburgh City Battalion)

Results from these raids varied. The 11th Borders sent over seventy-five men and came back with twenty German prisoners; these were not regarded as a very valuable catch as 'They were a poor lot of Saxons', but the Borders had lost half of their raiding party as casualties. Another raid (probably by the Ulster Division) brought back twelve prisoners, from trenches opposite Thiepval Wood. This time the raiders had no casualties and their prisoners were reported to G.H.Q. as 'cowed and glad to surrender'.

The 30th Division reported that two of their patrols had entered the German trenches and found the front line heavily damaged and empty. They had worked along the trench in both directions and even found the dug-outs empty; it was only on trying to reach the German support trench that any enemy was discovered. But not all the raids went so smoothly. In two nights, Hunter-Weston's corps attempted nine raids, but every one was beaten off by the Germans, some with heavy loss.

Near La Boisselle, the 3rd Tyneside Irish made two successful raids. They had prepared home-made bombs – a full can of petrol with a grenade attached – and, when they entered the German trenches, these fearsome missiles were thrown down the entrances to thirteen dug-outs. On the return of one of these raiding parties, the officer in charge found that one of his men was missing. He went back and searched No Man's Land but stayed out too long. A German rifleman spotted him in the growing light, a shot rang out and the officer was dead. His body was recovered the following night.*

The news of hungry and demoralized German prisoners and empty, flattened trenches encouraged the generals to think that the bombardment was achieving its object. The worse news, of raids being bloodily repulsed and wire defences not destroyed, was discounted as being exaggerated and unreliable.

The Germans were also raiding. The 12th Northumberland Fusiliers were holding the trenches near Fricourt when, just after dusk, the Germans put down a barrage, firstly on the wire and then on three sides of a short stretch of trench. 'After that, nothing seemed to happen, but when I stepped down from the fire-step, I nearly jumped out of my skin. Standing behind me was a German, armed with a revolver and grenade, but he surrendered at once, asked for a cigarette and seemed very pleased to be taken prisoner.' (L/Cpl H. Fellows, 12th Northumberland Fusiliers)

Another device used to harass the Germans was poison gas. This was released whenever the wind blew towards the German trenches. But it was a fickle weapon. When German shells burst open the gas cylinders or the wind blew sideways, the wrong people might be gassed.

While the bombardment was being fired an officer from a gas unit was killed in No Man's Land near Serre. He was said to be the son of a well-known politician and the battalion holding the line, the Hull Commercials, was ordered to recover the body. Two attempts failed, with the Hull men suffering casualties. Their C.O. was ordered to try again but refused. He was promptly relieved of his command.†

In spite of the build-up of men and the extensive preparations being made on the Somme front, G.H.Q. still tried to mislead the enemy as to the exact time and place of the attack. Haig had ordered his other armies as far north as Belgium to do all they could to confuse the Germans. New trenches and dummy gun emplacements were dug; sudden artillery barrages were put down and the guns tried to blow away stretches of the German wire. So that the increase in night raids on the Somme should not draw attention to that

* He was Capt. H. Price, a surveyor from British Columbia. His grave is in Albert Communal Cemetery.

† Lieut-Col. Dan Burges was later given another battalion in Greece. In 1918 he lost a leg but won the Victoria Cross. After the war he was, for ten years, Governor of the Tower of London.

front, other sectors had to do the same. Night after night, all along the front, the hated raids continued. These may have misled the Germans, but they were very costly; in one raid on the Maroc sector, near Loos, two battalions (Royal Sussex and King's Royal Rifle Corps) lost fifteen officers and 385 men in the raid and the retaliatory German barrage.

For some troops, however, there was a bonus. Leave had been cut almost to nothing in the Fourth Army and, to keep leave boats and trains running at the usual rate in June, Australian troops in the base depots were given extra leave to England.

The cavalry had been kept out of the way until the last day before the offensive, 28 June, but, as that day approached, they started to move up by easy stages, only at night and by carefully selected side roads, so as not to block the over-strained transport system. There were three full divisions of cavalry, containing some of the most romantic names in the British Army – Dragoon Guards, Hussars, Lancers, Life Guards, Royal Horse Guards and, in the 2nd Indian Cavalry Division, the Poona Horse, Hodson's Horse and the Deccan Horse with a full brigade of Canadian cavalry attached. Every trooper was armed with a sabre or lance, in addition to his rifle, and all were expecting action at last. 'Just before the battle we were told by our c.o., "Undoubtedly there will be a gap and, when you go through, I guarantee you will not be more than five days without fresh rations." ' (L/Cpl G. J. R. Wraight, 3rd Dragoon Guards)

Gough had once been the commander of the 7th Division, which had seen much hard fighting under him and had called itself 'Gough's Mobile Army'. The men on the Somme knew vaguely of Gough's presence and of his force of cavalry and infantry preparing for a breakthrough. The phrase 'Gough's Mobile Army' was revived and there was much talk of it amongst the troops. There were stories that when the cavalry galloped through the gap they would be accompanied by infantry carried in lorries and buses.

The infantry were being given last-minute orders and advice, although they were still not told the day or time of the attack. The leading battalions were to advance in a series of waves which had to enter No Man's Land at one-minute intervals and move forward at a steady pace of no more than 100 yards in every two minutes (less than two miles per hour), and the men were forbidden to cheer or shout, in case the enemy heard them coming. If faced by resistance, they were not to run until within twenty yards of the enemy, so as not to become exhausted. It was to be like a vast, complicated parade ground movement, carried out in slow motion. 'Assurance was given that the time honoured system of short rushes would, in this instance, be unnecessary.' (Cpl J. H. Tansley, 9th Yorks and Lancs)

'We were instructed not to attend to any wounded men but, in such cases, to take his rifle and place it vertically with the bayonet sticking in the ground in order to attract the attention of the R.A.M.C. We also received orders that no quarter was to be shown to the enemy and no prisoners taken.' (Pte R. Love, Glasgow Commercials)

This advice about prisoners was repeated in at least three different divisions but never by written order, always verbally. A brigadier-general in the 34th Division told the Cambridge Battalion,* 'You may take prisoners but I don't want to see them', and another, in the 18th Division, told the 6th Royal Berks that it would be difficult to get food through to the attacking troops and the fewer prisoners taken, the more food there would be for the Berkshires. At the other extreme, the 1st Bradford Pals (and many others) were told that any man who refused to go over the top would be shot on the spot by Military Police.

Battalion commanders had to decide which of their officers and men were to take part in the attack. In previous battles battalions had gone into action with the whole of their fighting strength and, if they had suffered heavy casualties, had found difficulty in rebuilding the battalion. Although the attack was expected to be a walk-over, battalions were ordered, on this occasion, to leave ten per cent of their fighting strength behind with the transport. In the event of a catastrophe, these would form the nucleus in rebuilding the battalions.

This process of deciding who was to go into action and who was to remain behind, potentially a life-or-death decision,

* The battalion, officially the 11th Suffolks, was recruited entirely in the city and county of Cambridge and will be referred to as 'The Cambridge Battalion'.

The Wave System

A battalion of the 21st Division deployed for attack

There were many variations of this layout: some battalions attacked on a two-company front. The battalion strength in attack was 23 officers (◆) and about 700 men (||||||)

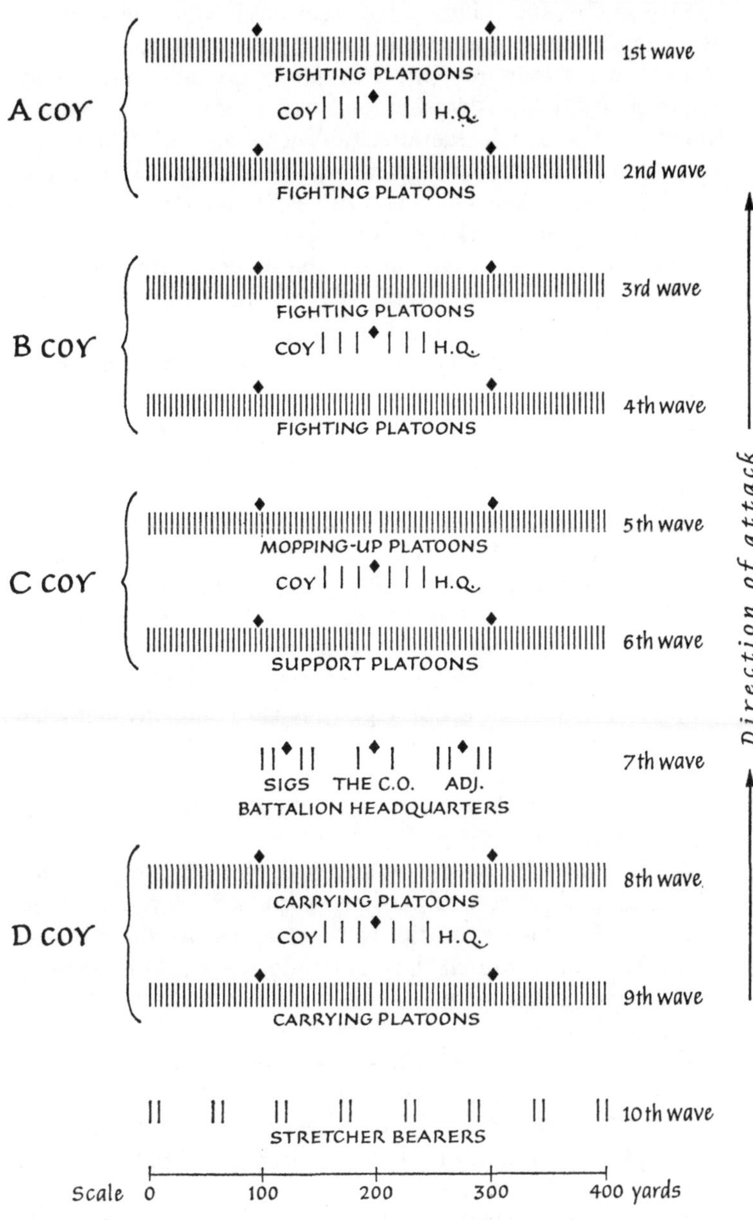

There were 5 yards between each man in a wave and 100 yards between each wave. When fully deployed the battalion covered 400 x 900 yards and took 9 minutes to pass a given point. When the carrying platoons had delivered their loads to the captured trenches, they became fighting platoons.

went on in every battalion. 'I had just joined the battalion on a draft but, because I could write shorthand, the adjutant put me in the office. Then a lance corporal came and gave me 120 extra rounds of ammunition. "You'll want these for the attack." Next they gave me a couple of grenades and finally a shovel. I didn't know whether I was to stay in the Orderly Room or take part in the attack. When I asked, the adjutant said, "On no account is that man to be allowed to go. He is the only man round here who can write shorthand!" ' (Pte T. A. Senior, 9th Yorks and Lancs)

The infantrymen were also being issued with their full loads of equipment and were only just beginning to realize the full weight of the burdens they would have to carry. Training had invariably been done without the full packs carried in action. A typical man from the first wave, in addition to all his packs, carried a rifle and bayonet, two gas helmets, 220 rounds of rifle ammunition, two grenades (which he was to give to the trained bombers to throw), two empty sandbags, a spade, a pair of wire-cutters, a flare and a variety of smaller items. The basic minimum load was about seventy pounds and most men had more than this.

The men in the rear waves were given even heavier burdens, such as duck-boards to be used for trench bridges, rolls of barbed wire and bundles of stakes for the barbed wire. 'My total load was about eighty pounds and my personal weight at that time was only eight stone.' (Pte E. G. Hall, 1/6th West Yorks)

Some of the loads given to men showed great originality, if some optimism:

A long pole with a pennant attached; this was to be erected at a certain point as a marker for the artillery.

Triangular pieces of tin were attached to the back of leading troops so that the sun's reflection could be seen by observers in the rear.

Carrier pigeons.

Two wine bottles full of water – a sensible idea.

Two signallers in the Tyneside Irish were given bags full of small pieces of paper. They were to follow the leading troops, laying a trail, so that other signallers could lay telephone wire after them.

The supreme confidence of Gen. Rawlinson that he would be able to take the German first line easily, having been impressed first upon his corps commanders, now began to find its way down to the ordinary soldiers. Battalions were paraded and addressed by senior officers, usually brigadier-generals. These are a selection of the reassuring speeches made to them. To the Newcastle Commercials:

> You will be able to go over the top with a walking stick, you will not need rifles. When you get to Thiepval you will find the Germans all dead, not even a rat will have survived.

To the 11th Sherwood Foresters:

> You will meet nothing but dead and wounded Germans. You will advance to Mouquet Farm and be there by 11 A.M. The field kitchens will follow you and give you a good meal.

To the 1st London Rifle Brigade (in Part Two Orders):

> Success is assured and casualties are expected to be ten per cent.

To the 8th K.O.Y.L.I.:

> When you go over the top, you can slope arms, light up your pipes and cigarettes, and march all the way to Pozières before meeting any live Germans.*

It all sounded very easy and the noise in the background of hundreds of their guns, firing night and day into the German lines, added reassurance.

Other speeches were on different themes. When Lieut-Col. Reginald Bastard's battalion was paraded, the brigade commander told them that he wanted the Lincolns to win many more medals. An unknown voice from the back shouted, 'It's all right for you, you won't be there.' As indignant N.C.O.s ran up and down looking for the culprit, the brigadier-general called back, 'No, I won't, but you will be.' This brought laughter from all ranks.

Occasionally the talks were less optimistic. 'Just before the battle our divisional commander took a group of us N.C.O.s and showed us our objective in the distance. He said, "I am willing to sacrifice the whole of the 101st Brigade to take that."' (L/Cpl A. Turner, Grimsby Chums) This was Maj.-Gen. Ingouville-Williams. His men would have to force the German defences astride the main road from Albert to Bapaume; Inky Bill's determination was very clear.

* I cannot guarantee the exact wording of the passages quoted above but I am satisfied that they are reasonably accurate.

While the generals were giving their pep talks, the five-day bombardment was entering its final stage. After three or four days of continuous shelling, most of the targets should have been destroyed. Of these targets the wire, a vital one for the infantry, was the only one where the damage could easily be assessed. Each night small patrols went out into No Man's Land and inspected the effect of the shelling. The reports were inconsistent: in some places the wire was well cut; in others there were a few gaps; but in several places the wire was still intact. One party, at least, found the Germans had come out of the trenches during a lull in the shelling and were calmly repairing the damage to the wire.

Renewed efforts were made on some sectors. The artillery was diverted from other targets for a fresh bombardment of the wire and the infantry went out at night with special explosive devices to destroy what was left standing. But these attempts were dangerous and only small gaps could be made, even when the raids were successful.

On those sectors where there were doubts about the wire, the infantry were most unhappy; at the same time as they were being told that the attack would be a walk-over, they could see, from their own trenches, that the German wire remained a barrier. One officer who was particularly worried was Lieut-Col. E. T. F. Sandys, commanding the 2nd Middlesex. His battalion had the doubtful distinction of having to cross a greater width of No Man's Land than any other involved in the attack. Its objective was the German trenches at the head of Mash Valley, 750 yards away from the Middlesex trenches. Sandys was an efficient and popular c.o. but he was very highly strung and had convinced himself that his battalion was to be launched against uncut wire and Germans who had survived the shelling.

During the bombardment the 2nd Royal Berks, which was in the same brigade as Sandys' battalion, raided the German trenches. Making a silent approach, they were surprised to hear the sound of singing coming from the deep dug-outs in the German trenches. Doubtless Sandys heard this discouraging news. He spent many daylight hours in an artillery observation post staring at the wire nearly half a mile away, but it was difficult to see clearly. At night he could not sleep but walked aimlessly around the camp where his men were bivouacked. He was so consumed with anxiety and felt the responsibility of his position so keenly that he complained to his brigade commander, and possibly even higher, but to no avail.

The Middlesex officers knew of their colonel's misery but did not share it. They could hear the guns firing day and night and they shared the widespread belief that the attack would be an easy success.

Infantry commanders like Lieut-Col. Sandys who raised objections were not well received, being told that they were exaggerating or that they were windy. Maybe a Fourth Army order had hardened the attitude; Rawlinson had warned, 'All criticism by subordinates . . . of orders received from superior authority will, in the end, recoil on the heads of the critics.'

Rawlinson's subordinates faithfully passed his optimism on to those further down the chain of command. A Brigade Major in the 31st Division records: 'The corps commander [Hunter-Weston] was extremely optimistic, telling everyone that the wire had been blown away, although we could see it standing strong and well, that there would be no German trenches and all we had to do was to walk into Serre.'*

How did the Germans react to the increased activity, the bombardment, the raids? The first emotion was surprise. 'When the British shelling started, one of our grenadiers put on his best uniform, went to the company commander and asked indignantly, "Who has started this silly shooting? In God's name, someone is going to get hurt." ' (Unteroffizier Paul Scheytt, 109th Reserve Regiment)

As the bombardment settled down, the German infantry took refuge in their deep dug-outs. While a hail of shells was falling on the trenches above, gradually destroying their carefully prepared defences or blowing away the barbed wire, most of the Germans were quite safe. They kept their rifles and machine-guns oiled and stacked boxes of ammunition and grenades by the stairways.

In the trenches lonely sentries had to remain on duty watching for the first sign of a British raid or the main attack. 'Behind our trench we had a mirror mounted on a post, so that we could see over No Man's Land. During the bombardment we had one sentry on duty in the trench all the time, watching

* Public Record Office, CAB 45/188.

the mirror. The ground was shaking as though the end of the world was coming and the mirror was quivering but it never broke.' (Soldat Wilhelm Lange, 99th Reserve Regiment) Some dug-outs had long periscopes which came out above the ground so that the look-outs could keep watch in safety.

The constant shelling made movement along the trenches almost impossible. Even behind the lines it was dangerous. 'Three days before the battle started I was fetching something from Miraumont to Grandcourt when an English aeroplane chased me for about ten minutes. I escaped by dodging among the willow trees along the Ancre.' (Feldwebel Felix Kircher, 26th Field Artillery Regiment)

Steadily the shelling took its toll. Electricity cables and water pipes were broken, emergency food and water supplies had to be opened. The entrances to the dug-outs became blocked and required constant work to keep them clear, an essential but dangerous task. Occasionally one of the heavy shells collapsed a dug-out, crushing and killing the occupants, but this was a very rare occurrence. On some sectors, articularly in the south near the Somme, the Germans evacuated the whole of their front-line trench, hoping to have sufficient warning of the attack to reoccupy it in time.

The reduced rate of the British shelling during the night gave some opportunity for essential movement. Ration carriers from the rear risked their lives to bring water and hot food to the forward dug-outs, but the British were firing on all likely approaches intentionally to stop this traffic. The food and water often did not get through.

The Germans had a daily beer ration and one party from a Baden regiment, isolated in a dug-out near Mametz, insisted that someone had to go back to fetch a fresh barrel. The youngest soldier was chosen and had a terrifying journey as he rolled the barrel over the torn-up ground, in darkness, with shells bursting all around; but the Badeners got their beer.

Routine reliefs of front-line battalions had to be put off; it was decided not to risk 1,500 men in the open trenches while two battalions changed places. A Bavarian battalion in the trenches at Montauban waited night after night, its relief long overdue.

Although the Germans were comparatively safe in their dug-outs, the bombardment was a terrible ordeal for them.

The long months when the Somme was a quiet sector had not prepared them for five days and nights of constant shelling. They could only wait; sometimes in darkness or candlelight where their electricity supply had failed; very short of water in conditions where tension and fear added to their thirst. The wounded could not always be evacuated; the dead, unburied, soon started to rot and stink in the heat. The days of *Trommelfeuer* (drumfire) continued and the Germans realized that this was no casual bombardment. At some time in the future, the shelling would stop and then, if they were not blown sky high by underground mines, they would have to scramble up the damaged stairways, man what was left of their trenches and fight for their lives.

'We could see sixteen English balloons and thought "That's the English for you; we cannot do anything about those." The English artillery – the English army – the masses of English aeroplanes over our heads always. We are finished, we shall all be wounded or dead.' (Grenadier Emil Kury, 109th Reserve Regiment)

Farther back, the German artillery could do little to help their suffering front-line troops. There were many batteries in the area, all carefully concealed, but every time one of them opened fire, a hail of British shells fell upon it, directed by the British aeroplanes that were everywhere.

The German gunners in turn were nearly blind; their own planes were driven off by the R.F.C. and their observation balloons destroyed as soon as they appeared in the sky. Even the German observation posts on the ground were vulnerable: 'I was the leader of a small observation troop. Our task was to watch the movements behind the English front by day and, by night, the flash of the English guns in order to fix their positions.

'We had three observation posts: the church tower at Pozières, the Hill 153, called Feste Staufen [by the English, Stuff Redoubt] and one near Serre. The church tower was the best; we could see about ten kilometres behind the English lines, the airfields, the gun positions and the movements of the infantry. But the English artillery hit the tower and, literally in the last second, we slid down the ropes of the bells and were saved.' (Feldwebel Felix Kircher, 26th Field Artillery Regiment)

However, the observers had done their work well in the

past few weeks. Thanks to their advantage of higher ground, the Germans knew to the metre the position of every British trench, most of their gun positions and every feature in No Man's Land. When the time came they would rely on this knowledge to put down defensive barrages in answer to pre-arranged signals from their front-line soldiers. So the German gunners held their fire, and the British assumed that they had located and destroyed most of the German batteries.

Except for the doubts about the wire, the five-day bombardment appeared to be going well for the British, as did all the last-minute preparations. But the weather was a source of anxiety. A series of heavy summer storms had broken out on 26 and 27 June and it was still raining heavily in the early hours of the 28th, only twenty-four hours away from zero hour. During the morning the weather cleared and the sun came out, but it would be some time before the roads and trenches dried out. Those considering a postponement were in a difficult position; some of the assault battalions were already in their trenches, others were on the way and it was doubtful whether there was enough ammunition available to maintain the bombardment at the previous rate. On the other hand, the infantry attack might be seriously impeded if the battlefield had been flooded. There were other factors – a longer bombardment would certainly help the wire-cutting programme, but some of the divisions had not had the bad weather and these were ready to attack on time.

At 11 A.M. on 28 June, just under twenty-one hours before the infantry attack, the decision was taken: there would be a postponement of forty-eight hours. The new time and date for the attack was decided – 7.30 A.M. on 1 July. Bad weather had decided that history would have an easily remembered date for a famous battle.

The staff immediately started on the enormous task of adjustment. Orders went out to the artillery that they must make their shells last another two days: immediately, their rate of fire slackened. The timetable of movements for nearly 200 infantry battalions and all the supporting units had to be amended. Battalions already packed tight in the front-line trench were marched out again; the larger number, which had not yet gone into the trenches, were stopped in their last-minute preparations and made to wait a further two days. The postponement was handled with the minimum amount of disorganization and was, for once, a triumph for the much abused staff.

For most men the next two days were to be a miserable time; they were all keyed up and had been ready for the battle on 29 June, now they had to wait an extra two days. There was not much for them to do, time passed slowly and tempers grew short. 'Rumours came back from the front line that the German wire was not all cut and many of our chaps were a bit jumpy. While we were sharpening our bayonets an argument broke out and one of my pals, the Sanitary Corporal who was being left behind, joined in. Someone said, "You shut up! You don't have to go in." He felt so bad that he went to his company commander and got permission to come in with us. He was killed.' (Pte H. C. Bloor, Accrington Pals)

'Our bank books were taken in and we were paid all our credit, which was substantial. Some of us had hundreds of francs, which immediately gave the impression to many of us that most were not coming back. The result was that the *estaminets* got most of it.' (Pte R. T. Tait, Durham Pals)

Some men could stand the strain no longer. 'A shot went off some yards away; a fellow had shot himself right through the knee. He had pluck, I think. It was a strange sight to see him being carried away on a stretcher under arrest, with a man at each side of him with fixed bayonets. I often wonder what happened to him.' (Pte W. J. Senescall, The Cambridge Battalion)

Probably the only soldiers to be really pleased with the new date were the Ulstermen; 1 July was the anniversary of the Battle of the Boyne and there could be no surer omen of success.*

One who took advantage of the postponement was William Noel Hodgson, one of the war poets. At Cambridge, Hodgson had been a contemporary of Rupert Brooke. Now he was Bombing Officer of the 9th Devons and had already won a Military Cross for bravery in 1915. As he waited in the trenches near Mansel Copse where Capt. Martin of the same battalion had forecast the Devons would be caught by German machine-gun fire, Hodgson wrote another poem: 'Before

* When the calendar was reorganized in 1752, eleven days were lost; this resulted in the Boyne now being celebrated on 12 July.

Action'. Maybe Capt. Martin's prophecy caused Hodgson to be uneasy, for his last verse reads:

I, that on my familiar hill
  Saw with uncomprehending eyes
A hundred of Thy sunsets spill
  Their fresh and sanguine sacrifice,
Ere the sun swings his noonday sword
  Must say goodbye to all of this!
By all delights that I shall miss,
  Help me to die, O Lord.

The King brothers made the most of the postponement. Dick had heard that his wife had given birth to their fifth child. It was a little girl and in the spirit of the day she was named Gladys Hope Verdun. Dick was due for leave and was looking forward to seeing the new baby, but most leave had been stopped for the battle. On their last full day before going into the trenches Dick King and his brother, Frank, obtained permission to visit the third brother in the next village. The two K.O.Y.L.I.s walked over and a grand family reunion was held in an *estaminet*, much food and wine being consumed. When darkness fell, Frank said it was time to be going but Dick refused. 'This is the last time we shall all be together. I'm making the most of it.' Dick stayed until dawn and only reached his battalion in time for reveille.

30 June dawned, once again the last day before the attack. The bombardment, thought by many to be over-long when planned for five days, now entered its seventh. The yellow weeds and red poppies that had once made the German trenches so pretty had long since been swept away. Now a white dust floated permanently above their trenches from the pulverized chalk. Above the German front-line villages, this dust was brick red from the shattered buildings being raked over and over by the shelling.

Those British soldiers who had been left to hold their front line were stupefied by the thousands of shells passing over their heads and bursting a few hundred yards away. Some had endured 150 hours of the uproar and there were several cases of shell shock There was even pity among them for 'poor old Gerry, copping it'. But, more than anything, they were impressed by this massive demonstration of their army's power. For Rawlinson and the front-line soldier alike, it was difficult to imagine anything surviving that fire. In the week that the bombardment lasted, 1,437 British guns had fired 1,508,652 shells into the German lines, at a cost to the British taxpayer of approximately £6 million.

As 30 June slowly dragged on, the last preparations were made. Even at this late hour there were changes to be made; sick men had hung on hoping to be fit on the big day and had to be ordered to the rear, their places being taken by reinforcements. One of these late-comers was Albert McMillan. He had joined the Public Schools Battalion in the last few days of June and, as they were short of men, he was detailed for the battle, although he had never been into a trench in his life. In spite of, or because of, his inexperience he was delighted to be joining in the attack.

The strain was telling on some of the older officers who had become C.O.'s of New Army battalions, and several had to report sick. This caused some comment among the men who felt they had been left in the lurch just when they needed their commanders most. At least three battalions – the 2nd Tyneside Scottish, the Sheffield City Battalion and the 8th K.O.Y.L.I. – lost their colonels for various reasons. In the 8th K.O.Y.L.I., it was left to a captain to lead the battalion into action on the following day.

The 2nd Lincolns were all ready for the battle so a concert party was arranged in a field next to the River Ancre outside Albert. A cockney soldier, an officer's batman, led a sing-song and 800 men joined in lusty renderings of such favourites as 'Burlington Bertie', 'Give Me Your Smile' and 'If You Were the Only Girl in the World'. When it was over, Reginald Bastard, standing on a small rise near the stream, talked quietly to his battalion. He concluded, 'I wonder how many of us will be here tomorrow night.'

As the time approached for the men to move off for the trenches, they made their final preparations, packed their kit and made up their loads. Percy Chappell had been soaked through in one of the rainstorms and could find no dry underwear or shirt. The only spare dry clothes he had were a pair of pyjamas, so he put these on under his uniform. As he did so he wondered what the Germans would say if he was taken prisoner.

Another soldier packed with optimism: 'We understood

that, when our division had captured Pozières, the 19th (Western) Division would pass through us and capture the important town of Bapaume. I had a pair of boots which needed attention and I packed these in my haversack, expecting to be able to get them repaired in Bapaume.' (Cpl S. F. Hill, 34th Signal Company)

6

The Last Few Hours

Late on the afternoon of 30 June, the men due to attack the next morning marched out of the villages where they had been billeted. It was a moment charged with emotion as all those remaining behind turned out to give the fighting men a good send-off. 'As second in command of a company, I had been ordered to stay behind. I remember saying to some of the men, "I'll see you in Pozières tomorrow afternoon." I was nearly in tears; these were my chaps and they were going in without me.' (Capt. E. E. F. Baker, 2nd Middlesex)

When the Robin Hoods marched out of their village, Bill Soar was amazed to see the normally fierce regimental sergeant major standing by the side of the road with tears streaming down his face. One man to be left behind when the 7th South Lancs left their billets was Lieut Henry Webber. Although his duties as transport officer would normally have kept the sixty-eight-year-old Webber out of any action, many men were finding excuses to go up to the trenches and his C.O. had specifically ordered Webber to remain behind.

As the battalions marched up to the front, their divisional or corps commanders turned out to watch them go by. When the men from the 7th Division marched past, a veteran brigadier-general could not control himself and burst into tears but some of the men had other emotions: 'My load was almost beyond human endurance. As we staggered up to the trenches, we passed, on the roadside, our divisional general with some of his staff. His words of cheer to us were, "Good luck, men. There is not a German left in their trenches, our guns have blown them all to Hell." Then, I suppose, he got into his car and went home to his H.Q. to wine and dine, while we poor benighted blighters tottered on our way to glory.' (Pte A. V. Pearson, Leeds Pals)

The infantry fell into a thoughtful silence as they settled down to march the remaining kilometres to the trenches. 'The feeling of comradeship among us seemed to grow as we marched forward into a common danger. In particular I have a lasting memory of the man who was closest to me as we marched. I was only eighteen at the time, having joined the army under age, and he was some years older than I. As he spoke to me I became aware of a feeling almost of tenderness in him towards me, as though he sensed my fears and was trying to reassure both himself and me. "Don't worry, Bill," he said. "We'll be all right." And he spoke as gently as a mother trying to soothe a frightened child.' (Pte W. Slater, 2nd Bradford Pals)

But the solemnity of the occasion could not restrain the more highly spirited of the men. 'Whereas most of us had been very silent when we set off, a few here and there started to sing. Whether this was the result of nerves or not, I do not know, but they sang and gave comfort and/or relief to others.' (Pte G. E. Waller, Glasgow Boys' Brigade Battalion)

As they got nearer to the trenches some saw parties of cavalry and were reminded of all the talk of a breakthrough. Even C.S.M. Percy Chappell, a veteran of 1914, seeing the cavalrymen, quite expected that this time there would be a victory.

Every battalion eventually reached and passed through the artillery lines where the guns were firing constantly. The infantry could see the gunners, stripped to the waist and sweating over their work, their eyes blood-shot and some bleeding from the ears after six days of serving their guns. Spare gunners ran over to the infantry, shaking their hands and wishing them luck. 'As we passed an Observation Post a major said, "Goodbye, boys. Sorry I can't come with you." Joke number one!' (Pte F. P. Weston, 7th Buffs) *

Not all men marched in full battalions. As Paddy Kennedy's had been split up to provide supporting and carrying parties, he found himself marching up with a party of only half a platoon strong. As the Manchesters passed the guns, they met a gunner carrying a dixie full of tea. The afternoon was very warm and the tea, immediately offered by the gunner, was very refreshing. The only problem was that Kennedy and his pals could not get at their cups, packed under several layers of equipment. This was soon solved when a steel helmet was produced for all to drink from.

Shortly afterwards, the Manchesters had a more sobering encounter. Two men were being escorted to the rear by armed Military Police – self-inflicted wounded. Kennedy

* The East Kents.

could sympathize with these men, but could not understand their attitude; he was going into his first attack full of confidence that the Germans and their defences were all destroyed and wondered why these poor men did not share his optimism.

For some battalions the march was a long one and they were allowed to halt and rest. During one such rest, men of the Sheffield City Battalion were startled to see several German balloons, flying high in a clear sky. In spite of all the R.F.C.'s efforts, the Germans had managed to fly these at this vital moment and were observing the roads up to the British trenches, where thousands of men were marching up to take their places for the attack. On the same part of the front, near the Sucrerie (a small sugar-beet factory) at Colincamps, the men were marched past several freshly dug, wide trenches – graves ready for mass burials.

As night began to fall, another battalion, a little later than the others, was given a rest near a light railway siding. The area was crowded and noisy, with the full battalion of infantry – the 12th Northumberland Fusiliers – the railway troops and a unit of Chinese labourers unloading railway wagons. It was a beautiful summer evening and a strong tenor voice could be heard singing above the bustle and chatter. Gradually all work stopped and every man became quiet, listening to 'My Little Grey Home in the West', beautifully sung. When the singer finished there was loud applause and calls for more. Once again there was silence as 'When You Come to the End of a Perfect Day' was sung. Not a man present could keep his thoughts from those at home and the coming battle at that poignant moment. But the spell was soon broken when the battalion was ordered to move on. The infantry shouldered their packs and set off into the deepening gloom while the workers on the railway siding went back to their work.

The communication trenches were packed with soldiers from various units searching for their allotted positions. Men took the wrong turning, were sent back again, and collided with others coming up behind them. The night was noisy with curses and shouts. Staff officers hurried about, trying to sort out the confusion, settling arguments, while the heavily burdened soldiers could only shuffle forward, a few paces at a time, waiting for the traffic to move on. In the darkness, it was not always easy to identify an obstacle: 'Orders were to lie down when star shells lit up the surroundings. On one such occasion, no more followed after the light from the star shells died out. After much shouting of, "Get a move on in front", the C.S.M. went along to find out why we were not moving. He found one of our second-lieutenants (nicknamed Charlie Chaplin on account of his splayed feet) waiting for the man lying in front to move, but he was lying behind a corpse.' (L/Cpl H. C. Lancashire, 1/4th London)

Bugler Bill Soar's route to the front line was by way of a communication trench called Roberts Avenue which had been badly shelled and, because of the recent heavy rain, was waist-deep in mud in some places. At one such quagmire Soar was ordered to pass a heavy Vickers machine-gun overhead. When he was passed the Vickers, he sank chest-deep into the mud and was hardly able to keep his feet. The newly commissioned officer in charge of the gun became very agitated and threatened to shoot Soar if he did not get on with passing the gun forward. Soar transferred the gun to the next man but only by pushing himself deeper into the mud. It took two heaving men to get him out again and the suction was so great that he lost both puttees. Once clear, he still had to find his rifle, buried somewhere in the mud, before he could continue on his way.

Five men from an Ulster platoon had an unpleasant surprise. They had been sent along to the assembly trenches in the wood opposite Thiepval as an advance party. When their company (C Company of the Co. Down Volunteers) arrived, 9, 10 and 12 Platoons were at full strength but all they could see of their own 11 Platoon was one private. While the five had been away a heavy German shell had burst on the platoon as it was parading; forty-two men had been killed or wounded, leaving this one dazed survivor, and he was soon judged to be shell-shocked and sent to the rear. This left 11 Platoon to go into action with just four men and a corporal.

Not far away, the c.o. of the Derry Volunteers went through a rotten duck-board in the bottom of a trench and broke his leg. He had to go to the rear and thus missed his battalion's first battle.

As the infantry struggled through the trenches, the senior

Δ A German battalion marching through a Somme village, 1916. The ceremonial helmets, *Pickelhaubes*, which some of these men are wearing, were much sought after by British troops.

∇ 'On the Somme, 1916.' German artillerymen with their 21-centimetre howitzer.

Men of the German 91st Reserve Regiment in their trenches at Gommecourt opposite the 46th (North Midland) Division, Spring 1916. The well constructed trench is defying the wet conditions.

Δ General Sir Douglas Haig, Commander-in-Chief of the British Expeditionary Force.

∇ General Sir Henry Rawlinson, commander of the Fourth Army, outside his headquarters at Querrieux Château.

Δ A British artillery observation balloon being hauled down near Fricourt.

∇ Major General de Lisle, commander of the 29th Division, talks to the 1st Lancashire Fusiliers two days before the attack.

Δ A 15-in. howitzer (nick-named 'Grandmother') firing on German positions near Thiepval. These were the heaviest guns the British had, but there were only six for the eighteen miles of attack frontage. The howitzer fired a shell weighing 1,450 pounds to a maximum range of nearly six miles.

Δ A 9.2-in. shell explodes on the German front line trench near Beaumont Hamel. The photographer was in the British front line.

∇ The effect of seven days of British shelling on the German village fortress of Mametz.

Δ Cheerful soldiers of the 2nd Royal Warwicks, 7th Division, enjoy a hot meal shortly before moving into the line for the attack.

∇ A platoon of D Company, 7th Bedfords, marches through a French village on its way to the trenches. The platoon commander, Lieutenant Douglas Keep, will go into action in Service Dress; he was killed in action one year later.

Δ The 1st London Scottish, 56th (London) Division, marching up to the trenches for the attack. The platoon commander, Second Lieutenant Coxon, is referred to in the text.

∇ Men of the Public Schools Battalion about to go into the trenches on the eve of the battle. They are being issued with new sandbags to add to their already heavy loads.

generals relaxed in their châteaux. The battle was out of their hands now and they could do little to influence what was to happen on the next day. Success, and the generals' reputations, would rest on the skill and courage of the ordinary soldiers. At Advanced G.H.Q. in Beauquesne village eleven miles behind the front lines, Douglas Haig made up his diary:

With God's help I feel hopeful. The men are in splendid spirits. Several have said that they have never before been so instructed and informed of the nature of the operation before them. The wire has never been so well cut, nor the artillery preparation so thorough.*

At Querrieux, Sir Henry Rawlinson had prepared a message for all the troops in his Fourth Army:

In wishing all ranks good luck, the Army Commander desires to impress on all infantry units the supreme importance of helping one another and holding on tight to every yard of ground gained. The accurate and sustained fire of the artillery during the bombardment should greatly assist the task of the infantry.†

At 10.17 P.M. this not very stirring message was sent out to all units in the Fourth Army. In the 34th Division, opposite La Boisselle, a harrassed staff officer was afraid that the message might not reach the forward units by hand through the crush in the trenches. As a result, he transmitted it over a field telephone, although the use of this equipment for important messages was forbidden. It was suspected that the Germans had a listening post that could pick up such telephone conversations.

Rawlinson, too, made up his diary:

What the actual result will be, none can say, but I feel pretty confident of success myself, though only after heavy fighting. That the Boche will break and that a débâcle will supervene I do not believe, but, should this be the case, I am quite ready to take full advantage of it. . . The issues are in the hands of the Bon Dieu.

Back in the trenches the confusion was eventually sorted out and the soldiers reached their allotted positions. Then they settled down to get what rest they could. Even though the attack was due to begin in a few hours, the usual raids and patrols were sent out so as not to give the Germans the

* *The Private Papers of Douglas Haig, 1914–1919,* page 151.

† The Official History, *France and Belgium 1916,* vol. I, page 392.

impression that this night was at all different from any others. Many last-minute attempts were made to destroy the German wire that was still standing. A Sheffield City Battalion patrol blew a gap in the German wire opposite them and then laid white tapes over No Man's Land from the gap, as a guide to the attackers next morning. A patrol from the North Midland Division found a dip in No Man's Land that could not be observed from the British trenches. In this hidden ground they discovered a wide belt of barbed wire, completely untouched by the bombardment.

Only a few men were engaged on these patrols. The majority could do nothing but wait. The trenches were very crowded and there was often no room to lie down. Some men did manage to doze, leaning against the side of the trench, but most of the attackers had to spend a sleepless night on their feet. Midnight passed: it was Saturday 1 July. In the 10th K.O.Y.L.I. the two King brothers, although in the same platoon, were separated by many men and were not able to meet. Dick King thought of his wife and children, especially the baby girl he had never seen, but also of his eldest daughter, Christine, realizing that today, 1 July, it was her ninth birthday. Percy Chappell, a veteran of many battles, thought of his wife at home in Somerset, but then he met four more old Regulars who had been out since the beginning and were all convinced 'that they would draw their rations for a long time yet'. These five sat and chatted quietly and, as the talk got round to the battle, they lightheartedly suggested flowers which they might place on each other's graves, the suggestions ranging from orchids to dandelions.

L/Cpl Charles Matthews and his section spent the night in a dug-out; they would move to a support trench at dawn. While they waited, an N.C.O. called and ordered one of the Northamptons to the rear. The others were first amazed and then envious to hear that the fortunate man was to go home on leave. Soon after this incident there was a loud report and a bullet ricocheted around the walls of the dug-out; a man's rifle had gone off by mistake. After much cursing and shouting, it was discovered that only one man was slightly wounded, the man who had fired the shot. He too went to the rear, one of the first casualties of 1 July.

By 4 A.M. there was enough light to see the German lines. The day dawned calm, misty near the rivers but clear on the uplands. Then a light rain began to fall and there were fears of another wet day in spite of the forecasts. 'It started to rain, so we got our dixies out and let the rain run into them from our tin hats. The rain didn't last long, but we caught enough to quench our thirst.' (Pte W. Gathercole, The Cambridge Battalion)

There were still two and a half hours before the usual morning barrage and three and a half before the infantry attack. Only at this stage were some men told the time of the attack. 'Then came some news which really did put the wind up us. In early daylight, our company commander came on his visiting rounds and informed us that zero hour was at 7.30 A.M. Up to this time we had expected the attack would be made just before dawn, which was the usual time for such occasions. But 7.30 A.M., why that would be in broad daylight!' (Pte A. V. Pearson, Leeds Pals)

Those belonging to the more efficient units received breakfast in various forms; the lucky ones had hot food. 'I remember frying bacon over candles in the battalion H.Q. dug-out. The C.O. and several other officers were there and everyone was very cheerful. Morale was very high.' (Lieut W. J. White, 3rd Tyneside Irish)

'I was ordered to fetch the breakfast from the kitchens about a mile away. On the way back, in the trench, we came across a covey of young partridges and, as we walked along, we were driving them in front of us. A lot fell in a sump which was full of water so they would surely drown. But I could not see them drown, so I pulled the top off and got them out, put them in my steel helmet and lifted it up to the top of the trench. There, their mother was waiting and she chuckled them all together and off they went, never to be seen by us again.' (Pte F. G. Foskett, 7th Bedfords)

What was more welcome than the food were the hot drinks. 'Petrol tins of hot coffee with a lashing of rum arrived. As we were standing in water-logged trenches, feeling cold and miserable, this was acceptable; and who minded the flavour of petrol anyway?' (L/Cpl W. Disney, 1/5th Sherwood Foresters)

Some units, for once, issued the men with as much rum as they wanted. Albert McMillan, looking round him in great excitement on his first morning in the trenches, was offered some, although he had never drunk it before. He took a large helping, which made him choke, but it cheered him up. Many of the younger soldiers had far too much rum with predictable results: 'Now the first of many silly things happened. They had laced the tea with rum; the rum out there was the goods, real thick treacle stuff. I had one sip and, whoa, I wasn't going to make myself muzzy for the job we were going on. Some chaps drank and had some more; they were soon tiddly. Two of them lay on the floor completely out. A sergeant major was kicking them both as they lay there to bring them round, although to no purpose.' (Pte W. J. Senescall, The Cambridge Battalion) Some Bradford soldiers were very upset when a captain, who was known to be a strict teetotaller, tipped the surplus down a sump hole.

There were some battalions, however, whose men got nothing – no food, no drink and no rum. Bad organization by the rear parties, or bad luck as carriers lost their way in the maze of crowded trenches, meant that these faced the battle on an empty stomach. Lieut Philip Howe realized that his men's rum ration was missing so he went to look for it and when he returned, successful, was very popular with his platoon.

The attacking troops took up their final positions. L/Cpl Charles Matthews led his section, already depleted by the loss of two men, from their dug-out to an assembly trench, behind the assault battalions they were to support. Matthews did not know that he was directly opposite the mine due to be blown at Kasino Point but, as he was not in the front line, he would be some distance from the explosion.

At 5.30 A.M. Reginald Bastard reported with his fellow battalion commanders to brigade H.Q. for a final conference. When the short discussion was over, those present checked their watches, wished each other luck and the four lieutenant-colonels set off back to their respective battalions.

The German artillery fire, which had not been heavy during the night, started to intensify. Some men wondered if the Germans knew or suspected that this was not just another day. Some British sectors escaped this fire but, on others, a steady barrage settled on trenches, approach roads and gun positions. The shelling caused surprise because the German batteries were thought to have been destroyed during the past week's bombardment.

The soldiers huddled lower in their trenches but they were packed so tightly that the German shells could not fail to score hits. Already dead men were being thrown over the edge of the trenches and wounded sent to the rear. These last may have been the lucky ones; it was well known that the beginning of a battle was the best time to be wounded, with all the medical units waiting. The others could only endure the shelling and many wished for the attack to start; anything was better than waiting helplessly under the German shells.

In Thiepval Wood, Billy McFadzean and his fellow bombers were making their final preparations in a short, very narrow assembly trench. Boxes of grenades had been opened and the bombs were being distributed. Shells were falling here and there in the wood as the Germans searched for likely targets in the Ulster Division positions. The shelling had not yet stripped all the foliage from the trees and the bright, early morning sun threw dappled shadows over the Belfast men as they worked. Suddenly, a box of grenades fell to the floor of the trench. No one seems to know exactly how the accident happened; perhaps an explosion, closer than the rest, dislodged it; perhaps it was just knocked over in the cramped trench. But the fall had knocked the pins out of two grenades. In four seconds they would explode. In that crowded, enclosed space the effect would be disastrous. While some stared in horror at the small metal objects, McFadzean pushed himself forward and threw his body over the grenades. A moment later the live grenades exploded and Billy McFadzean was dead. In giving his own life, he had saved his friends, for only one other man in the trench was slightly hurt. The shocked Ulstermen laid the shattered body carefully aside, hoping that someone would be able to bury it later, then they finished sharing out the grenades and waited sadly for the battle to begin.*

Each day for the past week, the British artillery had fired an intensive bombardment starting at 6.25 A.M. and lasting until 7.45 A.M. On this morning the bombardment would lift from the German front line at 7.30 A.M., fifteen minutes earlier than usual. It was hoped that this would induce the

* Billy McFadzean's heroic action was recognized by the posthumous award of the first Victoria Cross to be awarded to a member of the Ulster Division.

Germans to stay in their dug-outs for a few vital minutes, instead of manning their trenches when the British attacked.

On those parts of the British line where the German shelling was not heavy, the period before their own bombardment started was quiet. 'It was a perfect morning with a cloudless blue sky. There was not a breath of wind and one felt that it was going to be a very hot day. There was not a sound, it was weird, to say the least, so that when our main bombardment opened at 6.25 A.M. its effect was stupefying.' (Pte J. G. Hanaghan, 3rd Liverpool Pals)

For most infantrymen this was their first close-up view of the British barrage. They were delighted. They could see, sometimes just 200 yards away, the shells pounding the German trenches; surely, when they went over in an hour's time, nothing could stop them. The 1st Somerset Light Infantry sat on the parapet of their trench, cheering like mad, 'just as though they were watching a firework display in a London park'.

Even at this comparatively late hour it was still misty in some places: 'On the dawn patrol it was difficult to see what was happening on the ground. It was like looking at a bank of low cloud, but one could see ripples on the cloud from the terrific bombardment that was taking place below. It looked like a large lake of mist, with thousands of stones being thrown into it.' (Lieut G. Chetwynd-Stapleton, 9 Squadron R.F.C.)

In some places, the British barrage provoked equally heavy German return fire. This was particularly so at Gommecourt but, as the two divisions there were supposed to draw fire onto themselves, they were fulfilling their part of the plan.

Bugler Bill Soar was at the receiving end of these German shells near Gommecourt and a man beside him was struck by a piece of hot shell casing, which remained embedded in his neck. Soar had been trained as a stretcher-bearer; he pressed his knees on either side of the man's neck to slow the flow of blood and plucked the hot metal out, using his tunic to stop his fingers being burnt. As he did this, the wounded man screamed in agony, but Soar, with 'Too late, pal', dressed the wound. Having got permission from his platoon sergeant, Soar took the wounded man to the medical officer, but returned in time for the attack.

Again at Gommecourt: 'One of my platoon officers checked his watch with me just before 7.30 A.M. He had just left me when he was hit by a shell and killed. There was nothing else for it but to take his place as he should have been leading the first wave. It wasn't heroic, it was *force majeure*. It just had to be done.' (Maj. C. J. Low, D.S.O., 1st London Scottish) *

The patient British infantry were nearing the end of their long wait but it was now that the nervous tension pressed hardest upon them. Men knelt down and prayed – God seemed very near to them at this time; some took out their pay books and completed that page which contained a form for making out a will; others stared at photographs of their families which they kissed before returning to their pockets: 'I myself gave a sad thought of home. At this particular time it would be milking time. The cows would be coming in from the meadows and everything would be lovely and peaceful at my father's farm, in the little village at the foot of the Sperrin Mountains.' (Pte L. Bell, Derry Volunteers)†

For some the strain was too much. The innocent Albert McMillan could not understand why a near-by sergeant shook more and more as zero hour approached. A man in the Cambridge Battalion went berserk; his pals were ordered to hold him down until they went over the top and then to leave him. Officers and N.C.O.'s did their best to calm and encourage their men. C.S.M. Percy Chappell made a last-minute round of his men. Most were calm but one young soldier was crying.

Not all were sad: two cheerful Bradford soldiers played a game juggling with hand grenades, quite confident the attack would be a walk-over. ' "Fix Bayonets" was carried out with much laughter and bravado. The rum had begun to work.' (Cpl H. Beaumont, M.M., 1st Edinburgh City Battalion)

But the German shelling continued to take a toll on some sectors. 'Jerry retaliated with his Whizz Bangs and shrapnel, he knew what we were up to, but, in spite of everything, we were still in one piece. Just after 7.00 A.M. Lieut Aird said, "Eastwood, go to number 7 Platoon on our left. Give my

* The officer referred to by Maj. Low, 2nd Lieut H. A. Coxon, is the platoon commander shown in the plate of the 1st London Scottish, opposite p. 125.

† Bell was badly wounded but survived to return to the village of Moneymore.

compliments to the platoon commander (mannerly under all circumstances) and tell him Zero Hour is at 7.30 A.M." As I reached number 7 Platoon, the late lieutenant was being covered with a groundsheet. He had been killed instantly by shrapnel.' (Pte J. Eastwood, 1st Salford Pals)

At 7.20 A.M. the British barrage reached a crescendo as the gunners poured shells at the maximum possible rate into the German lines. They were joined by the closer range trench-mortars, which could put down a furious barrage for short periods. The German front-line trenches, their redoubts and fortified villages were battered by an awesome intensity of fire which made even the most doubtful men more confident.

Paddy Kennedy and about twenty others had spent the night in a shallow tunnel which ran out into No Man's Land from the front line. In the open end was a mortar and a big store of mortar ammunition. When the advance started, it would have been the duty of this half-platoon of Manchester men to carry this ammunition forward for the mortar crew. Suddenly there was a terrific explosion in the mortar post, the blast blew down the tunnel and the roof collapsed all around them. As it was being fired, one of their own mortar bombs had just grazed the edge of the gun pit. The resulting explosion had blown up the spare mortar bombs and killed all the mortar crew and some of the Manchesters. The remainder scrambled out as best they could and made their way back to the front line.

When the survivors had gained the cover of the trench, attended to the wounded and sent them to the rear, they found that out of the half-platoon there were only three unwounded privates, including Kennedy. There was no one to give them any orders and they had no idea what they were to do, so, like many others, they waited.

It was at about this time that the first infantrymen were allowed to move. A few commanders had decided to allow their leading waves to go out into No Man's Land just before zero hour and lie down nearer the German trenches. The soldiers clambered up the ladders, filed through their own wire and then spread out into the straight lines required by the plan, before lying down to get what shelter they could in the open. The crescendo of fire falling on the German trenches ensured that most of these men forming up in No Man's Land could do so in safety but some brave Germans were already manning their weapons. An observant officer in the 4th Middlesex estimated that his men were being fired on by at least six machine-guns, four from the ruins of Fricourt and two from the German trenches.

There remained one last act to be played out before the infantry attack opened – the blowing of the mines. Three large and seven small ones had been prepared at a vast expense in labour and with some loss of life; now the time had come to gain the benefit. The main salvo of mines was due to be blown at 7.28 A.M., allowing two minutes for the debris to settle before the infantry rushed the craters. There was one exception; the most northerly mine, that underneath the German redoubt on Hawthorn Ridge near Beaumont Hamel, was to be blown at 7.20 A.M. The decision to do this ten minutes before the infantry attack was a compromise between the corps commander, Lieut-Gen. Hunter-Weston, who wanted it blown several hours earlier and other officers who wanted a 7.28 A.M. firing. Hunter-Weston wanted his men to capture and consolidate the crater well before the main attack, but this was forbidden by G.H.Q. who thought that it would probably be the Germans who would take the crater.

The tunnellers had finished their work; the charges were ready and the circuits checked. The sapper officers knelt by their detonators anxiously looking at their watches, for in their job exact timing was vital. Above ground the infantry waited; many knew that mines were to be blown near them and were eager to see the results.

Opposite the Hawthorn Redoubt mine was young Albert McMillan, determined to miss nothing on this, his first day of war. He stood on the fire-step peering at the ridge only 500 yards away. Promptly at 7.20 A.M. the mine exploded and a huge column of earth and chalk spewed into the air.* McMillan was very impressed with the sight but also a little sobered. He realized for the first time the violence about to be released in the battle; maybe it wouldn't be such a lark after all. He did not have long to enjoy the view; within a few seconds the shock waves passing through the ground reached his trench, making it sway from side to side

* See plate following p. 204.

and throwing him to the ground. McMillan lay on the floor of the trench, winded, his kit all around him. His platoon sergeant stood over him: 'You silly little bastard.'

The decision to blow this mine at 7.20 A.M. had been unsound. Immediately the Germans put down a heavy artillery barrage on every British trench in the area. Their infantry too were alerted. 'I watched the enormous core of earth go up and, within five minutes, it seemed that every Boche machine-gun was shooting full belt, the bullets simply whistling like hail over our position.' (Capt. C. J. P. Ball, 15th Brigade R.H.A.)

Then, at 7.28 A.M., came the other mines, the biggest being the two on either side of the main road at La Boisselle, each with twenty-four tons of explosive. These were the largest mines that had been blown on the Western Front and the troops facing La Boisselle were a little anxious: 'We knew precisely when it would explode. A private braced himself against the side of the trench with one leg placed against the other side. When the mine exploded, the shock waves actually fractured his leg below the knee and, I heard later, it had to be amputated.' (Sgt H. Benzing, Grimsby Chums)

'We were out in No Man's Land, waiting. The whole world seemed to be moving; the earth moved sideways and back three times before the final explosion of the mine. I saw the debris rise hundreds of feet into the air and then it began to fall back with a noise rising above the bombardment. I thought, "This is it", and buried my head underneath my tin hat and arms, waiting for the first clout. However it missed me but caught some of the men on my left.' (Cpl H. Beaumont, M.M., 1st Edinburgh City Battalion)

Flying above La Boisselle was an R.F.C. machine and its pilot has described the scene from the air: 'The whole earth heaved and flashed, a tremendous and magnificent column rose up into the sky. There was an ear-splitting roar, drowning all the guns, flinging the machine sideways in the repercussing air. The earth column rose higher and higher to almost 4,000 feet. There it hung, or seemed to hang, for a moment in the air, like the silhouette of some great cypress tree, then fell away in a widening cone of dust and debris. A moment later came the second mine. Again a roar, the upflung machine, the strange giant silhouette invading the sky.

Then the dust cleared and we saw the two white eyes of the craters.' (2nd Lieut C. A. Lewis, 3 Squadron R.F.C.)*

There was now nothing between over 60,000 British soldiers in the eighteen miles of front-line trenches and the opening of the attack at 7.30 A.M. The men were ready, bayonets fixed, rifles loaded, the heavy uncomfortable packs finally adjusted. Young officers, many at school a year ago, stood with whistles in their mouths, looking at their watches as the last few seconds ticked away.

The battle was in the hands of these men, now; the generals could do nothing. For the first half hour it would not even be a battalion commander's battle. The outcome would be decided by captains and second-lieutenants, lance corporals and privates. Hearts thud, stomachs turn. 'For God's sake, let us get going.' (L/Cpl J. J. Cousins, 7th Bedfords)

* From his book *Sagittarius Rising*, p. 104.

7

Zero Hour

Exactly at 7.30 A.M. an uncanny silence fell over the battlefield. The British barrage suddenly ceased as it lifted from the German front line and gun-layers adjusted their sights for the next target. By a strange coincidence, the German guns, too, were silent. It was eerie; the sun was shining out of a cloudless sky, birds hovered and swooped over the trenches, singing clearly. To the men it seemed a weird anti-climax. 'Suddenly, for a few seconds, all seemed silent, the firing had quietened down. I walked up and down the footboards saying to the men, "It's a walk-over." I had almost a feeling of disappointment. It was short lived.' (Lieut M. Asquith, 1st Barnsley Pals)

After a few seconds the quiet was shattered as the British barrage fell upon the next line of enemy defences. In their own trenches whistles blew, shouts came from the platoon and section commanders. The Battle of the Somme had started.

The first away were those lying out in No Man's Land. The long lines rose, men looked to left and right as if to correct their dressing on a parade ground and set off after their officers at the steady, well-rehearsed pace towards the enemy. There was no rushing, no shouting.

For most, however, it was a case of over the top. First up the ladders were the platoon commanders; behind them the heavily loaded men struggled to get out quickly, urged on by those following. Officers ran along the parapet shouting encouragement, leaning in and giving a hand to pull the over-burdened soldiers up and out.

Before these men could form up in their waves they had first to pass through their own barbed-wire defences. Some units took duck-boards over with them and placed these on the wire to make bridges, but most had to file through paths cut the previous night before they could get into the open. Now that the action had begun most men lost their fear; they knew what they had to do, their friends were all around them, their officers leading. They pushed through the wire and took their places in the waves.

The Germans, however, were alert; their reaction was swift and deadly. An attacker at Gommecourt could hear a bugle as a look-out called the Germans from their dug-outs to man the trenches. The first machine-guns were soon in action and found easy targets. British soldiers struggling out of their trenches were hit and tumbled back, some dead before they fell. 'The German machine-gun fire was terrible. Our colonel was hit after only a few steps along the trench. I helped to prop him up against the trench side. Then, we climbed on to the top of the trench. I had not reached my full height when a machine-gun bullet smacked into my steel helmet. I felt as if I had been hit with a sledge hammer. I caught a glimpse of my helmet; it was completely smashed in.' (Pte W. H. T. Carter, 1st Bradford Pals)

The Germans spotted some of the gaps in the British wire and their machine-guns soon turned these narrow alleys into death-traps; men trying to avoid their dead and wounded comrades got caught and were themselves hit.

In spite of the unexpected opposition there was no hesitation as more and more men left the trenches and, if they could, formed up into their waves. They were bewildered; the Germans were all supposed to be dead. 'We had no idea what it was going to be like but a few yards from our trench, a Whizz Bang caught my platoon sergeant in the throat and his head disappeared.' (Pte J. Devennie, Derry Volunteers) There was no time for logical thought; discipline and training took control of their bodily movements. 'The only feeling I had was to get to the objective and stay there and the thought that was uppermost in my mind was the phrase "For England", which I seemed to be repeating continually. This is the truth and not put in for heroics. To be perfectly truthful, I was scared stiff.' (Pte W. L. P. Dunn, 1st Liverpool Pals)

At Gommecourt, the attack by the North Midland Division started badly; everything seemed to be going wrong. This sector had had the worst of the wet weather and some of the men had spent the night up to their knees or waists in mud and water. The German shelling had been very heavy during the night and there had been many casualties. A smoke-screen, although it may have shielded the attackers from the enemy, combined in some cases with a liberal rum issue to cause confusion. On the extreme left Bugler Bill

Soar went over with the second wave of his battalion but it was impossible to get the men lined up properly. Soar and those others who could be mustered were formed up in makeshift fashion and set off into the smoke-screen towards the German trenches.

In the 8th East Surreys, Capt. Nevill's four platoons, each with a football, competed for their company commander's prize. Nevill himself kicked off. 'As the gun-fire died away I saw an infantryman climb onto the parapet into No Man's Land, beckoning others to follow. As he did so he kicked off a football; a good kick, the ball rose and travelled well towards the German line. That seemed to be the signal to advance.' (Pte L. S. Price, 8th Royal Sussex)*

Those who had been able to get out of their trenches and form up into waves without being fired upon started their advance. As far as the eye could see, lines of men moved forward, their rifles held across their chests, bayonets glinting in the morning sun. 'As we advanced out of our trenches the sun was shining gloriously and it seemed as if every bird in the sky was trying to outsing the noise of the guns.' (L/Cpl L. C. Palmer, Glasgow Commercials) At La Boisselle another sound competed with the din of battle; the four Tyneside Scottish battalions' pipers played their men into action.

When the Sheffield City Battalion men went over they looked for the white tapes left out the previous night to guide them to the gaps in the German wire, but the tapes were gone. The Germans had pulled them in during the night.

All along the eighteen-mile front, the leading waves paced farther across No Man's Land, into ground where no man had stood in daylight for nearly two years. There were, as yet, few shell holes here and animals were still living amid the wild flowers and rank summer grass. At Gommecourt a subaltern in the London Division disturbed a hare which ran off from under his feet and across the battlefield; both were startled by the encounter.

It was in these open spaces in the middle of No Man's Land that the German machine-gunners found their choicest targets. From their trenches came the 'tac-tac-tac' of the guns as they traversed to and fro along the endless lines of

* One of the footballs is in the National Army Museum and another at the Queen's Regiment Museum, Howe Barracks, Canterbury.

advancing men. Whole waves were swept over by the fire. The dead lay in long rows where they had fallen, the wounded lay with them, pretending to be dead, or took cover wherever they could – in a fold in the ground, in one of the rare shell holes. Many huddled behind the body of a dead comrade. If a wave or part of it was missed by the first sweep, back would come the traverse of fire seeking out the survivors. 'The long line of men came forward, rifles at the port as ordered. Now Gerry started. His machine-guns let fly. Down they all went. I could see them dropping one after another as the gun swept along them. The officer went down at exactly the same time as the man behind him. Another minute or so and another wave came forward. Gerry was ready this time and this lot did not get so far as the others.' (Pte W. J. Senescall, The Cambridge Battalion)

'For some reason nothing seemed to happen to us at first; we strolled along as though walking in a park. Then, suddenly, we were in the midst of a storm of machine-gun bullets and I saw men beginning to twirl round and fall in all kinds of curious ways as they were hit – quite unlike the way actors do it in films.' (Pte W. Slater, 2nd Bradford Pals)

Just outside Mametz, the 9th Devons did not attack from their front-line trench which had been badly damaged by shell fire, but from the support line. As Capt. Martin led his company forward at zero hour, they were for some time sheltered by the small hill at Mansel Copse but, as the Devons topped the rise and moved downhill, they were in full view of any enemy who might have survived the bombardment.

A single machine-gun, built into the base of the crucifix on the edge of the village, exactly where Capt. Martin had forecast, was only 400 yards away – easy range for a competent machine-gunner. The crew had survived; the gun was not damaged and, when it opened fire, it caught the Devons on the exposed slope. Scores of men went down, among them Capt. Martin, killed at the exact spot by Mansel Copse that he had predicted from his model would be where his company would be doomed.

In spite of the terrible fire, the infantry kept going. Although the leading waves had been broken, individual survivors kept to their steady, disciplined pace. The waves behind them met the same fire and always a few men survived and kept going. Men could hear the German machine-guns; they could see, farther along their wave, comrades falling silently into the grass or crying out as bullets struck home; they could sense the fire scything towards them. They suffered a variety of emotions, from astonishment and anger to numbness or absolute terror, but few wavered.

When the main salvo of mines had gone off at 7.28 A.M., one had not exploded. The R.E. officer waiting to detonate the mine under the German-held position at Kasino Point was horrified to see British infantry all around him climbing out of their trenches and setting off across No Man's Land before he had blown the mine. He was in a dilemma. The mine (of 5,000 pounds) was all ready and a German machine-gun at Kasino Point was firing on the British infantry as they crossed No Man's Land. He decided to fire the mine and as he pressed the plunger there was the usual roar and blast of the explosion.

A section leader of the 10th Essex was out in No Man's Land as the mine went up: 'I looked left to see if my men were keeping a straight line. I saw a sight I shall never forget. A giant fountain, rising from our line of men, about 100 yards from me. Still on the move I stared at this, not realizing what it was. It rose, a great column nearly as high as Nelson's Column, then slowly toppled over. Before I could think, I saw huge slabs of earth and chalk thudding down, some with flames attached, onto the troops as they advanced.' (L/Cpl E. J. Fisher, 10th Essex)

In addition to the late firing of the mine there must have been a defect in the placing of the charge. It was while working on this mine that the tunnellers had broken into a German dug-out by mistake; perhaps the charge had been placed too shallow. Whatever the reason, the debris of the mine, instead of rising straight up and falling back around the crater in the normal manner, spread out and fell over a wide area. British soldiers from at least four different battalions were struck by falling stone and soil, suffering many casualties.

The late explosion certainly surprised the Germans. Their machine-gun post at Kasino Point had, of course, gone sky-high, the gun crew blown into eternity; nearby posts were also destroyed or badly shaken. The fire faltered, the British recovered and swept forward on either side of the crater and over the German trenches.

L/Cpl Charles Matthews and his section were about 300 yards away from the mine, still in the British reserve trench. The Northamptons knew nothing of the existence of the mine and as the debris flew into the air and started falling they presumed that it was an enemy mine blown under the British front line. A huge lump of chalk and earth crashed down onto the edge of the trench near Matthews and then, disintegrating, fell over him before he could move out of the way. So brutal was the fall that his rifle was broken and he was buried from the waist down. A bag of grenades Matthews had been holding was buried with him; fortunately no pins came out and they did not explode. He was the only one wounded and his companions started dragging the rubble away from him. But Matthews was so badly crushed that every movement caused him great pain.

Now a new danger menaced the British. The German artillery had, until now, been firing steadily on the British gun positions, the rear and the trenches. But once it was clear that the British were attacking, the German batteries opened their defensive barrage on the centre of No Man's Land and the British front-line trench system. The scale and accuracy of the German shell fire was a rude shock to the British, who believed that the seven-day bombardment had destroyed most of the German batteries. Along the centre of No Man's Land a long line of bursting shells could be seen. The accuracy was astonishing; as each battery fired, the fountains of earth and black smoke appeared as straight and as evenly spaced as a row of trees.

The first waves had mostly crossed before the barrage started but, as salvo after salvo fell, the following waves could not avoid challenging this new barrier. 'On my left I could see large shell bursts as the West Yorks advanced and saw many men falling forward. I thought at first they were looking for nose-caps (a favourite souvenir) and it was some time before I realized they were hit.' (Pte E. C. Stanley, 1/8th Royal Warwicks) 'Men were falling right and left of me, screaming above the noise of the shell fire and machine-guns – guns we had been assured would have been silenced by our barrage. No man in his right mind would have done what we were doing.' (L/Cpl J. J. Cousins, 7th Bedfords) 'Before we had advanced far, Jerry's guns had joined in the deafening roar and I actually saw a howitzer shell of large calibre plunge out of the air, bury itself, explode and blow one of A Company over backwards. He jumped up immediately and advanced with the rest. I don't think he was wounded in any way.' (Cpl J. Norton, 8th Norfolk)

So far, Dick King had been lucky. Before zero hour his platoon had gone out a few yards into No Man's Land and lain down waiting for the signal to attack. Promptly at 7.30 A.M. the platoon commander blew his whistle and the K.O.Y.L.I.s rose. At that very moment a German machine-gun opened fire on them and caused many casualties. His brother Frank was badly wounded just as he was getting to his feet by a bullet which passed through his arm and lung.

Dick King survived this moment of danger and made good progress with the Lewis gun team up a gentle, grassy slope. The sun was already hot, making them sweat under their loads, but in some ways it was a relief to be on the move. Then, without warning, the German barrage fell in the centre of No Man's Land, a salvo of heavy shells landing among the leading wave. When the survivors emerged from the smoke and dust, Dick King was not with them. One of the bursting shells had been so close to him that he had been, quite literally, blown to pieces.*

C.S.M. Percy Chappell's company of the Somerset Light Infantry was supposed to leave the British front line three minutes after another battalion, but before that interval had elapsed, more troops from the rear had arrived, anxious to get on. Chappell had consulted with his company commander, who decided not to wait. They had reached the far side of No Man's Land and were almost at the enemy wire before the barrage fell behind them. Chappell blessed the decision to start early which had put his company on the safe side of the shells. Looking back he saw the following companies of the Somersets advance without hesitation into the line of shell-bursts and reappear on his side just as steadily but pitifully reduced in number.

* His brother, Frank, lay out on the battlefield for several hours unaware that Dick had been killed only a few yards away.

It is easy to use words like courage and determination but this display by thousands of ordinary infantrymen, burdened down with their huge loads and facing several hundred yards of bullet and shell-swept open ground before they could get near the enemy, was superb. The British soldiers were showing themselves at their best as, keeping at the same steady pace, they walked towards what they must have thought was certain death.

Even some wounded men who could have been excused for taking shelter in the shell holes which were appearing all over No Man's Land or for turning back, kept going, determined not to let down their friends. 'For some time I walked across No Man's Land with a man who had a severe wound in his jaw and he kept going until he collapsed.' (Pte G. T. Rudge, 2nd Essex)

Those attackers who had survived the shells and bullets approached the German trenches, where they were at least free from the worst of the shelling, and, here, some met their first Germans, the unseen enemy who had been tormenting them for months. A Lewis gunner describes his first encounter: 'Up and over, the first thing I noticed, how the top of the tall grass was flying up in a bit of a mist; this was caused by the machine-guns traversing at waist height against us. Then we were calling Jerry everything. My men were falling all round, some shouting, "I'm hit" or "I've got it", and some not a word. Then, as we were advancing, a bunch of Jerries loomed up from nowhere. I let a burst into them but, when we got to them, we found they were surrendering.' (L/Cpl W. G. Sanders, 10th Essex)

'When I got near the German trenches I could see some of them coming out with their hands up but, when they saw how many of us had been hit, they changed their minds and ran back again.' (Pte A. Fretwell, Sheffield City Battalion)

Lieut Philip Howe had made a good crossing of No Man's Land. His objective was a German trench well behind their front line named Lonely Trench. He had been ordered to take his platoon, which was in the leading wave, and to stop for nothing until he reached his objective. Howe had gone over the top promptly and crossed No Man's Land as quickly as he could. He could hear bullets whistling all around him but, heeding his instructions, he kept going and did not bother about those behind him. As he reached the German wire he could see that it was well cut and in the German front-line trench he could see only one of the enemy.

This solitary German, an officer, came out towards them and started throwing grenades at the West Yorks, almost as though he wanted to take on the whole British Army on his own. There followed a short duel around some shell holes between Howe with his revolver and the German officer with his grenades, the affair being settled when the German was shot dead by one of Howe's platoon with a rifle. After this diversion Philip Howe set off again to his objective, Lonely Trench, which was still some distance away.

Where the British had suffered particularly heavily the few survivors could see the Germans were actually standing up on the parapets of their trenches, so confident and exultant that they were shouting and taunting their seemingly beaten foes. 'As I approached the German trenches, I could see a wall of German soldiers standing shoulder to shoulder right along the parapet of their front-line trench, waving to us to come on.' (Pte L. Ramage, Glasgow Boys' Brigade Battalion)

Next, the men arrived at that most controversial barrier, the German barbed wire. They had been told that the artillery and mortar barrage would have blown it away but patrols had come back with stories that it was intact. Were the rumours exaggerated? On a front eighteen miles long there could be no precise answer; as with so much in a big battle it was a matter of luck for each individual soldier. There were many like Philip Howe who had found the wire so well cut that they were able to pass over it and on to their objectives with nothing but a passing glance. Others found it partially cut but tossed into big coils up to ten feet high; if they were careful they could find a passage through. For most, however, the encounter was a tragic disappointment after the promises of their officers. They found themselves faced with a wide belt of uncut wire and, beyond that, the Germans.

At Gommecourt a soldier found one reason why the wire had not been cut. 'I was in the first wave. My first impression was the sight of hundreds of unexploded mortar bombs. As large and round as big footballs, I thought how like oranges they looked, they were bright orange-yellow. They were supposed to destroy the German wire which was almost untouched. I doubt if one had exploded.' (Pte G. S. Young, 1/6th North Staffs). These bombs, known as 'plum puddings' or 'toffee apples', were fired, attached to a stick, from a mortar; only recently introduced, the sticks often came off in flight resulting in duds.

Desperately, men struggled to get through the wire but only got more enmeshed; their equipment caught on the long barbs and made them helpless. They were picked off at leisure by the German riflemen, bodies jerking in their death throes, in the writhing, twanging wire. 'I could see that our leading waves had got caught by their kilts. They were killed hanging on the wire, riddled with bullets, like crows shot on a dyke.' (Pte J. S. Reid, 2nd Seaforth Highlanders)

On the worst sectors, frantic men ran along the wire searching for gaps but, if they did discover one, often found themselves in a death-trap. The German machine-gunners were covering every gap.

Isolated men finding themselves without support and faced with uncut wire took cover where they could and waited either for fresh waves to come up if the attack went well, or for the Germans to come out and kill or capture them.

After his long, hazardous crossing of No Man's Land, and if he was lucky enough to find the wire well cut, the soldier arrived at his first objective – the German front-line trench. In theory this, like the wire, should have been completely destroyed and the defenders all killed by the bombardment. But it was already painfully clear that the Germans were very much alive and determined to defend their positions. Although the trenches had been badly damaged by the bombardment there was still adequate cover for those Germans who had managed to survive. Instead of strolling over them 'with pipes lit and rifles at the slope', the British infantry had to fight hard to capture the enemy front lines, but it was essential that they did so, otherwise their rear waves and the follow-up battalions would suffer the same fate as the leaders coming across No Man's Land. There was one consolation; at last they were near enough to hit back at the Germans.

Only in a few places had the promise of the bombardment been fulfilled, with the German trenches destroyed and only little opposition. Where the losses coming across No Man's Land had been heavy, the men from the leading waves who survived and found an easy entry into the German trenches sometimes had to act on their own and some had weird, lonely experiences until the following waves caught them up.

'Out of breath and to gather my wits and strength I dropped into a shell hole just in front of the German wire. I peeped over the edge, fired a shot at a round hat on a German head that suddenly appeared, rushed the last few yards and jumped into the German trench. I saw nobody there, friend or foe. It was very eerie but I recall facing *our old* front lines and being appalled at the poor positioning of them. They were absolutely clearly overlooked by the enemy for all those terrible months preceding the battle. Sitting ducks we must have been, I thought.

'I then went on to the second-line trench and jumped in, to see a German soldier lying on the parapet. With fixed bayonet I approached, then I saw his putty-coloured face which convinced me he was mortally wounded. The German brought up an arm and actually saluted me. I understood no German language but the poor chap kept muttering two words "*Wasser*, *Wasser*", and "*Mutter*, *Mutter*". It took me a minute or so to realize he wanted a drink of water. The second word I could not cotton on to. I am glad to this day that I gave him a drink from my precious water.' (Pte G. R. S. Mayne, 11th Royal Fusiliers)

Some men had been ordered not to wait at the front-line trench but to push on to more distant objectives. 'I found the German wire well cut and their front-line trench flattened. There were one or two dead there, that's all. But only three out of our company got past there. There was my lieutenant, a sergeant and myself. The rest seemed to have been hit in No Man's Land. I had the wind up and the officer said, "God, God, where's the rest of the boys?"

'We could see a long way on either side of us, but we couldn't see a soul. We went on still further and nearly reached the village [La Boisselle]; then I felt a sharp stab in my arm and blood spurted out. The others helped me to take my equipment off and then they set off again. I thought to myself "They'll never get back" – and they didn't.' (Pte L. Dodd, 4th Tyneside Scottish)

Bugler Bill Soar, in the second wave, found that some of the first had managed to get through the wire and over the deserted German trench. Soar, with four others, the remnants of his wave, followed them. When they got over the front line they found that the leaders were under fire from the next trench, so the five took cover behind them. Soar looked round but could see no more Sherwood Foresters following. Instead, he watched three Germans in their shirt-sleeves emerge from a dug-out behind him. They were armed and immediately started firing rifle grenades at the Nottingham men.

After trying to dodge these for some time, Soar took stock of the situation. The men from the first wave appeared to have been killed or taken prisoner and there were no other British troops on either side of them. Soar had achieved the doubtful privilege of being the left-hand man of the whole eighteen-mile attack, but he and his friends were in an exposed position and obviously cut off. One of the men, Soar's close friend, had been badly injured in the foot by one of the rifle grenades and could not move.

Soar's predicament was a common one. While the lucky or skilful ones could carry on with their planned advance and were being backed up by the following waves, small unsupported parties like his were being cut off by Germans appearing behind them.

Elsewhere, there was no easy crossing or capture of the German trenches, but a hard fight to get into them. The British infantry took cover outside the wire and furious little battles developed. 'We dashed forward and I found, right in my line of advance, a patch of thistles and nettles. Reaching this, I pushed the Lewis gun through this small, but dense growth of weeds. This afforded complete horizontal cover to my number two with his ammunition, and for my body. Having pushed the gun through and dividing the nettles, I found my first target of the day, six or eight Germans in a trench firing at our men stranded in the open. One good burst of fire cleared that parapet.' (Cpl J. Norton, 8th Norfolks)

'We were soon obliged to fall flat in the grass to escape the hail of machine-gun fire. As we lay there, a comrade beside me raised his head a little and asked me in which direction were the enemy lines. These were the last words he uttered. There was a sound like a plop, he gave a shudder and lay still. The bullet had passed through his eye. It was about this time that my feeling of confidence was replaced by an acceptance of the fact that I had been sent here to die.' (Pte J. G. Crossley, 15th Durham Light Infantry)

At this crucial stage of the attack these fights were vicious, with no mercy shown by either side. The Germans had the advantage of cover and inflicted heavy casualties. If the British did eventually force their way into the trenches, some Germans, who had fought to the last possible moment, threw down their rifles and tried to surrender. But many left it too late and were shot down or bayoneted. Other Germans fought to the end: 'One German, only about ten feet away, shot me through the shoulder. Although the bullet came out near my hip, I was not hurt too badly and, instinctively, I threw myself at him and he fell down underneath me. Then the poor man died. He must have been hit before and had saved himself for this last effort. He was a plucky fellow.' (Maj. C. J. Low, D.S.O., 1st London Scottish)

These trench fights were the scenes of some very brave actions. C.S.M. Percy Chappell had been lucky getting across No Man's Land before the German barrage had fallen upon it but, at the far side, the battalion they were following, the 1st Rifle Brigade, was held up at the German wire and an indecisive bombing fight was taking place. Suddenly, a Rifle Brigade officer stood up and shouted, 'Come on, lads. Let them have it!' and the whole line rose and charged the enemy trench. This resolute action made the Germans bolt and freed the Somersets from being pinned down in the open. The Rifle Brigade and the Somersets found they were in the Quadrilateral Redoubt but the force that gathered there was very weak. Some started mopping-up and consolidating the maze of trenches, dug-outs and tunnels, while others pushed on to the next line of German trenches.

The losses in No Man's Land had been so heavy that in many places the fight could only be carried on by individuals in lonely and isolated actions. 'I found myself alone in front of a trench with three Germans firing their rifles. I returned their fire and took what cover was possible, which, at the time, seemed infinitesimal. I saw, some distance away, a young boy from our battalion break cover and run for the German trenches but he was set on by four or five Germans and killed with bayonets. I jumped into the trench, ready with my bayonet to encounter the three Germans but they were all lying about in such awkward looking positions with blood all over them and I laughed outright – the reaction, I suppose.' (Pte R. Love, Glasgow Commercials)

The British were fighting not only for the trenches but also for the craters left by the newly blown mines, their fresh chalk glistening white in the bright sunshine. These craters would be valuable prizes; the raised lips could dominate the surrounding German trenches; the interiors, still smoking and stinking from the recent explosion, would be a safe haven from the terrible machine-gun fire. As with all crater fighting, it was a race by both sides for possession. At Beaumont Hamel, where the Hawthorn Redoubt mine had been blown ten minutes before the infantry attack, a company of the 2nd Royal Fusiliers was ready. As soon as the debris had settled they rushed the crater and managed to secure the near side but not all of the far side. The Germans had been quick to react and had gained the remainder.

South of La Boisselle, the Grimsby Chums managed to beat the Germans to the Lochnager crater. They lined the lip nearest to the Germans and consolidated this important foothold in the German line. Gradually, wounded and lost men from many units found their way in from the naked expanse of Sausage Valley and took shelter in the crater. The prominent feature soon became the target for German fire. 'I saw a man near me, shot through his head. He rolled over and over right to the bottom of the crater.' (Cpl A. Dickinson, Grimsby Chums)

While the leading troops fought for the German trenches the following waves remorselessly continued to set off after them. These contained the rear of the first battalions – their H.Q.S, with the signallers and runners, and the mopping-up parties who would complete the clearance of the captured trenches. On some sectors more than one battalion was making the initial attack, the leading battalions being followed by another or even two more, so that within a few minutes of the opening of the attack, there could be up to twenty waves of men out in the open at once.

Just north of Fricourt, the 10th Green Howards were following a battalion of the Somerset Light Infantry. The Green Howards wavered as machine-guns sprayed the top of their trench. A company commander, Maj. Loudoun-Shand, jumped up onto the parapet and ran along urging his men forward, until he was hit and fell back into the trench. Even then, he insisted on being propped up and continued exhorting his men until he died. His heroism was recognized by the award of the second Victoria Cross of the day.

Opposite the Thiepval Spur, where a ruined château looked down on No Man's Land, the initial attack had been carried out by the 1st Salford Pals and the Newcastle Commercials. In each, the first three companies had attacked but the German machine-gun fire had cut down all six waves and not a man had reached the German wire. Both c.o.'s issued a sensible order: the last companies were not to go over. Instead, the men were ordered to man the fire-steps and fire on the Germans who could be seen quite clearly on the other side of No Man's Land, standing on their parapets, shooting at the survivors pinned down in the open. These orders certainly saved many lives but it meant that the attack on the vital Thiepval Spur had been abandoned, at least for the time being.

Near Kasino Point, where L/Cpl Charles Matthews was buried to his waist in debris, the whistles blew: it was time for his section, which was originally designated a mopping-up party, to go over. Matthews' best friend, Bert Smith, was prepared to disobey orders and stay behind to free him, but Matthews ordered Smith to go, assuring him that either stretcher-bearers would soon release him or some mortar gunners farther down the trench, who had now stopped firing, would come along and help. Reluctantly Smith left his friend and went over with the rest.* The frantic attentions of his friends had been so painful that Matthews preferred to be left for a more leisurely release.

So the following waves set off for their crossing of No Man's Land. In those sectors where the leaders had done well, the machine-gun fire had eased off but there was still the German barrage falling steadily all along the middle of No Man's Land. Here the waves crossed, losing men, but arriving at the far side in sufficient strength to renew the momentum of the attack. These were the lucky ones; for most the prospects of getting across safely were grim. There

* Smith, normally a mild man, was so enraged at Matthews' injury that he bayoneted three Germans within a few minutes. He was badly wounded three weeks later but recovered and survived the war.

were very few occasions, like that of the two battalions at Thiepval, where the attack was deliberately stopped. Most had to form up in their waves and walk into the fire-swept zone. They met fear-crazed survivors running back and badly wounded men dragging themselves along. They had to step over the bodies of the dead, torn-off limbs and torsos mangled by shell fire, or rows of bodies hardly marked but victims of machine-gun bullets, the eyes already glazing in death. Some did not get far. As with the leading waves, unsubdued German machine-guns soon found their range and whole waves of men were shot down. The attack faltered, the survivors jumping into the nearest shell hole, of which there were now many in No Man's Land offering protection for those who could reach them.

Opposite Ovillers, Lieut-Col. Reginald Bastard had watched the leading waves of his battalion attack. At first all had gone well, the straight lines of men had got half-way over No Man's Land without trouble, but then two things happened at once. The Germans, especially those in the fortified village just behind their own front line, poured heavy machine-gun fire into the Lincolns. At the same time the defenders fired red distress rockets which brought down the usual heavy barrage in No Man's Land. Immediately, the well ordered waves were thrown into confusion. Men went down on all sides and the second and third waves rushed forward to get out of the barrage and became mixed up with the leaders. The remnants who reached the other side fought hard and gained some footholds in the German trench.

Bastard could see only part of this as, with his battalion H.Q., he led the last company into No Man's Land. Ahead of him he could see the German shells throwing up huge showers of earth and hear the tapping of the machine-guns, but he could also hear the sounds of his own men fighting in the German trenches.

Near Serre, a follow-up party of Durham Pals went over. 'I was in charge of our small section and one man was carrying a six-foot stick with a red pennant on top; in my opinion a stupid idea. Other specialist squads were carrying a similar emblem of death – "Excelsior" had nothing on us.

'Then we got over the top and the first thing that happened in No Man's Land was a fight between the chap with the flag and ourselves. We threatened to bash him if he did not throw the damned thing away. In the end he left us and all he needed to complete the picture was a dog. We were, at this time, in very high grass, well above our heads, and only his flag could be seen.

'Later, after I had been wounded, I got back to our line and there, bejabbers, was the man, still holding the pole. Did Excelsior do so well?' (Pte R. T. Tait, Durham Pals)

One of the German front-line villages, Fricourt, had not been attacked. It was hoped that successful advances on either side would force the village to fall with a frontal attack. In the trenches facing the village was a Yorkshire battalion, the 7th Green Howards, who had been told not to move until ordered to do so. If Fricourt fell they would occupy the village; if not, they would have to attack it later in the day.

The officer commanding the right-hand Green Howards company watched the main attack; all seemed to be going well. Perhaps he thought the Germans in Fricourt must be dead; perhaps he misunderstood his instructions. For whatever reason, he ordered his company to attack. The German machine-guns in Fricourt immediately caught the exposed company of Yorkshiremen, and within moments the company's advance was halted. The news of this unnecessary disaster went back: 'I got a message to say that A Company on the right had assaulted at 8.20. I did not believe this but sent the adjutant to find out. He reported that it was true. I could only account for this by supposing that the company commander had gone mad. Later a report came in saying that what was left of the company were lying out in front of our wire and that they were being heavily fired on by machine-guns and snipers.' (Lieut-Col. R. Fife, 7th Green Howards) *

A Company had attacked with 140 men; 108 had become casualties due to this tragic mistake. The company commander was severely wounded.

In this vast battlefield, with thousands of men playing their parts, and where the overall plan was going hopelessly wrong, it was often left to each individual to decide his own destiny.

* Taken from Colonel Fife's diary. The Official History says that A Company attacked at 7.45 A.M.; the difference in times is not important. The C.O. never received an explanation from the company commander who did not return to the battalion and was killed in 1918.

One cannot blame lone survivors for taking shelter in shell holes but the devotion of many who, finding themselves alone, continued to do their duty, often to find death in the process, is one of the remarkable features of this desperate part of the day.

In Sausage Valley a young signaller set off, one of a party of five men whose task was to follow the leading troops with a large drum of signal wire. Four of the five were soon killed or wounded. The survivor paused to consider what he should do: 'Well, I suppose this is where the old discipline came in. I dare not stop. I was not wounded; so forward I had to go. I could not carry the drum myself so I did the unforgivable thing and left my rifle behind. Well, I pushed the drum along as well as I could and I had to negotiate corpses, shouting wounded men and large lumps of earth. Puffing and panting, I kept this up for a long time, as I was crawling along on my stomach and progress was slow. At last, I thought, I must have a look round. I had got some thirty yards from Jerry's trench. I could see the German hats moving about their trench top. That settled it – no use taking the wire to them.' (Pte J. W. Senescall, The Cambridge Battalion)

Not far away was being played out one of the morning's epics. La Boisselle, the fortified village on the main road, was the key to the advance to Pozières and any eventual breakthrough to Bapaume. The task of capturing La Boisselle had been given to Maj.-Gen. Ingouville-Williams's 34th Division. He had placed two brigades in the front line whose duty it was to capture the German trenches on either side of the village and then the village itself. Behind the British front line, and separated from it by Avoca Valley, was the Tara–Usna Line, astride the main road. Posted in this line was his third brigade – the four battalions of Tyneside Irish – the Irish names of Tara, Usna and Avoca forming a suitable setting for their exploits. Their task was to pass through the leading brigades after these had captured the German trenches and the village and push into the rear, helping to create the gap. If a real collapse of the German defences on the sector occurred, the 19th (Western) Division and the cavalry were to follow the Tyneside Irish – Gough's Mobile Army would get its chance.

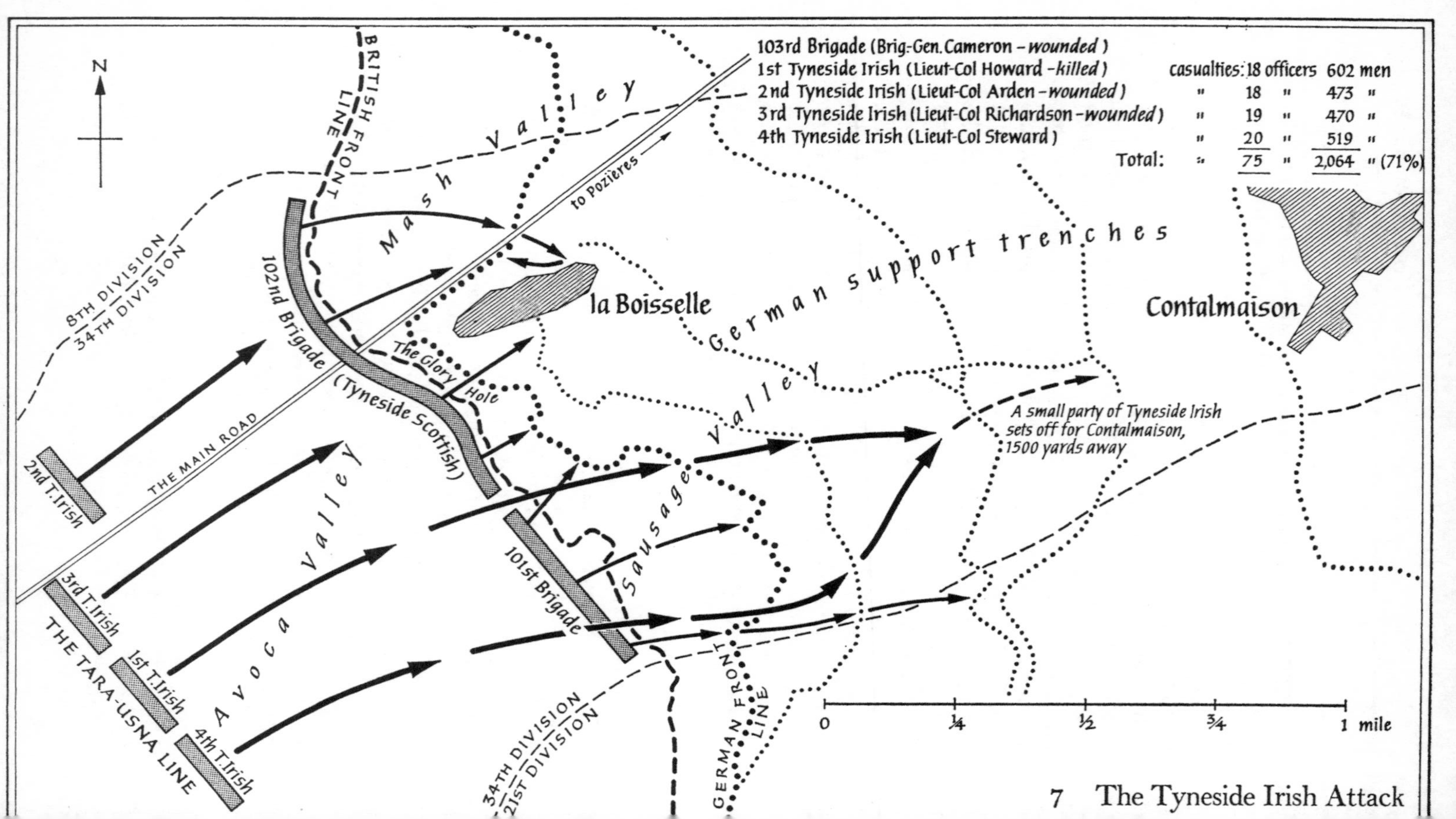

7 The Tyneside Irish Attack

The divisional commander's plan had been a straightforward one. At zero hour every battalion in his division would leave their trenches and advance; he left nothing in reserve. He was clearly determined to force the defences guarding the main road to Pozières. Precisely on time the Tyneside Irish Brigade, 3,000 men strong, rose from the Tara–Usna Line and advanced in waves down the open slopes of the Avoca Valley. They had to cover nearly one mile of completely open ground *before* they reached the original British front line.

Behind the German front line the defenders of La Boisselle had not been destroyed by the bombardment and the German machine-gunners there dominated all the surrounding ground. As soon as they saw these long lines of men coming steadily down the hillside in front of them, they raised their machine-gun sights and opened fire. An officer from a Pioneer battalion was watching the Tyneside Irish advance: 'As they moved forward, the sun gradually shone through the mist and the bayonets glinted. They then commenced to have losses but, as each man fell, the men behind increased speed and the pattern was maintained. No man was allowed to stop to assist casualties and the march continued to the beat of a single big drum, centrally placed.' (Capt. R. Wood, 18th Northumberland Fusiliers)

The effect of the German fire was dramatic. Wave after wave of the Geordies was cut down but still they kept coming on, individual men or small parties stepping out when all around them had gone down. 'I could see, away to my left and right, long lines of men. Then I heard the "patter, patter" of machine-guns in the distance. By the time I'd gone another ten yards there seemed to be only a few men left around me; by the time I had gone twenty yards, I seemed to be on my own. Then I was hit myself.' (Sgt J. Galloway, 3rd Tyneside Irish)

Furiously the German machine-gunners fired belt after belt of bullets into this fantastic target. The first to be extinguished were the two left-hand battalions, the 2nd and 3rd Tyneside Irish; very few of these ever reached the British front line. But on the right, the 1st and 4th kept going; their ground was not quite as exposed as that of their sister battalions.

Eventually, after twenty minutes, the survivors reached

the British trenches and the chance to shelter from the terrible fire. But they did not rest; their orders had been to follow the leading brigades and the survivors moved on into No Man's Land, across Sausage Valley, on the far side of which the trenches were still held by the Germans in some places. Still losing men, the Tyneside Irish crossed the 500 yards of No Man's Land, through the wall of German shell fire and through more machine-gun fire, and two small groups, the survivors of the two battalions, managed to reach the German front line. Here they found troops from the leading brigades holding out but, instead of taking shelter with them, the Tyneside Irish, still mindful of their orders, set off again to fight their way into the German rear completely on their own. Deep in the German lines the two isolated parties met each other and joined. Incredibly the C.O. of the 4th Tyneside Irish was still with them, but he was now recalled; the brigade commander had been wounded and he was needed at brigade H.Q. He did not realize that, apart from the men he was leaving, there was hardly any brigade left.

The Tyneside Irish were now down to less than fifty effective men. They were isolated 700 yards deep into the German trench system, having covered 3,000 yards under fire since starting out from the Tara–Usna Line. They had more than done their duty but in the distance they could see their final objective, the village of Contalmaison, H.Q. of a German division and protected by several more trenches. Undeterred, these brave men set off for Contalmaison. Kitchener's Army may have lacked skill but it had an abundance of courage.

All along the battle front the fight for the German trenches continued. The whole of the initial attacking force had now gone over; a second force of fresh battalions would continue later in the morning but these would expect the whole of the German front line to be captured and No Man's Land to be safe from machine-gun fire. Both sides knew that the battle hinged upon the capture or loss of these trenches and both sides fought hard, without regard to cost. It was trench fighting of the most confusing nature and this was where individual skill and determination mattered most.

The British were often in such small numbers that captured trenches could not always be regarded as secure; Germans would appear behind them from uncleared dug-outs or from nearby trenches. Ammunition, especially grenades, soon ran out because the carrying parties bringing fresh supplies were unable to cross No Man's Land. So many officers had been killed that small groups of men were often left leaderless, completely ignorant of how the battle was going. Their knowledge was confined to the few yards of trench in which they found themselves, the next bay was a mystery; they did not know whether it was empty, or occupied by friends or enemies. The sun was turning the morning into a very hot day and the dust and noise of battle was all around. Wounded men were a problem; often they could not be sent back over No Man's Land. Field dressings were applied to their wounds, they were given a little of the precious water and then made as comfortable as possible.

When rival parties did meet, the action was fierce. 'About a dozen of us got into Jerry's trench but then we had a tough fight. I was hit in the face by a grenade but the German had forgotten to pull the pin out and it didn't go off. The fight only lasted three minutes and we lost nine of our men and had to give up the trench.' (Pte A. Fretwell, Sheffield City Battalion)

'Now we came on to a German machine-gun post and there were all the twelve of the crew lying dead around the machine-gun; a short distance away we saw the body of one of our sergeants, formerly one of the king's footmen who joined up with us at Norwich. He had obviously accounted for the machine-gun crew, before he himself received his death blow. A strange feeling possesses one, at such a moment. It seems as if one is detached and merely looking at a scene of carnage from a great distance.' (Pte W. C. Bennett, 8th Norfolks)

Lieut-Col. Reginald Bastard emerged safely from the barrage in No Man's Land and reached the German trenches. He found his men fighting fiercely; they had joined up with the remnants of the 2nd Royal Berks and captured 200 yards of trench. Bastard was the senior officer present, the Berkshire's c.o. having been mortally wounded while crossing No Man's Land.

He took command of the mixed force and assessed the situation. The trenches on either side of him were held by the Germans; in front his men had a small footing in the next trench but could get no farther. A few men from a third battalion, the 1st Royal Irish Rifles, crossing after the Lincolns soon joined him but the barrage in No Man's Land appeared to have stopped all other support. The Irish Rifles had lost their C.O. too, so that Bastard was now commanding the remains of three battalions, but the whole force was still under 100 men. He was determined to hold the gains and, if fresh troops came, he would continue the attack. Bastard knew that a fourth battalion in the brigade had been held in reserve and would possibly be sent across to support them. Swiftly he organized the defence. On both flanks, men were ordered to block the trench with wire and hold off counter-attacks. The trench was searched for any German dug-outs that had not been cleared and for stocks of German grenades; their own were running out. He allocated his few men so that the foothold in the next trench ahead could be maintained. The wounded were collected and made comfortable.

The discipline and skill of a Regular officer had turned the survivors of three battalions into an effective force. But, as the Germans pressed their attacks, Bastard recognized that his force could not hold out indefinitely. His casualties mounted steadily and ammunition began to run out. Anxiously he looked back over No Man's Land for the reserve battalion.

There were many, like Bastard, who found themselves commanding small parties of men holding out in the German trenches: '2nd Lieut H. P. Hendin was actually the only officer of the 10th Lincolns to get into the enemy's trenches; he reached their third line with five men and hung on there. He beat off several counter-attacks with his small party and other men he had gathered together. He said, "It was just luck that I got across and luck that I was able to hold on. I shall never forget the experience and hope never to have another like it."' (Maj. W. A. Vignoles, Grimsby Chums)*

Another man in the German trenches was Lieut Philip Howe. Heeding his orders to push on to Lonely Trench, he had crossed three German trenches – all strangely empty. He still did not look behind, although he was conscious of much firing. Half an hour after setting off he arrived at his objective and this trench, too, was deserted. Then for the

* Again from the diary of Maj. Vignoles. 2nd Lieut Hendin was killed at Arras in April 1917.

first time he turned round, expecting to see the rest of the West Yorks following. To his amazement there were only twenty men, the remnants of two platoons. There was one other officer, a second-lieutenant who was wounded in the leg, and most of the men were wounded too. Of the rest of the battalion there was not a sign; he had no idea what had happened to them.

As they stood in Lonely Trench wondering what to do, a German appeared from the next bay and fired at him. The bullet passed right through the palm of Howe's right hand. Blood poured from the wound and he felt himself losing consciousness. He fainted, but, within ten minutes, recovered his senses to find that the others had driven off the German and put a field dressing on his wound.

Howe took charge again of the small group of men. They were obviously cut off deep in the German lines and surrounded, but they had found and taken their objective and were prepared to hold it. Finding a deep dug-out, they took shelter in it, placing the badly wounded at the bottom on the floor and the lightly wounded on the steps. The second-lieutenant, the only one who could fire a rifle, stayed at the top of the steps with Philip Howe behind him, ready to reload the rifle. They waited. Who would arrive first, the Germans or the British?

8

Review at 8.30 A.M.

Had Sir Douglas Haig and his army commanders been raised above the confusion of the battlefield at the end of this first hour and been able to see the progress of their troops and the casualties they had sustained, they would have been bitterly disappointed. Eighty-four battalions had attacked in the first hour, a total of some 66,000 men. Roughly one third, by hard fighting, skill and some luck, had gained all their objectives. Another third had nothing to show for their losses, except small and vulnerable footholds in the German trenches. The final third had been completely repulsed; not a living attacker was inside the German wire, unless as a prisoner of the enemy. Five out of the nine villages due to be taken during the day should have been captured in the first hour. Not one had fallen.

The right wing of Rawlinson's army had been successful. Attacking from the lower arm of the L-shaped front, three divisions, the 30th, 18th (Eastern) and 7th, had taken nearly all their early objectives. The Manchester and Liverpool battalions of the 30th Division, on the extreme right, had attacked alongside the French; all had gone well and the Lancashire troops were fighting their way towards Montauban, scheduled to be taken later in the morning. On their left the 18th (Eastern), too, had taken all its early objectives, in spite of the delayed firing of the Kasino Point mine which had affected some of its battalions. The 7th Division, Gough's old command, had captured the German front-line trenches but were held up by the fortified village of Mametz. This was a good, Regular division and its commander had ordered the attack to be halted to allow for a re-bombardment and for fresh troops to take over the lead. Few of the New Army divisions were as flexible.

Gen. Rawlinson's keenest disappointment would have been in the centre of his front. The reader will remember that it was here that the main road ran towards Pozières and Bapaume; it was behind this sector that the bulk of the cavalry was waiting for a breakthrough. If success was essential anywhere at all, it was here in Rawlinson's centre.

Five divisions were attacking on this four-and-a-half-mile sector. The two outside ones had made some progress but the centre three astride the vital main road to Bapaume had been bloodily repulsed. The alternate valleys and spurs in No Man's Land had become death traps, where the men from the 34th, 8th and 32nd Divisions had perished. In the 32nd Division, the Glasgow Commercials had captured part of the Leipzig Salient in a well-planned and executed rush as soon as the artillery had lifted off the German front line, but apart from this only a few small parties like Reginald Bastard's had gained precarious footholds in the German trenches.*

The vital, initial attack in the centre had foundered completely. One of the reserve divisions, the 19th (Western), had taken up position close to the front line and was ready, if ordered, to renew the attack. Behind these anxious infantry troops the cavalry could only continue waiting.

The fortunes of the most northerly of the five centre divisions deserve to be looked at more closely. The 36th (Ulster) Division, attacking north of Thiepval, had taken the German front line and was well into the Schwaben Redoubt just behind it. This had been no easy advance; the Germans had resisted stubbornly and continuous machine-gun fire had poured into the Ulstermen's flank from the untaken village of Thiepval on their right. They were also unsupported on their left, so that their advance had created a deep, narrow salient in the German lines. They were still fighting hard and pushing even farther into the enemy lines. If the divisions on either side of them could not get their attacks going again, the Ulstermen could be counter-attacked from three sides and risked being pushed right back again or even cut off and wiped out.

North of the Ancre, where Hunter-Weston's corps was to have formed a flank guard for the main attack, disaster loomed. This powerful corps had attacked with three full divisions, two of which were the precious Regulars, and two battalions from a fourth, on a frontage of under three miles, but it had captured only one German position, the

* Sgt James Yuill Turnbull of the Glasgow Commercials was posthumously awarded the Victoria Cross for holding a vital post in the Leipzig Salient for many hours until killed by a sniper.

Quadrilateral Redoubt. Here, the remnants of four battalions had gained the German trenches, but along the rest of the corps front there was absolute failure, with the exception of one company still hanging on to the edge of the Hawthorn Ridge mine crater.

At Gommecourt, where the two Territorial divisions from Third Army were making the diversionary attack, a complicated situation was developing. Attacking from the south, the 56th (London) Division had performed brilliantly. Making use of the new trench they had dug in No Man's Land and a smoke-screen, four battalions had captured the whole of the German front-line system. A fifth battalion had crossed over behind them and, following the plan, was preparing to push out an arm to link up with the other division behind Gommecourt.

North of the salient, however, it was a different story. The 46th (North Midland) Division had attacked with six battalions but they had not done so well. Only small parties had got into the trenches and these had been wiped out or cut off, making it very difficult for this division to retrieve the situation and complete the encirclement of the village.

The capture of Gommecourt was not vital. The attack on the salient had already fulfilled one of its aims, that of attracting fire which might otherwise have fallen on to VIII Corps, although Hunter-Weston's troops had not profited from this sacrifice. The vital issue now was whether the North Midland men could renew their attack and complete the encirclement of the village. If they were to fail, the Londoners would be left stranded in the German trenches.

What had been the cost of this first hour? It is impossible to say exactly but probably half of the 66,000 British soldiers who had attacked were already casualties – 30,000 infantrymen killed or wounded in just sixty minutes!

The commanders at G.H.Q. and at army level were completely unable to influence the opening stages of the battle. The difficulty of obtaining any reliable detailed information on progress made and of sending fresh orders forward made them helpless. Even if communication had been possible, radically different orders would have done more harm than good at this early hour. The most useful thing the C.-in-C.

himself could do was to keep out of the way of his army commanders. Gen. Haig intended to visit them in the afternoon when more news would be available. In the meantime, he waited at his advanced H.Q. in Beauquesne. He could hear the gunfire quite plainly and already ambulances were passing through the village to a nearby Casualty Clearing Station. It was a very anxious time for Haig. This was his first battle as C.-in-C. and one for which he had high hopes, but he was not an excitable man and he passed the morning calmly enough.

At Fourth Army, Gen. Rawlinson was up early to watch the opening of the bombardment and by 6.30 A.M. he was at an observation post on some high ground near Albert, four miles behind the front. From this vantage point, which some racing enthusiast had named the Grandstand, he could see shells bursting on the German trenches near Mametz, Fricourt and La Boisselle. He probably stayed there for an hour, waiting until the twin mines at La Boisselle were exploded, signalling the start of the infantry attack. He would then have heard the long bursts of German machine-gun fire faintly in the distance, had it not been for the continuous firing of the British batteries around Albert.

As Rawlinson made his way back to his headquarters at Querrieux, he passed units of the 2nd Indian Cavalry Division who were waiting in fields and woods, being careful not to get in anyone's way on the roads. After breakfast he went to his office in the château and settled down to receive the reports of his five corps commanders, for he had a direct telephone line to each of them. In adjacent rooms the members of his staff were also up early and working. They, too, were in telephonic touch with their colleagues at the corps H.Q.'s. It was too early yet to receive any detailed reports but, at 7.47 A.M., the officer keeping the Fourth Army Diary made the first entry of the day: 'Enemy barrage reported feeble.'* The infantry then crossing No Man's Land would not have agreed.

Even at the corps and divisional H.Q.'s it was too early to assess the situation, or attempt to influence the course of the battle. Many wounded were passing on their way to the rear but their reports could not be relied upon; the old army

* This and subsequent extracts from the Fourth Army Diary are in the Public Record Office, WO 95/431.

custom of claiming to be the sole survivor of one's platoon did not impress anyone at this stage. Others brought back more encouraging stories of captured German trenches and prisoners. Because these latter reports were more what the generals expected, more credence was given to them.

The brigade H.Q.'s had a better idea of what was happening and some were having an anxious time. Two, and sometimes three, battalions had gone over in the first hour and had been seen to fall under the German fire. The time would soon come for the remaining battalions to go over. According to the original plan, these uncommitted battalions had been supposed to cross a safe No Man's Land, help the leaders consolidate captured German trenches or penetrate farther.

Anxious battalion commanders rang up their brigadier-generals. Was there any change of orders? Must they throw away their battalions in attacks that were already quite clearly hopeless? The brigade commanders were in a dilemma. They realized the attack had broken down on their own front but they had no knowledge of what was happening on either flank and no time to find out. Reference to divisional H.Q. brought little help: 'You must stick to the plan. You must carry out your orders.' The brigade commanders had no alternative but to order their remaining battalions forward.

A staff officer has described the atmosphere in such a brigade H.Q. 'Brigadier-General Gordon fully realized the gravity of the order he was giving when he ordered the 11th Sherwood Foresters to continue their forward movement. There was a tense silence in the dug-out after he had given his decision and General Gordon was never quite the same again.' (Maj. W. C. Wilson, 70th Infantry Brigade H.Q.)* Lucky those brigadier-generals where the attack went well; they could order their battalions forward without such doubts.

News of the heavy losses was beginning to reach those soldiers who had been left behind when their battalions had attacked; some could even see what was happening with their own eyes. The Accrington Pals had left behind some of their signallers to follow when the German trenches had been taken. These men watched the attack from a mound behind the line: 'We were able to see our comrades move forward

* Public Record Office, CAB 45/187.

in an attempt to cross No Man's Land, only to be mown down like meadow grass. I felt sick at the sight of this carnage and remember weeping. We did actually see a flag signalling near the village of Serre, but this lasted only a few seconds and the signals were unintelligible.' (L/Cpl H. Bury, Accrington Pals)

These infantry observers were not the only ones who were powerless. The British artillery was firing to a carefully prepared programme. At zero hour the gunners had lifted their fire from the German front lines and, since then, had gradually been extending the range. But in most places the infantry had not crossed the German trenches and the shells were therefore falling farther and farther away from the area of decisive action. The complicated artillery plan now had little relevance to the infantry battle.

'I was an artillery Liaison Officer with the 18th West Yorks (2nd Bradford Pals) and was in an Observation Post about 300 yards behind the British front line. As soon as our infantry moved into the open, the Germans placed machine-guns on their parapets and enfiladed the flank of the 93rd Infantry Brigade, causing grievous casualties. The machine-guns and their gunners were clearly visible but all our guns were in the main barrage and were not to be brought back, except by order of VIII Corps H.Q.' (2nd Lieut T. Reilly, 170th (County Palatine) Brigade R.F.A.) It would have been a simple job for an experienced artillery officer to have destroyed these machine-guns or at least drive the crews back into cover. Helplessly, the gunners watched the carnage.

Farther back, those serving the guns were able to do so mostly without interference by the Germans, who were directing their own artillery only at No Man's Land and the British trenches. The enemy had given up counter-battery work for the more urgent task of providing close support for their own infantry. Some British gun positions which were immediately behind the front line were hit by German 'overs' but most were able to work in safety.

The gunners themselves imagined they were doing their best to support the infantry. As the layers gradually extended the range, the gunners, already exhausted after seven days of loading and firing, were working their guns harder than ever. They were not to know that their shells were falling uselessly beyond the battle area. Some batteries had been ordered to be prepared to follow the advance. Bridges had been built across the trenches and ammunition stocked well forward of them. The horses stood near by as the gunners waited for the orders to harness up and move forward. Those orders rarely came.

For a few the battle was already over, their duties had been completed, but even then they were still in danger. At Gommecourt, some men from the North Midland Division had been in a disused trench throwing smoke grenades into No Man's Land since dawn. This was partly to thicken the smoke-screen and partly to draw German shells onto an otherwise empty trench. They had indeed been shelled heavily, but they had been lucky and had suffered no casualties. 'As soon as we had finished, we got out to the rear as fast as we could. When we were clear of the trenches three of us stopped and we sat down for a breather. We were very pleased to be out of it safely. Just then a shell from one of our own guns burst prematurely, right over us, and the man in the middle was killed outright.' (Cpl J. Ward, 1/4th Lincolns)

If some men had completed their day's work, many others never got started. L/Cpl Charles Matthews, trapped in his trench, had watched his friends go over the top leaving him alone except for the three mortar gunners who had finished firing and were resting by their mortar. Matthews hoped that soon they would come and release him. It was at this moment that the German barrage fell on the British trenches and a shell burst near the resting mortar gunners. Two were killed outright and the third ran, screaming crazily, down the trench over Matthews, treading on his chest as he went by. Matthews cursed him for his thoughtlessness but, when the gunner had passed, could see that a piece of shell had removed most of the back of the poor man's head.

The German shelling continued and every four minutes a salvo of shells burst just outside Matthews's trench. The shelling was so regular that he listened for the 'plop' from well behind the German lines as the battery fired, followed several seconds later by the explosions a few yards away. Matthews realized that, if one of the German gun layers elevated his gun a fraction, a shell would burst in his trench and he, too, would share the fate of the mortar gunners. He was determined to move, despite the pain. Using his broken rifle and his one good leg, he started to lever himself upwards. He made some progress but, when half-way up, he could get no farther. His situation was now even more painful, for he could neither free himself nor could he get back to his old position. In this uncomfortable and exposed posture, he had to await further developments.

The units of the medical services, if not yet at full stretch, were rapidly approaching that state, for many wounded were coming back from the trenches. The Field Ambulances dealt with these quickly, often merely checking that the field dressings were secure. The walking wounded were directed down specially signed tracks and motor ambulances took the stretcher cases; all were making for the Casualty Clearing Stations.

Here the nurses and orderlies made the men comfortable, examined their wounds and classified them. The lightly wounded were, again, given a minimum of treatment; a cup of tea and the realization that they had a coveted Blighty wound, soon restored the spirits of these men. Those more seriously wounded were marked for the operating tents; already the surgeons were hard at work trying to save the lives, or limbs, of the worst cases. These lay in rows, patiently awaiting their turn. Those who died were taken outside to await burial; their stretchers were urgently needed.

The Casualty Clearing Stations were filling more rapidly than had been expected, but sufficient ambulance trains had been asked for and should be available nearby. Already there were enough cases awaiting evacuation to the base to be calling the trains forward.

For those many wounded out in No Man's Land there was little that could be done for the moment. Many stretcher-bearers following the attacking troops over the top had themselves become casualties; the remainder could not work in the open and were more often struggling through the congested British trenches. Thousands of wounded men in No Man's Land had taken cover in shell holes or lay out in the hot sun. A few in the shell holes received some treatment when their friends applied field dressings, but those badly wounded and out in the open got no help, and many bled slowly to death. It was still only 8.30 A.M.

. . .

On the other side of No Man's Land the attack had come as no surprise to the Germans. Their commanders had suspected for some time that the British would attempt to relieve the pressure on the French at Verdun. There had been no major effort by the British since Loos, over eight months earlier, and none since Gen. Haig had become their new c.-in-c. in December 1915. What the Germans did not know, at first that is, was the exact date and place of the coming offensive. By a series of unconnected incidents, however, they had been able to learn both of these vital pieces of information.

One of the first indications given to them was when the speech to the munitions workers, about the postponement of the Whitsun Holiday, had been reported in the British newspapers. Within a few hours, these were on sale in Holland and the German intelligence service took note of the hint that there would shortly be a British offensive. Soon after this, German observers at the front had noticed the increased activity on the Somme, as the British there prepared for the battle. Even before the bombardment opened, suspicion fell upon the Somme as the most likely place for the coming attack, although it was not thought that the French would be involved. The Germans were sure that the French, having lost so heavily at Verdun, had not sufficient strength remaining to join with the British in an attack.

So, by mid-June, the Germans knew roughly the 'when' and roughly the 'where'. Their agents abroad tried to obtain more specific information and the neutral Press was full of speculation, fired partly by the rumours sweeping London; but neither agents nor rumour could tell the Germans the exact 'when' or 'where'.

The German commanders were not unanimous in their forecasts. The commander of their Second Army, against which the blow would actually fall, was quite sure that he was to be attacked, but his superior, Falkenhayn, the German c.-in.-c., thought that the attack would be against the Sixth Army farther north and, as a result of this, no extra troops were sent to the German Second Army on the Somme. Before condemning Falkenhayn for this omission, it should be remembered that, while all this was happening, he was also fighting a major battle at Verdun.

When Rawlinson's bombardment opened, on 24 June, the Germans on the Somme could be even more certain that they were about to be attacked. The intense shell fire and the heavy concentration of British observation balloons flying on such a short front indicated to them the exact limits of the sectors to be attacked, although they still did not think that the French would be involved. The British diversions farther north were partially successful and Falkenhayn, thinking the British Fourth Army's preparations were so obvious that these were the diversionary moves, continued to think that the attack on the Somme would not materialize and still sent no reserves there. The Germans would have to hold the attack with the troops they had in the line on the Somme and the few local reserves. They were outnumbered by seven to one.

As the last day of June passed by, the German generals studied the latest reports and their soldiers waited in their dug-outs; all wanted to know the answer to the one final question. When? They were to be supplied with this vital piece of information by none other than a British staff officer. When Rawlinson's eve-of-battle message had been sent over the telephone to a forward unit in the 34th Division at 2.45 A.M., a German listening post at the Glory Hole had picked up the last part of it. It was sufficient to tell the Germans that the attack would begin that morning, and the message was passed on to all their nearby units.

It is possible that they learned by other means, too. 'During the night of 30 June/1 July, a small English patrol was sent out to inspect our wire and they were captured. Times were rough; the revolver was the best interpreter. It went from mouth to mouth that these prisoners had revealed the time of the attack to the minute.' (Unteroffizier Paul Scheytt, 109th Reserve Regiment)

Herr Scheytt's story is not recorded elsewhere, as far as is known, but there is no reason why it should not be true. A copy of the intercepted telephone message was found in a captured German dug-out at Ovillers a few days later. It is certain that Germans from as far apart as Gommecourt and Montauban, the limits of the front attacked by the British, were told, that night, that the British would attack in the morning.

When the British blew the Hawthorn Ridge mine at 7.20

A.M., they gave the Germans the final confirmation. The noise and vibration of this huge explosion, just ten minutes before the British attack, told the German soldiers that their long ordeal under the *Trommelfeuer* was over. The time had come for them to fight back.

'We ran out of food that night and I was sent to get some. At the field kitchen I was told, "Tell your comrades the English will attack tomorrow morning." It took me seven hours to fetch the food and when I got back I couldn't find my dug-out because the ground was so torn up. Then I saw one of my friends signalling to me.

'I told my comrades, "We must be prepared; the English will attack soon." We got our machine-gun ready on the top step of the dug-out and we put all our equipment on; then we waited. We all expected to die. We thought of God. We prayed. Then someone shouted, "They're coming! They're coming!" We rushed up and got our machine-gun in position. We could see the English soldiers pouring out at us, thousands and thousands of them. We opened fire.' (Grenadier Emil Kury, 109th Reserve Regiment)

The tension which had been building up among the German front-line defenders during the terrible days while they had been under bombardment was now released in action. When they realized that the British had not followed immediately upon the heels of the bombardment, but had allowed them time to man their trenches, the German soldiers' relief was enormous. They were not to be trapped in their dug-outs but, instead, were presented with targets that exceeded their wildest expectations as the waves of British infantry plodded stupidly into their machine-gun and rifle sights.

'We had lain for seven days under the drum-fire, in a mood of blind fury because we felt so defenceless; so that, when the moment of attack came, we felt good. At last we could get our own back. None of us thought we would be killed or wounded. Now we'd pay them back in their own kind.

'We heard the mines go up; then it was deathly quiet for a few moments. The English came walking, as though they were going to the theatre or as though they were on a parade ground. We felt they were mad. Our orders were given in complete calm and every man took careful aim to avoid wasting ammunition.' (Unteroffizier Paul Scheytt, 109th Reserve Regiment)

The Germans were amazed by the attack formation used by the leading British troops. 'The behaviour of the Highlanders seemed to us rather strange, for these came forward very slowly, either because of their heavy loads, or was it madness, without taking the least cover.' (Schneyer, 170th Regiment) *

The German infantry sent up coloured rockets, which were the pre-arranged signal to the artillery; immediately this brought down the heavy defensive barrage. With this combination of shell and bullet, the slaughter of the British infantry began. 'When the English started advancing we were very worried; they looked as though they must overrun our trenches. We were very surprised to see them walking, we had never seen that before. I could see them everywhere; there were hundreds. The officers were in front. I noticed one of them walking calmly, carrying a walking stick. When we started firing, we just had to load and reload. They went down in their hundreds. You didn't have to aim, we just fired into them. If only they had run, they would have overwhelmed us.' (Musketier Karl Blenk, 169th Regiment)†

So exhilarated were they with their release from the bombardment and with the complete mastery they had over No Man's Land, that the more exuberant of the Germans could not restrain themselves from jumping onto the parapets of their trenches, shouting with glee and taunting the defeated British. 'I scrambled up the back of the trench, took up my position with my rifle on a small rise and opened fire blindly into the crowd of English soldiers who were coming across No Man's Land. There were so many of them, they were like trees in a wood. We kept them out of our part of the line but they broke through on our left. I was standing up, firing, and my officer shouted to me, "Come down", but in my excitement I told him, "But they're not shooting", and the officer said, "You fool, can't you hear the bullets whistling?" ' (Soldat Wilhelm Lange, 99th Reserve Regiment)‡ This

* Herr Schneyer was facing the London Scottish at Gommecourt. This quotation is taken from a letter written in 1919 to Maj. C. J. Low of the London Scottish.

† Herr Blenk was facing the Sheffield City Battalion and the Accrington Pals at Serre.

‡ Herr Lange was firing into the left flank of the Co. Down Volunteers north of Thiepval.

reckless and foolhardy behaviour was to have tragic consequences.

So the first hour of the battle had ended in heavy loss and bitter disappointment for the British, and some relief for the Germans. But the day was still young. Was there no chance that the British could redeem their early failure? So far, they had committed less than half of their available strength to the battle. In addition to the remnants of eighty-four battalions still on the battlefield, forty-three more fresh battalions were due to renew the attack during the morning and behind them there were waiting a further seventy, if the British generals decided to use them. In addition to these reserves of infantry there was the powerful force of artillery, still intact. Now that the Germans had come out of their dug-outs and were having to fight, these British guns could be the decisive factor, if properly handled. The Germans had fought well in this first hour, but could their defence hold for the remainder of the day?

9

The Morning

Unlike the mass assault of 7.30 A.M., there was no regular pattern to the follow-up attacks to which the fresh battalions were due to be committed as the morning wore on. According to the original plan, these new units had certain specific tasks to perform depending on the importance of their sector, the anticipated strength of the opposition, the distance to the final objective and various other factors. Although they were not all to leave their trenches at the same time, it had been planned that their attacks should all take place before mid-morning. This time-table had already suffered severe set-backs, but this battle was on such a vast scale and news was so slow to reach the rear that there was little chance of these secondary infantry attacks being cancelled. The demands of the plan had to be met.

The men who had attacked in the first assault may have been nervous and frightened as they waited to go over but at least they were confident of success. Those who were to follow them could be under no such illusion. As they struggled forward through the communication trenches, often under heavy shell fire, they heard stories about or saw with their own eyes the devastation of the first attack. Many battalions suffered heavy casualties from this shelling before they even reached the front-line trenches. They met a continuous stream of wounded men from the first attack who left them in no doubt about the ferocity of the German defence. Even so, there is no record of any battalion hesitating in its attack.

Let us follow the steps of one battalion, the 11th Sherwood Foresters. It was the decision to confirm the attack of this battalion that had caused Brig.-Gen. Gordon such anxiety. The Foresters were to follow three other New Army battalions which had already gone over and, passing through these, were to be at the final objective, Mouquet Farm ('Mucky Farm'), 2,000 yards away, by 11 A.M. There, they had been promised a hot meal from field cookers which would follow their attack.

As they moved up to the front line the Foresters found

that the German shelling had caused terrible casualties among the men of the 9th Yorks and Lancs who had preceded them. 'Before the battle we had helped to dig assembly dug-outs just off the communication trench. These were not deep, having about two feet of head cover, but were each big enough to hold a platoon of men. When we moved up for our attack we found that many of these had been hit by German shells, killing or wounding the men inside. That place was full of dead men, torn-off limbs and badly wounded who begged for help, but we dared not stop. The communication trench almost ran with blood that morning.

'While we were waiting in our front line to go over, a German machine-gun was spraying the top of the trench, flicking up dirt from the parapet. When the whistle blew, the first man up my ladder was an American, Private Martin. As soon as he reached the top he was shot through the wrist. He came straight back. "I've got mine," he said. "I'm off." ' (Pte F. W. A. Turner, 11th Sherwood Foresters)

On many parts of the front, men had to face a fearful prospect: 'I found that I wasn't alone, as a second-lieutenant was standing beside me, shaking like a jelly, which nearly made me jittery myself. He was just a youngster, about my own age, and had just joined the battalion a few days before. I shouted at him to get over the top but he just looked at me forlornly and couldn't seem able to speak. I whipped out my bottle of rum, I had been saving it for several days, and offered it to him but he must have been a teetotaller as he only took a sip. I told him to take a good drink, which he did. You never saw a man find his courage so quickly. He pulled out his revolver, climbed the ladder and went charging after the men like a hare. If we hadn't had our rum, we would have lost the war.' (Pte G. Brownbridge, 13th Northumberland Fusiliers)

In most places the attacks of these follow-up battalions foundered almost as soon as they began. Since they were often the only troops out in the open on their own particular sector, they immediately drew fire from every German within range. Most got only a few yards before their attack wilted, leaving still more dead and wounded to join those already strewn across the battlefield. 'We set off across the open at 9 A.M. Casualties, of course, began at once and my impression was that, in spite of the noise and dust of the shell bursts, it was the machine-guns that were doing the damage. I hadn't gone far, I couldn't now and couldn't then be sure whether I had actually got to our own wire, so disfigured was the landscape by the shelling, when I felt a thud in the upper leg.' (Lieut A. Sainsbury, 2nd Royal Dublin Fusiliers)

'Imagine stumbling over a ploughed field in a thunderstorm, the incessant roar of the guns and flashes as the shells exploded. Multiply all this and you have some idea of the Hell into which we were heading. To me it seemed a hundred times worse than any storm. On top of all this we were losing a lot of men. When I say men, I should really say boys, because we had been drafted to a battalion of public schoolboys. They were a nice lot of lads and I hated to think of them going up against trained men of the German Imperial Army.' (Pte E. Houston, Public Schools Battalion)

There were always a few men, luckier or more persevering than the rest, who managed to get as far as the German wire, but all they could do there was to take shelter in shell holes and join the survivors of the leading battalions. On these sectors, the attack had broken down completely. The primary assault had failed; the secondary assault had failed.

On just such a sector, near Beaumont Hamel, was Pte Albert McMillan, the enthusiastic young Cockney who had been looking forward to his first day of war. The Public Schools Battalion had gone over the top in support of the leading troops and had immediately caught the usual German fire. Only a few reached the German wire but could get no farther; one of these was Albert McMillan. Sharing his shell hole was a man with a bad shrapnel wound in the back. He could not dress the wound himself so McMillan attended to him, although neither could move freely because their hole was so shallow. In his ignorance and haste, McMillan broke the top off his iodine bottle and poured the whole of the contents into the open wound. The man screamed with agony but McMillan secured the bandage and was relieved to see his comrade crawl away towards the British trenches during a quiet spell.

The Germans seemed quite content to defend their trenches without counter-attacking to drive the British away from their wire. On the whole eighteen-mile front the Official History only records one incident, throughout the morning, where a few Germans came out to clear away the Leeds Pals from their wire, but once this was done they soon returned to their own trenches: 'Away on the left, a party of Germans climbed out of the trench. They kicked one or two bodies; any showing signs of life were shot or bayoneted.' (Pte A. Howard, Leeds Pals)

Elsewhere the Germans merely manned their trenches, although some were so confident that they continued to stand up on the parapets to get a better aim or to jeer at the British. No Man's Land now contained many British soldiers in good cover, armed with powerful rifles and ample ammunition. They were unable to continue the attack, to force the enemy defences, but they could, quite easily, shoot the standing Germans off their parapets. The firing started gradually as some British soldier, more daring than the rest, gathered his wits after the terror of the earlier part of the morning, selected his target, fired and a German toppled back into his trench. Soon the German parapets were cleared but the sniping continued all morning from No Man's Land as the British found that they could hit back.

'Eventually I took shelter in a shell hole with two other men from the battalion; we were all wounded. I looked over the edge and could see the Germans in their trench again. I suddenly became very angry. I had seen my battalion mowed down by machine-guns and one of them trapped in the wire. I thought of my particular pal who had been killed a few days before by a shell. I thought we were all doomed; I just couldn't see how any of us would get out of it alive and, so far, I hadn't done anything to the Germans. I made up my mind to get one of them, at least, before I was killed.

'I took out my clips of cartridges and laid them out ready for use. I checked the sights on my rifle, settled myself into a comfortable position, took aim and fired. One of the Jerries threw up his arms and fell backwards and the others ducked down.' (Pte H. C. Bloor, Accrington Pals)

Probably the most frustrated of all the soldiers involved in the battle were the battalion commanders. The breakdown of the attack and the danger in any movement above ground level had robbed them of the ability to perform their proper function – the command of their battalions in action. Instead, they had to watch their fine commands of eager volunteers being smashed before their eyes. But one did not rise to command a battalion of British infantry and allow these things to happen without making every effort to regain control of the situation.

The lieutenant-colonels should have stayed in their own trenches, leaving their company and platoon commanders to lead the initial attack; no one could command a unit as big as a battalion in the confusion of No Man's Land. Indeed, many C.O.'s had been specifically ordered not to take part in the attack; they were to join their troops only when the objectives had been taken. But the C.O.'s not so ordered to remain behind invariably attacked with their men because their feelings prevented them from taking the safer but more reasonable course of action.

Those who had survived the crossing of No Man's Land set up their H.Q.'s in the captured trenches. Their big problem was the lack of fast and reliable communication. They had many devices for signalling back to the British trenches but few were successful under the conditions of that day. The visual methods, the flags, signal shutters and lamps, on which the signallers had spent hours of practice, often brought death to the operator as soon as he exposed himself. Rockets sometimes did more harm than good, for the Germans had rockets too and, from the British trenches, the observers could not tell whose rockets were being fired. Field telephone links suffered frequent breakdowns as shells cut the cables running back over No Man's Land, and there was a constant need for running repairs: 'As a linesman I had to run through No Man's Land with the cable in my hand until I came to the break. Then I squatted in a shell hole, patiently waiting for a signaller from H.Q. to trace his end. When he arrived we joined the two ends and tested the line with our portable telephones. This happened so often that we had to give up and revert to runners.' (Pte J. R. Parkman, 2nd Devons) In the last resort it was always the company or battalion runner who had to take the messages. As this was the infantryman's most dangerous job, the messages frequently did not reach their destination.

Lieut-Col. Reginald Bastard was one C.O. who suffered from this breakdown in communications. His mixed force in the German trenches, subjected to continuous counter-attack, was being pressed back gradually and still there was no sign of reinforcements. Eventually his force was so weak that the survivors were forced out of the German trenches altogether and took cover near the German wire. The Lincolns c.o. left them there with orders to hold on, while he went to fetch more men; he was determined to continue the attack.

Bastard managed to get back to the British trenches without being hit but found that the fourth battalion in his brigade, from which he had expected support, had been ordered not to go over. He rounded up every fit man he could find from the other three battalions and ordered them to go with him to reinforce the party he had left near the German wire. One can imagine the feelings of these stragglers as they were ordered over the top again in the middle of the morning, but they had to obey the lieutenant-colonel's orders. Bastard led them out into No Man's Land but they did not get far. Accurate German fire caused heavy casualties and he was soon down to thirty men.

Reginald Bastard had been very fortunate personally, for many of the c.o.'s who had gone over the top had become casualties, the duties of leadership making them prominent targets for German marksmen. Those who survived did their best but eventually had to recognize the inevitable and take refuge in shell holes.

Those lieutenant-colonels who had remained in the British trenches knew they could do little to help their battalions pinned down in No Man's Land, but every instinct led them forward: 'I was a field clerk with Colonel Machell and the adjutant. The previous day the c.o. had said, "If things go badly, I'll come up and see it through." Everyone was tense as no messages were received from the companies. The colonel was fidgeting and watching the progress of his men and eventually decided to go and lead them on himself but as soon as he left the trench he was shot through the head and killed. Then the adjutant was severely wounded as he leant over the colonel's body. The second in command had already been wounded. The c.o.'s batman, his bugler and two runners were all killed but I was only knocked over by a shell and stunned.' (L/Cpl F. Allan, 11th Border) Within a few seconds this battalion had become completely leaderless.

Another c.o. was saved by his bugler: 'Colonel Ritson had watched the leading companies in No Man's Land. I vividly remember him standing in the British front line, tears streaming down his face, saying over and over, "My God! My boys! My boys!" I had to restrain him from going over himself. He would have been killed if he had.' (L/Cpl S. Henderson, Newcastle Commercials)

Among those c.o.'s who had gone on to the battlefield the casualty rate was high. 'I was ordered to stay with Colonel Hind at all costs. When we got to the German wire I was absolutely amazed to see it intact, after what we had been told. The colonel and I took cover behind a small bank but after a bit the colonel raised himself on his hands and knees to see better. Immediately, he was hit in the forehead by a single bullet.' (Pte A. H. Tomlinson, 1/7th Sherwood Foresters)

Another battalion commander to become a casualty was Lieut-Col. Sandys of the 2nd Middlesex who had worried so much about the German wire in Mash Valley. Some of his men had in fact managed to cross the 750 yards of No Man's Land and a few had briefly occupied the German trenches before being turned out. But the battalion's casualties had been enormous. Sandys had followed his men and was soon hit himself. His wound was not serious but he had to go to the rear.

Even brigade commanders became casualties. Brig.-Gen. C. B. Prowse was so frustrated as German opposition held up his brigade's attack, that he went forward himself to organize a fresh attempt and was badly wounded. One report says that he was hit while attacking a German machine-gun post with a walking stick, but his wound was actually caused by a shell. He was rushed to a Casualty Clearing Station but died soon afterwards.

In all, two brigade commanders, fifty battalion commanders and an R.A.M.C. lieutenant-colonel became casualties during the day. Of these, thirty-one, an unusually high proportion, lost their lives.*

The Germans now began to eliminate some of the smaller and less secure of the British gains in their trenches. The German soldier was always very quick to react after being attacked and the British were often in such small numbers that it was inevitable that they should eventually lose some of their hard-won gains.

* A full list of senior officer casualties appears in Appendix 3.

After Lieut-Col. Bastard's second attack, his brigade commander realized that any further attempts would be hopeless and decided that no more were to be made. On receipt of these orders, Bastard crossed No Man's Land again, joined his men in their exposed positions by the German wire and gave instructions for the depleted force to withdraw. A captain from another battalion, wounded and sheltering in a nearby shell hole, watched their withdrawal. 'I spent the next few hours in a shell hole, but from there actually saw a platoon of the Lincolns come back to our line. They came back in perfect formation.' (Capt. K. E. Poyser, 8th K.O.Y.L.I.)* Even when retiring the Lincolns did things in style, for what the captain had seen was almost certainly Bastard's force withdrawing.

Reginald Bastard had now crossed No Man's Land four times under fire, besides spending some time fighting in the German trenches. He was extremely lucky to have come through unharmed. His story illustrates the determination of a good officer but, in the end, all his efforts and those of his men had been in vain.†

Elsewhere another eye-witness, this time in the British front line, watched a less successful withdrawal: 'We saw the survivors of a kilted battalion returning down an enemy communication trench [probably men from the 2nd Seaforth Highlanders]. Then they spread out in what is called Extended Order as though they were on a barrack square. The officer or N.C.O. in charge rose and held up his arm. On his signal they all set off at a trot in perfect line towards our trenches. Within seconds, a German machine-gun was traversing them until the last man fell. I remember standing on the fire-step and screaming "Bastards! Bastards! Bastards!" That was a word I never used.' (Pte W. E. Aust, Hull Commercials)

On the extreme left of the battlefield, near Gommecourt, Bugler Bill Soar and four other men from the Sherwood Foresters were isolated in the open just beyond the German front line. The attack there appeared to have broken down

* Public Record Office, CAB 45/190.

† For his determination on this day Lieut-Col. Reginald Bastard received a bar to the Distinguished Service Order he had won at Neuve Chapelle in 1915.

completely and three Germans in a trench behind them were both blocking any retreat and firing rifle grenades at the Nottingham men. Already one of Soar's fellow buglers had been badly hurt in the foot; he was urging Soar to leave him and attempt an escape.

Soar didn't want to leave his friend but he dared wait no longer or he would be killed or forced to surrender. He got up and ran straight at the trench. In spite of his heavy load of equipment he jumped clean over the heads of the three Germans; he could hear their gasps of surprise as he landed on the far side. He ran on, through a gap in the wire, heading for a large bed of reeds that he could see in No Man's Land. The Germans were so astonished by his tremendous leap that Soar gained this shelter without being fired upon.

The Germans could not believe that Soar seriously intended to escape and called out to him 'Come in, Tommy! Come in!' When this did not persuade him to surrender they started firing rifle grenades into his hiding place. Although one of these caused a painful injury to his arm, Soar kept perfectly still.*

Near La Boisselle, the remnants of the Tyneside Irish had decided to make for Contalmaison, their original objective, although they were completely alone in the German trenches. Someone in authority had realized by now that the attack on this sector had failed and an order was sent out that no further attempts should be made to advance. Unfortunately, the order failed to reach this Tyneside Irish party. Whoever was in command, probably a junior officer, led the Geordies towards Contalmaison, partly along German trenches and partly over open ground. It can only have been luck that allowed them to avoid any large numbers of the enemy on this journey, but when they reached Contalmaison their luck ran out; thirty or so men could not tackle a German village fortress completely on their own that day and survive.

As soon as they ran into the German fire they must have realized that they were doomed. Those who survived the brief fight turned in an attempt to retrace their steps, but they had left it too late. This small, determined body of men

* Bugler W. Caunt, Soar's friend, was taken prisoner but had to have a foot amputated. He was repatriated to England through the Red Cross in December 1916. Nothing is known of the fate of the other three men.

had achieved the distinction of advancing farther than any other unit during the day on the whole of the battle front. They had come 4,000 yards under fire since they started. They died 2,000 yards inside the German lines.*

The fate of some of the British soldiers who had got into the German trenches will never be known. Small parties, often without leaders, or isolated individuals, were hunted down by the Germans and eliminated. The ultimate casualty figures were to show that very few of these men surrendered. They fought to the end and met unrecorded deaths in some squalid corner of a German trench.

In some places the British had got into the German trenches in sufficient strength to keep their gains but were not strong enough to improve them. Just such a place was the Quadrilateral Redoubt (called by the Germans *Heiden Kopf*, after one of their officers). This position jutted right out into No Man's Land which was very narrow at that point. The Germans had previously decided that in the event of an attack it could not be held, and had left only one machine-gun crew, who were to inflict as much loss on the attackers as possible, and some engineers to blow a demolition charge when the machine-gunners had to withdraw. Through a fault, the charge had exploded earlier than planned, killing both engineers and machine-gunners.

Not far away, Sergeant Major Percy Chappell, with his company commander and some of their men, had fought his way through the first two German trenches and had reached a third which was found to be empty. Here the captain ordered his men to consolidate. The dug-outs were checked to make sure that they were empty and barbed wire pulled down to make barriers at each end of their little position. Besides Chappell and the captain, there was only a sergeant and nine men. Although the noise of battle was all around them, their immediate vicinity was clear of Germans and very quiet.

The company commander decided to reconnoitre still

* One report says that a party of the 16th Royal Scots also reached Contalmaison and were killed or captured. The Tyneside Irish story is told in such detail because, starting from the Tara–Usna Line, they had come twice as far, under fire, as the Royal Scots. It is hoped that the 16th Royal Scots (2nd Edinburgh City Battalion) will excuse this.

farther and ordered Chappell and the sergeant to accompany him. They set off up to an empty communication trench and reached the next German trench; still there were no Germans. It was a peculiar sensation to be so deep into the enemy lines and find them deserted. They were now joined by a wounded Somersets officer and, after the two officers had consulted together, Chappell was told to take charge of the men while the officers went back for fresh orders.

Chappell watched the officers go with some misgivings and he and the sergeant discussed what to do next. Their minds were made up for them when the noise of a fierce bombing fight behind them showed that they were cut off from their men, who were under heavy attack. At the same time a crowd of Germans appeared over a rise in front of them and started throwing grenades, which, fortunately, were falling short. Chappell and the sergeant were caught between two superior enemy forces. He had no intention of remaining to be trapped, so, calling to the sergeant to run for it with him, he set off in what he hoped was the safe direction. Making his way over open ground, dodging from shell hole to shell hole, he dropped into an empty trench. He looked back, but there was no sign of his companion.

Cautiously, Chappell looked around him. About 150 yards away he could see a line of British soldiers, but between him and them was a trench containing Germans. He hesitated, but when a grenade burst near him, he made up his mind to try to reach the British troops. He climbed over the parapet and ran. Bullets whizzed around his ears but Chappell was leading a charmed life. Crossing the German-held trench with a mighty leap, he ran on again without being hit and threw himself down among British soldiers.

Chappell was in the Quadrilateral and found himself near a lieutenant-colonel of the Seaforth Highlanders who was organizing the defence of the redoubt. The Germans in the trench he had just leapt were able to fire right into the British positions and the Seaforth colonel decided that they would have to be driven out. The order was passed along: when a whistle was blown every man would fire five rounds rapid and charge. But even while this message was being circulated, a Seaforth corporal collected an armful of grenades and walked steadily towards the Germans, shouting and swearing in broad Scots, throwing grenades as he went. He caused confusion and loss among the Germans, but as he reached their trench he fell dead, hit by several bullets. Inspired by this brave action, the whole British line rose and charged the enemy, shooting and bayoneting, until the trench was clear of Germans and the redoubt secure again.*

After this action things quietened down somewhat. There were men in the Quadrilateral from no less than five different battalions and the colonel ordered each party to make itself responsible for the defence of part of the redoubt. Chappell was delighted to find nearly fifty men from the Somersets but without an officer, so he took charge of them and prepared to defend their allotted section. They were very low on ammunition but a search of some dug-outs revealed a good stock of German grenades.

During the rest of the morning, the beleaguered garrison had to beat off several half-hearted German attacks, but there were also long periods of calm.

In spite of the early disasters on the majority of the British attack front, they had achieved three substantial, if separated, advances into the German trenches: by the London Division in the diversionary attack at Gommecourt; by the Ulster Division at Thiepval and by the four divisions on the right wing who were attacking alongside the French.

Two Territorial divisions from the Third Army were attacking the Gommecourt Salient, the 46th (North Midland) from the north and the 56th (London) from the south. It had been planned that, in the first stage each would seize the German trench system on the shoulders of the salient, and then they would attempt to link up behind the village, thus cutting off the garrison there.

The London Division was probably the best Territorial division in France at that time. Its battalions had seen much action yet still contained a high proportion of well-trained pre-war volunteers. The soldiers themselves were mostly well educated, intelligent men from London's commercial class and many would have become officers in other divisions.

* As far as is known, this man's bravery was not recognized by the award of a medal, but Walter Ritchie, a young drummer of the Seaforth Highlanders, was awarded the Victoria Cross for standing on the parapet of a captured trench near the Quadrilateral and repeatedly sounding the 'Charge' when nearby men were beginning to retire without orders. Drummer Ritchie survived the heavy fire of the Germans and the remainder of the war.

The Londoners' assault had started well. Within an hour four battalions – the London Rifle Brigade, Queen Victoria's Rifles, the Rangers and the London Scottish – attacking from their newly dug trench in No Man's Land had seized nearly every one of the German trenches which were their objectives. 'By 9 A.M. we had taken our final objective, although the German trenches were so badly smashed up, we didn't really know where we were. From my company of 150 men there were only thirty-five who were not wounded. That final trench was, then, the safest post in the whole countryside, for our own guns were not firing on it, nor were the Germans; they were not sure whether their own men had been ousted or not.' (Maj. C. J. Low, D.S.O., 1st London Scottish)

A fifth battalion, the Queen's Westminster Rifles, had followed the leading troops and was preparing to attempt the second phase, the link-up behind Gommecourt village with the North Midland Division. The infantry of the division all came from London, but the divisional Pioneer battalion was the 1/5th Cheshires. Some of the Cheshire platoons followed the London battalions to construct strong-points in the German trenches. The platoon with the Westminsters was commanded by a second-lieutenant, George Stuart Arthur.

At 9 A.M., the Westminsters were due to send a bombing party up the German trench which led to the rear of Gommecourt village and the projected meeting with the North Midland men. The Westminsters had suffered so many casualties that none of their own officers could be found to organize the bombers. But 2nd Lieut Arthur was there and, leaving his pioneer work, he took over the Westminster bombers and led the attack himself, although he had been slightly wounded in the arm.

The party succeeded in bombing its way up 400 yards of German trench until just short of the point where it should have met the North Midland men coming down from the other side of the salient. But the North Midlanders were not there. Instead, 2nd Lieut Arthur and his bombers met a strong force of Germans. A fierce bombing fight took place in which the Westminsters' grenades were soon exhausted. 2nd Lieut Arthur ordered his men to retire whilst he remained behind to hold the Germans a little longer. As the Westminsters made their way back to safety they could hear

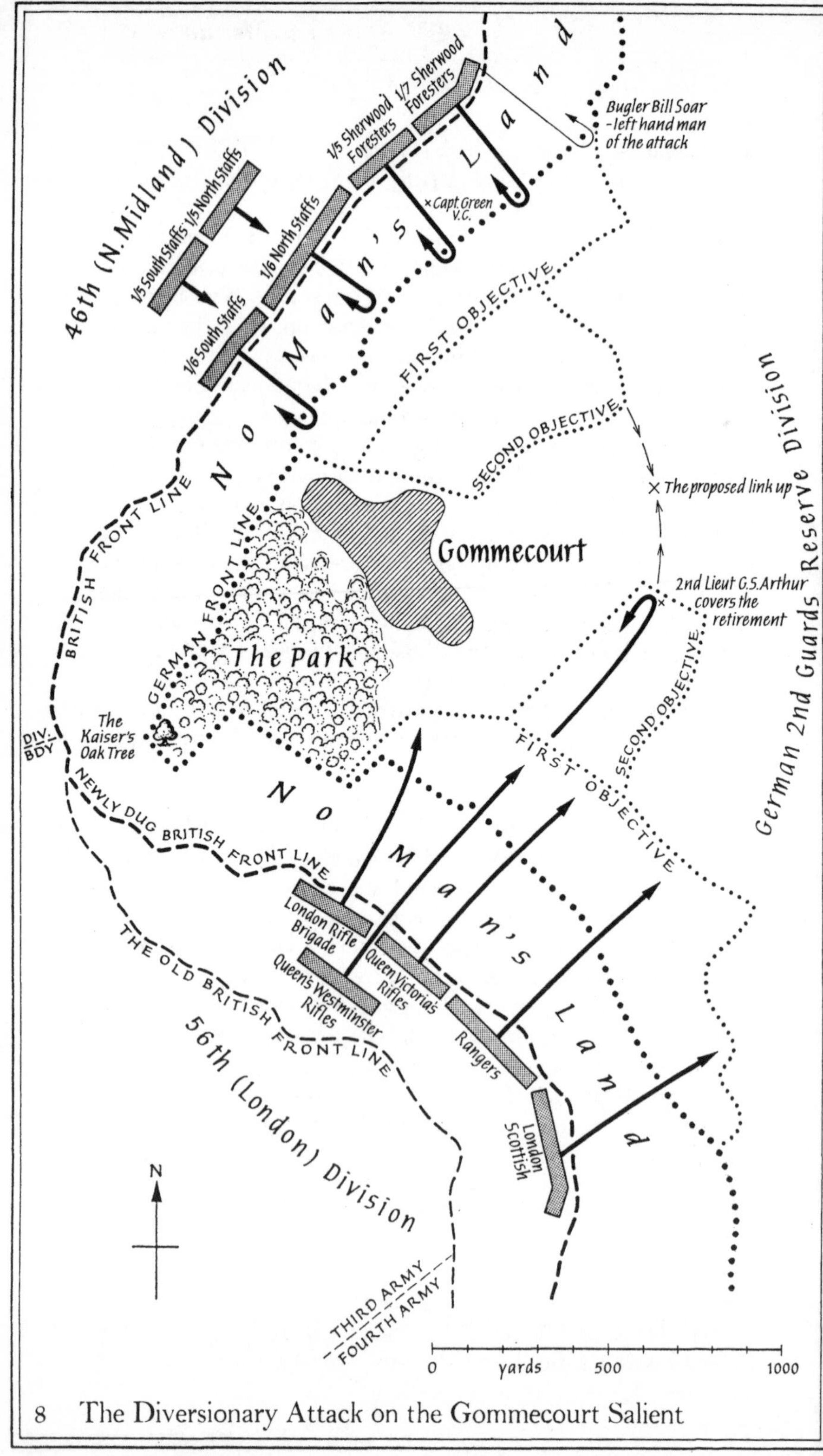

8 The Diversionary Attack on the Gommecourt Salient

the sounds of fighting as the Pioneer officer covered their retreat. He was never seen again.*

The most extensive and promising British success was that of the four divisions of Rawlinson's right wing. These had nearly all taken their first objectives; only Fricourt still held out in the German front line. Now the divisions were proceeding, with varying fortunes, to their next objectives.

In their captured dug-out in Lonely Trench, near Fricourt, Lieut Philip Howe's small force of 10th West Yorks had managed to keep the Germans at bay for most of the morning, but by midday their ammunition was dangerously low. Howe asked his men whether they wished to fight their way back to their own trenches, or whether they preferred to surrender. He was very relieved when it was agreed that they would give themselves up when their ammunition ran out. Just before this happened, however, they heard the sounds of bombing coming along the trench to their left. Howe and his men waited. If these were more Germans, they were finished.

But the men who came were friends, soldiers of the 10th Yorks and Lancs. All the trenches on the left were now securely held by the British. A delighted Philip Howe took his party through the British-held trenches and back across No Man's Land. As they approached their original trenches the second-lieutenant said lightheartedly to Howe, 'Let me put my arm around your shoulder and we can stagger in like wounded heroes', thinking to impress the rest of the battalion which they expected to meet there. Instead, they found that of the original 800 men, only forty could be mustered including Howe's party. The second-lieutenant went off to have his wounded leg treated but Howe decided to stay, in spite of the bullet hole in his hand, as there were no other officers. He spread his men out along the whole of the battalion front, for the trenches opposite them were still held by the Germans.

Five miles to the north, the 36th (Ulster) Division was performing a glorious feat of arms. Six of its battalions were to capture the German front line on a wide, open plateau

* Probably due to lack of witnesses and an uncertainty at that time of the exact identity of 2nd Lieut Arthur (a native of Halifax, Yorkshire), no medal was awarded for this action.

between the village of Thiepval and the River Ancre; two more, on the other side of the river, were to clear out some German positions on the edge of the marshy river valley. Behind the German front line in the division's main attack sector lay one of the biggest German redoubts, the Schwaben, and, beyond this, the German second main position. This sector was on that part of the front where Haig had persuaded Rawlinson to include the German second line in his objectives. For this purpose, the third Ulster brigade would follow the leading troops, pass through the captured Schwaben Redoubt and attack the German second line.

For their opening attack, the Ulstermen had one great advantage; their own front line was on the edge of the Thiepval Wood so that their assembly positions were hidden from the enemy. By 6 A.M., ten battalions had assembled in the wood; desultory German shelling caused some casualties (it was here that Billy McFadzean was killed in the grenade accident) but most of the attackers were safe.

The Ulstermen awaited the attack in a state of emotional, religious fervour. Many were members of the Orange Order and some had sent for the orange sashes of their order and wore these over their bulky equipment. Hymns were sung, prayers were said. The Ulstermen were ready for battle although at least one had succumbed to an old Irish failing: 'Next to me was a man who was a well-known drinker; his water bottle was full of some French stuff and he was drinking all night. When it was time to go over, he collapsed, drunk. I heard, later, that he came round, went over the top fighting mad and got taken prisoner.' (L/Cpl J. A. Henderson, Belfast Young Citizens)

The leading battalions had been ordered out from the wood just before 7.30 A.M. and laid down near the German trenches. On one part of their frontage they had the added advantage of a sunken road, which ran along No Man's Land, and many men assembled there. At zero hour the British barrage lifted. Bugles blew the 'Advance'. Up sprang the Ulstermen and, without forming up in the waves adopted by other divisions, they rushed the German front line. The wire was well cut; the Germans were slow coming up from their dug-outs. After a short, fierce fight, the front-line trench was captured along most of its length. By a combination of sensible tactics and Irish dash, the prize that eluded so

Δ These men are in an assembly trench soon after dawn on 1 July; some are still asleep. Scaling ladders will enable them to advance at zero hour.

∇ Loading a Stokes mortar bomb ('Toffee Apple' or 'Plum Pudding') near Beaumont Hamel. These were very effective in cutting wire but many of the bombs failed to explode.

The first British mine goes up. The eighteen tons of explosive under Hawthorn Redoubt explodes at 7.20 am. The photographer is nearly half a mile away.

Δ The crater left by the explosion of the mine on the edge of Mash Valley; the photographer is 650 yards from the crater. Immediately behind the trees, which line the Albert-Bapaume road, is all that remains of the village of La Boisselle.

∇ Men of the 1st Lancashire Fusiliers fix bayonets ready for the attack. The second lieutenant is one of the few officers to dress in an ordinary soldier's uniform.

Δ Troops of the 29th Division advance into No Man's Land. One man is already hit and falls into the British wire.

∇ The Tyneside Irish commence their ill-fated attack on the Tara-Usna Line. Another wave, in the trench, prepares to follow those already in the open. The hillside over which they will move is devoid of any cover.

Δ A dead British bomber in the trenches near Mametz. The original caption indicates that the trench was probably Dantzig Alley, taken on the afternoon of 1 July. The soldier may be from the 2nd Queens or from the 6th or 7th Manchester Pals.

∇ German prisoners coming out of the British trench system facing Mametz. They are probably Württembergers of the 109th Reserve Regiment. The lightly wounded British soldier (*centre*) has deliberately elbowed the German out of the line. The crowd of men in the background are a Pioneer battalion, the Oldham Pals, waiting to move up.

Δ German prisoners, headed by four officers, being marched to the rear behind the successful British right wing. Many British soldiers comment on the height of the men in certain German regiments; the tall officer seen here certainly towers above his diminutive escort.

∇ German dead in their front-line trench.

Δ British machine-gunners giving support near La Boisselle, 1 July. Judging from the angle of the gun, it would appear that they engaged in providing long-range harassing fire over the heads of attacking troops.

∇ A badly wounded man is rushed to the rear but he died thirty minutes after this picture was taken.

many, the capture of a long section of the German front line, had been accomplished.

Fresh men pressed forward from the wood and took the fight into the Schwaben Redoubt, but two things happened to hold up the Ulsters. The advance of the 32nd Division on their right had broken down almost as soon as it had started; the reader will remember how the c.o.'s of the battalions attacking the Thiepval Spur had refused to commit their last companies to an attack they thought had failed. From the ruins of Thiepval village and the château on the spur, a network of German machine-gun posts, having beaten off the attack on their own front, turned on the Ulster Division. These machine-guns could fire straight down the old No Man's Land outside Thiepval Wood and every Ulster soldier that followed the leading troops had to brave this fire.

The second obstacle was the fierce resistance of the Schwaben garrison. These Germans had not been caught in their dug-outs like some of the front-line defenders. The Ulsters had to fight hard for the redoubt but their Irish spirit was roused; they had captured one German trench, they could capture the Schwaben.

While the six leading battalions fought for the redoubt, the follow-through brigade, four Belfast battalions, moved up for their attack on the German second line. When they tried to cross No Man's Land they suffered heavy loss from the machine-guns in Thiepval and from the usual German artillery barrage. When some of his men wavered, one company commander from the West Belfasts, Maj. George Gaffikin, took off his orange sash, held it high for his men to see and roared the traditional war-cry of the battle of the Boyne: 'Come on, boys! No surrender!' This action drew a whole crowd of men after him over No Man's Land.

Instead of an easy passage to the German second line, the Belfast Brigade had to join in the fight for the Schwaben. There were now men from at least eight battalions fighting in the redoubt. No battalion staffs had been allowed across, by divisional order, but two lieutenant-colonels had disobeyed; one was killed as soon as he moved off from the wood, the other failed to get into the Schwaben. The fighting there was an uncoordinated, vicious, close-quarter mêlée: 'We were being fired at by a sniper; he got five or six of us before we found him. My boy-oh was wounded and sheltering behind a rolled-up stretcher. Our sergeant major took Jerry's rifle away from him and smashed it across his head.' (Pte J. Grange, Belfast Young Citizens)

'I was firing on some Germans when there was a loud explosion near me and part of the torso of a man, clothed in a khaki jacket, landed just in front of my Lewis gun.' (Pte R. Irwin, Tyrone Volunteers)

'Another chap and myself were in a shell hole, near a trench, and we could see a party of Germans coming down it, just their helmets showing. I told the other chap, "I'll take the first one; you cover the second." We had to wait some time, until they came into a shallower part of the trench, and then we both let fly. I think I got mine and the rest all scampered back like a lot of scalded cats. Later, I heard some bombing about 100 yards away, so I peeped over to have a look and found myself looking down the barrel of a German rifle, only twenty yards away. I got the hell out of it as fast as I could.' (C.S.M. R. S. Drean, M.C., East Belfast Volunteers)

'We came to three dug-outs, which we thought contained Germans. We threw the contents of three full bags of grenades down the steps. The yells and screams of those boys down there were wicked. The German dug-outs had fire-places with chimneys or they may have been ventilation shafts. Some of the men from our trench-mortar battery were there and were pulling the pins out of the trench-mortar bombs and dropping them down these pipes. We could hear them explode down below.' (Pte J. Devennie, Derry Volunteers)

'I found a German, badly wounded. I could see from his face that he was mad with thirst. I gave him my water, although it was against orders. Then I found one of our men; he was terribly wounded, shot in the head and his leg nearly off. He begged me to kill him but I couldn't do it.' (L/Cpl J. A. Henderson, Belfast Young Citizens)

It was in this fierce fighting that the Ulster Division earned its second Victoria Cross of the day. Capt. Eric Bell, a Tyrone Volunteers officer attached to a Trench Mortar Battery, advanced with the infantry into the Schwaben. His many acts of bravery included *throwing* trench-mortar bombs at the Germans. He was killed whilst leading infantrymen who had lost their own officers.

By mid-morning the fight was over. The whole of the

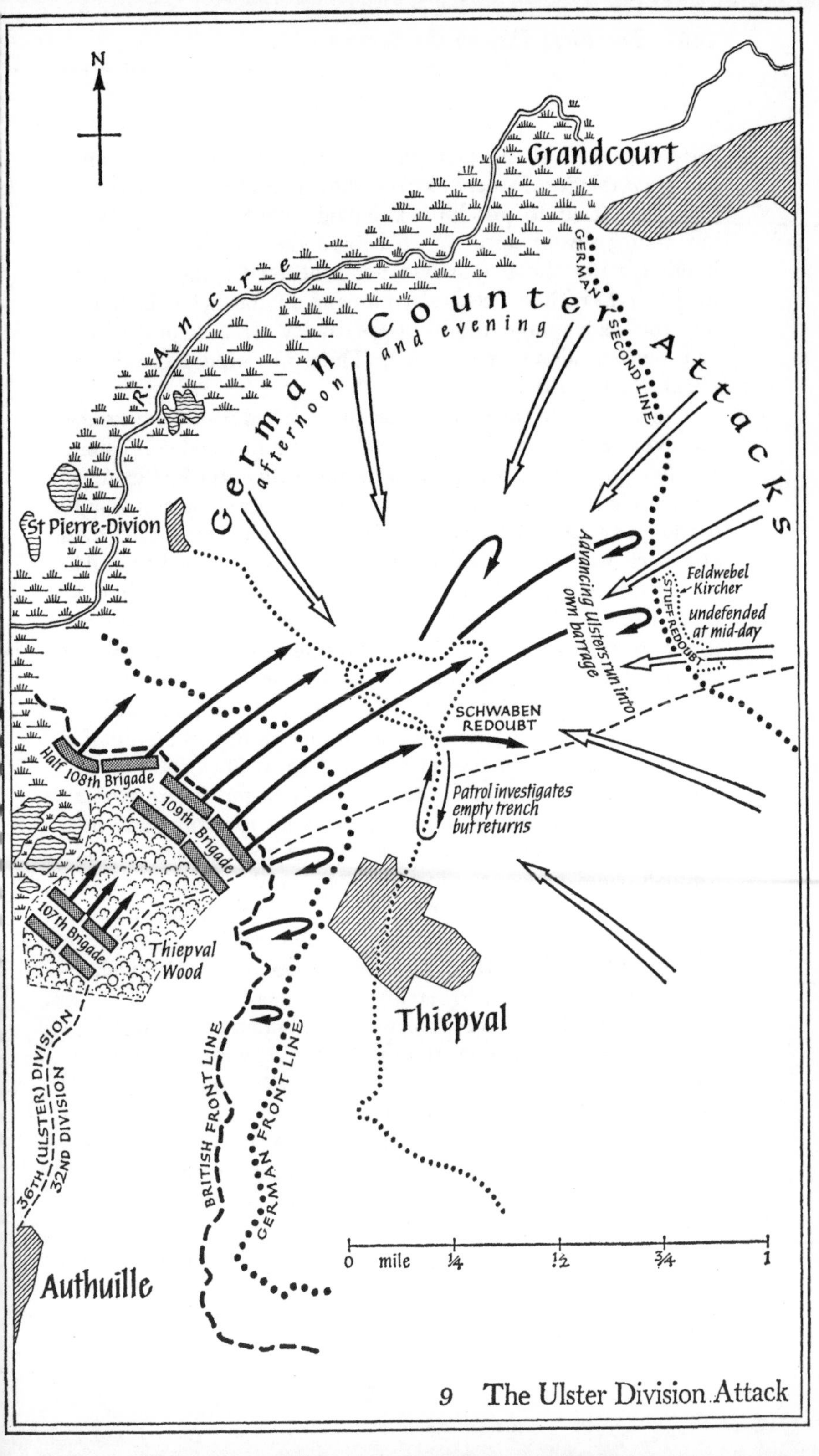

9 The Ulster Division Attack

Schwaben was in the Ulstermen's hands and 500 Germans had been taken prisoner. Patrols were sent out to the flanks; one, that tried to get into Thiepval village, was repulsed but another went up a trench behind the village and found it empty. But the troops had not rehearsed a move to the flanks and, with no central command in the Schwaben, no one took advantage of this opportunity. If a strong force had pushed along the trench, Thiepval could have been attacked from the rear.

The advance to the German second line had been rehearsed, however. But, instead of a brigade, casualties and confusion had left only two small parties to make this attack. Leaving the shelter of the Schwaben, these advanced over open ground to the wire of the German second line, but, for once, the attackers were ahead of schedule. A German soldier tells what happened: 'At 9 o'clock, I was down in a dug-out in the Feste Staufen (Stuff Redoubt) when someone shouted down to me in an amazed voice "The Tommies are here." I rushed up and there, just outside the barbed wire, were ten or twenty English soldiers with flat steel helmets. We had no rifle, no revolver, no grenades, no ammunition, nothing at all; we were purely artillery observers. We would have had to surrender but, then, the English artillery began to fire at our trench; but a great deal of the shells were too short and hit the English infantrymen and they began to fall back. If the English could have got through, they would have only met clerks, cooks, orderlies and such like. For a distance of several hundred metres to right and to left from us there were no German soldiers. It was a decisive moment.' (Feldwebel Felix Kircher, 26th Field Artillery Regiment)

Unfortunately, the advance was on too narrow a frontage and the Ulsters had spent too much of their strength getting across No Man's Land and through the Schwaben Redoubt. 'We were pinned down in the open just outside the German wire which was covering their second line. It was just Hell; the British artillery were at us, the German artillery were at us and rifle and machine-gun fire as well.' (Cpl G. A. Lloyd, West Belfast Volunteers)

'There were precious few of us who got to the next German line; the wire was hardly cut. I could see right through into what was left of Grandcourt village and saw, quite clearly, a crowd of Germans there, getting ready to counter-attack. We tried to get through but it was no good and we had to go back.' (C.S.M. R. S. Drean, M.C., East Belfast Volunteers)

The glorious advance of the Ulster Division was, for the time being at least, over. These were the only men to reach the German second line anywhere. It was a penetration nearly as deep as that of the Tyneside Irish and the Royal Scots near Contalmaison and certainly the farthest advance by a major unit. The Ulster Division had no Regular battalions attached to it as 'stiffeners', as had some of the New Army divisions, and it was fighting its first battle. But the Ulsters had committed every one of their battalions to the battle. The divisions on either side had still not resumed their attack; indeed, for four miles on either flank there was no advance to distract the German defence. As a result, the Ulstermen in the Schwaben Redoubt were being pounded by shell, mortar and machine-gun. The Germans were gathering reserves for counter-attacks and they so dominated No Man's Land that the Ulster Division was virtually besieged.

The most spectacular of the early successes was that of the 30th Division on the extreme right. The division contained four Liverpool and four Manchester battalions, whose first battle this was, and four Regular battalions, which had been in France since 1914. The initial attack had been completely successful. Four Pals battalions, three from Liverpool and one from Manchester, had stormed and taken the whole of the German front line. At the same time the French on their right and the 18th Division on their left had also successfully carried out the first phase of their attacks. The way to Montauban village, on the top of a slope 1,000 yards away, was open.

Three battalions had been ordered to pass through the leading troops and attack the village. They were the 1st and 2nd Manchester Pals, which would lead the advance, and a Regular battalion, the 2nd Royal Scots Fusiliers, whose C.O. was in overall command of the attack.

Paddy Kennedy and his two friends had been in the old British front line since their escape from the accidental explosion which had blown up the trench-mortar, the mortar gunners and most of the half-platoon of Manchesters who had been waiting to carry forward the mortar bombs in the advance. No one had given the three survivors any orders; they had no idea where their own battalion was. When more Manchesters reached this trench on their way to Montauban, the three decided to join them. Before doing so, Kennedy took off his heavy load and, keeping only a few items, dumped the remainder. He made careful note of its position, hoping that he could recover it later. When the 800 men of the 1st Manchester Pals moved on they were joined by these three self-appointed reinforcements.

At first all went well. As the three battalions advanced in perfect order up the slope, a few German shells fell among them, but the ground had been so pulverized by the British bombardment that the explosions in the soft earth caused few casualties. But the attackers were now in an exposed position with both flanks wide open, for the French had decided to go no farther and the 18th Division was held up by strong opposition.

On the left a single German machine-gun crew spotted the Manchesters and Scots Fusiliers and opened fire. The attack faltered. 'German machine-gun fire was dropping our men by the hundred and when we came to a sunken road we halted in it for cover, although it was wrong to do so. Fortunately our quartermaster sergeant, who was twice the age of most of us and had served his time as a Regular with the Coldstream Guards, came along and very quickly did the necessary rallying and urged us on with his great shouts of what I might call "cheerful command".' (L/Cpl F. Heardman, 2nd Manchester Pals) A Manchester Lewis gunner engaged the German post and silenced it, but not before it had caused heavy casualties to all three battalions, particularly among the officers. All the leading company commanders were killed or badly wounded, one major losing both eyes.

The machine-gun fire had thrown the leading troops into confusion and the meticulous formation of the early advance was lost. Two separate crowds of men charged the village. The capture proved to be easy; the Germans holding a trench outside the village surrendered with hardly a fight. The village itself was in ruins; a French heavy mortar battery had been firing on it for a week. The only living thing to be seen in Montauban was a fox. The Manchesters pushed on to the final objective, a trench just beyond, and this, too, was swiftly taken with more prisoners.

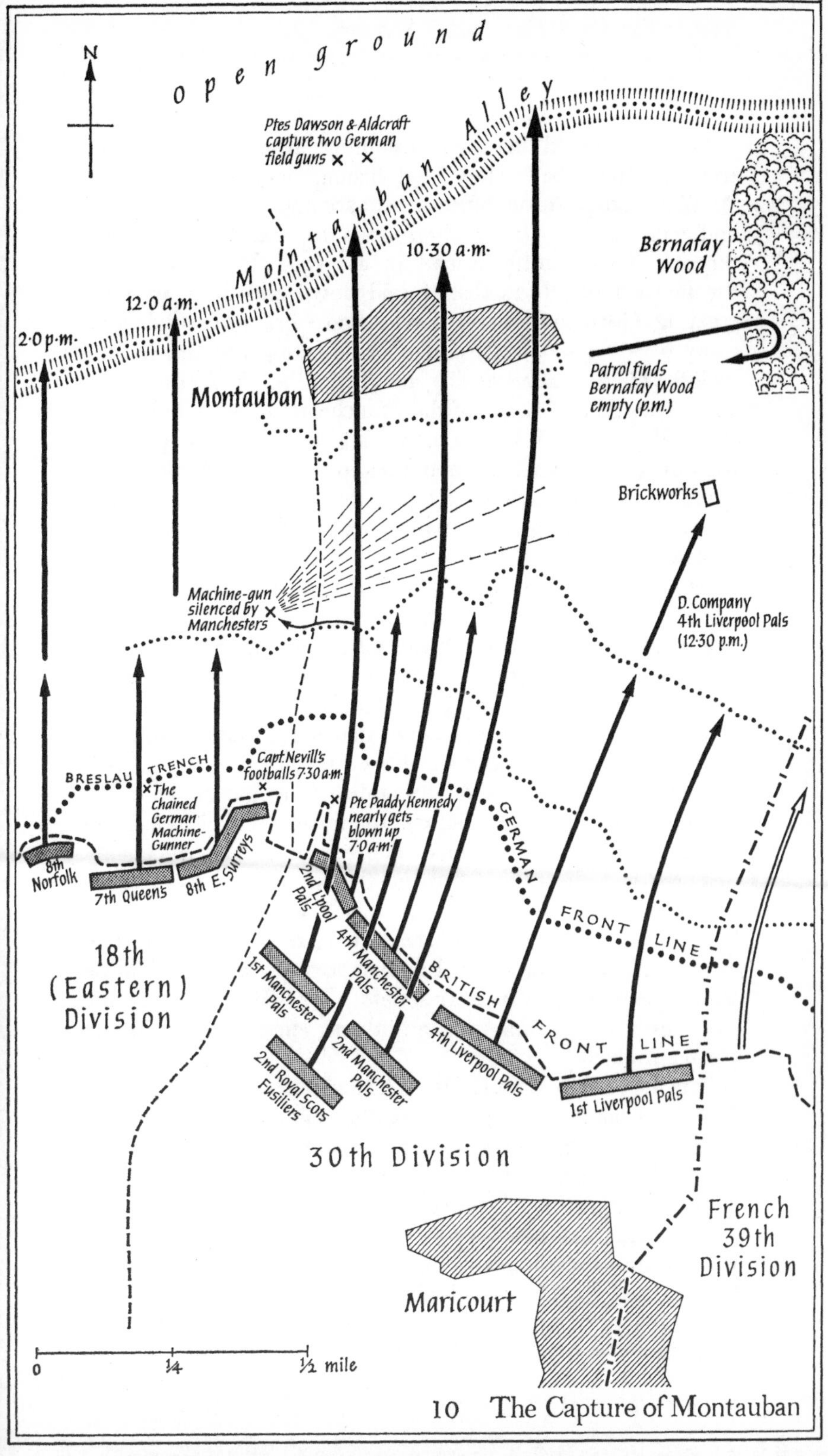

10 The Capture of Montauban

Germans could be seen streaming away from this last trench, Montauban Alley, and fleeing over a wide valley. Artillery observation officers had accompanied the advance and were able to bring their guns to bear on these easy targets. The infantry joined in as well. 'When I got to the far end of Montauban I laid down and fired at a retreating German gun team who were dragging their gun away by a rope. I well remember adjusting my aim for the weight of the bayonet, as taught.' (Pte A. A. Bell, 2nd Manchester Pals) Some of the Manchesters swept down into the valley and, killing or capturing the German gunners, took the guns and hauled them back in triumph to Montauban. Privates Dawson and Aldcraft of the 1st Pals claimed their capture by chalking their names and that of their battalion on two of the guns.

Meanwhile, the Scots Fusiliers had been clearing Montauban's cellars and the surrounding trenches. Over 200 prisoners were collected at the village pump. One of these was an English-speaking doctor who was put to work tending the wounded; many were to speak of his fine work. It proved so difficult to dislodge one sniper that R.E.s placed explosive against his concrete post and blew him up.

The successful troops in Montauban Alley gazed in wonder on an amazing sight. Before them they could see open country and peaceful woods. There was no sign of enemy defences and the only Germans they could see were those fleeing in the distance. Was this the beginning of the breakthrough they had all been told about? Would they receive orders to move still farther forward and seize these seemingly empty woods and fields? Or would the cavalry come up and, passing through them, spread havoc in the German rear?

The men of the 30th Division had achieved a great success. They had taken many prisoners, three field guns and Montauban, the first village to fall in the Battle of the Somme, although the heap of ruins that was all that remained of Montauban had little practical value. The capture of the village had cost nearly 700 casualties, mostly in the two Manchester battalions. A high proportion of this loss had been caused by the one machine-gun on their left flank.

What was particularly gratifying about the success of the 30th Division was that Gen. Rawlinson had been so uncertain of its ability to fulfil its task that he had nearly taken it out of the line before the battle and replaced it with another.

On these sectors where the British advance had been successful, the first task after the capture of the German trenches was the operation known as 'mopping-up' – the final clearance of German trenches and particularly of their dug-outs. Special parties of men, equipped mainly with hand grenades, had been detailed for this essential duty, but there were other methods: 'In clearing the dug-outs, which normally had two entrances, we first of all shouted for the occupants to come out. If this had no effect, we would throw a heavy stone down one entrance which would generally send them all racing out of the other end.' (Pte W. C. Bennett, 8th Norfolks)

'My platoon commander and I came to a dug-out; we thought there were Germans inside. I fired down the steps with a Lewis gun and then they surrendered. There were twenty-three of them, but they gave us no trouble; they were as scared as we were.' (Cpl T. McClay, M.M., Tyrone Volunteers)

'One of our bombers, ignoring instructions, pulled a hessian curtain aside in the entrance of a dug-out, instead of calling out first. As he bent down to call out, a German hiding behind the curtain delivered an upper-cut. Infuriated that a German should punch him on the jaw, he screamed at him to come out. It was a low entrance, the German had to emerge bending down. The bomber raised his knobkerrie and felled the German with one blow.' (L/Cpl H. C. Lancashire, 1/4th London)*

The British often over-estimated the value of their grenades which were not sufficiently powerful to kill all the occupants of a large dug-out. Because of this, dug-outs which had been 'cleared' once often came to life later with unfortunate results. One man soon found the answer to this problem: 'I remember my platoon sergeant kicking a full box of grenades with the pins removed down the steps of a dug-out but I didn't wait to see what happened.' (Pte W. B. Bird, 12th Middlesex)

After months of trench warfare, when the enemy had never

* A knobkerrie was a spiked iron ball on the end of a stick.

been seen, the taking of German prisoners made the British soldier realize that his opponent did indeed exist and that he could even be mastered in battle. 'I came face to face with a great big German who had come up unexpectedly out of a shell hole. He had his rifle and bayonet at "the ready". So had I, but mine suddenly felt only the size of a small boy's play gun and my steel helmet shrank to the size of a small tin lid. Then, almost before I had time to realize what was happening, the German threw down his rifle, put up his arms and shouted "*Kamerad*". I could hardly believe my eyes.' (L/Cpl F. Heardman, 2nd Manchester Pals)

It is not surprising that in the fury of the battle and after the advice given to them by their senior officers, some British soldiers should refuse to take prisoners. 'In the heat of the attack, a German came running past us, surrendering. One of us dropped a grenade with the pin out into his wide pocket and waved him back. When it went off we all laughed, me included.' (Pte T. S. Frank, 2nd Green Howards)

'We are filled with a terrible hate. Our actions are born of a terrible fear, the will to survive. Some of the Germans were getting out of their trenches, their hands up in surrender; others were running back to their reserve trenches. To us they had to be killed. Kill or be killed. You are not normal.' (L/Cpl J. J. Cousins, 7th Bedfords)

'I watched our troops bringing German prisoners back, trying to make them walk in the open alongside a communication trench. The Germans kept going down into the trench. This annoyed the escorts so much that, eventually, they threw some grenades among the Germans and left them to it.' (Lieut A. W. Lee, M.C., 22nd Infantry Brigade H.Q.)

Sometimes the killing of prisoners was more cold-blooded: 'I watched some Germans coming out of a dug-out and surrendering. They were holding up photographs of their families and offering watches and other valuables in an attempt to gain mercy but as the Germans came up the steps, a soldier, not from our battalion, shot each one in the stomach with a burst from his Lewis gun.' (Pte J. H. Harwood, 6th Royal Berks)

This killing of German prisoners was the exception rather than the rule. The British soldier was, by nature, a friendly man who treated his captives well when the heat of battle had passed. 'German prisoners were being rounded up and as they passed us, our chaps were giving them cigarettes. I heard one man say to a wounded German, "Give us your mum's address, mate – and I'll drop her a line".' (Capt. W. Chetham-Strode, 2nd Border)

A wounded Belfast man took shelter from German shelling in a captured dug-out and found himself alone with ten German prisoners. They treated him well, dressing his wound and making him comfortable in a bunk. The Ulsterman passed round a packet of Woodbines and soon struck up a friendly conversation with an English-speaking German. 'I asked him who would win the war. He replied that no one would win. If either Germany or England lost they would rise again as both nations were too strong to be kept down.' (Pte J. Grange, Belfast Young Citizens)

It was not always easy to get the captured Germans back to the British trenches. At Gommecourt, where the German barrage fell on No Man's Land all morning, the battalions of the London Division captured about 300 Germans. These were sent back but only 178 arrived; the remainder were either killed by their own barrage or escaped in the confusion. Similarly, the Ulster Division took many prisoners who were sent back with one Ulsterman as escort to every sixteen Germans. In a race across No Man's Land the Germans were reported to have won easily. Sometimes the British were so hard pressed that they could not spare sufficient escorts. 'I was detailed to take back about sixty German prisoners on my own. As they were being marched back I thought all that lot could easily have turned on me. I was only sixteen.' (Pte H. E. Bathurst, 8th Devons)

Once safely over No Man's Land and away from the worst of the shelling both prisoners and escorts could relax. The Germans were formed into groups and marched off to the waiting cages. These columns of prisoners were a source of great encouragement to fresh British troops moving up to the fighting. 'I saw a crowd of prisoners being brought back by the K.O.Y.L.I.s. One small German was whimpering and a much bigger one, next to him, threatened to hit him if he didn't behave. There were so many prisoners I really thought the war would soon be over.' (Pte J. P. Turner, 12th Northumberland Fusiliers)

Another group of Germans were more truculent. 'We watched some Germans being marched by. The leading one was very tall and as he passed us he spoke to the others and they all started laughing because we were wounded. We were near one of our field guns and an artilleryman, only a short man, put down the shell he was carrying and going up to the German, grabbed hold of him and hit him very hard. They all put up their hands promptly and stopped laughing. I felt very proud as I watched this.' (Pte J. L. Hunt, 6th Royal Berks)

Some soldiers from the Cambridge Battalion found a solitary German wandering about, lost, behind the British line. They took charge of him and solemnly made him salute a photograph of Lord Kitchener.

Once the mopping-up had been completed, calm descended on the captured trenches and those British troops without urgent business were able to look around. The favourite occupation of many was to go souvenir hunting; the ceremonial German helmets, binoculars and revolvers were great favourites. So quiet was it on one sector, that the post corporal of the 6th Royal Berks appeared in the captured trenches and calmly distributed the battalion's mail.

The British soldiers were able to examine at leisure the dead or captured enemy and their defences. Men from the 3rd Liverpool Pals sorted out the German dead in a trench they had captured and, choosing the largest and smallest corpses they could find, laid the two out side by side as a macabre contrast.

During the battle preceding the capture of these trenches, a single German machine-gun had sometimes held up a whole British battalion or even a brigade. These machine-gunners, specially chosen and trained in their work, often died at their guns, fighting to the last. 'We found a German machine-gun on its sledge, its dead gunner, a grey-haired, elderly man, still holding its handles, his head dropped forward as if asleep and in front of the gun, a pile of empties almost as high as the gun.' (Maj. J. K. Dunlop, 43rd Brigade Machine Gun Company) *

Again, a short distance away, men of the 7th Queens (the Royal West Surreys) captured in Breslau Trench a German chained by his ankle to a machine-gun. 'The man was wounded in the thigh; a real "tough" who obviously chained himself to his gun out of sheer bravado and not by order. He was

* Public Record Office, CAB 45/188.

probably a Bavarian.' (Capt. M. Kemp-Welch, 7th Queens)* After the battle the divisional commander ordered a Court of Inquiry to confirm the accuracy of this incident; it was accepted by him as being true, but gave rise to the story, often repeated but untrue, that the Germans manned their machine-guns with convicts and chained them to their weapons to ensure that they did not run away.

What amazed the British soldiers most was the depth and lavish scale of the German dug-outs. Men wandered from one dug-out to another, amazed at the German ingenuity and envious of the comfort and safety that their enemies had enjoyed. 'We went down into a dug-out and actually found the electric lights still burning. So much for the artillery preparation.' (Pte A. McMullen, Donegal and Fermanagh Volunteers) Coarse jokes were made when double beds and women's clothing, perfume and powder were found. The men were convinced that the Germans had actually entertained their French lady friends in the front line.†

Among the explorers was Paddy Kennedy. He found a small, nervous, black kitten, the pet of some German soldier. Kennedy took pity on the frightened animal and, deciding to take care of it himself, put it in his small pack and fastened it in. A further find was a bottle of perfume, which Kennedy and his pals lightheartedly splashed over their dusty uniforms. This revelry was interrupted by an officer who ordered them out of the dug-out. 'Don't you know there's a war on?'

The day was going well for the British on the right; but on the numerous sectors where they had been repulsed, there began, in mid-morning, the first of a series of small-scale, hastily organized attacks that were to continue through the day, as divisional and corps commanders tried to redeem lost situations and get their men moving forward again.

Opposite Beaumont Hamel, the commander of the 29th

* Public Record Office, CAB/189. Breslau Trench was held by the 6th Bavarian Reserve Regiment. Some books attribute the incident of the chained machine-gunner to the 6th Royal Berks but the capture was made by the 7th Queens.

† When interviewed, German soldiers indignantly denied this possibility; the garments and perfumes were either souvenirs of past leaves or presents for the next leave. For their part, the Germans heard rumours that the Allies had women in their trenches. 'The French were believed to be more active in this matter.' These stories were started by men in German listening posts who claimed they had heard female voices from the opposing trenches.

Division had attacked with two brigades but hardly a man had crossed the German wire. The third brigade was to have followed just over an hour later and gone on to the final objective. Before that hour was up, it was known that the initial attack had failed but not the full extent of the failure. Rockets had been seen to rise from the German trenches, but it was not known whether these were British or German. It seemed inconceivable to the divisional staff that, out of the eight battalions that had attacked, none was in the German trenches. The commander of the reserve brigade was informed that the original plan for his men was cancelled and he was ordered, instead, to mount an immediate two-battalion attack to clear the German front line. With so little time he had no choice in which battalions to use; the two nearest the front line would have to go – the 1st Essex and the 1st Newfoundland. The brigade commander issued the necessary orders to them.

The Newfoundlanders had heard the pre-attack bombardment, the explosion of the Hawthorn Redoubt mine and then the German machine-guns when the leading brigades made their attacks. An anxious wait followed while wounded and rumour brought the news that the attack had not been successful. 'But it was recalled that the awards awaiting them were not confined to the honours of the battle. For had not a prominent St Johns society maiden let it be known, by confiding to her friends, and they to all who would listen, that she intended to marry the first V.C. in the battalion?' (2nd Lieut C. S. Frost, 1st Newfoundland Regiment)

In his H.Q. dug-out, Lieut-Col. Hadow, the English officer commanding the battalion, received his orders by phone from the brigade commander. These were simple. The Newfoundlanders were to leave their present position as soon as possible and advance to the German front line. The 1st Essex, on their right, would also attack. Hadow asked questions: Were the German trenches held by British or Germans? He was told that the situation was uncertain. Was he to move independently of the Essex? Yes. Colonel Hadow must have been unhappy, but he had been given a direct order. He gave out his own orders and in a few minutes the battalion was ready.

The Newfoundlanders had to go 300 yards before reaching the British front line and then a similar distance across No

Man's Land. In view of the urgency of their orders they went straight over the top from a reserve trench, instead of going to the front line by way of congested communication trenches. As soon as they appeared in the open, the German machine-gunners spotted them and opened fire. No artillery bombardment kept the Germans' heads down; no other targets distracted them, for the Essex had not appeared. They concentrated their fire on the 752 Newfoundlanders advancing over the open ground less than half a mile away. Before the men could even get into No Man's Land they had to pass through several belts of British barbed wire. As the Newfoundlanders bunched together to get through the narrow gaps in this wire, the German machine-gunners found their best killing ground. Dead and wounded men soon blocked every gap, but those still not hit struggled on, having to walk over their comrades' bodies.

More experienced or less resolute men might have given up and sought shelter in such impossible conditions, but not the Newfoundlanders. Those who survived to reach No Man's Land continued towards the German trenches, but they had no chance. A few dozen men could not cross No Man's Land without any support in broad daylight and, inevitably, the German fire cut these down. The attack was watched by a survivor of an earlier attack from a nearby shell hole: 'On came the Newfoundlanders, a great body of men, but the fire intensified and they were wiped out in front of my eyes. I cursed the generals for their useless slaughter, they seemed to have no idea what was going on.' (Pte F. H. Cameron, 1st King's Own Scottish Borderers) Only a handful of Newfoundlanders reached the German wire. There they were shot.

The attack had lasted forty minutes. Rarely can a battalion have been so completely smashed in such a short time. Of those who had attacked, ninety-one per cent had become casualties – twenty-six officers and 658 men.* Every officer who had left the trenches had been killed or wounded, even some who had no right to be there at all: the quartermaster, a captain, whose normal duties kept him behind the lines, was one of the wounded.

* Some accounts give the casualties as twenty-six and 684, but those quoted above are from the battalion War Diary. Possibly the difference of twenty-six may be the officers having been mistakenly counted twice in the later accounts.

What had this battalion, which had sailed with such high hopes from St Johns a year and a half earlier, achieved? It is probable that not a single German soldier was killed or wounded by their attack and no friendly unit had been helped to improve its position. The more experienced Essex battalion had insisted on going up the communication trenches to the front line before starting its attack; this manoeuvre had taken two hours, by which time the Newfoundlanders' attack was over. The Essex, too, failed to reach the German wire, but their more careful approach kept casualties down to one third of the Newfoundlanders' terrible total.

As the morning drew to a close, the battlefield lost some of the noise and violence of the early, intense fighting. Where an attack had been successful, the troops rested on their final objectives, not yet much disturbed by the Germans. The small parties which had only precarious footholds in the German trenches had to fight to maintain their positions, but for these, too, there were quiet periods. The British artillery was still in action, but the firing of their guns and the explosions of their shells far away in the German lines had become a background noise, hardly noticed by the men on the battlefield. German shell fire too had slackened on some sectors, but it was quick to return if called for.

Over most of the front, No Man's Land itself appeared to be completely deserted except for the pitiful bundles of khaki which showed where men had been hit. To the onlooker there was no sign of the thousands of men who had gone to ground there. The sun, high in the sky now, was blazing from a cloudless sky. It was a very hot day and there was hardly a breath of wind. Overhead, an occasional R.F.C. aeroplane swooped close to the ground, looking for signs of life.

For the wounded out in the open the hours seemed endless and they were also in great danger. The Germans were furious at the persistent sniping from wounded British in No Man's Land. To them the British were defeated, the attack completely broken. Released from the tension of the week of shelling in their dug-outs, they had thrown caution to the winds and jumped up onto their parapets, convinced the British would accept the defeat. To be sniped at from No Man's Land, especially by wounded men, was, to them, treachery.

Angrily, the Germans retaliated. They shot to kill at anything that moved. No longer was a wounded man shown any mercy. They watched bodies for any sign of movement. If a wounded man moved involuntarily, a shot rang out and he never moved again. Either he was dead or he had learned his lesson. 'I had been wounded in both legs early in the attack and had fainted from loss of blood. Later in the morning I came round and found my steel helmet was off. I felt terribly exposed without it and reached forward very slowly to try and put it back over my head but as soon as I moved a bullet hit me in the shoulder.' (Pte H. Kemp, Grimsby Chums)

Those who were safe in shell holes could do little but watch in anguish. 'It was a real shame to see poor fellows with lovely Blighty wounds being picked off as they tried to crawl away.' (Pte A. Fretwell, Sheffield City Battalion)

At Gommecourt, Capt. John Green, the medical officer of a Derby Territorial battalion, was hit as he searched for wounded in No Man's Land. Despite this, he went to help a machine-gun officer, badly hurt and caught fast in the German barbed wire. Capt. Green succeeded in freeing this officer and dressed his wounds in a nearby shell hole, although the Germans were throwing grenades at them the whole time. Capt. Green then dragged his patient over No Man's Land and had almost reached safety when he was, himself, hit again and killed. The machine-gun officer died that night. Capt. Green was awarded a posthumous Victoria Cross.

Those who were unhurt had settled down in shell holes to make the best of their enforced rest. Provided they stayed out of sight, they were fairly safe: 'I suppose a shell hole is not the best place from which to admire anything but, believe it or not, waving about just over my head were two full-blown red poppies which stood out in pleasant contrast against the azure blue sky.' (Pte G. E. Waller, Glasgow Boys' Brigade Battalion)

Others became pessimistic about their chances of survival: 'As I crouched there in a shell hole I became so weary of the whole ghastly business that I began wishing that if I was going to be killed I could get it over quickly. I don't remember praying, although I had been a devout Anglo-Catholic before joining the army. I was more curious about death than afraid of it. Would there be a sudden blackness, like the switching off of a light and would one be aware that this blackness was death? As each approaching shell seemed likely to explode on top of me in the shell hole I braced myself to meet the threatened oblivion. What really frightened me was the possiblity of being shattered by a shell but not killed outright, and then having to lie there unattended until I died miserably and painfully.' (Pte W. Slater, 2nd Bradford Pals)

10

Review at Noon

At noon, after four and a half hours of bitter fighting, the fortunes of the day were almost decided. For the British commanders and their men, the second part of the morning had brought no dramatic improvement despite the commitment to the battle of nearly 100,000 British infantrymen from 129 battalions.

In Gen. Rawlinson's Fourth Army the right wing was the only sector which could give cause for real satisfaction. The divisions attacking northward, from the lower arm of the 'L', had all made good progress, although none had done as well as the 30th with its spectacular capture of Montauban. The 30th Division was the only one of the thirteen assaulting divisions to take and hold all its objectives during the morning.

Turning the corner of the 'L' it was mostly a heartbreaking story of failure on the remainder of the Fourth Army front all the way to Serre nine miles away, the only exception being the blazing success of the Ulster Division near Thiepval. Astride the main road to Pozières and Bapaume, on Rawlinson's vital centre, there had been no improvement. Similarly, Hunter-Weston's attack with three divisions, which would have formed the northern flank guard, had been completely repulsed. But as there had been no progress in the centre, there was now no flank to be guarded. On all these sectors some of the earlier captures of small stretches of German trenches had been lost, the attackers having been driven out, as were Reginald Bastard's men, or wiped out like the Tyneside Irish party.

In the diversionary battle at Gommecourt the North Midland Division had fared badly and those few of its men who had got into the German trenches had been forced back, killed or captured. When 2nd Lieut Arthur and the Queen's Westminsters' bombers pushed through behind the village, the Germans had been in complete control of all their positions on the north of the salient. The London Division still held most of its captures, although it had recoiled from its farthest advance.

What was the best course of action open to those directing the actions of both the London Division and the Ulster Division? The Londoners belonged to the Third Army and were taking part in a diversion, the Ulstermen were part of the main Fourth Army attack; but the problems facing the commanders in both cases were identical: what to do about a successful division stranded in the German lines. Each division still had a firm grip of the German trenches, albeit on a narrow frontage. Properly reinforced and directed, these lodgements could be exploited to the flanks and used to bring about the collapse of further German positions. The hard-won early successes would not then have been in vain. But could the divisions be reinforced and could further operations be competently directed? A second option would be to press the divisions alongside the Ulsters and Londoners to resume their attacks. Or again, the commanders might assess the prospects of further success as slim, refuse to risk any more troops and recall the men in the German trenches with the least possible loss. The worst policy of all would be to do nothing and leave the survivors unsupported in the German lines where they would surely be overwhelmed.

It was on decisions being made in various army and corps headquarters that the fate of the Ulster and London Divisions depended.

Looking once more at the whole battlefield, there was complete failure on two thirds of the attack front, while on the right wing there was success and, at Gommecourt and Thiepval, partial success but potential danger. An estimate of the losses at midday shows that nearly 50,000 British soldiers had been killed or wounded. Whatever the afternoon brought, it was going to be a black day for the British Army.

On the fringes of the battlefield were all those arms of the army whose role it was to support the infantry. Where the battle had gone according to plan they had done their duty well, but elsewhere they found it almost impossible to help their infantry comrades.

The newly formed Machine Gun Companies had had a particularly frustrating morning. Their heavy Vickers machine-guns were too vulnerable in the open and, from their position in the British trenches, could give little close support to the infantry in the confused fighting. Even those who had managed to get across No Man's Land and set up their positions in captured trenches could give little help, since the fighting was mostly with grenade and bayonet. Similarly, the Trench Mortar Batteries which had joined in the last few minutes of the artillery bombardment just before the infantry attack had been able to give little support since then, because of the difficulty in knowing which trenches were held by their own troops and which by the enemy. Both the machine-gunners and mortar gunners had suffered heavy casualties from German shelling.

The main task of the Royal Engineers and the Pioneer infantry battalions was to construct new communication trenches across No Man's Land. Shallow tunnels had often been dug there before the battle, leaving only the head cover to be removed on the day of the battle and so provide ready-made trenches. Where the battle had gone well they had been able to do this, but more often the shelling and machine-gun fire had prevented them working and the tunnels had collapsed under German shell fire or become blocked with frightened or wounded infantry. Other sappers and pioneers had been ordered to build trench bridges and clear away barbed wire to enable field guns and cavalry to follow the advancing infantry. But these plans, like so many others, were now irrelevant.

The large number of wounded and the heavy shelling had turned many of the British trenches into a nightmare of congestion and suffering. It was difficult enough to get a badly wounded man away on a stretcher in normal times but, with dead and wounded everywhere, shell fire levelling the trenches and bullets from machine-guns passing just overhead, the stretcher cases could not be moved in any quantity.

Strangely, other trenches were almost deserted. 'The trench was now almost blocked with dead and wounded. One of the latter with both legs shattered was screaming in agony but, scrambling my way a little farther along in the blown-in remains of the trench, I realized that I was now entirely alone. For some time I remained in the ruins of one of the bays, accompanied only by the corpse of a man in number 5 Platoon and a mole, disturbed from its burrow by a shell.' (Pte R. N. Bell, Leeds Pals)

Still alone and trapped by fallen debris in a British trench was L/Cpl Charles Matthews of the 6th Northamptons. He had managed to raise himself to a half-sitting position, but no farther. He had been stuck in this painful attitude until a passing soldier had laid him down again but then hurried away. Matthews spotted a small niche in the side of the trench a few yards away in which he could shelter, but because of his injured leg he could only edge his way forward slowly, using chin and elbows. Every few minutes he had to flatten himself to the floor of the trench as what he was coming to regard as his own personal German battery fired a salvo which exploded a few yards away.

This crawl was interrupted by another visitor, a soldier badly wounded in the face and wrist, who suddenly dropped into the trench beside him. He could not speak but, by mime, appealed to Matthews to dress his wounds, offering only a filthy handkerchief to staunch a prodigious flow of blood. Matthews did what he could but still the blood spurted out, so he directed the wounded man down the trench towards the rear. The poor man would not go but clung to Matthews, soaking his tunic in blood. With his own painful injury, the constant shelling and this man refusing to leave him, Matthews began to think he would go crazy but was saved when a passing signals officers, out inspecting his cables, led the wounded man away but left Matthews to continue his crawl. When he reached the niche, it had taken him just three hours to crawl four yards. He felt exhausted and in severe pain, but at least a little safer from the nearby shell bursts. At midday he was still there wondering whether he ever would be rescued.

There were many wounded, like Charles Matthews, whose condition was desperate. 'A shell landed next to me and I was hit all down my left side. I was in insane agony and took a handful of my morphia tablets and was just going to swallow them when one of my men knocked them out of my hand. He said, "Stop that, you daft bugger."' (Lieut W. J. White, 3rd Tyneside Irish)

'One incident impressed on my mind was one of my company, wounded in the head and apparently dead. I noticed a movement in his scalp and, on examination, saw his brain pulsing where the bone of the scalp had been smashed. I found a stretcher party and the casualty was taken back and I heard, later, that he had survived.' (P e N. H. Norton, 8th Norfolks)

All along the line those wounded who were able to do so were getting out of the trenches as best they could. 'I saw wounded coming down our trench and, to my astonishment, one of them was my brother, who was wounded in the knee by shrapnel, using his rifle and shovel for crutches. I remember asking him if he had any fags as we hadn't a smoke between us. He gave us a 50 tin of Capstans. He made our day.' (Pte E. Green, 23rd Brigade Machine Gun Company)

'The wounded were coming back and passing within two yards of our Lewis gun position. One sergeant shouts to me, "Give them hell; they've shot my bloody lug off." And sure enough his right ear hung in shreds.' (Cpl J. Norton, 8th Norfolks)

By midday the medical services were at full stretch. The divisional units, the Field Ambulances, were coping well, despite the huge number of wounded coming back to them. Those of the divisions actually in action were being helped by the Field Ambulances of nearby reserve divisions, whose own infantry were not yet fighting. From the Field Ambulances the wounded were being passed back as quickly as possible to the Casualty Clearing Stations (c.c.s.'s), so that the forward medical units could continue to accept casualties.

At the c.c.s.'s, however, something had gone wrong with the evacuation process. In spite of Gen. Rawlinson's personal request for eighteen ambulance trains for his army, only one had arrived by midday. At 9 A.M., No. 20 Ambulance Train had left Vecquement for the base hospitals at Rouen with a load of 487 patients, but more than half of these were sick and most of the remainder were wounded from the previous day.

Nearly every c.c.s. had, by now, accepted large numbers of patients from the forward units, and a steady stream of motor ambulances was bringing in more with every hour. Most of the tents and other accommodation were full and the latest arrivals were having to be left outside, laid in long rows in a field on either a blanket or some straw. Harrassed orderlies tried to provide some shade from the hot sun for the wounded outside and attend to their other needs, but were hard pressed to cope with so many. R.A.M.C. officers were ringing up the local railway officers, wanting to know where the ambulance trains had got to.

The British artillery was still potentially the decisive weapon which, properly handled, could have eased the lot of the infantry by shelling the German machine-gun posts which dominated No Man's Land and breaking up the counter-attacks which the Germans were beginning to mount. Some brigade and divisional commanders ignored higher orders and brought their guns back on to more realistic targets, but the danger of hitting friendly troops, whose exact position was unknown, prevented the closest support. Serre and Thiepval, two villages that were full of Germans and were causing heavy British casualties, hardly received a British shell all day because of mistaken reports that British troops had been seen in them. Serre was, however, shelled by the Germans; the confusion was not all on one side.

When the divisions making the initial attack had left their trenches, their places on some sectors had been taken by the reserve divisions which theoretically should have joined the cavalry in any penetration of the German rear. When the Tyneside Irish left the Tara-Usna Line, astride the main road outside Albert, eight battalions from the 19th (Western) Division started to take their place there. These troops marched through the outskirts of ruined Albert and by 10 A.M. were installed in the trenches. They could see little of the battlefield only a mile away because of the smoke and dust; but the long bursts of German machine-gun fire, the absence of prisoners and the stream of returning British wounded soon showed them that the attack on this sector had broken down. They waited here all morning, wondering if they would have to attack in the afternoon where others had failed.

It was quite possible for one part of a unit to be fighting furiously while the remainder, left out of the battle, spent the day in relative safety. A company commander in the London Division's Pioneer battalion describes his day while a fellow-officer, 2nd Lieut Arthur, was losing his life leading a bombing party in the German trenches: 'My recollection, after all these years, is of being in a trench discussing the rumours, helping with the wounded (we had four men killed) and occasionally lying in a bit of shelter, reading *Pickwick*

Papers and watching the activities of a fat and grey rat.' (Capt. P. H. Jolliffe, 1/5th Cheshires)*

Farther back, reserve battalions were on the move, the long columns of men tramping towards the front being covered with dust from passing ambulances, supply lorries and despatch-riders; the motor cyclists shouting out their snatches of news, before disappearing on their urgent business. 'At first the rumours were good: "Gommecourt is taken." "Serre has fallen." "The French have broken through." But later the news became worse. "The K.O.S.B.s only gained a foothold." "The London Scottish were cut up at Gommecourt." "The 46th Division has been wiped out." "Two generals have committed suicide."' (Cpl J. T. Brewer, 1/6th Gloucesters)

Also waiting just behind the front were the three divisions of cavalry. These had risen before dawn and moved up as near to the front as they could. At first the troopers sat in their saddles, ready for action, but as the morning wore on they were allowed to dismount and ease their horses. One cavalry division, the 2nd Indian, was deployed behind the successful infantry divisions on Rawlinson's right wing, admirably placed if it was decided to exploit the infantry success there in the afternoon.

After the clearance of the early morning mist it had become ideal operating weather for the R.F.C.† A succession of aircraft kept watch over each sector of the front trying to maintain visual communication with the attacking troops and passing details of their progress back to the infantry H.Q.'s, observing the fire of the British heavy artillery batteries or keeping German aircraft from the battlefield.

The ground patrols were often fruitless since the British infantry, too close to the Germans, refused to reveal themselves. All morning, the planes flew up and down over No Man's Land and the German trenches hoping to be able to report progress. But the other R.F.C. operations were more successful. The British were so superior in the air on this day, that no German aircraft was able to interfere in the battle.

* Such was the fog of war that Capt. Jolliffe had never heard of the manner of 2nd Lieut Arthur's death when asked about it in 1970. Arthur's story was built up by assembling fragments from many sources.

† Four of the squadrons in action during the day were from No. 9 Wing, R.F.C. The officer commanding the wing was Lieut-Col. Hugh Dowding, later Air Chief Marshal Dowding, who led Fighter Command in the Battle of Britain.

'Just as we were consolidating our position three German planes flew over from their lines and, before we could say anything at all, *one* of ours appeared from out of the blue and went after the Fritz planes. They just turned tail and disappeared.' (Pte W. R. Thompson, 6th Northamptons) In all, nine 'dog fights' took place and one German aeroplane was shot down.

Over the German rear, the artillery-spotting planes went about their work, finding plenty of targets as the Germans were at last forced to reveal the position of their artillery batteries. Using primitive morse 'buzzers', the aerial observers sent back messages which were picked up, if all went well, by R.F.C. wireless operators who were attached to the artillery batteries. These ground operators, who often suffered casualties because they were so close to the front line, rarely saw the rest of the R.F.C. and regarded themselves as the forgotten men of the air arm, but they provided the essential link between the observing planes and the guns.

Above Pozières, a British airman directing artillery fire watched the results of his efforts: 'A Hun 4.5-battery behind a hedge was still firing. This battery was a good one and the commander a sportsman, as he was being heavily strafed by several of our heavies and lighter guns and shells were falling on and round his battery, but he refused to stop firing. Eventually only one gun was left which he kept in action and was still firing when we returned to our 'drome.' (Lieut T. W. Stallibrass, 3 Squadron R.F.C., from his log book)

During the day, forty bombing flights were made by the R.F.C. and a total of four tons of bombs was dropped on such targets as billets, artillery positions, trenches and various forms of transport. A direct hit was claimed on an ammunition train at Cambrai, twenty-five miles behind the front. One pilot was in the air for over five hours, a feat of endurance in the open cockpits of 1916. Another, Lieut J. C. Turner of 27 Squadron, could not release one of his two bombs while bombing Bapaume. In spite of being under attack by two German planes, he flew over the target twice more, finally making the bomb fall by pushing at it with both hands whilst flying the aeroplane with his knees.*

* Lieut Turner, aged twenty, was shot down and killed in Belgium nine weeks later.

The British H.Q.s farther away from the front were now getting more accurate reports of what had happened to the attacking divisions, and decisions were being taken that would affect the progress of the battle in the afternoon. Sometimes it was a fresh formation that was ordered forward to join in the battle; at others, battered units that had failed in the morning received orders, which were backed up by the whole weight of the chain of command, that somehow their attacks should be renewed. Brig.-Gen. Gordon, who three hours earlier had ordered his last battalion into a hopeless attack, was in turn pressed by his divisional commander to attack again. Gordon's quiet reply on the telephone was, 'You seem to forget, sir, that there is now no 70th Brigade.'*

The corps commanders controlling the battle at Thiepval and at Gommecourt had both reached decisions about their divisions which were all but cut off in the German trenches. Both were far from admitting that all hope of success had passed and were determined to continue the attack. Lieut-Gen. Morland's main move was to send part of his reserve division into Thiepval Wood with orders to cross No Man's Land and reinforce the Ulster Division in the Schwaben Redoubt. Lieut-Gen. Snow of VII Corps at Gommecourt chose a different tactic. His 46th (North Midland) Division had failed to penetrate the German trenches on the northern part of the salient in the morning. Snow ordered that division to repeat its attack in the afternoon, in a fresh attempt to encircle Gommecourt village. Snow must have known that the attack of his corps had already fulfilled its diversionary function. By this fresh order, either he, or his army commander, Gen. Allenby, was turning Gommecourt into a separate little battle in its own right.

At Fourth Army, reports had been coming in from the corps all morning, but either the corps were reluctant to repeat the truth and were only sending back the more optimistic reports, or the staff officer responsible for keeping the Fourth Army's Diary was himself an incurable optimist.

8.46 A.M. A wounded captain from the 10th Lincolns reports: 'Germans had had heavy casualties . . . . Lincolns have got over No Man's Land with very few casualties.'

The captain was either a fool or had been misquoted. The

* Public Record Office, CAB 45/188.

Grimsby Chums had lost nearly 500 men and very few of the remainder were in the German lines.

9 A.M. 10th West Yorks are in the northern edge of Fricourt.

Except for Lieut Philip Howe and a handful of men, no one knew where the 10th West Yorks were. They had disappeared.

9 A.M. 29th Division held up in German wire.

This was the first adverse report in the Diary.

11.8 A.M. Ovillers and north of the Bapaume Road is very quiet with hardly any shelling.

Also at Fourth Army H.Q. was Lieut-Gen. Gough, the commander of the cavalry, with a small staff. The only order he sent to his three cavalry divisions during the morning was one at 11.30 A.M. telling them that they would not be moving until 2 P.M. at the earliest. As Gough watched the Fourth Army staff officers marking up their maps, he must have wondered whether Rawlinson would allow him to use the 2nd Indian Cavalry Division to exploit the infantry success of the right wing. Some of its units were quite close to the old British front line opposite Montauban. How Gough must have longed for the order to come.

But to many staff officers, 1 July was just another routine day. 'In the middle of the battle, two runners were sent from brigade with a message; one was hit on the way and the other handed over the message to me. It read, "Please resubmit drawing of the foot of Pte Warke, size of boot 13." Pte Warke, who had particularly big feet, was in the middle of the Schwaben Redoubt at the time. I was furious that such a stupid message should be sent at such a time and stamped it into the mud.' (Capt. N. Strong, Derry Volunteers) *

Another unknown staff officer circulated the following order to many of the units which were in action:

PORK AND BEANS

Certain complaints have been received that no pork can be found in the tins. . . Troops must not be misled by the name *pork* and

* Later Sir Norman Strong, Speaker of the Northern Irish Parliament.

beans, and expect to find a full ration of pork; as a matter of fact the pork is practically all absorbed by the beans.*

For the German soldiers it had been a long morning. The frenzy of the opening attack had passed in most places but sometimes the Germans had to fight hard to maintain their positions against attacks which had been partially successful. 'We built a block in the trench between us and the English who had broken into the trenches on the left. We couldn't see very well when they were coming, but some of our men behind us had better observation, so they would call out to us every time the English approached and then we threw grenades for all we were worth. I've no idea how many we threw; these people attacked us at least fifteen times. We had a big advantage because our grenades were on a stick and with the extra leverage we could throw further.' (Soldat Wilhelm Lange, 99th Reserve Regiment).†

On the British right wing the Germans appeared to be fighting a losing battle. Many fought to the end but there were also others who allowed themselves to be taken prisoner. The fighting was confused and bitter. The following quotations all come from men of a Baden regiment who were gradually succumbing to the attacks of the 7th and 18th (Eastern) Divisions between Mametz and Montauban.

'There were five of us on our machine-gun when I saw an English soldier about twenty metres away to our left. Then our eldest soldier, a painter who came from Pforzheim and had five children, was shot in the forehead and dropped without a word. Next I was shot in the chest. I felt blood run down my back and I fell; I knew the war was over for me. He shot three of us before I even had the chance to use my rifle. I would like to meet that English soldier. He was a good shot.' (Grenadier Emil Kury, 109th Reserve Regiment)‡

'One of the men in my group went completely mad from thirst during the day. He was foaming at the mouth and, despite our shouts, he ran blindly out of our trench towards

* Public Record Office, WO 95/684. The order was definitely sent to all units in III and VIII Corps and possibly to others as well.

† Herr Lange was on the edge of the Schwaben Redoubt. German soldiers usually used the word 'English' when talking of their opponents. He did not realize he was fighting the Ulstermen.

‡ The marksman who wounded Herr Kury was almost certainly a soldier of the 8th Devons.

the English and was shot down.' (Unteroffizier Paul Scheytt, 109th Reserve Regiment)

'We were being fired on from the rear. We thought this was our own infantry, so we jumped out of our trench, all waving and shouting "Higher! Higher!" Then we saw two or three of our men drop wounded and we realized it was the English who were behind us, so we jumped back into our trench. There we had a conference as to whether to surrender. One or two wanted to fight on but there were many in our regiment who were over forty and, unlike the younger men, these had family ties and were the first to suggest surrendering. In the end the others were swayed. We tied a handkerchief to a rifle and waved it and the English came and rounded us up. We were very depressed but we knew that once we had surrendered the English wouldn't shoot us. We could see from their faces that they were as pleased as we were that it was all over, but they took all our watches from us.' (Unteroffizer Gustav Luttgers, 109th Reserve Regiment)

But, on the majority of their front, the Germans were able to look out triumphant, if tired, on to their beaten enemies in No Man's Land. Outside Serre, 'There was a wailing and lamentation from No Man's Land and much shouting for stretcher-bearers from the stricken English. They lay in piles but those who survived fired at us from behind their bodies. Later on, when the English tried again, they weren't walking this time, they were running as fast as they could but when they reached the piles of bodies they got no farther. I could see English officers gesticulating wildly, trying to call the reserves forward, but very few came. Normally, after 5,000 rounds had been fired we changed the barrel of the machine-gun. We changed it five times that morning.' (Musketier Karl Blenk, 169th Regiment)

There were at least nine more hours of daylight left. Could the British yet recover? Would the Germans still be dominant on these sectors at the end of the day?

11

The Afternoon

The afternoon opened with a curious lull that lasted until 2.30 P.M., when the first of several British efforts was made to renew the offensive on sectors where there had been failure in the morning.

Lieut-Gen. H. S. Horne, the commander of XV Corps, had ordered an attack on Fricourt. This village had not been directly assaulted during the morning; it had been hoped that successful advances on either side of it would force the village to fall, but this had not happened. The afternoon attack was to be carried out by a brigade of the 17th (Northern) Division. The handling of this brigade, the 50th, was to have serious repercussions and it would be well to examine the command structure.

XV Corps, under Horne, had two divisions in the line, the 7th on the right and the 21st on the left. The other division in the corps was the 17th (Northern), under Maj.-Gen. T. D. Pilcher, which was officially in reserve. However, the corps commander had ordered Pilcher to detach one of his brigades and hand it over to the 21st Division for the day. Accordingly, the 50th Brigade had gone into the line in the corps centre, opposite Fricourt. Maj.-Gen. Pilcher had no say whatsoever in the handling of the brigade; it was under the command of the 21st Division.

Until midday the only battalion from the brigade to have attacked had been the 10th West Yorks, but it had failed and only Lieut Philip Howe and a few men had returned to the British lines. As a result of the corps commander's orders that Fricourt should be attacked frontally, the commander of the 21st Division sent orders to attack Fricourt at 2.30 P.M.

Soon after 2 P.M. Philip Howe was surprised to see a large number of men taking over his trench. These were from C and D Companies of the 7th East Yorks, arriving for the proposed attack. Howe greeted the East Yorks C.O., whom he knew well, and gave him a report on the morning's happenings. He was somewhat disconcerted when the lieutenant-colonel invited him to join in this second attack;

within a few hours Howe had come to be regarded as a veteran among these New Army troops, one who had actually been over the top and returned. He had little option but to comply.

At exactly 2.33 P.M. all was ready. The whistles blew and the attack started. It was broad daylight; there had hardly been any artillery bombardment; the Germans were ready. The East Yorks C.O. was first up the ladder, Howe just behind him. To right and left the East Yorks rose and moved forward. One German machine-gun opened fire, traversing along the line of men before they had gone twenty yards. A bullet grazed Philip Howe's face and the sling of the rifle he was carrying was shot through at each end. It was clearly hopeless to continue and the East Yorks were ordered back to their trench. In three minutes 123 men had been killed or wounded.

As the remaining East Yorks took over his trench, Philip Howe gathered his men together and moved off to report to brigade H.Q. On his way he met another lieutenant-colonel, the C.O. of the 7th Green Howards. This battalion too had just attacked and had lost even more heavily that the East Yorks.

The Green Howards had already suffered one disaster when one company had attacked in error that morning. To avoid a similar occurrence the C.O. had withheld details of the afternoon attack until the last possible moment. This decision caused some of his men to miss their beloved rum. 'We had a gallon jar of rum in the dug-out with us but we were never allowed to touch it. Our officer said we had to have a tot just before zero. At 2.30 P.M. zero came; a runner came along shouting, "Zero. Over the top." One chap said, "What about our rum issue, sir?" "No time for that now," he replied, "I'm taking it with me. We'll drink our health in Jerry's front line." I doubt if he ever got there. We mounted the parapet; some of us got out, some of us didn't but we were under a murderous attack of machine-gun fire. We were falling like ninepins.' (Pte A. W. Askew, 7th Green Howards)

The Green Howards C.O. invited Philip Howe and his men to join him for yet another attack. Howe was appalled. He had already escaped death twice; surely no one should be expected to go over the top three times in one day. He pointed out his wounded hand, his grazed face, his exhausted men and was excused.

The afternoon attacks of these two battalions had cost 400 casualties and achieved nothing.

A similar pathetic attempt was made on the extreme left of the front at Gommecourt. The story of this attack by the 46th (North Midland) Division is an excellent illustration of how unrealistic orders were received by the officers in the chain of command between a corps H.Q. and the front line, and what the results of such orders could be.

The corps commander, Lieut-Gen. Snow, had ordered the North Midland Division to attack again at 12.15 P.M. to attempt a link-up with the London Division which was being counter-attacked in the German trenches on the other side of the salient. This attack was postponed first to 1.30 P.M. and then to 3.30 P.M.

One can imagine the feelings of the divisional commander, Maj.-Gen. Hon. E. J. M. Stuart-Wortley. His division of Territorials had suffered nothing but ill-luck since crossing to France in 1915. Firstly, it had held a dangerous part of the Ypres Salient with many casualties but no chance for glory. Then in October, as part of the Battle of Loos, it had been thrown, in broad daylight, against the notorious Hohenzollern Redoubt and had lost 3,700 men in ten minutes. Finally the division had come to the Somme, not to take part in the main attack, but in a diversion of doubtful value. Six battalions had attacked during the morning; all had been repulsed. Five of their C.O.'s were dead or wounded; the men had suffered heavily too and the survivors, like Bill Soar, were still lying out in No Man's Land. Now Stuart-Wortley was being pressed to attack yet again, in what he knew were hopeless conditions.

The major-general could not put off the attack indefinitely. Behind him the corps commander was insisting on a full effort, in front of him brigade commanders were pointing out the hopelessness of the idea. Stuart-Wortley's answer was a compromise. He would attack again, but only a token effort of two companies, one each from the Sherwood Forester Brigade and the Staffordshire Brigade. The story is taken up by the Sherwood Forester company commander: 'I was promised an artillery barrage and a smoke screen.

I pointed out that most of the mortars that fired the smoke bombs were out of action but I was told the attack must go on. The trenches were so muddy and so crowded with wounded men that I had great difficulty in deploying my four platoons, but eventually they were ready. My own C.O. came up ten minutes before the attack was due to start and watched the smoke screen and bombardment, which were quite inadequate. Just before we were due to go over he ordered me to cancel the attack. I sent runners off, at once, to the four platoons; only three managed to deliver their messages on time. The other platoon attacked but every man except one, the platoon sergeant, was hit.' (Capt. V. O. Robinson, M.C., 1/6th Sherwood Foresters)

There was also an eye-witness in the Staffordshire Brigade: 'At about 3 o'clock a runner clambered along amongst the dead and wounded and said we were to attack again. At that moment I had found two others unwounded in my company and thought that I was the only survivor in my platoon. Our clothes were torn and a mass of gluey mud, and our rifles caked and useless. We were attending to the wounded and the idea of cleaning our rifles for another attack never entered our heads. No officer had survived and we made jokes as to who would blow the whistle for the attack, if we could find one on a dead officer. Fortunately the attack was cancelled.' (Pte G. S. Young, 1/6th North Staffs)

The direct orders of a corps commander, that a division should attack, had been so resisted by officers at different levels that, in the end, only one platoon had attacked. Many lives had been saved but, again, there were to be repercussions.

By mid-afternoon the Ulster Division was in a desperate position. The battalions, which had done so well that morning, had been fighting in the Schwaben Redoubt for over seven hectic hours and were now exhausted, their numbers dwindling under the fire from three sides. 'One remark was passed by one of the lads that I will always remember. He said, "We should call it a draw and I'll give our garden in with it." ' (Pte F. G. Gardner, 109th Trench Mortar Battery) Ammunition and water were running low, even rifle cartridges were being used to keep the machine-guns firing.

Behind them No Man's Land was impossible. The Ulster's Pioneer battalion had tried to dig communication trenches across it but had been unable to work because of the machine-gun fire from the untaken village of Thiepval. The sunken road from which the attacking battalions had assembled for their first attack was to be so full of corpses by nightfall that it was renamed Bloody Road.

Gradually the Germans started to co-ordinate their counter-attacks and the Ulstermen were driven in from their farthest gains. The first signs of cracking began to appear: '3 P.M., a lot of men from the 8th and 9th Royal Irish Rifles [East and West Belfasts] have broken under Bosch counter-attack from the direction of Grandcourt. We had to stop them at revolver point and turn them back, a desperate show, the air stiff with shrapnel, and terror-stricken men rushing blindly. These men did magnificently earlier in the day, but they had reached the limit of their endurance. At 4 P.M. I received a message from Capt. Willis of our D Company that he was hanging on but hard pressed. He was never heard of again.' (Lieut-Col. F. O. Bowen, Belfast Young Citizens)* The Ulsters in their first battle had done as much as could be asked of even the most experienced soldiers. They needed help.

The corps commander had already ordered forward his reserve division, the 49th (West Riding). These Yorkshire Territorials had started the day in the shelter of Aveluy Wood, but by 9 A.M. the first battalions had moved on to positions nearer the front, their way taking them over the marshy Ancre valley. 'We crossed the river on a very rickety bridge. German prisoners were wading through the water, holding on to the sides of the bridge. Some of our fellows were hitting them on the hands and head, knocking them back into the water. I was horrified at the sights – dead men floating in the water, and wounded shouting for help.' (Pte J. G. Dooley, 1/6th West Yorks) Crossing the Ancre, they soon reached the shelter of Thiepval Wood which went right up to the old British front line and here they remained until mid-afternoon.

'I was an officer's servant and had to go with him to a conference where the brigadier (I think) met all our officers. He informed them that we had to be at the row of apple trees

* Public Record Office, CAB 45/188.

in Thiepval village at 4 o'clock. Our colonel tried to point out that this was impossible in the time. The answer was, "Those are the orders." We moved off, got into the first communication trench and found it full of prisoners. We turfed them out and proceeded towards the front line.' (Pte E. T. Radband, 1/5th West Yorks)

But the moment the Yorkshire battalions left the shelter of the wood, they were caught by the machine-guns in Thiepval. 'We went forward in single file, through a gap in what had once been a hedge; only one man could get through at a time. The Germans had a machine-gun trained on the gap and when it came to my turn I paused. The machine-gun stopped and, thinking his belt had run out, or he had jammed, I moved through, but what I saw when I got to the other side shook me to pieces. There was a trench running parallel with the hedge which was full to the top with the men who had gone before me. They were all either dead or dying.' (Pte J. Wilson, 1/6th West Yorks)

No Man's Land was still clearly impossible to cross and the West Yorks were told to stop trying. The Ulsters would have to hang on until dark.

Not all the British efforts during the afternoon were failures. The task of capturing the village of Mametz had been given to the 7th Division, Gough's old command.* Although officially classed as a Regular division, six of its battalions were from the New Army – four of Manchester Pals and the 8th and 9th Devons. During the morning, the men of the division had captured all their early objectives and had reached the outskirts of Mametz, but here bitter opposition had stopped them. Two further attacks had been mounted, each preceded by an artillery bombardment, but still the Germans denied Mametz to the 7th Division.

The fighting hereabouts was fierce, hand-to-hand combat. 'I went over the top at 2.30 P.M. in the second wave with

* 2nd Lieut Siegfried Sassoon, M.C., the famous war poet and writer, was serving in this division. His battalion, the 1st Royal Welch Fusiliers, took little part in the attack and Sassoon spent the day watching the fighting around Fricourt from a vantage point in the British trenches. Another officer in the division was Capt. Richard O'Connor who commanded the divisional signals unit. As the commander of the Western Desert Force, the forerunner of the famous Eighth Army, Gen. O'Connor conducted a brilliant campaign against the Italians in North Africa in 1940 and 1941.

our bombers. Just as I was about to jump into the German trench, a Jerry made a lunge at me with his bayonet, but I stepped back a little and he just took a small piece out of my thigh. Instead of a rifle I had a knobkerrie, which the bombers used for trench fighting. I hit out at him and sank it deep into his forehead. In the scuffle his helmet came off and I saw that he was a bald-headed old man. I have never forgotten that bald head and I don't suppose I ever will. Poor old devil!' (Pte J. Kirkham, 5th Manchester Pals)

At 3 P.M. yet another half-hour bombardment was ordered. Again the 7th Division men attacked and this time, after another bitter fight, the village was theirs. One British soldier was particularly pleased with this victory. 'I had been wounded in the morning attack and captured by the Germans, who took me to a dressing station in a very deep dug-out. It was lit by electric light and was full of wounded Germans waiting for treatment, but preference was given to me and I was bandaged up right away, put on a wire netting bed and given some bread and cheese and a bottle of pop. In the afternoon our artillery started another heavy bombardment. The lights went out twice and the whole place shook. Soon afterwards, the Germans rushed out along the tunnels and I was left alone. A few minutes later a sergeant-major from the Manchesters came down the steps.' (Pte A. Wilson, 1st South Staffs)

And so Mametz fell, the second village of the day to do so. As at Montauban, the Manchesters had a hand in the capture, their 6th Pals being one of the battalions making the final assault.

The capture of Mametz extended the earlier success on the British right wing to a frontage of three miles, for the 18th (Eastern) Division had also taken all its objectives between Mametz and Montauban.* The scenes that had followed the taking of Montauban were repeated. The old No Man's Land became safe to cross, the captured trenches were cleared and German guns and transport could be seen fleeing in the open valley beyond the new front line. 'Straight in front we could see Longueval village across a valley which was unscarred,

* A certain Capt. A. E. Percival of the 7th Bedfords won the Military Cross for his part in this fighting. In 1942, Lieut-Gen. Percival was in command of the ill-fated Singapore garrison which was surrendered to the Japanese. Part of this garrison was another 18th Division, again made up of battalions from Eastern England, but they went into captivity almost as soon as they landed at Singapore.

not like the ground we had captured farther back and the trench area we had lived in. The trees in the distance had full foliage, such a change from the blackened and scarred stumps we had left behind. The air seemed sweeter, not that stinking smell of cordite and fumes from the shells of the battlefield in the rear.' (Cpl J. Norton, 8th Norfolks)

Some men wondered how quickly the success could be exploited: 'It was then very quiet, with only an occasional long-range shell from Gerry coming over. From my own point of view, I should have thought a small force of cavalry could have followed up and inflicted enormous damage to the German lines of communications. Quite a number of same were lying in reserve.' (Pte N. H. Norton, 8th Norfolks)

As the French had also taken all their first phase objectives during the morning on a three-mile sector between Montauban and the River Somme, the whole German front-line system had been captured on a six-mile front. Many men, having seen the complete defeat of the Germans, were asking the same question as Pte Norton of the Norfolks. 'Where was the cavalry?'

There had been ten hours of daylight remaining after the capture of Montauban. The only action there during the afternoon was at 12.30 P.M. when, after an artillery bombardment, a company of the 4th Liverpool Pals had dashed out from their recently captured trenches to the remains of a brickworks, the Briqueterie, an important German position opposite the junction between the British and French sectors. So swift was the Liverpools' rush that they caught the Germans underground. Their prisoners formed an impressive list: the commander and adjutant of a German infantry regiment, seven other officers, over 100 men and several machine-guns.

When the 7th and 18th Divisions had extended the Montauban capture in the late afternoon, there were five daylight hours left. The German defence had obviously collapsed and the British had both ample infantry reserves and part of a cavalry division, the 2nd Indian, immediately behind the front. Lieut-Gen. Congreve was the corps commander with the best opportunity to exploit the success; his neighbour, Horne, was still preoccupied with the obstinate Fricourt. Congreve went up into the new front line. He saw his victorious infantry, he saw the open ground void of Germans, he saw the silent woods – Bernafay, only 200 yards from the Liverpool Pals in the Briqueterie, Trônes and, away to the left, Mametz Wood.

Congreve was a real fighter who had won the Victoria Cross in the Boer War. He hurried back to his H.Q., rang up Rawlinson at Fourth Army and sought permission to advance again; he had his own infantry and he could use the Indian cavalry regiments. The answer that Congreve received from Rawlinson was to become one of the controversial aspects of the day's battle.

Leaving the scene of success on the right let us look at what was happening in those places where small, isolated bands of British soldiers were still holding out in the German trenches. There had been several such places in the morning but, by midday, only two remained – the Quadrilateral Redoubt and the Leipzig Salient where Sgt Turnbull of the Glasgow Commercials won his posthumous Victoria Cross. The British troops in these redoubts must have wondered, as the day wore on, what would happen to them. The Germans had drawn a tight net around their lost positions and every attempt by the British to exploit their gains had failed. If the Germans were to make really determined efforts to recover their losses, it was doubtful if the British could hold on until darkness gave them either the chance to escape or brought them reinforcements.

Fighting raged around the Leipzig all day but in the Quadrilateral the afternoon was mainly peaceful. 'It became very quiet, so first I had a sleep and then I wandered around, talking to some of the men. There were only eleven from our battalion and we simply hung around waiting for something to happen.' (Pte E. C. Stanley, 1/8th Royal Warwicks) A seventeen-year-old soldier had helped to beat off a German bombing party. 'This was the first time I had killed anybody and when things quietened down I went and looked at a German I knew I had shot. I remember thinking that he looked old enough to have a family and I felt very sorry.' (Pte G. T. Rudge, 2nd Essex)

Towards the end of the afternoon C.S.M. Percy Chappell looked out over No Man's Land towards the British lines and was amazed to see a familiar figure walking calmly towards the Quadrilateral. It was his friend the Somersets regimental sergeant major who arrived swinging a walking stick as calm as could be – he was even wearing a soft service cap – but the news he brought to Percy Chappell was bad. Their C.O. had been killed and so had Brig.-Gen. Prowse. Chappell was particularly saddened by this last loss. Before the war Prowse had served in the Somersets and for some time had been Chappell's company commander. The R.S.M. promised to send fresh supplies of ammunition to the men in the Quadrilateral and returned safely the way he had come.

In the captured German trenches at Gommecourt, the London Division still appeared to be in a strong position in the early afternoon. Despite their disappointment at the failure of the North Midland Division to link up with them behind the village, the Londoners still held most of their early gains. But the local German commander soon realized that the North Midland Division had failed and that the Londoners represented the only real threat to him, so he was able to concentrate all his reserves against them. As in so many places, German fire completely dominated No Man's Land. During the morning a company of the Kensingtons and a machine-gun section from the London Scottish had managed to cross, though with heavy loss, and reinforce the early attackers, but these were the last to do so. During the morning and early afternoon the Germans mounted three carefully prepared, full-scale counter-attacks, each preceded by a short but intense bombardment. With every hour that passed German strength grew but that of the Londoners only became weaker.

Gradually the battalions in the German trenches began to disintegrate. The battalion commanders had not been allowed to go across with their men and control of the battle fell to the company commanders who frequently became casualties. The first sign of a break-up came at 1 P.M. when small parties of lightly wounded men began to leave the captured trenches. There was never a divisional order sent to the force that they should retire but, as individual groups ran out of ammunition or were forced back, the officers in charge decided to withdraw before it was too late. Sometimes the decision was taken by a lieutenant-colonel watching from the British trenches: 'Another runner and myself were given a sealed message to be delivered to a captain in the German trenches. As I left, I passed the C.O. and the adjutant standing on top of a dug-out, watching the battle through binoculars, just as though it were Ascot Races. We had to go about 800 yards along a sunken road and the air was screaming with bullets. About half-way across, the other man was hit in the wrist so I bandaged his wound and he went back. I carried on, but then I heard a shell coming. I threw myself full length and buried my head in the earth. After the explosion I was surprised to find myself in one piece; I stretched out a hand and could touch the crater. Eventually I reached the German trenches but could not find the captain; I found out later that he had been captured. A sergeant took my message and I returned the way I had come, faster than sound.' (Rfmn A. Hollis, 1st London Rifle Brigade)

By 4 P.M. the Londoners had been so forced back that they held only the German front-line trench. They shared out their ammunition and prepared to fight on. During the next few hours the line they held gradually dwindled but, incredibly, at 9 P.M. there was still one party of five officers and seventy men holding out. Then came the end. A few brave men volunteered to form a rearguard. The last few bombs and bullets were given to them, and the rest escaped as best they could. Just before dusk, the last German counter-attack was delivered. It was all over.

The London Division had carried out every task demanded of it. It had captured the complete German front-line system; it had reached out to the back of Gommecourt. But now it had lost everything. These Territorial soldiers had fought with the utmost gallantry and had suffered grievously. This one story typifies their spirit: 'My company sergeant major, Matt Hamilton, was only nineteen, one of the best men I ever met. He was shot through the knee within a few yards of leaving our own trench but he apparently crawled all the way over No Man's Land and three German trenches, because he finally arrived at our objective where he was hit again and killed.' (Maj. C. J. Low, D.S.O., 1st London Scottish)

From the seven battalions that had attacked, over 1,700 men were dead; some 200, mainly wounded, were prisoners of war and 2,300 were wounded, most of them still lying out in No Man's Land. One battalion, the London Scottish, had suffered 616 casualties from the 871 men taking part in the attack. Another, the Queen's Westminster Rifles, had sent twenty-eight officers into action. Every one had become a casualty. Such was the cost of an operation that had only been a diversion.

Despite fierce local fighting, the greater part of the battle front saw no major action during the afternoon. Sunset was not until late evening so, between the breakdown of the first attack and the coming of darkness, the thousands of men out in No Man's Land had to endure up to fourteen hours of waiting. The luckier ones had been able to take shelter in shell holes and had long since settled down for the day. The bigger holes often accommodated several men, sometimes friends, sometimes complete strangers. The members of these little communities did not always get on well together: 'I was wounded twice in the leg and managed to get into a shell hole. It already contained five men, two of whom were dead. The others were all right, but they weren't pleased to see me. They didn't want to make room for me, so I had to spend the day between two corpses. The other men were signallers from my own battalion and I told them off for neglecting their duty; they had not been hurt. I told them I would have shot them if only I had a rifle. Later in the day they left for the British trenches, but they never offered to take me.' (Sgt A. Ingall, 2nd Lincolns) *

The hot sun continued throughout the afternoon and the biggest problem for most men was thirst: 'Late in the afternoon I slithered into a shell hole and, having lost an enormous quantity of blood, I was really thirsty. In the shell hole I found a bottle of Vichy water and a loaded revolver, which had probably been discarded by an officer. I tried to prize the metal top off the bottle but, with only one hand in use, I failed. There was only one way out, either blow the neck off with a revolver shot or clout it with the butt. I chose the latter, but I must have hit it too hard as the bottle broke into smithereens and I didn't get one drop.' (Pte T. C. Clynes, 1st London Scottish)

In spite of the proximity of the Germans and the danger of their position, some of the men in No Man's Land found relief in sleep. After a night without rest and the violence of

* The fierce Sgt Ingall, a Regular soldier, was eventually saved but he never soldiered again. He was discharged as a cripple in 1917.

the morning, the long hot hours under the sun had brought a drowsiness which some, especially the younger ones, could not resist and they slept the sleep of the exhausted, sometimes within a few yards of German-held trenches.

It was a far more nerve-racking experience for those men who could not reach the shelter of the shell holes. 'After our attack had failed, I lay down in a bit of dead ground, flat on my stomach with my haversack sticking up. A German sniper spent the day smashing it to pieces, each shot just missing my head. The Germans later bombarded the area and I was covered with fumes and smoke until the whole of my uniform was canary yellow.' (Cpl D. E. Cattell, Sheffield City Battalion)

Most men stayed where they were until nightfall but some were prepared to risk the journey back to their own trenches. Bugler Bill Soar, in his bed of reeds, was so close to the Germans that he felt he had to move. Discarding all his equipment and abandoning his rifle he ran to the nearest shell hole. After spending a considerable time waiting in it he made another dash of a few yards. A long wait followed each move as he tried to outwit the watching Germans. Several times his moves brought a burst of fire but on each occasion he was able to jump into a new hole in time. Soar was distressed to find that many of the shell holes contained dead or badly wounded men from his battalion. By dusk he was still only part of the way across No Man's Land.

The early sniping by the British soldiers marooned in No Man's Land gradually died down, discouraged by the German retaliation, but it never stopped completely. Here and there, a brave soldier kept up the fire as long as he had ammunition. A sergeant of the Glasgow Boys' Brigade Battalion found himself with a Lewis gun in a position from which he could fire into a German trench. Using first his own ammunition and then getting more from dead carriers, he fired off a total of twenty-four drums of bullets at the enemy during the day. Albert McMillan was another who was determined not to accept defeat. Whenever he thought it safe, he peered over the edge of his shell hole and exchanged shots with the Germans. It was a risky procedure; several German bullets 'pinged' off his steel helmet when he was slow in ducking back again.

For most of the day the Germans continued searching No Man's Land with their fire to finish off the wounded whenever they could spot a movement. The upturned rifles placed near the wounded during the morning attack were sometimes the cause of their doom. The Germans watched for any sign of movement besides these rifles and fired as soon as a body stirred. Outside Serre a bored German rifleman had another pastime: 'From my shell hole I could see a dead man [probably from the Accrington Pals] propped up against the German wire in a sitting position. He was sniped at during the day until his head was completely shot away.' (Lieut R. A. Heptonstall, 1st Barnsley Pals)

The British soldiers who were pinned down in Sausage Valley had to endure heavy shell fire for long stretches of the day. 'A very large shell fell some little distance on my left. With all the bits and pieces flying up was a body. The legs had been blown off right up to the crutch. I have never seen a body lifted so high. It sailed up and towards me. I can still see the dead-pan look on his face under the tin hat, which was still held on by the chin strap. He kept coming and landed with a bonk a few yards to my left.

'Then, during the afternoon, Jerry started shelling No Man's Land in a zig-zag fashion to kill the rest of us off. As each shell landed they gave a burst of machine-gun fire over where it fell, to catch anyone who should jump up. As they worked towards me I knew when my shell was coming. Sure enough it came and landed a few yards behind me. Over came the bullets as well but I kept perfectly still.' (Pte W. J. Senescall, The Cambridge Battalion)

Only a few yards away many men had taken shelter in the huge Lochnager mine crater but, even here, they were not free from danger. 'Shells from both sides were falling into the crater, the Germans' exploding on one side and ours on the other. We didn't know where to go to get away from them. Then an aeroplane flew over, very low, and one of our chaps took the shirt off a dead man and waved it. The plane flew off and soon afterwards the British shelling stopped. That pilot was a brave man.' (Pte W. T. Parkin, Grimsby Chums)

But another occupant of the crater, a wounded officer, has a slightly different version. 'For some unknown reason, our artillery started shelling us. Our planes were sailing close overhead and, though I shone a mirror up, they took no notice. In the end I sent an orderly to Colonel Howard to ask for permission to use a red flare, which he gave. As soon as we lit it our planes went straight off home and our batteries shut up, but of course the Boche redoubled his efforts, though we escaped without further casualties.

'I found my flow of language very useful several times; especially when the fit men wanted to bolt for it and leave a good hundred wounded who couldn't walk. I asked them what the — — they thought they were doing and they all meekly went back, much to my surprise.' (2nd Lieut J. H. Turnbull, Grimsby Chums) *

Although the fighting had died down on some sectors during the afternoon, the conditions in many of the British trenches were still chaotic. Continuous German shelling had smashed the trench system still further and caused more casualties. The lightly wounded were able to take themselves to the rear but thousands of the more seriously wounded still remained mixed in with the dead. There were some frightful scenes: 'Back in the trench I came upon one of our platoon, laid on his back with a huge baulk of timber across his legs. When I got to him, I saw that one of his legs had been severed but the heavy timber, as it laid across his legs, was acting as a tourniquet and had stopped the bleeding. I ran down the trench to get hold of stretcher-bearers but ran slap bang into an officer of the Bradford Pals who stopped me and demanded to know where I was going. I told him about Jim with his leg off and that I was seeking help. "Never mind him. Get a rifle and fall in with my men." Abandoned rifles and equipment were lying about everywhere, I picked one up, gave it a wipe, and followed on – but the first opportunity I had, I "lost" him and made my way back to what was left of our own H.Q. Jim was found that night and was carried out, attended to and sent home to Blighty – he is still alive today.' (Pte A. V. Pearson, Leeds Pals)

It could take two stretcher-bearers over an hour to take one wounded man to a Dressing Station and many had

* This extract was taken from a letter written by Turnbull in July 1919. He had been hit in the spine on 1 July 1916 and was still in hospital at Oxford. The letter was kindly loaned by Maj. C. H. Emmerson of Grimsby. Colonel Howard was the C.O. of the 1st Tyneside Irish. He died soon afterwards.

become casualties themselves. Those who remained had been struggling all day and were exhausted. Two Leeds Pals bearers took a well-earned break: 'Well, we were just about all in, still at it till close on night, having no rest. On our way back to the trenches, we came across a case marked "Headquarters Mess", so we took good care of it. Inside was a tin of bacon, coffee, biscuits, etc., so we had a good feed. It was a Godsend.' (L/Cpl T. H. Place, Leeds Pals)

Some soldiers in the trenches who were in a position to help had been expressly forbidden to aid the wounded, but to attend to their own duties. They had to watch the agony of these men for most of the day: 'The worst sights were in our own trenches where some of the badly wounded had managed to crawl. We were not allowed to help any of them, but kept our machine-gun mounted on the parapet in case of a counter-attack. The wounded were trying to patch each other up with their field dressings. A chaplain tore his dog collar off in front of me and, with curses, said, "It is a mockery to wear it." ' (Pte C. A. Turner, 97th Brigade Machine Gun Company)

Conditions had improved a little for L/Cpl Charles Matthews. Soon after midday, the German shells that had been dropping near him all morning ceased. An hour later he was startled when a duck-board was suddenly thrown across the trench above him and two stretcher-bearers crossed with a wounded man. Matthews shouted out to them and asked them to come back for him and they promised to do so. Another eternity of time passed and Matthews felt the bearers had forgotten him but, true to their promise, they eventually returned. His helpers' faces fell when they saw his blood-soaked tunic and began cutting it away, fearing he had a severe body wound. They were very pleased when Matthews told them the blood was not his, that his leg was crushed and that no dressings were needed. With their new load they laboured over the churned-up ground. With every lurch causing Matthews severe pain, he was very thankful when, after half an hour, he was left at a Dressing Station in the village square at Carnoy. It was eight hours since he had been injured by the mine debris.

There was one body of men who were still attending to their own grim duty – the Military Police. Their orders were to stop any fit man leaving the trenches without permission and to ensure that, when an attack had been ordered, no one remained behind. 'After I had been wounded, I came back to our trench and saw two very young soldiers. They were terrified and had been too scared to follow their mates over the top. Soon after I had left them I met two "Red Caps" with revolvers who wanted to know where I was going. I showed them my wound and they let me pass. I had only gone a few yards when I heard two pistol shots from close by. I feel *sure* that these two unfortunate boys had been "executed for cowardice".' (Pte J. Kirkham, 5th Manchester Pals)

All day the battalions of the 19th (Western) Division had remained in the trenches of the Tara–Usna Line, just outside Albert. As the initial attack on this sector had failed completely, there was obviously no chance that they could undertake their original task – the exploitation of the gap, the advance with the cavalry on Bapaume. Instead, just after midday, four Lancashire battalions – the 7th King's Own, the 7th Loyal North Lancs, the 7th South Lancs and the 7th East Lancs – received fresh orders. They were to attack the German front line at 5 P.M. after a thirty-minute bombardment. All afternoon the nervous Lancashire men waited. After only half an hour's barrage they were to attack where a complete division had failed after a week-long bombardment.

The battalions of the 19th Division were to be joined in this attack by those reserve battalions of the 8th Division which had missed the morning's fighting. 'In consequence of the proposed new offensive I was instructed urgently to send out a patrol to discover if the German line opposite our right company was held, and by whom. Accordingly, as soon as arrangements could be made, 2nd Lieut Fraser with one sergeant and five privates from D Company stole forward. This was the smallest number of men we could employ, compatible with carrying out the order; they were told to go very carefully, returning at once if seriously fired on. . . Later, the patrol reported back in our trenches having been heavily fired at; Fraser was missing, believed killed, to my profound sorrow.

'Shortly before the hour of the meditated attack we were informed of its cancellation owing to the possibility that some of our troops might still be holding out in the German trenches. . . By now, however, I was almost past caring, personally, whether we attacked or not.' (Maj. J. L. Jack, 2nd Scottish Rifles) *

The four Lancashire battalions were ordered to turn back and march to the rear. With lighter hearts, the soldiers turned their back on the battlefield. When Lieut Henry Webber with the battalion transport met the 7th South Lancs that evening, he was greeted by smiling friends. The gulf between the horrors of the battlefield and the peace of the rear could be immense. 'The attack was cancelled only minutes before it was due to start and we went out to some high ground behind Albert where we had refreshment and, illustrating the incongruities of war, were addressed by a visiting bishop and entertained by the divisional band.' (Pte C. B. Mawbey, 7th Loyal North Lancs) †

All through the afternoon and into the evening the fine midsummer weather had continued. Not a drop of rain had fallen since the drizzle of dawn, not a cloud had marred the sky since the early morning mist. The shadows lengthened and the sun prepared to set on this terrible day.

Pte Paddy Kennedy had taken part in the capture of Montauban in mid-morning, but then he had been sent back to the old British front line to fetch a load of grenades. As he picked his way over the torn-up ground of No Man's Land he was very upset to see so many wounded men lying out in the hot sun, calling out for help, but under strict orders to return quickly with his grenades, he dared not linger. On his return he was sent to join men from the 1st Manchester Pals, who were manning Montauban Alley. He still had no idea where his own battalion was and was content to stay with his fellow-Mancunians. All afternoon he had waited there, playing with his new-found pet kitten or looking out over the wide empty valley. It was so peaceful he felt that the war might be over.

There were many men like Kennedy who had now spent several hours in the new front line which stretched from Montauban to Mametz. The Germans seemed to have disappeared; there was hardly any shelling. But, in spite of

* From *General Jack's Diary, 1914–1918*, p. 149, edited by John Terraine.

† The identity of the visiting bishop is uncertain. One report says it was the Bishop of London, but the Roman Catholic Bishop of Khartoum visited other units of the division on 2 July.

all the fine talk before the battle of breakthroughs and cavalry, nothing had happened. The men who had been so successful earlier in the day were baffled and profoundly disappointed. They were convinced that a great chance was being allowed to slip away.

The refusal by the British to move on their right had also deterred the French from advancing farther. A British officer on liaison duty remembers: 'The French had taken all their objectives north of the Somme and could easily have gone farther; they could have taken Péronne if they had wanted. I knew the British right wing had done well too and I was almost biting my nails down to the palms with frustration.' (Capt. E. L. Spears, French Sixth Army H.Q.) Péronne was six miles away and was to the French what Bapaume was to the British.

Gen. Rawlinson had expected the Germans to counter-attack their lost positions but, on the right wing, they were still so off balance that the few, pathetic attempts they did make were easily frustrated.

Paddy Kennedy was involved in one such attack. At 9.30 P.M. a party of Germans crept up in the gloom to within a few yards of Montauban Alley and shattered the evening calm with a grenade attack. Paddy panicked, fumbling in his pouches to get at his ammunition, but his neighbour, an old soldier with Boer War medal ribbons, advised him to put down his rifle, get out all his ammunition, lay the clips out carefully and, only then, to open fire. Within a few minutes the little fight was over, the Germans beaten off.

The Germans were having more success with their counter-attacks on another sector, however. During the afternoon the Ulstermen near Thiepval had been forced back until all they held was the German front-line trench and the Schwaben Redoubt just beyond it. All afternoon the Germans had pounded away at the exhausted Ulsters with artillery, with machine-guns and with at least three more infantry assaults. 'We could see the muzzles of some light field guns firing at us over open sights, the barrels parallel to the ground. They were pumping out shells as fast as they could. It was awful; there was hardly any escape from them.' (Pte J. Devennie, Derry Volunteers) The Ulsters had beaten off every attack but each had left them with more dead, fewer defenders and less ammunition.

By evening they were in a desperate position. Nearly every officer who had attacked was a casualty; their ammunition was almost gone; no reinforcements had been able to reach them. Late in the evening came yet another German attack – delivered from three sides. It was the end for the Ulsters. A major gave the order to give up the redoubt and return to the former German front line for a last stand. But the Germans too had had enough and the Ulsters' withdrawal was carried out safely and in good order.

Ironically, as they retired, the Ulsters met the reinforcements they had been looking for since midday. Eight full companies of the West Riding Territorials had at last managed to cross No Man's Land in the gloom. The Schwaben Redoubt must have already established an evil reputation. 'As I was coming out I met the relieving troops moving up. I have never seen such a look of terror on the faces of human beings.' (L/Cpl J. A. Henderson, Belfast Young Citizens) But the reinforcements were too late to save the redoubt; the Germans had it back again now.*

The 36th (Ulster) Division, which had taken the Schwaben Redoubt, which had been the only division to reach the second German main trench system, had lost nearly all its gains. At no time during fourteen hours of fighting had it received any help from the divisions on either side. It handed over its only remaining capture, 800 yards of the old enemy front line, to the West Yorks and retired grimly to the British lines. Over 2,000 men from the old province of Ulster died by Thiepval, 2,700 more were wounded and 165 were taken prisoner. They had paid the price of their own success. It was to be over three months before British troops took the Schwaben Redoubt again.

At long last the sun set on the battlefield.† The moment has been remembered by two men; one's attack had been

* Cpl George Sanders, a Leeds Territorial soldier, held on with a small party to one corner of the redoubt for the next thirty-six hours. During this time, eleven of his thirty men became casualties, some wounded Ulstermen were rescued and several German attacks beaten off. For his leadership, Sanders received the Victoria Cross. Later in the war he was commissioned, won the Military Cross and became a prisoner of war.

† Sunset at Albert was at 9.02 P.M. by the newly introduced British Summer Time (H.M. Nautical Almanac Office).

successful, the other's had failed. 'The sun went down that first evening back over our old trenches, in gold which turned to blood, and it seemed symbolic. We had kept our nerve and at the end of the day were where we were supposed to be and that seemed triumph enough to be going on with.' (Pte H. L. Wide, 9th Devons)

'At long last, evening came and the light began to fade. I ventured a look forward and there was Gerry out of his trench, moving among the fallen. Now, I thought, I am going to Berlin too soon. That decided me; I jumped up and ran as best I could, for I was stiff. I kept treading on wounded and they called out to me for help. Gerry let me have a few more shots as I ran, but the light had now gone. Anyway, he couldn't hit me that day in daylight, could he?' (Pte W. J. Senescall, The Cambridge Battalion)

12

Review at Dusk

Gen. Rawlinson at Fourth Army H.Q. in the château at Querrieux had received two important callers during the afternoon. His visitors were Gen. Haig, the British C.-in-C., and Gen. Foch, commander of the French group of armies fighting alongside the British. Alas, Rawlinson could not deliver the good news of victory and breakthrough for which his chief and his ally were hoping. Haig returned to his Advanced G.H.Q. before evening, for he too was expecting an important visitor, Field-Marshal Sir William Robertson, the Chief of the Imperial General Staff. When Robertson arrived in the evening he would be disappointed at the mixed news from Haig. London had had high hopes of this day.

However, there was one general who was well satisfied. As Gen. Foch drove south from Querrieux he knew that France had got what she wanted. Foch was a humane man. He would have liked to have seen a British victory, but whether there was victory or not the British were, at least, fighting. The Germans would be diverted from Verdun and the French Army saved from destruction.

What action had Gen. Rawlinson taken since midday? Had he done anything to exploit the success of his right wing? Had he done anything to retrieve the failure of the remainder of his army? These questions can only be answered by studying a few known facts, one or two statements recorded by Rawlinson in his diary, and some deduction.

Absolutely nothing had been done to exploit the victories of the divisions on the right wing. Rawlinson had refused Congreve permission to advance one yard beyond his original objectives and, as early as 12.15 P.M., Rawlinson had already made up his mind about the cavalry. 'There is, of course, no hope of getting the cavalry through today.'* By 3 P.M. the cavalry divisions had received their orders: they were to turn round and retire. These orders were sent from Gough's Reserve Army H.Q., but there can be no doubt that the orders originated with Rawlinson.

* The Rawlinson Diaries.

As for that greater part of his front, where the morning attacks had failed, there was little that Rawlinson could do. No doubt he had urged his corps commanders, with some vigour, to try and try again, but on these sectors the attacking divisions had been so badly smashed that they were beyond the pressure of generals. There were adequate fresh divisions available, but the trenches were so shelled, so full of dead and wounded, that they would never have reached the front line, let alone have carried out a successful attack.

By the evening, Rawlinson had a good idea of what progress his troops had made and the extent of his failures. His diary entry for 7.30 P.M. gives a résumé of the battle that, in spite of the confusion, is remarkably accurate but for one detail: 'Casualties to date, 16,000.' The units of the Fourth Army had, in fact, suffered over 50,000 losses.

At about this time there was an important change in the command structure. Rawlinson's army was a big one, containing five corps, three of which were obviously in trouble. As a result of a telephone conversation between Rawlinson and G.H.Q., Lieut-Gen. Gough, the cavalry commander, was sent to take over the command of the two northern corps of Fourth Army. These were Hunter-Weston's VIII Corps, which had fared badly north of the Ancre, and Morland's X Corps, whose only success had been the capture of the Schwaben Redoubt by the Ulster Division. At the same time, control of the cavalry divisions passed directly to Fourth Army.

The move is an interesting one. Rawlinson had decided some hours previously that there was to be no cavalry action and thought that Gough could do a more worthwhile job looking after the two infantry corps. Gough had a reputation as a thrusting general, and might be expected to drive the failing corps to further efforts and possible success.

What is more interesting is Rawlinson's attitude to the change. In theory he and Gough were both army commanders and equals, although Gough still lagged behind by one rank. Haig had the final say in the move but in his diary Rawlinson stated bluntly: 'I am putting Goughy in command of VIII and X Corps.'

Gough appears to have relished the prospect of something to do. With his Chief of Staff he set off at once by car to see the two corps commanders. He had trouble on the way with military policemen who tried to persuade him to drive without lights, but Gough refused. He was in a hurry and preferred the remote risk of death or injury by aerial bomb to the more likely danger of crashing in the dark.

Gough's first call was at Hunter-Weston's VIII Corps, which was still under Rawlinson's order to make a fresh attack in the early hours of the next morning. Gough summed up the position quickly and came to the conclusion that such an attack would be hopeless. Although he was not supposed to take over until 7 A.M. on 2 July, he immediately cancelled the attack. This swift assessment and his decision to ignore previous orders shows high moral courage in Gough and it undoubtedly saved many lives. Leaving Hunter-Weston, Gough went on to his other corps where he arrived in time to learn that its only success, the capture of the Schwaben Redoubt, had turned to bitter defeat as the Ulster Division had been forced out of its gains.

As darkness fell, the medical services were faced with their biggest test. The casualty list had exceeded all estimates and the two attacking armies had suffered over 35,000 wounded men between them. Many of the lightly wounded had already reached the Casualty Clearing Stations, especially those from the sectors on the right wing where the attack had been successful. Now that it was dark, the thousands of men in No Man's Land were available for recovery too. These were in far worse condition. Their wounds had been left untreated for up to twelve hours, and some had been wounded several times. The evacuation process was about to come under its maximum strain.

The first stress to appear was among the stretcher-bearers, who had the difficult and hazardous job of recovering the badly wounded, firstly from the battered British trenches and, later, from No Man's Land. Heavy casualties among the bearers themselves had thrown an extra burden on those who had survived. Every spare man – pioneers, infantry, artillery, engineers and the rest – was pressed into service and every device was used to get the wounded away: 'As we had no stretchers we had to use sheets of corrugated iron and by the end of the day we had all cut our fingers.' (Sgt A. P. Britton, 8th Lincolns) 'We abandoned the communication trenches and carried over the open. We even carried two wounded to a stretcher and our men lost the use of their hands, but carried the stretchers by slings around their necks without complaint.' (Sgt F. F. Webber, 94th Field Ambulance)

First stop for the wounded man on his way to the rear was often the battalion Aid Post, where his own Medical Officer was in charge. Being so close to the fighting and having few facilities, the M.O.'s could give only rudimentary treatment. If a case could possibly go farther back without treatment he was waved past, leaving the M.O. to deal with the most desperate cases only. On the worst sectors, the scenes at these Posts were among the most harrowing of the whole battlefield. 'I managed to crawl half a mile to Basin Wood where I saw the most horrible sight. Our M.O. was working at a trestle table in his vest, and bodies were piled like sand-bags all around him.' (Cpl A. Wood, 1st Bradford Pals)

Immediately behind the trench system were the Dressing Stations operated by the Field Ambulances. Again there were no facilities for surgery here but men had their wounds dressed properly before being sent back to the C.C.S.'s. A typical Dressing Station had been set up in the basilica at Albert: 'Wounded flooded in on foot, or were brought by stretchers, wheelbarrows, carts – anything. Their wounds were dressed and then they were laid out on the floor to await evacuation. Soon the whole church was packed and we were ordered to stop any vehicle that passed and make them take wounded to the rear. I even put three cases in a general's staff car. Those who were not expected to survive were put on one side and left. It was very hard to ignore their cries for help but we had to concentrate on those who might live. We worked for three days and nights without rest. It was the bloodiest battle I ever saw.' (Pte H. Streets, 58th Field Ambulance)*

Even at the Dressing Stations the wounded were not finally out of danger. German shells sometimes crashed against the basilica, but the massive structure had survived nearly two years of shelling and the wounded inside were safe. Not so the men like Charles Matthews who were laid out

* Harry Streets' twin brother worked in the same unit. Another brother, Will, was a sergeant in the Sheffield City Battalion and was killed in the attack on Serre.

in the open in the village square at Carnoy. Matthews was given no treatment there, as he had no open wounds, but all afternoon he waited with hundreds of others under the hot sun. It was a terrifying experience to be lying helpless and vulnerable to random German shrapnel shells bursting overhead. A medical orderly covered his face with a newspaper to protect him from the burning sun. Matthews was touched by this thoughtful action and felt in some absurd way that the paper would protect him from the plunging shrapnel balls.

Those men who had only been lightly wounded and were still able to walk were expected to get themselves to the rear. Once their wounds had been dressed, often by themselves or by their friends, they were directed along specially marked tracks: 'The walking wounded started coming out of the trenches in ones and twos, but later they came in droves. It was just like watching a crowd leaving a football match. Most had left their rifles and equipment behind and were only half dressed.' (Gnr H. W. Beaumont, 170th (County Palatine) Brigade R.F.A.)

From the Dressing Stations to the Casualty Clearing Stations was a distance of some ten miles, covered by motor ambulances running a shuttle service. Even when they had been loaded into the ambulances, the wounded were still in danger from German shells for the first part of their journey. One man met an old school friend while waiting for the ambulance. Because there was only room for one when his turn came, he stayed behind with his friend, and watched the ambulance blow up fifty yards down the road.

All day the ambulances had been bringing the wounded to the C.C.S.'s, but how had the next part of the evacuation process, from the C.C.S.'s to the base, been operating? Before the battle, Gen. Rawlinson had formally requested eighteen ambulance trains for his Fourth Army and had been assured that there would be no delays. Using the procedure laid down in the new G.H.Q. instructions, the Fourth Army C.C.S.'s had called for twelve of these trains. The response had been disastrous. Only three ambulance trains had been standing by in the Fourth Army area. One had run in the morning and the other two in the afternoon. Urgent messages were sent to other parts of the British zone, calling for more trains, but by midnight only two more had arrived, making a total of five for the day.

These five trains had only taken 3,217 cases to the base. Of these 647 were sick and many of the wounded were cases left over from previous days. At least 32,000 men had been wounded in Fourth Army, whose C.C.S.'s had proper accommodation for only 9,500 cases. 10,000 had already reached the C.C.S.'s and most of the remainder were about to descend upon them. Less than 1,000 of the day's wounded had been evacuated to the base. All the carefully laid plans to avoid congestion had failed.

So it was that at 10.50 P.M., with thousands of wounded men coming in from the front, the Director of Medical Services in Fourth Army entered in his War Diary:

Ambulance Trains not yet arriving and all C.C.S.'s in Southern Area are full except those at Vecquement and these are filling rapidly.

And at midnight:

All arrangements except trains are working smoothly.*

Fortunately, there was no such problem in Third Army. 4,000 men from VII Corps had been wounded at Gommecourt, but all the medical facilities of Third Army were available to absorb them and there was no hold-up at any stage.

What did the shortage of ambulance trains mean to the Fourth Army wounded? Those who had been placed out in the open at the C.C.S.'s, had to spend the night there, in pain, often with their wounds untreated, and all hoping that it would not rain. Motor ambulances, bringing more wounded from the front, were turned away from those C.C.S.'s which were full and sent elsewhere. The drivers, already tired, had to motor farther in the dark, trying to find someone to take their loads.

At the front there was an immediate effect at the Dressing Stations. The War Diary of the 25th Field Ambulance reports:

7.0. P.M. Urgent demand for more stretchers, indented on C.C.S. Corbie without avail. 8.30 P.M. 36 C.C.S. and 38 C.C.S. at Heilly closed. By midnight choked with cases, opened several barns for temporary accommodation.†

The wounded men in such places as the basilica at Albert and the village square at Carnoy had to wait longer than

* Public Record Office, WO 95/447.

† Public Record Office, WO 95/1703.

would otherwise have been necessary for their turn to be taken to safety in the ambulances.

For some the wait was too long. They died of serious wounds, denied the attention of the surgeons at the c.c.s.'s, or they died as German shells fell amongst them. Someone would have to answer for the missing ambulance trains.

If the British soldiers were relieved when darkness fell, the Germans were equally pleased that the day was nearly over. Their regiments were defending a twenty-six-mile front, for they were having to fight the French as well as the British, and had done their work well in spite of the numerical superiority of their attackers. The long months of toil when they had worked on their defences and the pre-war years of conscription which had given them such a high degree of proficiency had paid their dividends.

True, there were parts of the front where their enemies had been successful, the German front-line defences had been lost and the defenders had suffered heavy casualties: 'By the afternoon we were very low in numbers and were nearly out of ammunition. We took all we could from the dead and wounded but we were not strong enough to hold out for long. The day closed with another English attack which we fought standing up in the open. When our last cartridge had been fired we retreated through the enemy barrage to Klein-Bazentin [Bazentin le Petit]. When the regiment collected in Le Transloy that evening, my company consisted of twenty men.' (Unteroffizier Paul Scheytt, 109th Reserve Regiment)

On his way back to Bazentin, Scheytt took part in a small diversion: 'We found a battery of our own guns completely deserted and, out of pure cussedness, we decided to fire them although we were only infantrymen. So we fiddled about with all those little levers and eventually got two guns loaded and fired two rounds. The English immediately replied, so we cleared off as fast as we could.'

The following story shows how difficult it was for the British to be sure they had completely cleared a dug-out: 'I was wounded quite early in the morning and remember lying semi-conscious and seeing British soldiers jumping over our trench but we were not rounded up and several of us took shelter in a dug-out. Once, during the morning, an

English grenade came down and exploded with a loud crash. No one was hurt and one of my comrades said "Pardon me" as if he had made a rude noise. We laughed. A second grenade followed and again no one was hurt. Then an English soldier came down but we all hid in a dark corner and weren't seen. It was many hours later that one of our men went out with a white handkerchief and we were taken prisoner by two soldiers from the Devonshire Regiment. They were very friendly and the doctor who attended to me asked me where I came from. When I told him "Freiburg", he told me that that was where he had studied and asked me about certain girls that he knew there.' (Grenadier Emil Kury, 109th Reserve Regiment)

In spite of these British successes, the Germans were still greatly relieved. The attack on such a long frontage had surprised them and there were few reserves behind the southern part of their front. For many hours the sector opposite Montauban had been virtually naked; only two battalions had moved forward half-heartedly during the afternoon. The seemingly empty woods and fields that the British troops had gazed on all afternoon had indeed been empty for long periods. The German second main trench system was over a mile away and that too was not fully manned. The Germans could have done little to stop a determined British advance on this sector. They were both amazed and pleased when nothing happened. 'What puzzled me most all day was the lack of further forward movement by the British. The whole of our line had collapsed and it would have been a simple matter for them to have advanced much further than they did.' (Soldat Emil Goebelbecker, 109th Reserve Regiment)

The sudden advance of the Ulster Division near Thiepval had again caught the Germans without local reserves and for some time the issue there had been in the balance. 'We were force-marched from Grandcourt up to the line; we were nearly running. We came under artillery fire, both shrapnel and gas, and had to put on our gas masks. We straggled all over the place. We heard that one of our companies had been taken prisoner. Then came the order that we wouldn't have to attack, after all, as the English had been held.' (Soldat Lorenz Schneider, 8th Bavarian Reserve Regiment)

At one place on the edge of the Schwaben Redoubt there

occurred the following curious incident. 'About 2.30 in the afternoon the attacks had stopped. I heard music from a bit farther along the trench where the English were. I told my mates and they didn't believe me. Then we all listened and sure enough we heard something like a zither or guitar. So I propped up my rifle and went along to have a look. At about 100 metres distance, I could vaguely see some people so I went back to my mates. We all took our rifles and fired off a few rounds at them. There was a short silence and then they replied with a machine-gun. We didn't hear the music again.' (Soldat Wilhelm Lange, 99th Reserve Regiment)

On most of the front where the British had attacked the Germans were more than satisfied. They had been tested by everything that their enemy could throw against them – a week-long artillery barrage and massed infantry attacks – and they had emerged victorious. The evidence of their victory was before their eyes, the bodies of hundreds of dead British hanging on the barbed wire and strewn thickly across No Man's Land. Their badly wounded enemies could be seen dragging themselves painfully away and fugitives sprang up from shell holes and ran back into the gloom. These latter were pursued by a few scattered shots, but the passion and fury of the day had abated and the Germans were mostly content to let them go. There had been enough killing.

The anger had turned, in some cases, to pity and compassion. The Germans had been prepared to allow truces for the removal of the British wounded as early as 2 P.M., on some sectors, but these daylight cease-fires had not been successful. Sometimes the British artillery had unwittingly spoilt the work of mercy by continuing to fire on German trenches. The Germans had also taken advantage of the truce by coming out into No Man's Land, less to help the wounded than to collect Lewis guns, which they calmly loaded onto stretchers and carried back to their trenches. This was reported to the nearest British brigade H.Q. which issued a stern order that no truce was to be allowed and that the Germans were to be fired upon. This was only carried out with some reluctance, but the spell was broken and firing started again from both sides.

When it became dark the front-line troops were able to

resume their local armistices without interference by their superiors. 'During the night I was approached by an officer of the Rifle Brigade [the 1st London Rifle Brigade]. He had a white flag and asked if he could remove the wounded. I could speak English and told him I would put his request to my leutnant. My officer gave permission but he only informed the troops on either side, not the H.Q. in the rear. We helped the English to find their wounded. Sometimes we carried them over to their own side, sometimes the English laid a white tape to the wounded men so that their stretcher-bearers could find them in the dark. When it got light we received orders that we should stop what we were doing but, by then, most of the good work was done. We fired warning shots to tell the English that the truce was over.

'We were hardened, experienced soldiers. It wasn't fair to send these young soldiers against us. Some of them were only students and we felt very sorry for them.' (Gefreiter Hugo van Egeren, 55th Reserve Regiment)

This incident was at Gommecourt. Not all the Germans were so cooperative; only where their domination was complete were they prepared to help.

13

The Night

With the coming of darkness No Man's Land became alive, as thousands of British soldiers decided that it was safe to move. The men limped, crawled and felt their way over ground which had been green and level at dawn but was now a mass of shell craters, littered with discarded equipment and dead bodies. 'I kept falling into shell holes which had men in them but, when I tried to get them to come in with me, I found they were all dead. Sometimes there were eight or nine in one hole.' (Pte A. Fretwell, Sheffield City Battalion)

One of the fugitives was Bugler Bill Soar. Although he was injured in the arm he managed to reach his own barbed wire easily enough but there a burst of machine-gun bullets, passing just above his head, forced him flat to the ground. A nervous sentry was challenging all comers in this fashion and Soar had to identify himself before he was told to come in. Then he got caught in the barbed wire and only freed himself by abandoning his trousers. He had already lost his rifle, helmet and all his equipment, and returned to his lines in just his tunic. His wound was not serious and he walked back to a Dressing Station.

The Glasgow Boys' Brigade sergeant, who had fired twenty-four drums of Lewis gun ammunition while he had been in No Man's Land, came in at dusk, asked for more ammunition and declared his intention of resuming his private battle in the morning. He was ordered to go to the rear and rejoin his battalion.

For those who had been pinned down close to the German trenches, escape to their own lines was not always possible; as it became dark the Germans left their trenches and rounded up prisoners before the British could get away. 'Four of us decided to wait until it was completely dark, so that we could make a run for it, but the Germans were soon all around us and stick grenades started coming at us. We decided it was hopeless and stood up to surrender. This action did not deter about twenty Germans from making a lunatic charge at us with fixed bayonets. A split second before connecting my stomach with a bayonet, at which I nearly passed out in terror, a terrific shout of "Halt!" came from somewhere and, showing how disciplined the German soldier is, the one coming at me slid flat on his back, his rifle went straight up in the air and his legs shot between mine.' (L/Cpl T. R. Short, 1st London Rifle Brigade)

'I lay by the German wire from about 7.45 A.M. till after nightfall, receiving a shrapnel wound in the foot and a bullet wound in the hand during the course of the day. When darkness fell, the Germans threw volleys of hand grenades into the wire and then came out to pick up the pieces. I was carried into the German front-line trench and taken down into a dug-out where I was searched and my wound dressed.' (2nd Lieut J. W. Stansby, 1/6th North Staffs)*

Pte Albert McMillan had been very close to the German trenches and would have liked to escape but, at dusk, a sergeant-major from his own battalion told McMillan and others nearby that the Germans had them covered and ordered them to put down their rifles, take off all their equipment and surrender. German soldiers then came out and rounded them up. McMillan noticed that their rifles were fitted with telescopic sights and that they wore metal breast plates on which were painted red crosses. He wondered whether the cross was a regimental insignia or a trick to avoid being fired at; it was probably the Landwehr Cross, a symbol worn by Reserve and other units. His captors were men of the 119th Reserve Regiment.

One of the Middlesex men, who had been badly wounded in the groin, was being passed down carefully into the enemy trench, when a watching German jeered, '*Nicht mehr Kinder machen*' ('No more children for you'). Albert McMillan found that his steel helmet was scored in several places where German bullets had struck it. One bullet had even pierced it and grazed his scalp. Pte Albert McMillan's active participation in the Great War had ended in less than twenty-four hours.

Back in No Man's Land some of the British soldiers could not, or dared not, move. The severely wounded had to stay where they were and hope for help. Already stretcher-bearers were out looking for them, but it would be a long job. Every-

* From the papers of the late Mr J. W. Stansby kindly loaned by his widow, Mrs J. Stansby, Yelverton, Norfolk.

thing was against the searchers – their own barbed wire, the torn-up ground, the difficulty of distinguishing dead from wounded in the dark, the firing which occasionally broke out and the very number of the wounded. There was not much more than six hours of darkness on this night and many could not be reached before daylight stopped the work. For some, help would come too late and they would die, alone, unconscious or in agony.

Where they had captured the German trenches, the British soldiers settled down for the night. They were weary but braced by their first taste of success: 'We got a ration of rum, which may have been slightly larger than usual owing to there being several casualties. We were, nevertheless, quite sober but feeling very pleased with ourselves at having taken our objective. We were so pleased with this and the fact that so many of us were still alive that we started singing some of these war-time songs, "It's a Long Way to Tipperary" and "Keep the Home Fires Burning".' (Pte R. G. Robertson, 4th Liverpool Pals)

Some battalions, in taking their objectives, had suffered heavily and sent for reinforcements from the men they had left behind in reserve. Near Fricourt, a tall, thin lieutenant, shown in the battalion diary as B. H. L. Hart, led a party of the 9th K.O.Y.L.I. up into the captured trenches. Every officer in this battalion and its sister battalion near by, the 10th K.O.Y.L.I., had become a casualty and Lieut Hart had to reorganize the remnants of both. What he saw that evening and later on the Somme left a lasting impression on the young officer who, as Basil Liddell Hart, became a leading military thinker and a critic of British military policy. But papers written by him in September 1916 show that he still admired his leaders then. This transformation, from enthusiastic infantry officer to bitter critic, is typical of the way many soldiers changed their views over the years.

Many of the smaller groups of men had been sent back from the Quadrilateral to the British lines but C.S.M.Percy Chappell's force of Somersets still formed part of its garrison. By nightfall, Chappell and his men were extremely hungry, so he selected two well-known scroungers and ordered them to search the German dug-outs for food. The foragers soon returned with a haul of dark bread, cold stew, cigars and,

Stretcher-bearers tending wounded men in a British trench in the 29th Division's area on the morning of the battle. Very few pictures of British trenches choked with dead and wounded were released; by 1916 the effect of propaganda images was fully appreciated.

Δ the Deccan Horse, part of the 2nd Indian Cavalry Division. On 1 July this was the nearest cavalry regiment to the successful British right wing, being in Happy Valley, three miles behind the lines. This photograph was not taken on 1st July.

∇ 18-pounder field guns move forward near Mametz after the successful infantry advance there. The gun team is wheeling to avoid the body of a man from the 2nd Gordon Highlanders.

∆ A carrying party (possibly the 1st Royal Irish Rifles, a reserve battalion of the 8th Division) resting in a communication trench on the day of the battle.

∇ Walking wounded of the 7th Division near Minden Post.

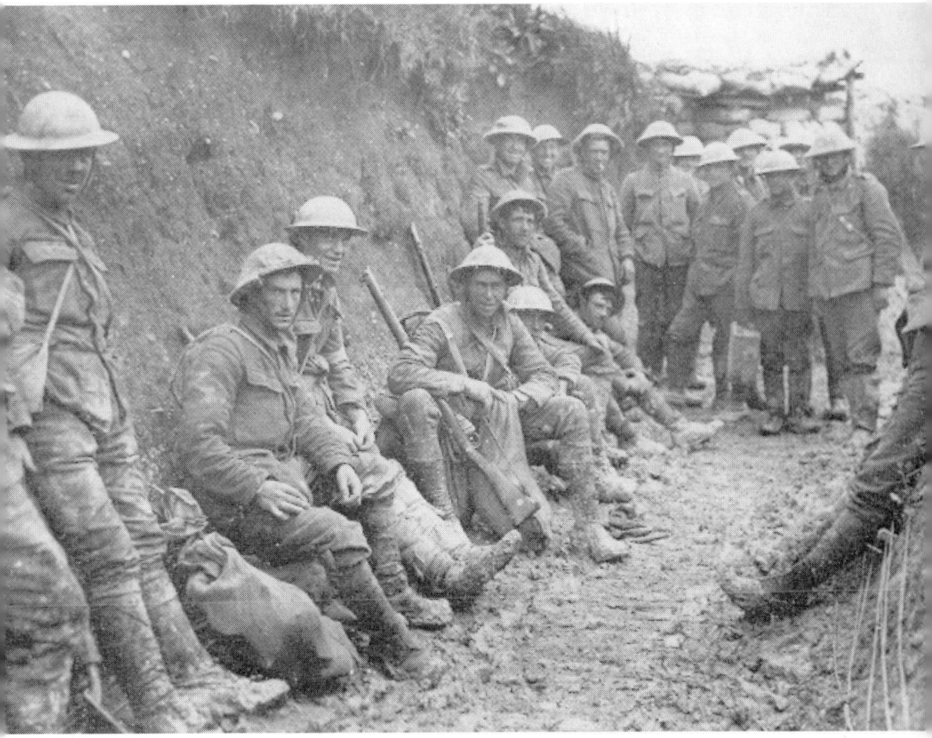

Δ This photograph, taken on 2nd July, shows the difficulty experienced in evacuating stretcher cases from the trenches.

∇ British prisoners being marched to the rear near Pys. They are probably men from either the 29th Division or the Ulster Division and are obviously from a good battalion. Although there are only eight men, they have formed fours and are marching in step.

Δ German machine-gunners with captured Lewis guns which were regarded as valuable booty. These guns were not necessarily taken on 1 July as the caption merely says 'Battle of the Somme, 1916'.

∇ 'Here rests the brave English Captain.' The Germans honour a dead British officer at Gommecourt. He was in fact Captain F. H. M. Lewes, adjutant of the 1/5th Sherwood Foresters. His grave was lost and he is now commemorated on the Thiepval Memorial.

Δ Men of the 1st Lancashire Fusiliers answer a roll call in a reserve trench after the battle (compare with photograph on page 19). This battalion suffered 483 casualties in the unsuccessful attack on Beaumont Hamel.

∇ The cemetery in Blighty Valley in 1921. On 1 July 1916, the 8th Division attacked just beyond the rise behind the cemetery.

Δ Blighty Valley Cemetery now. This picture shows how the War Graves Commission transformed the military burial grounds into permanent cemeteries. It also shows how the countryside has recovered from its war-time desolation.

∇ The Thiepval Memorial to the Missing. The names of those whose graves were never found are carved into the stone panels on the columns.

The Golden Virgin on the rebuilt basilica of Albert.

surprisingly, several tins of British bully beef. The bread and stew were left untouched as it was feared that the Germans might have poisoned them. There was much speculation as to the source of the bully beef; the Germans must have raided the trenches of a British battalion and made off with their rations. The Somersets dined on bully beef and water, and followed their meal with German cigars.

The following incident illustrates how precarious the position of the men in the Quadrilateral was. Under cover of the dark, a company of the 1st Royal Irish Fusiliers had crossed to the redoubt as reinforcements. During the night one of their sergeants was searching for wounded men, when he heard German voices. The sergeant threw a grenade in the direction of the voices, and either killed or drove off the Germans. He found they had been erecting two machine-guns which, in the morning, could have fired straight into the British-held part of the redoubt. He toppled one gun into a deep shell hole and called for help to bring back the other and deliver it to his officer.

Back in the British trenches, the breakdown of organization on some sectors was complete; few plans had been made for such a complete failure. Three groups of men should have been on the move: the wounded being evacuated, those involved in the attack being relieved, and fresh troops taking over the front line. The trenches themselves had been badly battered by shell fire and the movement of troops from different units, with conflicting duties, was adding to the congestion and hampering the clearance of the dead and wounded.

The suffering of the wounded was grievous. There were so many seriously hurt mixed among the dead bodies that, in the darkness, some were even trampled to death or pressed into the mud and choked in the slime. On the worst sectors the stretcher-bearers were so overwhelmed that badly wounded men had little chance of rescue. 'That night a captain begged me to shoot him as he was so badly hurt, but I couldn't. I went back next morning and he had died in the night.' (Pte A. Morrison, East Belfast Volunteers) Again, 'I was sent back from the Quadrilateral but, when I got back to our trenches, an officer's servant stopped me coming in. His lieutenant was dying and the soldier was straining to catch his last words. I heard the officer giving instructions for a watch to be sent back to his family. Then he died and I was allowed to come in.' (Pte E. C. Stanley, 1/8th Royal Warwicks)

It was feared that the Germans might take advantage of the confusion and attack during the night. Certainly, there would have been little to stop them taking the British trenches, had they wished to do so. One brigade reported that its front line was manned by only twenty-five men. The nearest unit, in this case a Pioneer battalion, was rushed up to man the line.

Those men who had been in the attack were sometimes allowed to retire. 'We were told that if we could clear the trench of dead and wounded sufficiently, we would be relieved. We propped the dead in rows at the back of the trench and sat the wounded on the fire-step and we waited to be relieved. There were three of us left in my platoon.' (Pte G. S. Young, 1/6th North Staffs)

The British trenches opposite Serre were being held by a company from a Hull battalion that had not been in the attack but, as they had been holding the trenches for over a week and had been shelled all day, were very tired. The company commander decided to concentrate his men in the reserve trench but wanted eight volunteers to man a post in the front line and fire a warning rocket if the Germans attacked. 'To a man we had frightful headaches and had had so much concussion that we were all suffering from varying degrees of shell shock. We stood there in stony silence, which was finally broken by a shell bursting just outside the trench and a piece of shrapnel knocking off the tin hat of the man standing next to me. The captain then said that he was left with the unpleasant task of detailing someone for such a mission and, as bombers were best suited for these isolated posts, he detailed *my* bombing team.

'And so, at dusk, we moved down the remnants of the trench to the front line. The last hundred yards was solid with men killed whilst waiting to go over. It was impossible to do other than walk on these bodies and I finally reached a man on a stretcher, with a bearer lying dead at each end. I raised my foot to place it on the chest of the man on the stretcher, when, to my amazement, he popped his head up and said quietly, "Mind my leg, chum", and then just laid back again.

'Reaching the front line we had a job to find a habitable bit of trench, but we got our rockets fixed and sentries posted and then set out to spend the longest night of our lives.' (Pte W. E. Aust, Hull Commercials)

As orders that they were to be relieved reached them, the battalions prepared to leave the trenches from which they had attacked with such enthusiasm that morning. It was a pitiful spectacle; a few dozen exhausted, dirty men were sometimes all that were left. Many had lost their rifles and equipment, or wore blood-stained field dressings. Quietly, they were called together by an officer or N.C.O., and led to the rear. An artillery officer witnessed the departure of Lieut-Col. Sandys' battalion: 'In the evening fresh troops took over the line and I watched the 2nd Middlesex, to which I had been attached as Forward Observation Officer, march away. There was one officer and twenty-eight men, all that remained of a very gallant battalion.' (Lieut F. L. Lee, 33rd Brigade R.F.A.)

The ten per cent reserve of officers and men which had been left behind was often called forward to help with the reorganization of the battalions. These meetings were tense occasions. On one side, the shabby survivors; on the other, the fresh, smart soldiers who had escaped the holocaust. There was a gulf between the two parties which would take time to bridge.

Lieut Philip Howe had been to his brigade H.Q. and reported all he knew of the fate of his battalion. When he had sent the wounded off to be treated, the 10th West Yorks consisted of himself and twenty men. The reserve joined them and another officer, senior to Howe, took charge. Philip Howe was very angry. He had come to regard himself as the acting battalion commander, even though his battalion had been less than a platoon strong. The other officer was not one of the original members who had formed the battalion in 1914 and he had not been in the attack. Howe's tired, unreasonable mind resented this man taking away his command, but soon exhaustion overtook him and he slept.*

The Ulstermen returned from the hell of Thiepval. 'Our C.Q.M.S. had promised champagne to those who came back; sure enough when I got back the champagne was there. Every now and then another straggler came in and we got talking about those who had been hit. Many of us broke down and started howling, but some were ready to go back next day and

* For his actions on 1 July, Philip Howe was later awarded the Military Cross.

look for the wounded. One man in particular, a fat man called Hamilton, was ready to go, but we had to laugh because his rifle had been hit and was twisted like a corkscrew and he didn't know it.' (L/Cpl J. A. Henderson, Belfast Young Citizens)

'We stayed up during that night to wait for the battalion to come in. They straggled in. First there would be a man on his own and then, maybe a couple, one helping another who was exhausted. I vividly remember some of them screaming and demented with shell shock. They had obviously had the shock of their lives. None of the chaps in my draft, who had trained with me and who had only just joined the battalion, came back. My shorthand had saved me.' (Pte T. A. Senior, 9th Yorks and Lancs)

Many men had become separated from their battalions and were lost in the dark. 'I tried to find the others but I had to give up. I went down into a dug-out in Observation Wood and slept there. When I woke up in the morning, I found that the only other occupant was a dead machine-gun officer.' (Pte A. Fretwell, Sheffield City Battalion)

In the North Midland Division, so few men had returned from the attacking battalions, that senior officers refused to believe that the remainder had all been lost. 'We battalion scouts were sent for by the c.o. and he asked for volunteers to go out into No Man's Land to find out what had happened to the rest of the 1/7th. He hinted that the highest possible award might go to anyone who could find Colonel Hind. I set off with other volunteers but, when we got to the front line, another officer stopped us going out.' (L/Cpl H. Hickman, 1/8th Sherwood Foresters)

A report was received that some of the Foresters were still holding out in the German trenches and a fresh battalion, the 1/5th Lincolns, was ordered to find and relieve the trapped men. This move, by one company of the Lincolns, was hastily organized. It was dark; the men did not know their exact position, the aim of the attack or the identity of nearby troops, but were simply ordered to attack the German front line. One platoon deployed in the open but were facing the wrong way. A sergeant, their acting platoon commander, turned them in approximately the correct direction but refused to move off until he had been given more precise information. Even when warned that this might be interpreted as mutiny, the sergeant stood firm, insisting that the absence of clear orders did not give his men a chance; the platoon never did advance.*

At midnight two platoons reached the German wire but they were caught by the light of flares and came under heavy fire. It was obvious that there were no longer any Foresters holding out in the German trenches and the Lincolns were ordered back. They withdrew in good order, but forty-eight of their men had been killed or wounded. This incident, on the extreme left of the battlefield at Gommecourt, was the last action of the first day of the Battle of the Somme.

Some 21,000 soldiers, representing the cream of the manhood of Great Britain, Ireland and the colony of Newfoundland, had been killed or would die as a result of their wounds. Over 35,000 more had been wounded and nearly 600 were prisoners of war.

At midnight, Lieut-Col. Reginald Bastard was in the process of handing over his trenches to a relieving battalion; all but one of his officers and two thirds of his men were casualties. Lieut Philip Howe and twenty survivors of the 10th West Yorks were asleep in a field. Lieut Henry Webber's battalion was in the outskirts of Albert, but had not been touched by the battle.

Paddy Kennedy was playing with his kitten in a captured German trench, thinking that the war was nearly won. Sergeant Major Percy Chappell was in a captured German redoubt, but surrounded by enemies.

L/Cpl Charles Matthews and Bugler Bill Soar were in Dressing Stations. Matthews was drowsy from the morphia that he had been given to ease the pain of his crushed knee but Soar only had a flesh wound in the arm.

Albert McMillan was in German hands after his first and last day of war.

Dick King and Billy McFadzean were dead, lost to their families and to their country.

* No action was taken against the sergeant for his refusal. Later, as C.S.M. W. E. Hamp, D.C.M., M.M., he was killed in action at Arras, in June 1917.

14

The Aftermath

The Battle of the Somme lasted for the remainder of the summer and well into the autumn of 1916, but midnight of the first day brought to an end a distinct phase of the campaign. The diversion at Gommecourt and the attack of the two corps that Gough had taken over were immediately closed down. On 2 July only three divisions were involved in serious action compared with fourteen on the previous day. The fighting of 1 July can be classed as a separate battle in its own right. It can be argued that, for the British at least, it was the turning-point of the First World War. Before going on to examine the long-term effects, however, a look should be taken at the immediate aftermath of the battle – on the battlefield itself, in those places where the generals and politicians wielded power and in the homes of the ordinary soldiers.

In the days following the battle, the remainder of the men who had fought on the first day were withdrawn. In the early hours of 2 July it was decided that the Quadrilateral Redoubt could not be held, so a staff officer crossed to it and ordered the garrison to withdraw. C.S.M. Percy Chappell gathered together the survivors of the 1st Somerset Light Infantry and led them back to the British front line. There were seventy-eight in all, including twenty walking wounded.*

The last to leave the Quadrilateral was the Royal Irish Fusiliers company, which arrived back at its battalion H.Q. next morning. 'Their arrival caused a merry interlude. The company commander was slung with German equipment of every shape and description, and his company were also replete with souvenirs. They still guarded a few sulky looking prisoners from whom they seemed reluctant to part. If the colonel had not intervened they would, in all probability, have been led about in triumph for the rest of the war.' (Capt. W. Carden Roe, M.C., 1st Royal Irish Fusiliers)

* Percy Chappell was awarded the Distinguished Conduct Medal for his good work and was also given a battlefield commission. This was a rare honour; only four members of the various Somerset Light Infantry battalions received such commissions during the war.

Paddy Kennedy remained for three days in the new front line at Montauban. To the amazement of these forward troops, they received no further orders to advance. Several small German counter-attacks were beaten off and there was obviously little to prevent the Manchesters and the other battalions here from occupying the nearby woods.

On 4 July the whole of the 30th Division was withdrawn for a well-earned rest. Kennedy went straight back to the place in the old front line where he had dumped all his heavy equipment and found everything as he had left it. When he reported back to his own battalion, the 3rd Pals which he had not seen since 30 June, he still had the kitten he had found in the German dug-out at Montauban. Paddy gave it to the company cooks for a mascot.

On the unsuccessful sectors, the clearance of the British wounded from No Man's Land went on for several days. At dawn on 2 July most of the work of recovery in the open had to cease, as the Germans were rarely prepared to allow the British to move freely.

Some stretcher-bearers and their helpers did not wait for darkness to come again, but risked their lives by continuing to work in daylight. Two examples of gallantry in this respect are recorded by the Ulster Division, on that part of its sector where the Germans still dominated No Man's Land.

Before the war Robert Quigg had been a worker on the MacNaghten estate at Bushmills in Co. Antrim. Now he was Pte Quigg and soldier-servant to twenty-year-old 2nd Lieut Sir Harry MacNaghten, the 6th Baronet, who was one of the missing on the evening of 1 July. Next day Quigg went out into No Man's Land seven times searching for his officer, and each time he brought in a wounded man, the last dragged in on a groundsheet from within a few yards of the German wire. In the end, Quigg had to give up through sheer exhaustion. Sir Harry was never found.*

In the same area Lieut Geoffrey Cather, the adjutant of the Armagh Volunteers, fetched in three wounded men during the night following the battle. Next morning, in full view of the enemy, he brought in another but, while giving a fifth a drink from his water bottle, he was killed by a German

* On Sir Harry MacNaghten's death, the baronetcy was inherited by his brother Douglas who was serving as a subaltern in the Rifle Brigade, but he was killed only ten weeks later near Delville Wood.

machine-gunner. For their bravery in the fighting on 1 July and for these rescue attempts both Quigg and Cather were awarded the Victoria Cross, making a total of four such awards in the Ulster Division.*

During the afternoon of 2 July there was a shower of rain near Thiepval and, shortly afterwards, some men could be seen crawling towards the British trenches. Fearing a German attack, the defenders called for artillery support, but cancelled this just in time when they realized that the 'attackers' were British wounded who had been revived by the shower.

As soon as darkness came again, full-scale rescue work was resumed as stretcher-bearers and many volunteer helpers combed the battlefield for the rest of the wounded. One of the searchers in Sausage Valley was Maj.-Gen. Ingouville-Williams. One wounded Newfoundlander had taken shelter from further German fire between the bodies of two of his dead comrades. Being a recently arrived reinforcement and unfamiliar with the area, he did not know which trenches were German and which his own. He stayed between the two bodies until 3 July, when he decided he would have to take a chance and crawled towards one of the belts of barbed wire. Fortunately he chose the right one.

In front of the 29th Division, one survivor was so demented that he had removed all his clothes. Another, also crazed, or having lost all sense of direction, fired at the British trenches every time a man showed himself there.

The attitude of the Germans to the wounded and their rescuers was unpredictable. Sometimes, as in Lieut Cather's case, they shot at anyone who moved, but at other times they were merciful. As late as 5 July, it was known that many wounded were out in No Man's Land near Beaumont Hamel so the British decided upon a bold scheme. 'A large Red Cross flag was slowly raised above the parapet. When, after a few minutes, no shots had been fired, two M.O.'s stood up on the parapet beside the flag. Still the enemy held their fire. The two officers then advanced across No Man's Land with the flag. A mass of curious heads appeared above the German parapet and a German M.O. and some orderlies came out to

* In all, nine V.C.'s were awarded for actions connected with the first day of the Somme Battle; six of these were posthumous awards. A full list is given in Appendix 5. During the First World War an average of two V.C.'s were awarded to British servicemen each week.

meet ours. The officers of both sides stiffened to a ceremonious salute. The Germans carried our wounded from near their wire to the middle of No Man's Land and handed them over to our bearers. This great work of humanity went on until all the wounded were collected then, again, the officers saluted. Not a word had been exchanged all afternoon.' (Capt. W. Carden Roe, M.C., 1st Royal Irish Fusiliers)

Some of the wounded managed to survive in the open for long periods and individual soldiers continued to be rescued from No Man's Land for many days. At Gommecourt, a lieutenant of the London Rifle Brigade came in three days after the battle – blinded by a head wound. The following day another lieutenant, from the 1/7th Sherwood Foresters, was recovered. He had been fired on whenever he moved and had been hit seven times. A week after the battle an artillery officer spotted movement in No Man's Land. That night he went out with an infantry patrol and rescued two men of the Rangers; they had been living off water from the bottom of shell holes. The record appears to have been held by a private of the 1/4th London, again at Gommecourt, who was found fourteen days after the battle. He was stuck fast in the mud and had to be dug out, but his wounds had not turned septic and he recovered after a year in hospital.

In spite of the good weather and the devotion and bravery of the stretcher-bearers, many of the wounded succumbed and met lingering, solitary deaths out in No Man's Land. 'The body of Lieut-Col. J. Addison, 9th Yorks and Lancs, was not found until the battlefield was searched in September, when it was found with a short diary, showing that he must have lived at least two, if not three days before he died.' (Lieut-Col. H. F. Watson, D.S.O., 11th Sherwood Foresters)*

After the fall of Ovillers two weeks later, two Tunnelling Company officers walked across Mash Valley, to inspect a mine crater which they had blown on 1 July. They were horrified to see that all the dead infantrymen of the 8th Division lying on the German side of the old No Man's Land had been bayoneted in the throat and that the bodies on the German wire had all had the back of their heads smashed in. They were convinced that German patrols had come out during the night after the battle and had finished off the wounded and mutilated the dead. The two officers wrote a report on what

* Public Record Office, CAB 45/191.

they had seen and one sent it by registered post to his father, a barrister, with the request that it be put before a committee, then sitting in London investigating German atrocities. The letter was never delivered. It was probably removed from the post by the Army Censor.

Another problem facing the British after the battle was the clearance of the dead and wounded from their own trenches. The worst conditions were in VIII Corps' sector where three divisions had been beaten off by the Germans, with heavy loss. Here there were many harrowing scenes. 'Our original front and support lines were full of wounded men from all the various units and it took three days to clear them. Heavy rain came on 2 July and made the trenches impossible, and many wounded were actually drowned.' (Maj. V. N. Johnson, 12th Infantry Brigade H.Q.) *

The men involved in this distressing and arduous work, many of whom had fought in the battle, became exhausted and irritable. On one occasion, after three days and nights of back-breaking work, two stretcher-bearers took a short rest but their M.O., as tired as they were, insisted that they resume work. 'My pal was so tired he threatened to shoot him. The M.O. got even angrier and, in turn, threatened to shoot my pal but in the end they both calmed down and we went back to work.' (Pte J. W. Stevenson, Sheffield City Battalion)

Nearby, two Accrington Pals signallers were helping the stretcher-bearers. 'A group of staff officers appeared and we stood to attention. One of them asked our corporal, "Why haven't these men shaved?" I could have shot him without compunction.' (L/Cpl H. Bury, Accrington Pals)

'I was out in No Man's Land until late on 2 July and I made up my mind I had to move. I was hurt in the foot and I more or less fell into our trench. There were no troops manning it and no stretcher-bearers but lots of wounded. There was a chap sitting on a box but he didn't reply when I spoke to him. I spent that night in a dug-out with some other wounded. Next morning I crawled up into the trench and the man was still sitting on his box; he had been dead all the time. An officer told me, "If you want to get out of here lad, crawl!" ' (Pte H. C. Bloor, Accrington Pals)†

* Public Record Office, CAB 45/189.

† Harry Bloor received his first medical treatment that night, sixty hours after being wounded. He was discharged from the army after a year in hospital.

Communal graves had been prepared behind the trench system but, with priority being given to the wounded, it was many days before all the dead bodies could be cleared. 'A large number of corpses were got out of our trenches by means of a very good trench-tramway, but from there it was a slow job to carry them away to the communal graves. The result was a large stack of corpses which was extremely bad for morale.' (Capt. H. F. Dawes, 12th Infantry Brigade H.Q.) *

Four battalion commanders of the 11th Infantry Brigade had been killed. Their men recovered the bodies from the battlefield and buried them side-by-side in the mass grave at the Sucrerie, near Colincamps, past which they had marched on the eve of the battle.†

Not all the dead were disposed of so methodically. Abandoned trenches or large shell holes formed the last resting place for many. The bodies of those Newfoundlanders who had been killed before reaching their own front line were collected and buried *en masse* in a disused assembly trench.

Many miles to the south, near Mametz, burial parties found the bodies of Capt. Martin and those of his men who had fallen in front of Mansel Copse, exactly where he had predicted they would be caught by a German machine-gun. His body, and those of 159 other men from the 8th and 9th Devons, were buried in a trench in the copse. When the grave had been filled in, a notice was put above it:

The Devonshires held this trench.
The Devonshires hold it still.

After the failure of the ambulance trains on the first day, strenuous efforts were made to get the wounded away to the base, in order to relieve the congestion at the forward medical units. The complicated instructions, recently introduced by G.H.Q. for the handling of ambulance trains, were ignored and every available train in the B.E.F. worked round the clock. As

* Public Record Office, CAB 45/188.

† The four dead C.O.'s were Lieut-Cols. J. A. Thicknesse, 1st Somerset Light Infantry; L. C. W. Palk, 1st Hampshires; D. Wood, 1st Rifle Brigade and E. A. Innes, 1/8th Royal Warwicks. The brigade had been reinforced for the battle by two Birmingham Territorial battalions and all its senior officers became casualties. The brigade commander (Prowse) and the four battalion commanders mentioned above were killed; the two remaining C.O.'s were wounded.

soon as one arrived, it was sent straight to a Casualty Clearing Station and loaded.

During the three days following the battle, there was a mass movement of wounded between the Somme Front and the bases that was, fortunately, never to be seen again in the war. Ambulance trains made fifty-eight journeys, carrying 31,214 wounded, from Fourth Army alone. This all-out effort shows what might have been done on the first day, when five trains had taken only 2,317 patients.

The trains were supplemented by other forms of transport on the long journey to the base hospitals on the coast; by barges that chugged slowly down the River Somme; by lorries and even by buses, some of which were still marked 'London General Omnibus Company' – a nostalgic sight for wounded Londoners. But it was the trains that were the vital factor, evacuating nearly ninety per cent of the wounded who went to the base.

The effects of the unexpectedly high number of casualties, made worse by the ambulance train failure on the first day, continued to be felt for some time. Devoted work by the R.A.M.C. men relieved some of the suffering, but it was several days before the congestion was completely cleared. An examination of the records available shows that approximately 10,000 of the first day's wounded were still in the battle zone at 10 P.M. on 2 July and, of these, half had still not been accepted by a medical unit. It was not until the morning of 4 July, that the Fourth Army's Director of Medical Services declared himself satisfied that all his wounded were being properly cared for.

The wounded continued to suffer much hardship. 'After being wounded, I walked to Bray, where I spent five nights in a field with only a ground sheet and a blanket. By then my arm was in a very bad state.' (Pte A. R. French, 7th Royal West Kents) One Field Ambulance, a unit near enough to the front to be under shell fire and which had accommodation for about 500 wounded, reported at one stage that it held 3,700, of whom 2,000 were outside in fields.

'I was brought in from No Man's Land on Monday 3 July and had a rough dressing put on a bullet wound in my foot, but no more. The same day I was taken to a C.C.S. at Corbie and remained there until the Friday night, with no medical attention at all. When I was taken to the Base

Hospital at Wimereux, the dressing was removed and my foot and all the way up my leg was completely gangrenous. Within a few hours I had to have a mid-thigh amputation, from what had been a simple wound in my foot.' (Sgt H. Benzing, Grimsby Chums)

An additional hazard that sometimes overtook the wounded was hunger, because the rations at the forward medical units were soon eaten by the unexpected influx of men. 'I walked from one medical unit to another until, after several days, I finally arrived at a place where my wound was dressed. By this time I was in agony and my leg was swollen. Here, too, were refreshments at a canteen but they had to be paid for and I had no money. I was desperately hungry until I met a man from my own company and he gave me fifteen francs.' (Pte J. A. Deary, 2nd Liverpool Pals)

In the confusion strange things happened. 'I have a vague memory of getting rough injections with jagged needles on half-a-dozen occasions and being left on the side of the road for hours; then into wagons and ambulances of all descriptions. I must have fallen into a coma for I woke up somewhere in Belgium. A lovely Canadian nurse was trying to work out where this Irishman had come from, with his Shamrock badge and shoulder tabs.

'Later, at the base, I was robbed while I was being given a bath. Someone took £30 in francs, which was sewn into the lining of my tunic. It was prize money that I had won in various sporting events, also several weeks of pay. Was I mad? And you know how mad an Irishman can get!' (Sgt J. A. B. Maultsaid, Belfast Young Citizens)

The thief was not the only opportunist. 'After my wound had been treated at the battalion Aid Post, a man who was on "light duties" there with a swollen toe was told by the M.O. to take me as far as the ambulance. No one noticed him in the confusion and he managed to stick to me all the way back to Southampton. When we landed, he shook my hand and congratulated himself on his escape from France.' (Pte J. Singleton, 1/7th Sherwood Foresters)

So the wounded came to England – to the Blighty of their songs. Day after day, packed hospital ships left French ports – Rouen, Le Havre, Dieppe and Boulogne. Southampton was the main English port used and for over a week trains were leaving there at the rate of nearly one an hour, taking the wounded to military and civilian hospitals all over Britain. So swift was the evacuation process, that some of the men who had been wounded early in the battle on 1 July could be in an English hospital within twenty-four hours; but these were the fortunate few.

As the flow of wounded continued, the hospitals in England began to fill up. Some effort was made to send men to hospitals in or near their home towns. 'Unfortunately I had been reported missing to my next of kin, who was my fiancée, but, by the afternoon post the same day, she received another letter telling her I had been admitted to Vernon Park Hospital, Stockport, just a few miles away from her home.' (Pte L. Welch, 1st Edinburgh City Battalion)

The wounded sometimes had so little treatment in France that their wounds were still covered by the field dressings applied by their pals in No Man's Land; their uniforms were torn and filthy; their boots caked in the mud of the Somme. 'You can imagine my joy when I was dumped into a nice clean bed, in Bristol Hospital, in my muddy uniform and well sprinkled with lice; and wasn't I sorry for the poor nurse who had the job of cleansing me.' (Sgt A. S. Durrant, Durham Pals)

'When I got to Orpington, six days later, they took the shrapnel out of my leg. The doctor said, "It's missed the bone by a hair's breadth, laddie." And then a dark-eyed, luscious maiden of twenty *kissed me*.' (Pte J. W. Allsop, Leeds Pals)

For twelve British officers and 573 men the war was over – they were prisoners. Of these, 399 came from the two divisions, 36th (Ulster) and 56th (London), which had first captured many of their objectives and then had to withdraw. Considering the scale of the attack – 120,000 men had gone over the top – it was a remarkably small figure, indicative of the complete German success on many sectors but, also, it was a tribute to the resolution of those attackers who had gained the German trenches and then been cut off there. These men often preferred to fight on and die rather than surrender. No doubt some of the prisoners felt ashamed and despondent but, in view of the fearful casualties suffered later in the war, many would say that these prisoners were the luckiest of all.

For the Germans this was the biggest bag of British prisoners taken in France in one day since the retreat from Mons in

1914. Their most important captive was the only officer taken from the Ulster Division. This was Capt. Charles Craig, the Member of Parliament for South Antrim, who had been one of the leaders in raising the division in 1914, when he had ordered the first 10,000 uniforms. He was badly wounded in the Schwaben Redoubt late in the afternoon, just as the Ulsters were being forced back, and had to be left behind. Craig was a large man whom the Germans considered too heavy to be carried on a stretcher. They found a wheelbarrow and pushed him back to an ambulance.*

The Germans were not always so considerate. 'There were six of us taken prisoner; one was a London Scottish bloke wearing a kilt. The Germans argued for a long time among themselves, whether to take us back or not. Eventually we set off and the London Scottish man helped me as I was wounded. The Germans kept hitting him with rifles; they hated the "Kilties".' (Pte H. B. Barr, 1/4th London)

Pte Albert McMillan was in a party of about 100 prisoners who were assembled behind the German lines. He noticed a five-foot-high pile of German corpses, neatly stacked criss-cross fashion, and covered by a sheet. These were victims of the British bombardment, awaiting a decent burial, but the sight of this and similar stacks on other occasions gave rise to the rumour, still believed by some, that the bodies were awaiting transport to special factories so that scarce raw materials could be extracted from the corpses.

The men in McMillan's group were asked by the Germans to explain the working of a captured Lewis gun. As each prisoner refused, he was hit across the face and kicked on the shins. Later, McMillan was interrogated by a German officer. One of the questions asked of him was why the British had not attacked on 29 June – a question which indicated that the Germans had known the original date of the attack.

That night McMillan and the other prisoners set out on a march to Cambrai, thirty kilometres away; a distance covered without any night stop which caused great hardship to those of the party who were wounded. But once at Cambrai the spirit of the British soon returned. They were housed in an old French barrack room, high up on the wall of which the Germans had painted '*Gott strafe England*'. Within a short

* Capt. Craig's brother, James Craig, later Lord Craigavon, became Northern Ireland's first prime minister.

time the British had managed to change this to *'Gott strafe Deutschland'*; the Germans were furious.

When wounded prisoners of the North Midland Division were taken to a hospital at Le Cateau, a German doctor greeted them with the following speech: 'If you are good fellows you will be well treated and if you are bad fellows you will get kick up arse.'

Three days after the battle a German aeroplane flew over the British lines at Gommecourt and dropped a list of the men of the London and North Midland Divisions who had been captured there. Soon afterwards a British aeroplane returned the courtesy.

When the unwounded survivors of the battle had returned to the villages or billets from which they had marched only a day or two earlier, battalions were paraded and roll calls were held. In the hardest hit battalions this was a sad occasion as less than 100 men answered out of 700 or more names that were called. Sometimes the fate of the absent was known; they had been seen to be killed or taken away wounded, but of many there was no news, and they were marked as 'Missing'. Those who had been left out of the battle were uncomfortable spectators at the roll calls; many felt guilty and ashamed at being spared the ordeal that had taken so many of their friends.

In the 1st Somerset Light Infantry, C.S.M. Percy Chappell was the senior rank to return unhurt from the battle; every officer was dead or wounded. Percy looked for his four sergeant friends who had joked on the eve of the battle about choosing flowers for each other's graves. All four were casualties.

The winning footballers of the 8th East Surreys were unable to collect the prize money from their commander. Capt. Nevill was dead. Another company commander to be killed was Maj George Gaffikin who had rallied the West Belfasts with his Orange Order sash. Gaffikin had been badly wounded in the Schwaben Redoubt and died at a Casualty Clearing Station.

One of the 9th Devons' casualties was Lieut William Hodgson, the poet. He had been killed in the fighting for Mametz and buried in the Devons' trench grave in Mansel Copse.

Only one man answered his name when the roll was called for 14 Platoon of the 1st Rifle Brigade. The platoon had been forty strong before the battle.

The 2nd Edinburgh City Battalion had recruited the complete First Eleven of the Hearts of Midlothian Football Club and, to July 1916, the battalion's football team had never been defeated. Now, most of the footballers had become casualties.

For the survivors, these roll calls produced mixed emotions. The strongest was that of disappointment. They had been led to believe that nothing could stop their victory, that the Germans would surely be beaten. Now, for so many, came the realization that this was not to be and that the war would be long and bitter. There was great sadness that so many of their friends were dead, but there was also relief that they themselves had survived. For all they knew, many of their friends might turn up as stragglers or be back in an English hospital, only slightly wounded, while they had to continue at the Front.

There was, however, one consolation for the survivors. For some time, parcels continued to arrive for those men who were missing and these were shared out among those who remained. 'I chose two tins of sugar from a parcel. On opening them, there were four half-crowns in each tin – one from Mother and one from Dad. It all seemed so ghastly. You can understand why they did not allow you to brood, but kept you fully occupied with inspections, etcetera, followed by fatigues and duties that gave you very little time to think.' (Rfmn A. Withers, 1st Rifle Brigade)

The generals, who before the battle had been so confident in their talks to the men, now toured their units, commended them for their courage and put as good a face as possible on the disappointing outcome. Where the battalions had been successful, the men were congratulated on their victory. The Territorials and New Army battalions were told that they had proved themselves as good as the Regulars – a compliment that would never have been paid a week before. For those who had failed, the theme was usually the same: by their gallant efforts they had held the attention of the enemy and contributed to success elsewhere.

The Ulster Division's commander did not endear himself to his men. 'Major-General Nugent addressed us after the battle and said, "Men, you've done very well, but you might have done better." There was a lot of murmuring in the ranks and some thought he was anything but a gentleman.' (Pte S. Megaw, Belfast Young Citizens)

Lieut-Gen. Hunter-Weston was particularly diligent in visiting his corps. In the weeks following the battle, he visited every battalion that had attacked and personally thanked the soldiers. During one of these visits, he had a narrow escape: 'General Hunter-Weston had assembled us all and told us that the whole of the VIII Corps had made a sacrifice so that troops on another part of the front could advance. Just then a German artillery spotting plane flew over and, not before time, we got the order to disperse. Then came the whine of approaching shells and a big one went off a few yards from where the General had been standing. A lump of shell killed one of our heavy grey horses. The pair had been out since Mons; they used to pull the field kitchen. It was a sad loss!' (Rfmn A. Withers, 1st Rifle Brigade)

When they had been raised in 1914, the Tyneside Scottish had been refused the right to wear kilts. Now each man was given a small square of tartan, immediately christened 'sand-bag tartan', which he could wear behind his cap badge as a tribute to the Tynesiders' bravery. 'One Geordie sat quietly studying the three-inch square of cloth. "Man, we'll have to fight a hell of a lot of battles before we get our kilts!" ' (Pte T. Easton, 2nd Tyneside Scottish)

For several days the senior generals remained unaware of the full extent of the losses suffered. By the afternoon of 2 July, estimates at Fourth Army and G.H.Q. were still forty per cent below the actual casualties incurred.

The only way of knowing what Haig and Rawlinson thought when the full extent of the losses was reported to them, is from a scrutiny of their respective diaries. In neither is there any direct reference to the final casualty list, nor did either of them show any sign of remorse, nor give any explanation for it. Haig did make one entry that was to earn him the disfavour of many ordinary soldiers. On the eveniny of 1 July he wrote: 'North of the Ancre, VIII Corps said they began well, but as the day progressed, their troops were forced back into the German front line, except two battalions which occupied Serre Village, and were, it is said, cut off. I am inclined to believe from further reports, that few of VIII

Corps left their trenches.'* This was an example of the deplorable communications that existed between the front line and the H.Q.'s. The divisions of VIII Corps – the 4th, 29th, 31st and part of the 48th (South Midland) – had lost 662 officers and 13,636 men between them during the day. To his credit, Haig made no attempt to conceal this entry when the true facts emerged.

On some sectors, the results had been so disastrous that some commanders felt uncertain as to their own future. The first general to lose his command and reputation during the Battle of the Somme was not in the Fourth Army, which had carried out the main attack and suffered most of the casualties, but one who had been involved in the diversionary attack at Gommecourt. There was more than one general who was apprehensive on account of Gommecourt. The Third Army commander, Allenby, was not popular at G.H.Q. and thought that he might be blamed for the failure to capture the village, especially after his two divisions had lost nearly 7,000 men.

The corps commander on the spot, Lieut-Gen. Snow, was also under suspicion. He had been away for ten days' leave before the battle and had been criticized by Allenby for not paying sufficient attention to the preparations. Allenby may have considered sending Snow home, but he needed the backing of the C.-in-C. and this he was not sure of getting.

The final possibility was Maj.-Gen. Stuart-Wortley, commander of the North Midland Division which had failed to link up with the London Division behind the village. It was Stuart-Wortley who had taken over VII Corps, temporarily, while Snow was on leave.

Immediately after the battle, Allenby ordered a Court of Inquiry to investigate the handling of the attack of Stuart-Wortley's division. Its members were a brigadier-general, who had not been involved in the battle, and two lieutenant-colonels, one each from the two attacking divisions.

The court held its first sitting in a hut on 4 July and took evidence from fourteen witnesses from the North Midland Division and from two R.F.C. pilots. The junior member of the court, the C.O. of the London Rifle Brigade who on 1 July had watched the attack 'as though it were Ascot Races', had to take down all the evidence in longhand. That night the court adjourned with the intention of resuming two days later.

* *The Private Papers of Douglas Haig, 1914–1919*, p. 153.

But early the next morning there came a dramatic move. At 6.50 A.M., Stuart-Wortley received orders from Allenby that he was relieved of his command and was to return, at once, to England. Even so the Court of Inquiry sat once more and heard another twenty-five witnesses, but one suspects that the proceedings had become a mere formality.

What of the generals in Fourth Army; was no one to blame for the loss of 50,000 men in one day? Rawlinson, who had refused Haig's advice when formulating his plan of attack? Hunter-Weston, whose corps had lost so many men without a single success, and where confusion reigned for days after the battle?

What about G.H.Q.? Haig had been in overall command of the battle and was ultimately responsible for it. Maxwell, the Quartermaster General, had placed only three ambulance trains in Fourth Army area on the first day after Rawlinson had requested eighteen trains, a failure which had led to such unnecessary suffering among the wounded.

Haig and Rawlinson were protected by the sheer enormity of the disaster. It was several days before the full extent of the losses were known in France, let alone in England. By then the battle had moved into another phase and the opportunity for a swift recall to England had passed.

Hunter-Weston and his corps staff were moved from the battle area before the end of the month to a quiet sector far from the Somme. This was almost certainly requested by Gough, who had taken over Hunter-Weston's part of the front. Gough tried to get rid of his other corps commander, Morland, who had handled the attacks on Thiepval and the Leipzig Redoubt, but this time Gough was out of luck. Haig turned down the request.

Some time during the second half of 1916, a suggestion came from the War Office that Lieut-Gen. Maxwell should return to England; possibly this was a result of the ambulance train fiasco of 1 July. Haig, always loyal to his subordinates, resisted, and Maxwell retained his position.

However, there was still one more 1 July general to go. Maj.-Gen. Pilcher, commander of the 17th (Northern) Division, had been ordered to detach his 50th Brigade to another division on the first day, and had had to stand idly by while it suffered heavy losses. One of its battalions was Philip Howe's, the 10th West Yorks, which had suffered more casualties than any other battalion in the whole battle on 1 July.

During the next few days the division sustained further heavy casualties, under Pilcher's command now, but subjected to relentless pressure from the corps commander, Lieut-Gen. Horne. On 11 July, Horne sent for Pilcher, accused him of not driving his division hard enough, and sent him home. Horne was certainly a demanding master, for he relieved another major-general the same day.*

Pilcher was much aggrieved by his dismissal. 'It is very easy to sit a few miles in the rear and get credit for allowing men to be killed in an undertaking foredoomed to failure, but the part did not appeal to me and my protests against these useless attacks were not well received.' (Maj.-Gen. T. D. Pilcher, 17th (Northern) Division)†

Neither Stuart-Wortley nor Pilcher was ever again given an operational command. Stuart-Wortley was posted to Ireland and Pilcher remained in England. Almost without exception, the soldiers who had served under them in France thought that they had been removed for losing too many men, whereas in both cases their dismissal was caused by their unwillingness to sacrifice still more. There was no room for soft-hearted generals on the Western Front in 1916.

In contrast to the 'degommering' of Stuart-Wortley and Pilcher, the hard-driving Horne was soon promoted. In October he was given command of the First Army. He had been a corps commander for only five months, but his methods were those in fashion.

If it had taken several days for accurate reports of the battle on 1 July to reach the H.Q.'s in France, how much more difficult was it, then, for the ordinary folk at home to find out what had happened?

For the first few days, their only source of information was the press which, in turn, was mostly dependent on official releases. Already, on 1 July, the evening papers had published excitable, optimistic, but vague, reports of the morning's battle. Reuter's correspondent reported in the London

* This was Maj.-Gen. I. Phillips, commander of the 38th (Welsh) Division, whose division was not in action on 1 July. The Official History makes no mention of any of these dismissals.

† Public Record Office, CAB 45/190.

Evening News that the German front line and many prisoners had been taken, at small loss to the British.

The Sunday papers had little further news, but by Monday the dailies were full of reports. The *Daily Express* claimed the capture of 9,500 prisoners and many villages, among them Contalmaison and Serre, neither of which had actually fallen, but it also added ominously: 'The New Tactics – Warnings Against Undue Optimism'. It was left to *The Times* to give the most reliable account of the battle. It had picked up the German official communiqué from a neutral paper; this proved far more accurate than the British versions.

The newspaper reports were soon supplemented by first-hand accounts of the wounded soldiers returning from France. Most of these were eager to recount their version of the battle and their listeners were subjected to many conflicting and exaggerated stories. Soon, the whole of the country was seething with rumour. The ordeal of the relatives of men serving at the Front was pitiful. The local character of many of the New Army battalions meant that some towns and cities soon found that their menfolk had suffered heavy losses, but accurate information was very hard to get. Crowds besieged council and newspaper offices and local drill halls demanding news. In Accrington it was rumoured that only seven men had survived from their Pals' attack! No one would confirm or deny the report and the townspeople surrounded the mayor's house in an angry mood, convinced he was withholding news from them.*

Gradually more details came from France and the Post Office was kept busy delivering thousands of telegrams to the homes of the casualties. Mrs Emma King was away from home, resting with her parents after the birth of her baby, and it was some time before she returned to her other four children at Tickhill. She found there a telegram which had stood unopened on the mantelpiece for many days. It told her that her husband Dick was dead. Two other men from the same mining village had also been killed on 1 July.

The window blinds were drawn in working-class streets all over industrial England as the people mourned their dead. Local newspapers published rows and rows of photographs of

* The townspeople of Accrington were only partly right; the Pals had suffered heavily, losing 585 men from approximately 700 who had gone into action.

young men who had 'fallen for their King and Country'. On 12 July, Orangeman's Day, all traffic in Belfast was halted at noon and the whole city fell silent for five minutes.

The greatest anguish was among those whose men were reported missing, and relatives tried every means to find out what had happened to them. They visited hospitals, searching for wounded men from the same battalion; they wrote letters to the missing men's pals or officers in France. Advertisements appeared in newspapers, appealing for news of loved ones. Some resorted to spiritualism.

There had been such confusion in France that many men who had been posted as missing were later found to be wounded, and as further advances were made, the bodies of some of the remainder were recovered and the news passed to their next-of-kin. Others were reported to be prisoners of war. Five months later, relatives of the remainder were told that the missing men were officially presumed to have been killed in action. Over the years some received more definite news but many never discovered what had happened to their husbands, sons or sweethearts.

Lieut-Col. Sandys, the officer who had been so concerned over his battalion, the 2nd Middlesex, had been evacuated to England where he soon recovered from his wounds. But he still brooded over his men, convinced that he could have done more for them. Early in September he sent letters to two of his officers who were also in England. To one he wrote that he wished he had been killed with his men on 1 July and, to the other, 'I have come to London to take my life. I have never had a moment's peace since July 1st.'

On 6 September, in his room at the Cavendish Hotel, the tormented man shot himself in the head with his revolver. He was taken to St George's Hospital, but died a week later without regaining consciousness and was buried in Brompton Cemetery. At his inquest, which was well covered by the press, the jury found that Sandys had committed suicide while temporarily insane. It was a tragic end for a much-loved officer. The War Office seemed to ignore the suicide. The official record states that Lieut-Col. Sandys died of wounds received on 1 July. Nine days after his death it was announced that he had been awarded the D.S.O. and he was also mentioned in Haig's Despatches in January 1917.

15

The Cost

For the British, who had staked so much on 1 July, the meagre achievements were a bitter disappointment. In simple terms, the right wing of their main attack had been successful; the centre and left had failed. At Gommecourt, the attack had not eliminated the salient even if the diversionary function had been fulfilled.

Territorially, the lower arm of the huge letter 'L' of the front line had been moved approximately one mile farther north, but the new front line here faced north towards the rest of the German lines rather than eastwards towards their rear.

The attack had taken three of the German fortified villages: Montauban, Mametz and Fricourt – the last being evacuated during the night following the battle – out of the thirteen which were in the day's objectives, plus certain trenches, dug-outs and redoubts that had taken much labour to build. At no point had the German main second line been breached.

To achieve these results the British units involved on 1 July had suffered shattering losses. The first returns, made up from the roll calls taken as the battalions came out of action, showed nearly 62,000 casualties:

	Killed or died of wounds	*Wounded*	*Missing*	*Total*
Officers	721	1,531	339	2,591
Other ranks	7,449	34,357	17,419	59,225
Total	8,170	35,888	17,758	61,816

There was obviously an unknown number of stragglers who had lost their units and wounded still to be fetched in from No Man's Land. It was hoped that, as these returned, the large number of missing would be reduced.

During the following days, the stragglers gradually returned to their units. Lists of prisoners were received from the Germans and many men, previously marked as missing, were now posted as killed as their bodies were found or witnesses to their death came forward. The final casualty list showed that, of the 17,758 men originally posted as missing, just over a quarter returned unharmed to their units or were taken prisoner, while 10,705 were found to be dead. The fate of the remaining 2,152 men was, in most cases, never discovered. They had been killed and their bodies lost.

The final return showed a total casualty list of 57,470 officers and men:

	Killed or died of wounds	*Wounded*	*Missing*	*Prisoners*	*Total*
Officers	993	1,337	96	12	2,438
Other ranks	18,247	34,156	2,056	573	55,032
Total	19,240	35,493	2,152	585	57,470 *

Even allowing for the size of the force involved and the ferocity of the fighting the casualty list was an amazing one. Almost exactly half of the men in the 143 battalions who had attacked had become casualties. The figures for officers alone were far higher; only one in every four of those who had gone over the top remained unhurt at the end of the day – a seventy-five per cent casualty rate!

Most officers had attacked with their distinctive uniforms, complete with polished Sam Browne belts, revolvers or swagger sticks. The adjutant of the 9th Devons is reported to have carried a sword. The 2,438 officers who became casualties on 1 July certainly upheld the traditions of leadership and self-sacrifice of their class, but many were the victims of a code of conduct and dress which had not yet been adapted to the conditions of the Western Front. Seventy-eight battalions recorded their officer casualties in detail, and these figures indicate that the most dangerous rank to have held on 1 July

* This, and the preceding table, are taken from the Official History. To compile the second table a researcher on the Official Historian's staff spent six months examining the Part II Orders of every infantry unit which took part in the battle on 1 July.

was that of captain. The least dangerous position was almost certainly that of the private soldier.

The British Army's casualties, on 1 July, were the equivalent of seventy-five battalions or of more than six full divisions of fighting infantry.* For every yard of the sixteen-mile front from Gommecourt to Montauban there were two British casualties.

The exact German losses for the day's fighting on their front facing the British attack will never be known, as their units only made a casualty return once every ten days. However, because the action was so heavy, many German units did make special note of the day's casualties. Based on these samples, a rough estimate would place German losses at about 8,000 men from Gommecourt to the boundary between the British and French armies. Of these, 2,200 are known to have been taken prisoner, leaving under 6,000 killed and wounded. A simple mathematical calculation shows the losses on 1 July to have been seven to one in the Germans' favour, an exact reverse of the British and German numbers involved. The British had paid a high price for the relief of their ally at Verdun.

On certain sectors the ratio was even more in favour of the Germans. The boundaries of the British 8th Division, attacking up Mash Valley and against Ovillers, coincided almost exactly with those of the defending German 180th Regiment. Here, a mere two German battalions faced the 8th Division's attack and, during the whole day, they had to call in only one company of the reserve battalion to repel the attack.

The 8th Division suffered 5,121 casualties, the 180th Regiment only 280 – a proportion of eighteen to one in favour of the German defenders.

With nearly 60,000 casualties, how does this one-day battle compare with other battles in which the British Army has been involved? Is there any rival to 1 July 1916 in the extent of its loss? Before 1914, the bloodiest battle had almost certainly been that at Waterloo, when the Duke of Wellington, with the Prussians, had defeated Napoleon's French. British

* When this book was being written, in 1970, the British Army contained only fifty-four infantry battalions.

losses at Waterloo had been 8,458 men, or twenty-five per cent of Wellington's force; this was less than the average number of casualties sustained by any one of the six corps employed by Haig on 1 July.

Even the First World War, easily the bloodiest in Britain's history, could not produce another day's fighting which approached that of 1 July. The opening of the two big offensives of 1917 – at Arras in April, and at Messines in June – both of which employed troops on a similar scale to that of the opening of the Somme, cost 13,000 in three days and 24,500 in seven days respectively. The worst day after 1 July 1916 was probably 21 March 1918, when the Germans launched their spring offensive. Figures are not available for the first day, but British losses in the first eleven days were 165,000, of which a high proportion were prisoners.

The British Army had its fair share of pitched battles in the 1939–45 war, but this was a war waged on a completely different scale to its predecessor: D-Day – 4,000 British and Canadian casualties; El Alamein – an average of 1,125 per day for eleven days. The only comparable day in the Second World War was that on which Singapore fell and some 80,000 British, Australian and Indian troops were taken prisoner by the Japanese.

The casualties suffered by the British on the opening day of the Battle of the Somme stand comparison, not only with other battles, but with complete wars. The British Army's loss on that one day easily exceeds its battle casualties in the Crimean War, the Boer War and the Korean War combined.

A study of the War Diaries of the units involved in the battle shows that it was the infantry who had sustained the overwhelming majority of the casualties. As some units were not as meticulous as others in recording every casualty, the first table overleaf is the best estimate one can make of the casualties suffered by the different arms during the day.

In the supporting arms, the moderate losses of the artillery and R.A.M.C. included a high proportion of officers. These were the Forward Observation Officers and Medical Officers who had been attached to the infantry.

Several General Staff officers had become casualties when they went forward in attempts to co-ordinate the efforts of struggling infantry battalions.

Type of unit	*Casualties*	
Fighting Battalions	54,335	all manned by the infantry
Machine Gun Companies	1,080	
Pioneer Battalions	1,020	
Light Trench Mortar Batteries	350	
Royal Engineers	450	
Artillery	170	
Royal Army Medical Corps	60	
Royal Flying Corps	5	
Total	57,470	

There is no record of any casualties among the cavalry. The three cavalry divisions of Gough's Reserve Army certainly escaped without loss, but it is possible that a few men from the corps cavalry regiments were hit by long-range shells. The North Midland Division reported one mounted military policeman killed.

There is further interest in the distribution of the casualties among the different divisions which had taken part in the battle.

Division	*Casualties*	*Type of division* *
34th	6,380	N.A.
29th	5,240	REG.
8th	5,121	REG.
36th (Ulster)	5,104	N.A.
4th	4,692	REG
56th (London)	4,314	T.F.
21st	4,256	N.A.
32nd	3,949	N.A.
31st	3,599	N.A.
7th	3,410	REG.
18th (Eastern)	3,115	N.A.
30th	3,011	N.A.
46th (North Midland)	2,455	T.F.
Part divisions		
17th (Northern) 3 battalions	1,115	N.A.
48th (South Midland) 2 ,,	1,060	T.F.
49th (West Riding) 5 ,,	590	T.F.

* REG. – Regular Army; T.F. – Territorial Force; N.A. – New Army.

One of the most obvious conclusions to be reached from this table is that success, in this case, had been cheaper than defeat. The three divisions which had advanced on the right wing, the 7th, 18th and 30th, are all near the bottom of the main table. Their leading waves had captured the German front line quickly, allowing the follow-up troops a comparatively safe crossing of No Man's Land. This was the all-important factor, because No Man's Land, not the German trenches, had been the big killing ground for the divisions that had suffered the heaviest losses.

The table shows the terrible losses suffered by Maj.-Gen. Ingouville-Williams's 34th Division, composed of the Tyneside Irish and Tyneside Scottish Brigades, two Edinburgh battalions, the Cambridge Battalion and the Grimsby Chums. Of its three brigades, two, the Tyneside Irish and Scottish, had each suffered more casualties than any other brigade in the battle. In their assault on La Boisselle, guarding the main road to Bapaume, they had lost one of their two brigade commanders, seven out of eight battalion commanders and each battalion had averaged 600 casualties. For this loss, the two brigades had captured a portion of German-held ground twenty acres in extent, the only result of the drive on Bapaume nine miles farther up the road. So shattered were the two Tyneside brigades that they were immediately detached from their division and sent to a quiet sector on Vimy Ridge. It was months before they were again fit for battle.

For a unit as large as a division to lose nearly three-quarters of its infantry in one day was a grisly achievement, even for the First World War, and shows both the strength of the German defences guarding the main road and the courage of the men from the 34th Division who tried to force those defences.

The presence of three Regular divisions in the first five places in the table shows how their battalions had preserved the traditions of the Old Army by pressing their attacks to the limits of their strength, but the sacrifice of these divisions had brought not a single yard of German trench as a permanent capture.

The position of the North Midland Division at the bottom of the main table shows how Maj.-Gen. Stuart-Wortley had managed to save most of his division. It had cost him his command.

Some divisions had cause to regret their success and comparatively low casualties on 1 July. Those who had done so well, notably the 18th and 30th Divisions at Montauban, gained such a reputation that they were used over and over again as 'stormers' during the remainder of the war. When peace came, very few of the original members of their battalions remained.

If heavy casualties could affect the character and performance of units as large as a division, what then of the battalion, the infantryman's home? Many had suffered terrible casualties with only a handful of men returning from the 700 or 800 who had taken part in the battle.

It would be tedious for the reader to examine more tables and figures, but two battalions stand out from the rest as having virtually disappeared.

The 10th West Yorks, of which Lieut Philip Howe was the only officer who remained, and he slightly wounded, had suffered 710 casualties, probably the highest battalion casualty list for a single day during the war. The West Yorks had mostly crossed the German front line easily enough but were held up by the next trench. No one had cleared the dug-outs of the front line and no other troops followed the attack, so that when Germans came up from the front-line dug-outs, the West Yorks were trapped in the open between the two German-held trenches. Worse still, they were on a hillside in full view of the German machine-gunners only 200 yards away in the ruins of Fricourt, which had not been attacked. Philip Howe's small party, all from the first wave, had escaped by pressing on hard to its objective. Trapped on the open slope, there had been no cover for the remainder of the battalion, and those who were not hit at once remained in full view of the enemy. This day-long purgatory had resulted in nearly sixty per cent of the West Yorks casualties being fatal – a very high proportion.

The other great tragedy of the day had been that of the Newfoundlanders. Their ill-planned attack in mid-morning had caused them a loss of 684 men. Fortunately a higher proportion of these had been wounded, but it was still a terrible casualty list.

The destruction of some battalions had been so complete that no one will ever know what really happened to them.

Every battalion was supposed to enter a daily account of its activities in its War Diary, this becoming the official record. The 1st Hampshires had suffered so severely that no one could be found at the end of the day to describe, reliably, what had happened. Its War Diary entry for 1 July reads:

> Our casualties in officers amounted to 100% and was also heavy in other ranks.*

And that was all that could be found to describe the battle in which the Hampshires lost twenty-six officers and 559 men.

Besides the 10th West Yorks and the 1st Newfoundland, two other battalions, the 1st Tyneside Irish and the 4th Tyneside Scottish, had suffered over 600 casualties each, and twenty-eight more battalions had lost over 500 men.†

Many communities at home suffered terribly because of the intense local nature of so many battalions. Certain areas suddenly found they had lost a large number of their menfolk as, by tragic chance, their battalions had seen fierce action while those from more fortunate areas had missed the worst on this occasion. The parts of the country that appear to have suffered most were:

Yorkshire	9,000
Ulster	6,000‡
Lancashire	6,000
the North-East	5,500
London	5,500
Scotland	3,500

Most of the English counties had their share of casualties, but Wales had escaped lightly with no more than about 500 casualties; its turn came in other battles. The Southern Irish regiments had lost less than 1,000 men, but this is not conclusive as many Irishmen were serving in English and Scottish units.

Particular cities had suffered grievously. The list is a long one: London – over 5,000 casualties; Manchester (with Salford) – 3,500; Belfast – 1,800; Glasgow, Edinburgh, Newcastle, Bradford, Leeds and Birmingham – all over 1,000;

* Public Record Office, WO 95/1495.

† Appendix 5 gives casualty figures of the thirty-two battalions which suffered more than 500 casualties.

‡ The old province, that is the six counties now in Northern Ireland, together with Donegal, Monaghan and Cavan, now in Eire.

Durham, Liverpool, Sheffield, Derby, Nottingham, Wolverhampton, Cambridge and many more – each with several hundred casualties. Then there were the smaller communities – Accrington, Barnsley, Grimsby; the country towns and villages of Ulster; the mining villages of Tyneside and south Yorkshire; the fishing villages and lumber towns of Newfoundland. For all these, and for many more, 1 July was to be a day of mourning and sad remembrance for the next fifty years.

In the days following the battle, large drafts of men arrived from the reinforcement camps and the battered battalions were soon restored to strength, taking their place in the line and, in many cases, taking part in later stages of the Somme battle. But the new men were not always from the battalion's parent regiment; one London battalion, the Queen Victoria's Rifles, was made up with men from nine different regiments. Other battalions received men of every description; there were second-line Territorials, Lord Derby men, dismounted Yeomanry and, before long, conscripts. It was the beginning of the end for the unique, volunteer Army of 1916.

To the Regulars and Territorials this rebuilding process was nothing new; the hard core of old soldiers who seemed to survive every battle soon knocked the new men into shape.

Many of the battalions of Kitchener's New Army, however, underwent drastic changes in their character. They were more mature now; the success of their 18th and 30th Divisions, the only ones to have taken all their objectives when more experienced divisions had failed, ensured that there would be no more looking down on the New Army. Kitchener's raw battalions had suddenly come of age, but in doing so they had lost part of their mystique. The bonds which had held the men so tightly together had been loosed. The new men who came to fill the huge gaps in the ranks were good men, but they were no longer from the same select area or background as their predecessors; they could never replace the band of brothers who had formed the original battalions in 1914.
'The memories of those heart-breaking days will last forever. The name Serre and the date July 1st is engraved deep in our hearts, along with the faces of our "Pals", a grand crowd of chaps. We were two years in the making and ten minutes in the destroying.' (Pte A. V. Pearson, Leeds Pals)

'The battalion was then re-organized and brought up to

strength with men from all sources and so ended the era of a battalion composed of the "Clerks and Warehousemen of Manchester" who so eagerly enlisted early in September 1914. It was never again a "Manchester City Battalion".' (Pte A. E. Hall, 2nd Manchester Pals)

One division which suffered greatly from these changes was the Ulster Division. For political reasons conscription was never enforced in Ireland and the division was made up with whatever men it could find. In doing so it lost its wholly Protestant nature, for some of the new men turned out to be Catholics.

Men who had sworn to remain with their friends as privates, on finding these friends dead, left to become officers. Others who had gone home wounded asked, when they had recovered from their wounds, to be transferred to other arms, many to the R.F.C. or to the newly formed Tank Battalions. They knew that if they went back to their old battalions they would find most of their comrades gone.

Perhaps the differing attitudes between the Old Army and the New can be summed up in two quotations. The history of the Essex Regiment, whose losses had nearly all been in its two Regular battalions, describes 1 July as 'A trying day on the Somme'.* To them it was just another bad day in a long war.

By contrast, the 9th Yorks and Lancs, a New Army battalion of South Yorkshire miners which had lost 423 men in its first battle, was to write of this day:

So ends the Golden Age.†

* *Essex Regiment in the War, 1914–1919.*

† *The History of the 9th (Service) Btn, The York and Lancaster Regt., 1914–1919.*

16

An Analysis

David Lloyd George, who was to become Prime Minister before the end of the year, described 1 July 1916 as a watershed in the war for Britain. It can be argued that not only was it a turning-point in the war, as Lloyd George suggested, but it was the most tragic day of the war for Britain. In doing this let two questions be examined, admittedly with all the advantages of hindsight: firstly, was there no alternative, political or strategic, to this head-on clash; and, secondly, if there was none, what had gone wrong, tactically, with a battle whose outcome had been awaited with almost universal optimism?

In June 1916, Britain's senior ally, France, had appeared to be in danger of collapse. Weakened by her heavy losses of 1914 and 1915, she claimed that she could not hold the German pressure at Verdun indefinitely. Britain's other allies were faring little better; Italy had been severely mauled by the Austrians in May and Russia's attack, the Brusilov Offensive, had petered out. It was unthinkable that Britain could stand idly by and watch her partner go under, for Britain too would share the stigma of defeat. She had, therefore, two alternatives – to fight hard and divert the Germans, or to attempt to make peace.

It was at precisely this moment, June 1916, that the Germans, for the second time at least, sent an emissary to the French Government suggesting the possibility of discussing peace terms. Germany was in a strong bargaining position and would have wanted to settle on terms reasonably favourable to herself. But the Allies were not yet defeated; France had not broken and Britain and her Empire had not yet been fully engaged. Any peace could only have been a compromise settlement leaving many issues unresolved, but at least the fighting would have stopped.

In spite of their supposed desperate position at Verdun, the French sent a haughty reply: if the Germans would, as a preliminary, return all French, British and Russian prisoners, they, the French, would then consent to talk. While the

Germans were digesting this Gallic masterpiece, July arrived, the British attacked and no one was in the mood to discuss peace for a long time.

Only a handful of the British leaders – the king, the prime minister, the C.I.G.S. and Haig among them – knew of the peace moves. The War Committee was probably not told, although some of its members may have heard rumours. The ordinary man in the street and the soldier in France, of course, knew nothing. But would it have made any difference if they had known? Consider the climate of popular opinion when these select few were considering the fate of their country. The war was still very popular to all but a few front-line soldiers; the handful of pacifists and conscientious objectors were treated as outcasts. Britain believed herself to be on the eve of a great offensive that would save the French and win the war.

In France, the generals were convinced they could break the deadlock. On 23 May, Rawlinson wrote in his diary:

> There are rumours of peace amongst the politicians, so it will be as well to have a go before they can mature. If we could win a decisive victory, it would certainly put us in an immensely improved position for discussing terms.

The realistic Rawlinson went on to add:

> I do not think there can be peace before this time next year – more probably the Autumn of 1917.

When Rawlinson spoke of 'peace' he meant, of course, 'victory'.

Public and military opinion would have regarded a compromise peace as no better than defeat. It is doubtful if any British prime minister could have secured the support of the country if he had attempted to negotiate at this time. In theory, peace had been possible; in practice, it had not.

If there was no political alternative to the continuation of the war, was there no military alternative to a pitched battle on the Somme? Could not Britain use her sea power; her island position? Was there no indirect approach? Both sea power and the indirect approach had been tried at Gallipoli and had failed. There was talk of a sea-borne landing on Germany's North Sea or Baltic coast many times during the war, but this would have been a hazardous venture. A landing in Holland to outflank the Germans in Belgium might have produced results, but Britain had gone to war over the violation of a neutral country; she could not, now, make use of that expedient herself.

The Royal Navy had imposed a very efficient blockade upon German sea-borne supplies as soon as the war had started, but the results were slow to affect German resistance and time was the one thing that Britain did not have in 1916. The French had stated, categorically, that they could not hold on at Verdun after June. No one appears to have suggested that the French should give up Verdun and withdraw to a new line, a move which might have given them time to catch their breath. The relationship between Britain and France did not extend to Britain, the junior partner, offering such advice. Moreover, a voluntary withdrawal would be utterly alien to the military philosophy of both countries.

Everything drew the main British effort to the Western Front. The best troops were there and the generals were convinced it was the only place where Germany could be beaten. If there was to be no peace, then this was the place for the fighting.

Given that the Western Front was the obvious choice, was there still no alternative in the method of attack to an infantry assault on a near-perfect German defence system? Haig would have liked time for his new divisions to become more proficient and to await the arrival of tanks, but tank production was being continually delayed and the French would not wait. Haig would have loved, also, an opportunity to use his large force of cavalry, but cavalry were of value only after a real advantage had first been gained by the artillery and infantry. The dominant motive for the British attack on 1 July was the French insistence that they be relieved. In the circumstances prevailing at the time there was no alternative to an infantry attack. The only choice left, and this was a real option, was on which part of the Western Front the attack should be made. Strategically, the Somme was a negative choice; behind the German lines there was absolutely nothing of any importance to either side. But, for the British, the Somme held several attractions. It was next to the French and the only place where a joint attack with them could be mounted. There was open ground; no mining area this, like Loos. There was dry ground, too, unlike the marshy lands of Ypres.

There was another attraction. The Somme had never been tried before. One cannot help thinking that the British were drawn to the clean, open land of Picardy because it was a fresh place for them to seek the victory for which they longed. It was a tragedy that the Germans recognized the British intention in time to make their defences there so strong. But in a war based on long artillery barrages followed by massed infantry attacks, it was hardly possible to prepare a major offensive with secrecy. In the end, it probably made little difference to the outcome. The British could have tried anywhere from Ypres to Albert; the result of the plan of attack used on 1 July would have been the same.

The Allied decision to fight on 1 July, rather than accept a compromise peace, doomed all the combatant countries. In June there had been a slender chance, given goodwill and common sense, for Britain, France and Germany to stop the war, and the other warring nations would have had to conform. But afterwards Britain, up to then almost an amateur in the war, had invested so much prestige and blood on this one day that she could not pull out without getting what she considered the only just return for that investment – a total victory.

Germany, her peace feelers rejected in such a dramatic manner, realized that she could not get at the conference table what she considered her rights from her 1914 victories and would have to fight on, in the hope of some chance of winning later.

France was happy. Now, she had a totally committed partner. Gone were the days when she had had to bear the full brunt; more and more, the British would do the fighting.

This commitment to a long war had far-reaching effects upon Britain. Above all else was the cost in human life, which eventually brought mourning into nearly every home in Britain. The exact proportion of the losses stemming from 1 July is not often appreciated. Eighty per cent of Britain's casualties occurred after the opening of the Battle of the Somme. Most of Britain's losses were on the Western Front; 522,206 casualties were sustained there up to the end of June 1916; 2,183,930 afterwards.*

As with the human loss, the financial cost, too, was the

* Figures taken from *The Military Effort*, page 253.

greater in the second half of the war. The full cost of the war to the United Kingdom was £8,742,000,000, seventy-three per cent of which was incurred after 1 July 1916. Between then and the end of the war, the National Debt increased exactly three times over.*

Although there was no practical alternative to a Somme, it is reasonable to ask whether the battle could have been better handled. It is easy to write of 'the generals', but just over 100 officers of general's rank were involved in the battle of 1 July, from the C.-in-C. down to the brigadier-generals who commanded the infantry and cavalry brigades. Some of these enhanced their reputations; others did not. But once the political and strategic decision had been taken, that an offensive should be launched on the Somme, one general above all others had dominated the battle – Gen. Sir Henry Rawlinson, commander of the Fourth Army.

Rawlinson's plan was based on at least three assumptions:

1. That his army was unskilled;
2. That his artillery was powerful enough to destroy the German defences, line by line, but not more than one line at a time.
3. That there was little possibility of a breakthrough followed by cavalry action.

This appreciation was never set out on paper; it may not have occurred, in this form, in Rawlinson's mind; but this plan can only be explained by accepting that these were his assumptions.

As there was to be no breakthrough, it was unnecessary to concentrate a decisive force at any particular point and so both infantry and artillery were spread out equally all along the front to be attacked. The infantrymen were to leave their trenches at zero hour and advance in a rigid wave system, carrying all their needs on their backs. There was to be no rushing of the German front line as soon as the artillery

* *The National Debt*

1914	£700 million
July 1916	£2,500 million
April 1919	£7,500 million

Of this, £1,200 million was borrowed from the U.S.A. A total of £640 million was repaid to them, but only £110 million of this was capital, the remainder being interest. All 1914–18 loan repayments were suspended by agreement in 1932; but, in theory, Britain still owes the U.S.A. £1,090 million from the First World War. (Figures supplied by the Information Division of the Treasury.)

barrage had lifted from it, despite Haig's advice that this should be done. Rawlinson's infantry was simply to occupy ground already conquered by the artillery and there await counter-attacks. This was the new doctrine of attack as pioneered by the Germans at Verdun. Rawlinson did not quarrel with anyone about the cavalry; he merely produced a plan which made no provision for its use.

If Rawlinson's plan had succeeded, it would have been hailed as a masterpiece of simplicity. The guns were spread along the attack front and fired shells, day and night, until the first line of German defences was destroyed. The infantry was then to walk over and occupy these, while the guns moved up and commenced the destruction of the next line. The whole process was to be repeated, indefinitely, until the Germans broke.

The list of mistakes made on 1 July is a long one but many would have been avoided but for the basic assumption that a week-long artillery bombardment would destroy all the German defences – the trenches, the dug-outs, the wire and the Germans themselves. The force of artillery available to the British and the ammunition for the guns was far greater than in any previous battle. Unfortunately neither the guns, nor the shells, were appropriate to their allotted tasks. The destruction of the dug-outs, in which the Germans were sheltering, demanded a quantity of heavy artillery that the British did not have. Although there were more heavies than ever before, the attack front was twice as long as in any previous battle. The heavies available were shared out fairly between all of the attacking corps but none of them had sufficient to complete the destruction of the German dug-outs on its sector. It was only on the right wing, where the French artillery lent a hand, that the dug-outs were sufficiently damaged to permit success. The French were lucky; they had nearly four times as many heavy guns for each mile of front as did the British.* The effect of what heavies the British did have was further reduced by the fact that up to one third of the heavy shells failed to explode.

The task of shooting away the German barbed wire had been given to the British 18-pounders, which accounted for sixty per cent of the total number of artillery pieces used.

* The British had 467 heavies for sixteen miles of front; the French had 900 for eight miles.

The ammunition return of III Corps, which attacked La Boisselle, shows that exactly seventy-five per cent of the 18-pounder shells it fired during the bombardment was shrapnel; the proportion would have been similar in the other corps. As we have seen, the margin for error in cutting wire with shrapnel was so slight that great stretches of the German wire still faced the infantry when they attacked.

Rawlinson had always wanted a long artillery preparation, while Haig, in a letter written on 12 April, favoured a 'short, intense bombardment'. By 16 May, Haig had compromised and he sanctioned a 'methodical bombardment, continued until the officers commanding the attacking units are satisfied that the obstacles to their advance have been adequately destroyed'.* These were sound sentiments but, at the end of June, they did not withstand the pressure of the timetable, with the French clamouring ever more insistently to be saved from defeat at Verdun. There was never any real attempt to relate the barrage to the reported observation of the units scheduled to attack. On the last day of the month, the unhappy Lieut-Col. Sandys and many other front-line officers were definitely not satisfied that the German defences had been 'adequately destroyed'.

In the end, both heavy and light guns failed to destroy all their targets and, instead of the infantry walking over to occupy a smashed defence system, they were faced by intact barbed wire and by machine-gunners emerging from undestroyed dug-outs. Rawlinson's plan for the infantry had not countenanced the possibility of trenches still manned by an aggressive enemy. The standard infantry tactics of this period, adopted by all armies and certainly taught in the British Army, was that an assault on a position such as this would include bombing parties, armed with grenades and light weapons only and carrying a minimum of equipment. These men would go out into No Man's Land, lie as close to the barrage as they dare, even at the risk of suffering casualties from shells that fell short. Then, at the very moment that the artillery barrage lifted, they would rush the enemy trench and keep the defenders down in their dug-outs until the more heavily armed main body of infantry arrived to complete the capture of the position.

* The Official History, *France and Belgium 1916*, vol. I, Appendices 9 and 11.

In May, Rawlinson issued the Fourth Army Tactical Notes, which contained detailed recommendations to the operational units taking part in the opening attack. For the infantry, the basis was the wave system described earlier in this book. Both Haig and the corps commanders protested at the absence of rushing tactics. Rawlinson, confident that the artillery preparation would destroy the Germans and fearful that his inexperienced battalions would become disorganized if the attack was too complicated, was adamant that his advice should be followed. It is uncertain whether corps and divisions were formally ordered by Rawlinson to adopt the recommended tactics, but it is certain that intense pressure was put on them to do so.

It is significant that two of the three divisions of the Fourth Army that were so successful in their initial assault did not conform blindly to the Tactical Notes. Both the 36th (Ulster) and 18th (Eastern) Divisions sent substantial numbers of their men right out into No Man's Land before zero hour; the third successful division, the 30th, probably owed its success to the support of the French heavy artillery. The Ulster Division's tactic may have been the result of native impetuosity rather than careful planning but it paid off. The Eastern Division, however, was commanded by the best training general of the period, Maj.-Gen. Ivor Maxse, a hard-swearing, intolerant man but a brilliant exponent of infantry tactics. His battalions had never been in battle before but Maxse had trained them thoroughly. The leading battalions were ordered to get right up to the barrage before zero hour, and told they must accept six per cent casualties from their own shells. The German front-line trench fell to their first rush.

It may be significant, also, that both of these divisions were from the New Army. It is possible that the intelligence of the New Army men proved, on this occasion, more successful than the blind obedience of the Regulars. What is certain is that those divisions, Regular or otherwise, which most closely followed Rawlinson's advice, suffered the heaviest casualties and achieved the least success.

The French, who did not use the wave system but sent all their men forward in small groups, captured the entire length of the German front-line trench in the first hour of their attack but, once again, any conclusions should be qualified by consideration of their greater concentration of heavy artillery.

The common criticism of the British infantry attack on 1 July was that the men were hindered by having to carry too heavy a load. This is not completely just. The spare ammunition was certainly needed in the bitter trench fighting that followed. What was wrong was that *all* the men had to carry the full loads. When Pte Paddy Kennedy dumped his heavy kit before joining in the attack on Montauban, he was doing what every man in the first wave of the attack should have been encouraged to do. It was the senselessness of sending up to eight waves of heavily laden men across open ground, without any sort of advance guard, that caused a high proportion of the casualties.

The mistaken assumption that the artillery would destroy the German defences, followed by the failure to provide skirmishers, caused the ensuing failure and the terrible casualties. If only one of these two mistakes had been made, Rawlinson would probably have got away with it. Together, they brought disaster.

Exactly two weeks later, thirteen of Rawlinson's battalions, twelve of them from the New Army, made a brilliant attack on German trenches near Mametz Wood. For the planning of this attack, Rawlinson consulted his corps commanders; the Official History records that the plan he made was 'in agreement with the whole body of infantry opinion'. The men were deployed in the dark near the German barbed wire and, after a bombardment of only *five minutes*, rushed and captured the German trenches in the half-light of dawn. The Germans were slow coming out of the dug-outs and either surrendered or were bombed to death. The dug-outs this time had become death traps.

The lack of heavy artillery at this stage of the war could not be helped, but imagine what might have happened if Rawlinson had taken the precaution of using standard infantry tactics on 1 July, as were used on 14 July. When we consider the success of this attack, as well as the progress made by some units on 1 July, it is reasonable to suggest that Rawlinson's men lost the battle on 1 July by a matter of seconds – the interval between the lifting of the artillery barrage and the arrival of the first wave at the German trenches. If the British infantry could have fallen upon the German front line quickly, it is possible that the day would have ended very differently.

These two terrible mistakes having been made, a further defect in the Fourth Army Tactical Notes was revealed. Just as Rawlinson had bound the infantry to the wave system, the artillery was shackled to a rigid programme after zero hour had passed. The Notes had declared:

Experience has shown that the only safe method of artillery support during an advance is a fixed time-table of lifts to which both the infantry and artillery must conform. . . . No changes must be made in the time-table by subordinate formations without reference to corps H.Q.'s, or confusion is sure to ensue.*

The average corps H.Q. was in a château five miles behind the trenches.

The infantry attack had been timed for 7.30 A.M., a late hour by normal standards. This had been done, mainly on French insistence, to allow the early morning mists to clear, giving good visibility for the dozens of officers who were observing for the artillery. Having secured this advantage for the gunners, at the expense of the infantry who were thus denied the chance to attack under cover of the half-light of dawn, Rawlinson threw the advantage away by issuing the above instructions. If only a proportion of the guns had been placed at the disposal of the Forward Observation Officers, the story of the vital first hour might have been different. Later in the day the rigid rules were relaxed, but by then it was too late. Once again, Rawlinson refused to credit his troops with having any skill and robbed them of all chance to use their initiative.

There were many other minor, local mistakes, the result of faulty decisions by subordinate commanders who had little experience of an attack on this scale and who had been over-rapidly promoted, factors unavoidable in the circumstances; but their shortcomings were remorselessly exposed once the basic errors had been made, and so the casualty list lengthened.

There was a sector on the left of VIII Corps of exactly one mile that was not to be attacked. It formed the gap between the northern part of the main attack, at Serre, and the diversion at Gommecourt. 'A few days before the attack, I pointed out to General Hunter-Weston that the assembly trenches

* The Official History, *France and Belgium 1916*, vol. I, Appendix 18.

stopped dead on the left of the 94th Brigade and that not a spade had been put into the ground between me and the subsidiary attack at Gommecourt. Worse still, no effort at wire-cutting was made on that stretch either. A child could see where the flank of our attack lay, to within ten yards.' (Brig.-Gen. H. C. Rees, D.S.O., 94th Infantry Brigade) * On the day of the attack the Germans were able to ignore this mile-long sector and concentrate their artillery fire on the British troops attacking on either side of it.

The narrow paths cut through the British wire were, in many places, completely inadequate to allow the infantry to deploy swiftly. The few paths that were provided were sometimes prepared so long before the attack that the Germans knew their exact positions. 'The advertisement of the attack on our front was absurd. Paths were cut and marked through our wire days before. Bridges over our trenches, for the second and third waves to cross by, were put up days in advance. Small wonder the M.G. fire was directed with such fatal precision.' (Capt. A. Stair Gillon, 87th Infantry Brigade H.Q.)† This was one reason for the heavy losses of the Newfoundlanders, who had to struggle under fire to get through their own wire. These were the very gaps about which Capt. Stair Gillon later complained. In one gap alone, the bodies of sixty-six dead Newfoundlanders were found after the battle.

No advantage was taken of many of the mines that had been prepared at such great labour. It was known that all the debris would fall to the ground within twenty seconds of the explosion, yet cautious commanders had ordered the mines to be blown two minutes before zero hour. The Germans often won the ensuing race for the craters. Ironically, the most successful mine had probably been the one at Kasino Point. In spite of the casualties it had inflicted on British troops, and most of these were caused by the shallow setting of the mine which resulted in the debris being distributed over a wide area, the late firing completely demoralized the German defence.

The commander of the London Division, by his bold action in digging a new advanced trench half-way across No Man's Land, had shown how it was possible to reduce the amount of open ground his men had to cross. Other divisions had pre-

* Public Record Office, CAB 45/190.
† Public Record Office, CAB 45/191.

pared long, shallow tunnels under No Man's Land, which disgorged attackers near the German wire, or became rudimentary communication trenches when the head-cover had been taken down or had fallen in under shell-fire. All these measures had saved life. But some divisions, over-confident, thoughtless or lazy, had done nothing. They had not dug advanced trenches. They had not dug tunnels. Their men were condemned to be exposed over as much as 800 yards of a bullet-swept No Man's Land.

Perhaps the greatest loss of life due to a single mistake by a junior officer was that which should have borne on the conscience of the brigade major in the 34th Division who, against orders, had sent Rawlinson's eve of battle message to a front-line unit by telephone.

Having surveyed the obvious mistakes made, there are at least two controversial aspects of the battle that should be examined. These are the diversionary attack at Gommecourt and the failure to exploit the success of the British right wing. Although Gommecourt and Montauban were as far apart as could be on the British attack front, there is a direct relationship between the two.

Some sympathy should be spared for the Third Army generals who had to plan the diversion at Gommecourt, for they had little say in the major decisions – the sector to be attacked, the date, or even the hour of the attack itself. In addition, they were ordered to make their preparations as obvious as possible. In the event of victory, the main glory would go to the Fourth Army; if defeat, the men at Gommecourt would die in vain. What a disheartening prospect!

In direct results, the attack at Gommecourt inflicted upon the Germans nearly 2,000 casualties, including those caused by the seven-day bombardment, and on the day of the attack it drew fire from the artillery of three German divisions, fire which would otherwise have been directed onto other targets. On the face of it, these were the only benefits, because Hunter-Weston's corps, on the immediate right, did not advance a yard. To achieve these meagre results, 6,769 of Britain's best Territorial soldiers had been lost.

But the effect of the diversion reached further. The Germans expected to be attacked at Gommecourt and, as they could not believe that the British would attack on a front as long as they actually did, they neglected their front opposite the British extreme right wing. The complete success of the British right wing was, partly, the result of Gommecourt.

In summing up the Gommecourt diversion, there are a number of questions for which it is difficult to find conclusive answers. Was Gommecourt the best place for a diversionary attack? Allenby would have liked it to be farther north, but then the German artillery at Gommecourt would have been free to fire on the main British attack.

Was a full-scale diversion necessary at all? Would it not have been better to have made the obvious preparations for an attack and to have fired the long bombardment, but then, at 7.30 A.M. on 1 July, to have made only a brief infantry demonstration? This would have held German attention at Gommecourt right up to that time and would have saved at least 5,000 British casualties there. But this would have allowed the Germans to turn, at once, from Gommecourt and attack the flank of the Fourth Army.

Finally, was the dismissal of Maj.-Gen. Stuart-Wortley justified? Of all the troops attacking on 1 July, the men of his North Midland Division had the bleakest prospects. Theirs was the wettest and muddiest part of the front – witness Bugler Soar on the night before the battle, struggling to pass along a machine-gun while trapped in the mud. Also, being the most northerly division of the attack, they were fired on by the German artillery in front of them and from as far north as there were guns within range.

The preliminary orders sent to Stuart-Wortley in May had included this note: 'The objective of the first bound should, therefore, be restricted to occupying the ground that is won by the artillery.'* They were signed by Brig.-Gen. F. Lyon, VII Corps' chief staff officer. The morning attack of Stuart-Wortley's division had been as brave and determined as any. Six battalions had lost 1,700 men, including five of their C.O.'s, against defences that had, quite clearly, not been 'won by the artillery'.

Stuart-Wortley was not a popular, dashing general. 'He was a worn-out man, who never visited his front line and was incapable of inspiring any enthusiasm.' (Brig.-Gen. F. Lyon, D.S.O., VII Corps H.Q.)† Fair comment, maybe. But Lyon was

* Public Record Office, WO 804/95.

† Public Record Office, CAB 45/135.

a staff officer; he did not have to bear the responsibility of ordering men to certain death.

One feels that Stuart-Wortley was a scapegoat; that Gen. Allenby and Lieut-Gen. Snow were afraid that any hesitancy on their part, any failure at Gommecourt endangering the Fourth Army attack, would result in their being sent home. They need not have worried. Fourth Army, its own attack a disaster, could never accuse the Third Army men of letting them down.

Many of the men who fought at Gommecourt never knew they were taking part in a diversion. Over half a century later, some still could not accept that their friends died simply to draw German fire.

It is commonly supposed that there was no place for cavalry in France after the lines of trenches had become established late in 1914: But I would contend that, for a few hours on 1 July, there occurred an opportunity when cavalry should have been used. Why had Rawlinson refused Congreve's request to advance farther, when his two divisions on the right wing near Montauban had taken all their objectives? Why had three divisions of cavalry been brought up and then, at 3 P.M., been ordered to retire, although regiments from one of these cavalry divisions had been just behind the successful Montauban sector?

Haig, the cavalryman, had always longed for an opportunity to use the cavalry divisions. It was he who had sent these forward and formed them into the Reserve Army under Gough. It was he who visualized what might be achieved if the German lines could be broken. Haig wanted the army to be a tiger, tearing into the German rear. His orders to Rawlinson had read:

> Opportunities to use cavalry, supported by guns, machine-guns, etc. and infantry should be sought for, both during the early stages of the attack and subsequently.*

But Rawlinson had constantly resisted this course of action and the presence of Gough with the cavalry divisions. His plan, eventually accepted, was for a gradual battering down of the German positions. To him, the army was an elephant trampling the German lines down one by one. Never has a

* The Official History, *France and Belgium 1916*, vol. I, Appendix 9.

family motto more suited the character of the man, for that of the Rawlinson family was '*Festina Lente*' – 'Make Haste Slowly'.

Was there, in fact, the opportunity for which Haig had hoped? Were the infantrymen in the new front line of Montauban Alley being practical when they looked for the cavalry to come through? Were the Germans waiting in strength to smash any impetuous move forward by the British?

In fact, the Germans on this sector could not have been in a more desperate position. Germany was fighting in Russia, in Italy, in Belgium and in France; although she had a large army it was committed to a huge length of line besides being heavily involved in the Battle of Verdun, and the limited number of German reserve divisions had to be carefully hoarded. It has been seen in an earlier chapter how the diversion at Gommecourt and the threatening moves made by the other British armies in the north had completely misled the German c.-in-c., Falkenhayn, as to where the main attack would fall. He had also assumed that the French had been so mauled at Verdun that they would not join in the British attack. When the German commanders on the Somme had pointed out the British balloons, the obvious preparations and the long artillery bombardment there, Falkenhayn thought that these were merely diversionary moves and sent no extra reserves to that front.

On 1 July, the commander of the German XIV Reserve Corps had only two weak divisions as local reserves for the eighteen-mile front from Gommecourt to the River Somme, and by the afternoon he had been forced to commit battalions of both to the fighting. On a four-mile sector facing the British right wing there were no more than four scattered battalions and most of the German artillery here had been put out of action. The construction of the second main line on this sector had been neglected and consisted of a single shallow trench. A scratch force of clerks, cooks, batmen and 200 recruits was rushed up to man this trench, and they were all that faced Congreve until midnight when fresh battalions arrived. Against this Congreve had the two divisions that had attacked that morning and a reserve division, the 9th (Scottish); in addition the French had indicated that they were willing to advance, and cavalry regiments of Gough's Reserve Army were near by.

One reason given for the neglect of the cavalry was that they could never have crossed the trenches, barbed wire and shell holes of the old battlefield. But these obstacles existed on every other part of the front; if the objection is valid, why had three divisions of cavalry been brought up at all? Once Montauban had been captured, the ground between the village and the former British front line became peaceful. Sappers started to lay a light railway; an old road was repaired and brought into use; teams of horses brought forward field guns, using duck-board bridges to cross the old trenches. The cavalry could have advanced over this ground.

Let it be stated that Rawlinson, as army commander in sole charge of operations on this front, had every right to choose whichever course of action he thought best suited to his overall plans. When Congreve made his telephone call, there were at least four possibilities open to Rawlinson.

'We had been told that if we made our three miles the cavalry would follow through with thirty miles.' (Pte A. A. Bell, 2nd Manchester Pals) This was the first of Rawlinson's options: an attempt at the breakthrough using some of Gough's cavalry and the infantry of Congreve's corps. Such an operation would have been a gamble, would have needed a complex command arrangement and the cooperation of the French on the right flank, but it could have opened up the most glittering possibilities. It was certainly what Haig, the C.-in-C., desired.

The clerks and cooks in the German second line might have broken and the Germans, with few local reserves and no strong lines on which to fall back, might have been

> forced to retire on a broad front and take up a new position, which could not be made so strong as the one abandoned. . . Whilst the Germans were fully engaged at Verdun there seemed to be every chance of a definite breakthrough.
>
> Whether the successes gained at Montauban on the 1st . . . could have been exploited in the sense of Sir Douglas Haig's conception must for ever remain an unsolved question: all that can be said is that no attempt was made to do so.

These quotations are all by the Official Historian, Sir James Edmonds, who had once been a member of Haig's staff.

A less risky alternative to an attempted breakthrough was a limited cavalry operation. If a small cavalry force had gone out from Montauban and wheeled left, exploiting the ground which lay between the German front-line system and the second line, such a force would have found open ground, no barbed wire and only a rare, probably unmanned communication trench. There was hardly any German infantry in this intermediate zone, but there were artillery batteries and administrative units which would have been most vulnerable to cavalry action. Such an operation would have been in the nature of a raid. Mametz Wood could probably have been taken, and Fricourt and Contalmaison threatened. After a week-long bombardment and heavy fighting all day, the sudden appearance of British cavalry behind them might well have caused the German infantry still holding the front line in the centre to break.

There would have been dangers, of course. The cavalry might have been caught by long-range German machine-gun fire or British artillery fire; their return route might have been closed behind them. But, considering the slaughter of the British infantry farther north, these would have been risks that the cavalry would certainly have accepted. Two or three cavalry regiments, boldly handled, could have achieved results out of all proportion to their numbers.

A third and even safer course open to Rawlinson was to permit a modest infantry advance in conjunction with the French. The two woods, Bernafay and Trônes, which were just outside Montauban, could easily have been occupied. Patrols did go into Bernafay, found only a few Germans whom they took prisoner, and then returned, leaving an empty wood. Indeed, the Germans assumed that both of these woods had been occupied by the British. Some of the open ground between Montauban and the German second line could have been occupied too. There was little risk in these moves.

But Rawlinson chose the safest course of all. In refusing Congreve's request to advance he was sticking to his original plan; the new front line in Montauban Alley was a perfect defensive position from which to beat off the expected German counter-attacks. When these did come, however, they were so weak that they were easily dealt with.

Nothing further happened on the right wing until the afternoon of 3 July. The Germans were still so disorganized that two Scottish battalions took Bernafay Wood at a cost of only six casualties. Rawlinson was now prepared to move farther, but the French, unimpressed by the British lethargy on the first day, had lost interest in this sector and were attacking elsewhere. Five more days of inaction followed, then the 30th Division, back in the line again, moved on Trônes Wood. But they were too late; the Germans had recovered.

The fighting for Mametz Wood, Trônes Wood and the open ground, some of which could have been taken so easily on 1 July, went on for days. The casualties incurred in their subsequent capture were enormous and might have been avoided by bold action on that day.

Little wonder that Pte Norton of the Norfolks had looked in vain for the cavalry, that Soldat Goebelbecker was 'puzzled by the lack of further forward movement by the British' and that Capt. Spears was 'almost biting his nails down to the palms in frustration'.

In attempting to assess whether this opening day of the Battle of the Somme was a success or otherwise, one faces several difficulties. It is not easy to look at the military aspects without the political, to treat the British attack apart from the French, or to separate the first day from the remainder of the battle.

Only with the massive use of hindsight can it be seen that Britain should not have fought the battle at all. The failure of the political and military leadership to recognize the stalemate, or their refusal to accept it, committed the soldiers to a war of attrition that resulted in the loss of the cream of a generation of young men and created problems in Europe that led to the Second World War. But this is an academic conclusion, much divorced from the realities of the period. It would have needed a genius and a very brave man to have turned Britain from the path she chose on the Somme rather than make a compromise peace with a hated enemy.

Whether the Battle of the Somme in its entirety was a victory for the Allies, as has often been suggested, is a subject of controversy. Looking back at Haig's three original aims for the battle, all seem to have been fulfilled. The French were relieved from defeat at Verdun; the positions held by the Allies at the end of the battle were better than on 30 June; losses were inflicted on the Germans. But the Battle of Verdun was probably waning, with both sides nearing exhaustion, before the Somme started, and the final Allied positions on the Pozières Ridge were rendered valueless when the Germans retired the following spring. Only the third achievement cannot be argued against: it was on the Somme that the Germans lost the core of their battle-hardened army.

In dealing with the first day alone, it can be claimed that 1 July was a British success, for the Germans immediately started closing down their attack on Verdun. But the British assault had been on such a scale that success, in this limited sense, had been inevitable. The terrible losses made it a success hardly worth having.

How should history judge the individuals who were involved in making the major decisions for 1 July? The ultimate responsibility rested with Asquith and his War Committee, but its members should not be judged too harshly. They represented a country which was still fully behind the war. In supporting their ally and pressing for military victory, they were doing what nearly every patriotic Briton expected of them. Many of the politicians did not know of the German peace offers; none suspected that the battle would be so grossly mismanaged.

Douglas Haig, that much maligned soldier, is another to whom too much blame should not be attached. Once he had chosen the front to be attacked – and the Somme was no worse than any other – and given his army commanders their instructions, his main duty was to provide them with the best troops and resources available, and there is no evidence that he failed in this. His ambitious plan to capture Bapaume with cavalry and then roll up the German lines to Arras may seem unrealistic, but it was a contingency plan in the event of a breakthrough occurring. It has been seen just how close the cavalry came to being needed.

On one count, however, Haig can be criticized: that was his reluctance to impose his will on Rawlinson. He felt that Rawlinson's plan of attack was wrong, but Haig, not long at G.H.Q. and an ex-cavalryman, would not overrule his ex-infantry subordinate. It turned out to be a tragic error.

Of the army commanders, Rawlinson emerges very badly. His Fourth Army had taken only a quarter of its objectives and had suffered 50,000 casualties in one day. He had been responsible for three major errors, one each for the artillery, the infantry and the cavalry.

Rawlinson was not to blame for the shortage of heavy artillery but he had failed to recognize the depth and strength of the German dug-outs it was supposed to destroy. He ignored the doubts of infantry officers on this score and the evidence of the captured dug-out on his Touvent Farm sector. It seems incredible that no one at Fourth Army H.Q. knew of this or suspected that the Germans had dug down so far.

Rawlinson had ignored both the current War Office manual on tactics and the advice of all around him in refusing to rush the German trenches. By insisting, instead, on his own rigid attack plan he had robbed his men of any opportunity to use the intelligence and initiative which they surely possessed. Rawlinson must take full responsibility for this, the worst mistake of the day and the one which had caused most of the casualties.

Rawlinson had a poor opinion of his neighbours, the French. On the eve of the battle he wrote;

> If we do bring off a great success they will be jealous; if we do not, they will say it is hopeless to try and break the lines and will begin, again, to talk of making terms. This makes one's relation with them very difficult, for they are like children in many ways.*

These were unworthy sentiments. On the following day, the French took four fifths of their objectives and twice as many prisoners as did Rawlinson. The French heavy artillery support and their successful infantry advance did much to help Rawlinson's only real success, the advance of his right wing.

Perhaps it was the antipathy that Rawlinson felt towards his ally which influenced his other mistake – the refusal to allow the right wing to exploit its success. It is easy, however, to write these lines after many months of research and thought, but picture the situation when the corps commander at Montauban telephoned his chief to ask permission to advance farther. Rawlinson had spent months planning this battle; he had given every appearance of having complete confidence in the result. But now, as he sat in his office at Querrieux with the hot sun streaming through the windows, his hopes were crumbling away. His other corps commanders were reporting disaster, confusion, or an ignorance that could mean anything.

Then, suddenly, from a sector where he had least expected success, came a report of victory. Rawlinson had heard other reports like this one during the morning; they had turned out to be false. To accede to Congreve's request, Rawlinson

* The Rawlinson Diaries. (See footnote on page 78.)

would have to trust the French, whom he did not trust; he might have to use the cavalry, in which he had no confidence; he would have to switch his attention from the centre, where his main hope lay, to a sector as far from the centre as could be. The proposed advance was against all Rawlinson's instincts and against his own carefully prepared plan.

Rawlinson did not have weeks to sit quietly coming to a decision. He did not have an hour. He should have grasped the opportunity to do something on the right wing, especially in view of Haig's orders about using cavalry, but he failed to do so under such great pressure.

The first two of Rawlinson's mistakes were the direct cause of the failure of his army to take many of its objectives and of the fearful casualties it had suffered. The third ensured even more casualties in the days that followed.

Of the other army commanders, Allenby had the unenviable task of making a diversion against Gommecourt. His plan showed imagination but he was over-ambitious in including the encirclement of Gommecourt village in the objectives. His failure to recall the London Division as soon as the attack had broken down, and his insistence that the battle be resumed in the afternoon, when his troops had already performed their diversionary function, only added to the casualty list. Also the summary dismissal of the North Midland Division's commander seems harsh, particularly after the advice about the limited nature of the attack given to Stuart-Wortley before the battle.

Lieut-Gen. Gough of the Reserve Army was blameless. His voice in the major decisions and his influence on the battle were non-existent.

The mistakes of the lesser generals were mainly due to an inexperience that was unavoidable in the circumstances; some of the corps and divisional commanders had done extremely well. If those who had not had all been replaced, it is unlikely that their successors would have done any better. One wonders, however, whether Haig was right to retain the sixty-four-year-old Lieut-Gen. Maxwell in his position as Quartermaster General after the ambulance trains' failure.

The only good to emerge from that terrible day was the display of patriotism, courage and self-sacrifice shown by the British soldiers. Theirs is a memory that their country should always cherish.

17

The Years that Followed

For the soldiers on both sides on the Western Front, the remainder of 1916 was dominated by the fighting that continued to rage in Picardy until early winter. Always it was the British or the French who were attacking; always the Germans defending, clinging desperately to each position. There was never a repeat of the massive assault of 1 July; instead, a series of attacks on a smaller scale, but all marked by the same ferocity. The whole later became popularly known as the Battle of the Somme, although it was never officially recognized under that name. After the war, each phase of the battle was given a separate title, that of 1 July becoming part of the First Battle of Albert.

Nearly every British division in France took its turn on the Somme; many attacked twice, some three times. Steadily, the Army of 1916 melted away.

On 21 July, Lieut Henry Webber's battalion, the 7th South Lancs, which had just missed being thrown into the battle on the afternoon of the first day, moved up to relieve a battalion in the front line near Mametz Wood. That night, Henry Webber took up supplies as usual with the battalion transport. Leaving his men to unload the horses, Webber went over to where the c.o. was talking with a group of officers. Into this routine, peaceful, evening scene, there suddenly dropped a single, heavy German shell. When the smoke and dust had cleared, it was found that twelve men and three horses had been hit. Henry Webber lay unconscious, badly wounded in the head. He and the other wounded were rushed to a Dressing Station, but for Webber it was too late. He never recovered consciousness and died that night.

The news of the death of this sixty-eight-year-old warrior was noted in high places. His family received special messages of sympathy from the King and Queen and from the Army Council – unusual tributes to a dead lieutenant of infantry. Webber's devotion to duty was further honoured when he was mentioned in the c.-in-c.'s Despatches. Webber's wife never recovered from the shock of his death and died two years later but, ironically, his three soldier sons all survived the war. It is probable that Henry Webber was the oldest member of the B.E.F. to be killed in action during the war.*

The day after Henry Webber's death, the Army of 1916 suffered another notable casualty. Maj.-Gen. Ingouville-Williams, commander of the 34th Division, had always been ready to share the dangers of his men and had cared so much for them that he had gone out into No Man's Land like a common stretcher-bearer, searching for wounded after the battle on 1 July. Like Henry Webber, he too went up to Mametz Wood and was hit by a shell and, like Webber, 'Inky Bill' died.

As the battle continued, the casualties inexorably mounted. Even the highest families in the land were not spared. In September the prime minister, Mr Asquith, visited the Somme and met his two sons who were serving there. Within a fortnight one of them, Raymond, a Grenadier Guards officer, was dead.

Another to die was a Maj. W. Congreve, son of the corps commander who had captured Montauban on 1 July. Maj. Congreve was killed while serving in a division in his father's corps. He was awarded a posthumous V.C., a medal also held by his father.

All through the summer and autumn the battle raged. The weather grew wet and cold; the attacks floundered in the Somme mud. The enthusiasm and high hopes with which the soldiers had greeted the opening of the battle began to fade. Towards the end, when an attack by a tired 30th Division had failed, a member of one of its battalions was court-martialled for cowardice. The man was only a recently arrived reinforcement but had not been able to explain how he had got lost during the attack. He was found guilty. The battalion was paraded; the accused man was brought forward and the sentence announced: execution by firing squad. His comrades were quite convinced that, after the abortive attack, someone in authority had decided to make an example of one man and that this poor wretch had been chosen as an example to the others.

Paddy Kennedy and five other privates had already been

* The youngest was probably Pte J. Condon, a fourteen-year-old Waterford boy, who was killed with the 2nd Royal Irish in the Second Battle of Ypres, May 1915. His grave is at Poelcappelle (Poekapelle) British Cemetery, Ypres.

given a day's rations and sent to a remote village; they were to be the firing party. That night the condemned man and his escort of military policemen joined them. The officer in charge encouraged the prisoner to get drunk, the usual procedure; but the drink was refused. Early next morning, the firing party went out to a nearby quarry. Kennedy and the others had their rifles taken away and later returned, loaded: one with a blank round, the others with live ones. No one knew who had the blank round.

The condemned man refused to walk out to the quarry and had to be dragged there. He was then tied to a chair, blindfolded and a white handkerchief pinned over his heart. The officer gave the firing party their instructions: 'Aim straight. I don't want to have to finish him off.'

After the crash of the volley, the prisoner was found to be alive, although badly hurt. Kennedy and the others watched, sickened, as the officer drew his revolver, put it to the man's head and pulled the trigger. Military justice, 1916 style, had been done.

On 14 November the battle ended. No one could ever agree on the final casualty figures, but it is certain that in the 140 days that the battle had lasted Britain's share was over 400,000. For this loss, Haig's troops had advanced exactly six miles and were still four miles short of Bapaume, which the cavalry had hoped to take in the opening attack.

The total casualties on the Somme were over 1,300,000, divided almost equally between the Germans and the Allies. Conceived as the 'Big Push' that might end the war, it had turned into a ghastly battle of attrition.

What of the mood of the people at home while the Battle of the Somme was being fought? Although the casualty lists continued to cause individual grief, comprehensive totals were not published and the country as a whole was content to read the optimistic official reports of the battle and assume that their men were winning a series of great victories. Perhaps inspired by the battle, a young composer, Haydn Wood, was writing a haunting, sentimental song – 'Roses of Picardy'. By the end of the year it was a hit song.

Fortunately, there exists an interesting guide to the civilians' thoughts at this time. In October there was a by-election in the constituency of North Ayrshire. There were only two candidates. One, a clergyman, the Rev. Chelmers, was standing as a Peace Candidate. The other was Lieut-Gen. Hunter-Weston, whose VIII Corps had suffered so disastrously on 1 July. He had been given leave from France and stood as a Unionist. The general received 7,419 votes; the peace-seeking clergyman only 1,300.

For one soldier, 1917 opened well. On 3 January, Gen. Sir Douglas Haig was promoted to the rank of field-marshal, the highest in the army. Haig and the other military leaders were pleased to see the New Year. After its disappointing predecessor, they were confident that 1917 was to be the Allies' year of victory.

The first actions of the year were political rather than military. Germany made fresh efforts to secure peace and throughout January diplomatic notes passed among the capitals of Europe but, again, nothing came of the peace moves. In desperation the Germans turned to unrestricted submarine warfare, hoping to starve Britain out. Instead, the submarines helped to bring the United States into the war, on the side of the Allies, in April.

'I was pleased when I heard that the Americans were on our side. We seemed to have borne the brunt of the fighting for so long and I felt the Americans were similar people to us and would be steadier than some of our other allies.' (L/Cpl H. Hickman, 1/8th Sherwood Foresters)* But it would be nearly a year before American troops were ready to fight in France.

In the meantime, those who remained of the 1916 men had to get on with the war. They were the 'old hands' now, the experienced men who would teach the conscripts the art of war. Philip Howe and Bill Soar had recovered from their wounds and returned to their own battalions, but for many the war was over. Charles Matthews spent eight miserable months in military hospitals; his knee was still 'the size of a football' and he could not walk at all. Eventually, he was offered a medical discharge and went home, thinking he was crippled for life at the age of twenty. Fortunately for Matthews, a civilian doctor became interested in his injury and sent him to the Great Portland Street Hospital, where a specialist found that his knee-cap was broken into five pieces. An operation was

* The ranks and units of 1 July 1916 will continue to be used in quotations such as these, which are all from men who were on the Somme on that day.

performed and Matthews walked out a month later. He was to have a stiff leg for the rest of his life, but he was able to resume work before the post-war rush for jobs began. It was six months after he had been injured before Matthews discovered that he had been crushed by debris from a British mine. He had always assumed that the debris came from a mine exploded by the Germans, to hinder the British attack.

There were many like Matthews. He had served only a few months in France, been wounded in his first battle and, with a typical Blighty wound, had escaped the long years of the war. Matthews realized he had been lucky and the men in France thought the same. 'Many went over the top on 1 July 1916 after a week or so in France, were wounded and went home as heroes. Perhaps they were, but what about those few of us who served all through!' (Cpl J. T. Brewer, 1/6th Gloucesters)

Before the Battle of the Somme had finished, the Germans had started to construct a new defensive system, over ten miles behind the front line, and work continued on it all through the winter. Then, in February 1917, the Germans did something that the British and French generals would never have done. They withdrew to this new line and voluntarily gave up nearly 1,000 square miles of territory, ten times more than the Allies had captured in 1916. When the British and French troops reached this new line, they found a perfectly sited defensive system waiting for them, as strong as the one they had so painfully forced the previous year. They would have to start all over again.

When the Germans retreated from Gommecourt, Bill Soar and other men who had taken part in the attack on 1 July were asked to help with the identification of the corpses which still littered the old No Man's Land. The bodies of twenty Nottingham men were taken from the German barbed wire and more were found in nearby shell holes. They were decomposing after being in the open for eight months and, when they were moved, flesh fell away from the bones. Despite this, many were identified; one captain from the distinctive boots he had always worn. Another body found was that of Capt. J. L. Green, the Medical Officer of the Derby battalion who had been awarded a posthumous V.C.; his body too was identified from the clothing. Bill Soar found the body of his best friend. This unpleasant work made Soar and many of the others sick but they were still pleased to have been able to give their dead comrades a proper burial.

Later that year Bill Soar was in Nottingham, on leave, and happened to meet the mother of one of the men he had identified. She had always refused to believe that her son was dead, even when notified that his body had been found. Soar was forced to tell her that he had personally recovered and identified his body. She died within a month.

All through 1917 the battles of attrition continued. The British, at Arras, and the French launched massive offensives in April; both ended with little gain but heavy losses. There were no more French attacks that year. Their soldiers had mutinied; they were prepared to defend their trenches but refused to take part in any more futile attacks. Once more, the British had to keep attacking to help the French. Their summer offensive opened well, with the capture of Messines Ridge, but soon degenerated into the mud and misery of Passchendaele.

The last attack, in November at Cambrai, started brilliantly with a successful tank attack by the British but, when the Germans counter-attacked, all the early gains were lost.

Reginald Bastard, Percy Chappell, Philip Howe and Paddy Kennedy all took part in the big battles of 1917. Bill Soar did not, however; the North Midland Division was still regarded with disapproval after its disappointing performance at Gommecourt and remained as a line-holder.

Reginald Bastard was wounded at Messines and had to return to England. In doing so, he lost his temporary rank and became, once again, a major. When he recovered he was sent to a Senior Officers' School at Aldershot to instruct future battalion commanders. It was an excellent place to spend the winter.

The cat, Nigger, which Paddy Kennedy had taken from the German dug-out at Montauban, left France in the summer of 1917 with a young soldier who took it home on leave, hidden under his jacket. He left the cat with his parents in Rochdale, where it settled well and survived the soldier, who was killed at Passchendaele soon after his leave.

For the Newfoundlanders, 1917 was a mixed year. At Arras, they suffered terrible casualties again, in another badly planned attack, but, after Cambrai, the king honoured them with the 'Royal' prefix. This was the only occasion that a unit was so honoured during the First World War, although many received the title afterwards.

Two more of the 1916 generals left France during the year. Gen. Allenby had directed the costly Battle of Arras and, soon afterwards, he was ordered to hand over the Third Army and was sent to command the British Forces in Egypt and Palestine. This move was regarded by some as a relegation, punishment for his poor showing at Gommecourt in 1916 and at Arras. However, Allenby did very well in the Middle East and finished the war with a higher reputation than any of the generals he left behind in France. But a month after Allenby left France, his only son was killed in action in Belgium.

Then, at the close of the year, the C.I.G.S. again requested the recall of the sixty-five-year-old Quartermaster General, Lieut-Gen. Maxwell. Again Haig tried to keep Maxwell, but this time London insisted and Maxwell went home and retired from active duty.

By the end of 1917, those of the 1916 men who were left were tired beyond description, and morale, at this time, was probably lower than at any other period in the war. Many of the men had been at the Front for up to two years with hardly a break; there was no system of relief for the battle-weary. Those who had been wounded were sent back to the trenches time and time again and, after each big battle, fewer and fewer of their friends remained. After the hell of Passchendaele and the disappointment of Cambrai they began to think that the war would never end; that they were doomed to fight on until they were all dead. Their ideals and patriotism had long since departed.

The infantryman's devotion to his immediate comrades and his inborn sense of duty helped to keep him going, but he became very bitter about that part of the army not in the trenches and about all civilians. The longing for an honourable release, in the form of a Blighty wound, was almost universal.

Most men stood by their duty; a few did not. Self-inflicted wounds, almost unheard of in the early days, became a great problem. Men tried all the old dodges such as chewing cordite or sleeping in wet towels to induce sickness, and being gassed almost became a court-martial offence. Successful desertion was difficult to achieve; the penalty for being caught could be death by firing squad.*

It would be unwise to generalize too much on this theme; there were wide differences between individual units. Possibly the Regular and early Territorial battalions kept going better than those which were without a tradition of discipline and lacked the nucleus of pre-war men who were prepared to accept more readily the casualties and appalling living conditions.

It is certain, however, that officers in general did not become as depressed as did the other ranks. Compared with their men, officers were in greater danger of being killed or wounded but, against this, the privileges of rank could be immense in those things which mattered to front-line soldiers. Leave, pay and decorations were received in direct proportion to the rank held, with the private soldier being worse off in all respects. The officers had the best and often the only dug-outs in the trenches, and did not have to undergo the trials of the exhausting carrying parties and labouring duties which faced the men as soon as they came out for a 'rest'.

Those officers whose nerve gave way were somehow got rid of, to the rear or to England, but, for the private soldier, 'battle fatigue' was rarely recognized as a disease and men who suffered in this way were condemned to a private hell in the trenches until they became a casualty, or cracked and committed an offence which sometimes led to a firing squad. A few could not face the future at all and took their own lives. One must feel pity for those desperate men who, in the solitude of a trench bay, ended their troubles in this way. No figures for such deaths will ever be available; suicides were usually posted as Killed in Action.

'Towards the end of the war, we were so fed up we wouldn't even sing "God Save the King" on church parade. Never mind the bloody King we used to say, he was safe enough; it should have been God save us. But we worshipped the Prince of Wales.' (Pte J. A. Hooper, 7th Green Howards)

'By the end of 1917 we didn't care who won as long as we

* Of all death sentences, only about ten per cent were carried out. In the B.E.F. an average of one soldier was executed every five days, mostly for cowardice or desertion. The Australian Government refused to allow executions in their divisions.

could get the war over.' (Cpl L. Jessop, 1st London Rifle Brigade)

There were many like Pte Hooper and Cpl Jessop but, although the B.E.F. contained thousands of cynics and war-weary men, the character of the British soldier and the discipline of the army were such that no battalion of the B.E.F. ever deserted its trenches or failed to obey an order to go over the top. The only mutiny, and that was short-lived, was at one of the base camps and was a protest against the bullying methods of instructors who had rarely served at the Front.

The heavy casualties of 1917 had left the B.E.F. in France considerably under strength. Although there were large numbers of men under arms in England, the government refused to send these out to replenish the depleted battalions. No one had the courage to dismiss Haig; instead, the War Cabinet sought to prevent him launching new offensives in 1918 by keeping him short of men.

In an attempt to overcome this shortage, the B.E.F. introduced a reorganization that was to have a lasting effect. In February and March 1918 a total of 153 battalions were disbanded or merged and, from that time, divisions were reduced to only nine battalions of infantry. The men released by this move were used to restore the strength of the remaining battalions. Introduced as an expedient, the nine-battalion division still remains as the standard British infantry unit.

As the Regular battalions were all spared, the greatest cuts were in the New Army. Many of the proud and eager battalions which had been raised in 1914 and had fought so bravely on the Somme passed quietly from the scene, their short lives over.

The first attack of 1918 was made by the Germans. On a foggy morning late in March, they launched a massive offensive against the southern part of the B.E.F.'s front. Using a short but very heavy artillery barrage, followed by infiltrating tactics against the under-strength British divisions, the Germans did what no other army on the Western Front had been able to do since 1914 – they broke through the opposing lines. For ten days they advanced, at the farthest point for thirty-five miles; the ground between Albert and Bapaume, over which the British had struggled for more than four months in 1916, was recaptured by the Germans in one day.

Bill Soar's battalion, the 1/7th Sherwood Foresters, had been transferred to another division in the recent reorganization and he was in the front line on the first day of the German offensive. For hours, massed ranks of Germans assaulted their position and Soar, for the first time in the war, was able to shoot many of them, until a German bullet hit him in the neck. Before he could be evacuated their position was overrun and virtually the whole battalion killed or captured. Soar's wound was not treated for three days, but he survived this, and an operation performed without anaesthetic, to spend the remainder of the war in Germany.

Philip Howe, still in the 10th West Yorks and now a captain, had to retreat over the old Somme battlefield. At one stage, whilst in charge of a small rearguard, he found that the Germans were all around him. Neither side opened fire but the Germans called on him to surrender. Howe shouted back 'No!' and, surprisingly, the Germans did not shoot but allowed Howe and his men to go. Both sides were sick of killing.

A few days later, from a position just outside Albert, Howe watched hordes of Germans enter the town; he was surprised when they did not reappear for two days. The Germans were exhausted and had also found a large store of drink.

Albert turned out to be the limit of the German advance at this point. They switched their efforts to fresh places and, for the next two months, continued their attacks. Casualties on both sides were enormous and this period saw the end of most of the 1916 veterans who were still at the Front.

The 2nd Lincolns were involved in the fighting and their c.o. was wounded, so Reginald Bastard was recalled to France and, within a few days, he was in command of his old battalion again. After further heavy fighting the Lincolns were taken out of the line, filled up with raw recruits and sent with several other weak battalions to hold a quiet part of the French Army's front on the Aisne. Here they were to rest and take the opportunity to absorb the new men.

Unfortunately the Germans had chosen just this place for their next offensive. After a sudden, intense bombardment, the Germans attacked. In a few hours the British positions were overwhelmed. Only two officers and thirty men escaped from the Lincolns. Reginald Bastard was not among them. He was a prisoner.

When Hubert Gough had taken over part of the Fourth Army in the evening of 1 July 1916, his command, which became the Fifth Army, did well for many months, but his hard-driving methods at Passchendaele in 1917 earned for him a reputation as a 'butcher'. In 1918, it was Gough's Fifth Army which had taken the hardest blows in the German March offensive and had been forced to give much ground, the worst offence a British general could commit. Gough was dismissed and left France in disgrace. His Fifth Army was disbanded. Many thought that he was being unjustly treated and had been made a scapegoat by those who had kept the B.E.F. so short of men.

All was quiet in France during midsummer while the two sides recovered. The British units were completely exhausted and many had almost ceased to exist. The 30th Division, which had gained such a high reputation on the Somme, had been used over and over again since then and had fallen so low in numbers that the whole division was temporarily disbanded; an unusual occurrence. When the 3rd Manchester Pals were broken up and the men sent to other divisions, Paddy Kennedy found that he and three others were the only men left in the fighting part of the battalion from the original members who had joined in 1914. This was the cost of being part of a 'stormer' division.

One night Capt. Philip Howe was out on a routine patrol in No Man's Land when he was fired at by a machine-gun. He escaped by jumping into a shell hole but impaled himself on a bayonet that was sticking up there. Although this was quite accidental, Howe was very worried that he would be charged with having a self-inflicted wound and it was several hours before he came in. His explanation was accepted and he went home to an English hospital, but it is a sad comment on the prevailing state of nerves and low morale that a company commander and a holder of the Military Cross should have feared being accused of wounding himself in order to get away from the Front.

All the time that the Germans had been attacking in the spring and early summer, Haig had been trying to build up a reserve, hoping to be able to launch his own attacks when the Germans had worn themselves out. It was August before he was ready for his first effort and, in three respects, it was 1916 over again: the sector chosen was the Somme, the attack was made by a new Fourth Army and the army commander was, again, Henry Rawlinson.* But here the similarity with 1916 ended for, this time, Rawlinson's attack was a brilliant success. This opened the way for a series of further successes, but the divisions which gained these victories contained few survivors from the Army of 1916. It is to be hoped that Rawlinson will be remembered by history as much for his 1918 victories as for the reverse of 1 July 1916.

By November the Germans were beaten and sued for peace, this time on the Allies' terms. An armistice was signed and, at 11 A.M. on 11 November, all fighting on the Western Front ceased.

Of our ten men of 1916, only two remained at the front. Paddy Kennedy had refused all offers of promotion and remained a private to the end. In three years he had had only fourteen days of home leave and had fought in nearly every big battle after the Somme. He had been awarded the Military Medal and been mentioned in Despatches three times. It was a fine record of service but, when the fighting stopped, he was utterly worn out and a sick man.

Percy Chappell was a major and second-in-command of a New Army battalion of the Somerset Light Infantry. He was one of the very few men to have gone out with the B.E.F. in 1914 and remain right to the end. He had served the whole war in France and had suffered nothing worse than a bout of the Spanish Influenza which swept Europe in 1918.

Three more of the men were in Germany as prisoners. Reginald Bastard was in an officers' camp but the other two had been put to work by the Germans, Albert McMillan in a coal mine and Bill Soar repairing railway engines at a Krupps factory in Essen.

Philip Howe was at home recuperating from his third wound of the war but was still in the army. Charles Matthews was a civilian and had a permanent limp to remind him of the British mine at Kasino Point which had hurt him so badly on 1 July.

* Due to the reorganization of the armies, in late 1917 and early 1918, the old Fourth Army had ceased to exist and Rawlinson had been sent as a British representative to the Supreme War Council at Versailles. When Gough was dismissed and the Fifth Army disbanded, the Fourth Army was re-formed with Rawlinson in command.

To Billy McFadzean, Dick King and Henry Webber, the end of the war meant nothing. Their bodies, buried on the Somme, were with those of the 725,557 British servicemen who had died on the Western Front.*

'*Il ne subsiste alors que le nom, la gloire et les ruines.*' So reads a plaque in the Hôtel de Ville at Albert describing the appearance of the town at the Armistice.

When the war ended, Albert, the surrounding villages and the once pleasant countryside were a completely devastated wasteland. This part of the Somme region had been fought over four times. Not a house remained intact and most of the inhabitants had left.

When Albert fell to the Germans in March 1918, the British were determined that their enemies should not use the tower of the basilica for artillery observers as they themselves had used it for so many months earlier in the war, and British heavy guns were turned onto it. The tower was destroyed and the golden Virgin finally fell into the square below. It has been estimated that the church had been struck by some 2,000 shells since 1914. The statue was lost; rumour had it that the Germans took it away for its scrap metal value. The soldiers' legend that the fighting would end only when the Virgin fell had been true, for within a few months the war was over.

The devastation was so complete that, at first, the French Government planned to make the whole area into a national forest, without attempting to rebuild the villages or reclaim the land, but gradually, the former inhabitants started to return. Slowly the area returned to life. Working from old plans found at Amiens, the new villages and even most of the individual houses were built on the exact sites of their predecessors. Special labour units were sent to clear the land and fill in the old trench systems. It was feared that the numerous tunnels and dug-outs might attract bandits, so orders were issued that all the entrances to these were to be blocked. In course of time, most collapsed.

The mayor of Mametz returned to his village, found the garden of his old house and dug up a supply of wine he had buried there in 1914. It was in perfect condition. The troops of the 7th Division who captured Mametz in the broiling heat of

* Figures supplied by the Commonwealth War Graves Commission.

1 July might have made short work of this wine if they had known of its existence.

Salvage contractors were allotted particular areas of the old battlefield and could claim all war material found in their area. Many thousands of tons of dud shells and other metal were removed in this way. At ploughing time it was a common sight to see women and children with baskets, searching for the millions of shrapnel balls to be found in the fields.

In 1927 work started on a new basilica at Albert, on the site of the one that had been so familiar to the British soldiers. The son of the original architect was found and, from his old plans, an exact replica of the former church was built. By 1929 the work was finished and, once again, a golden Virgin and her Child looked out over the Somme.

The difficult process of recovery was made easier by the help given by British cities and towns. In the decade following the war, it became the custom for British communities which had lost many men at a particular place to 'adopt' the nearest French town or village. In this way, Serre was adopted by Sheffield, whose City Battalion had fought its first and greatest battle there. Montauban was linked with the Kentish town of Maidstone; when the Manchester Pals captured the village on 1 July, it had been the 7th Royal West Kents of the 18th Division who had come up and fought alongside them there.

The North Midland Division had held trenches facing Gommecourt for nearly a year; while it did so its base had been in the ruined village of Foncquevillers (Fonky Bleeding Villas to the soldiers). Gommecourt was adopted by Wolverhampton, in memory of the South Staffords who fell there on 1 July and Foncquevillers by Derby, for the shelter its ruins had given to the Sherwood Foresters.*

Probably the most lasting memorials to the great battle of 1 July will be the beautiful military cemeteries established by the Imperial War Graves Commission after the war.†

When the cemeteries came to be given permanent names, the Commission retained, where possible, those that the

* Other Somme 'adoptions' were: Albert by Birmingham; Fricourt by Ipswich, and Mametz by Llandudno; but these were in memory of other battles than that of 1 July.

† For those interested in the work of the Commission, now the Commonwealth War Graves Commission, there is a very good book, *The Unending Vigil* by Philip Longworth.

soldiers had used. Thus, there is Blighty Valley and Railway Hollow, sheltered spots just behind the old British lines; Bapaume Post, by an old kilometre stone on the main road out of Albert, and Dantzig Alley, a German trench near Mametz.*

Others were named after the battalions who had buried their men in their own burial ground. That of the 11th Border became the Lonsdale Cemetery, although others are buried there, among them Sgt Turnbull, the Glasgow Commercials V.C. The trench grave used by the 8th and 9th Devons, in Mansel Copse, became the Devonshire Cemetery. Nearby is the Gordon Cemetery, which contains the bodies of ninety-nine men from the 2nd Gordon Highlanders who were buried in one of the trenches from which they attacked.

A large battlefield cemetery was established in the old No Man's Land between Thiepval Wood and the Schwaben Redoubt, and in it were buried many of the Ulstermen who attacked there on 1 July. The army had named this the Connaught Cemetery, either after the Duke of Connaught, the reigning king's uncle, or after the Southern Irish province of Connaught. One wonders why it was not named the Ulster Cemetery.

In all the Somme battlefield was searched at least six times for lost bodies and isolated graves. The graves of the dead of 1 July can now be found in some fifty cemeteries on and around the old battlefield.

The War Graves Commission worked hard in the post-war years to transform the old burial grounds of the Somme into beautiful, permanent cemeteries. Most of the work was done by British ex-soldiers, many of whom married local girls and settled permanently in Albert and the villages.

For those thousands of men who have no known grave, the Commission erected special memorials. One of these was built on the site of the château that had stood on Thiepval Spur, an appropriate place, since the German machine-gun posts there had inflicted grievous loss on 1 July and for many weeks following. The maze of trenches and underground tunnels caused great difficulty to the builders, but eventually a huge

* The most original cemetery names are probably behind the old Ypres Salient. There can be found three cemeteries, which were once alongside Casualty Clearing Stations, now named Bandaghem, Dozinghem and Mendinghem. (Bandage 'em, Dosing 'em and Mending 'em were the war-time names of the Clearing Stations.)

red brick and stone monument on sixteen massive pillars was completed. On these pillars were carved the names of the 73,412 men who were killed on the Somme and Ancre up to February 1918 and have no known grave. Most of these are from the 1916 battles. The Thiepval Memorial was opened in 1932 by the Prince of Wales, who had been such a friend to the front-line soldiers in the war years.

Some regiments or communities built their own private memorials. The Newfoundland Government purchased forty acres of the ground, near Beaumont Hamel, over which its men had attacked with such disastrous results on 1 July and made a memorial park there. The original trenches and barbed wire were preserved for the future interest of visitors and a bronze caribou, commemorating the battalion, was unveiled by Field-Marshal Haig. Sheffield erected a memorial to its City Battalion on the edge of Serre and a fine stone seat, commemorating the attack of the Tyneside Irish and Tyneside Scottish, was built on the main road at La Boisselle. On the old German front line, near the Schwaben Redoubt, the people of Ulster built a memorial tower in honour of their division's exploits there.

If the post-war years had been kind to the Somme, they were not so to the soldiers who were trying to settle down to civilian life, back at home. Even before most of them had left the army, there had been a General Election at which Lloyd George had promised them 'a land fit for heroes'. It was a phrase he was soon to regret.

At first, there was plenty of work, of a kind, for the returning soldiers. Those firms which had promised to keep jobs open for their workers who went off to war in 1914 did what they could, but were not always able to keep their promises. No one had known that the war was going to last for over four years. The ex-soldiers found the best jobs held by men who had never been to the war. They often had to take orders from men who had spent the past four years in what the soldiers called 'funk holes'. Before long, however, an economic depression settled on the country. It brought mass unemployment, short-time working, low wages and years of human misery. The men who had served in the trenches felt, especially after Lloyd George's promise, that they had been betrayed.

'I signed on for twelve months at the Labour Exchange. They used to call us the 29th Division because we got 29*s*. a week.' (L/Cpl C. O. Law, 89th Brigade Machine Gun Company)

'One universal question which I have never seen answered: two or three million pounds a day for the 1914–18 war, yet no monies were forthcoming to put industry on its feet on our return from that war. Many's the time I've gone to bed, after a day of "tramp, tramp" looking for work, on a cup of cocoa and a pennyworth of chips between us; I would lay puzzling why, why, after all we had gone through in the service of our country, we have to suffer such poverty, willing to work at anything but no work to be had. I only had two Christmases at work between 1919 and 1939.' (Pte C. A. Turner, 97th Brigade Machine Gun Company)

'When I was out of work, I had to go before a Means Test Panel. There was a very fat lady on the Panel, cuddling a Pekinese on her lap. She said, "We've all got to pull our belts in a hole or two these days". I was fed up and told her, "Your words belie your appearance. That bloody dog's had more to eat today than I've had." There was a lot of argument and it ended in a row. My chair went over; papers and ink-wells went flying and the dog was yapping and squealing. I was charged with common assault and got three months in Wormwood Scrubs.' (Pte G. Kidd, 9th Devons)

Some of the hardest hit were the coal-miners. Many had been prisoners of war and had worked in the German mines, where they were much impressed by the superior working conditions: 'It was 1945 before our pits became as safe and efficient as the German pits were in 1918.' (Pte T. Easton, 2nd Tyneside Scottish) Conditions and pay in British mines were very poor. In 1926, the coal-owners tried to cut pay even further. The whole industry went on strike, with the slogan 'Not a penny off the pay. Not a minute on the day.'

'Of course, I have been angry and bitter concerning the betrayal of promises made to the men of the 1914–18 War, "A land fit for heroes" etcetera. Many of my miner friends suffered long periods of unemployment and poverty. The greatest of all indignities was to watch their children having to line up at soup kitchens.' (L/Cpl W. J. Evans, 8th K.O.Y.L.I.)

The biggest sufferers were the war-disabled; there were

thousands of these with little chance of getting work, striving to exist on pensions that were often mere pittances. 'Although I have survived to reach the ripe old age of seventy-five, I look back, not with pride, but with disgust at the treatment meted out to the disabled ex-servicemen of my generation.' (Pte F. P. Weston, 7th Buffs)

'More than anything I hated to see war-crippled men standing in the gutter selling matches. We had been promised a land fit for heroes; it took a hero to live in it. I'd never fight for my country again.' (Pte F. W. A. Turner, 11th Sherwood Foresters)

In Ireland there were political as well as economic difficulties. The men of the Ulster Division had done more than kill Germans when they stormed the Schwaben Redoubt on 1 July. 'The Ulster Division has lost more than half the men who attacked and, in doing so, has sacrificed itself for the Empire which has treated them none too well. The much derided Ulster Volunteer Force has won a name which equals any in History. Their devotion, which no doubt has helped the advance elsewhere, deserves the gratitude of the British Empire. It is due to the memory of these brave heroes that their beloved Province shall be fairly treated.' (Maj. W. Spender, 36th (Ulster) Division H.Q.)* This is part of a letter, written after the battle, by the man who was later to be the Head of Northern Ireland's Civil Service. When the majority of Ireland became the Free State in 1921, most of Ulster was not forced into the unwanted union with the Catholic South. The sacrifice by the men of the Ulster Division in the war, especially on 1 July, was a factor influencing the granting of this controversial concession, just as Maj. Spender had hoped it would be. Even then, three Ulster counties, Donegal, Monaghan and Cavan, counties which had sent their own battalions to fight at Thiepval, became part of Eire, and Protestant ex-soldiers there found themselves unwilling members of a mainly Catholic country.

There was, for many years, a suspicion among a few people in Ulster that, because of its association with the illegal Ulster Volunteer Force, the Ulster Division was given the task of attacking the strongest part of the German line, at Thiepval, and the time of the attack deliberately revealed to

* Public Record Office of Northern Ireland, D 1295/4.

the enemy in the hope that the Force would be wiped out, thus obviating the necessity for dealing with it after the war. It is an interesting theory, but not supported by fact. Religion and politics continue to be troublesome subjects in Northern Ireland and the Ulster Volunteer Force is still in being over half a century later.

Those of our ten 1916 soldiers who had survived the war appear to have coped with the problems of peace better than many of their comrades.

Reginald Bastard retired from the army in 1920. He had served for exactly twenty years and through two wars. He married the widow of another 2nd Lincolns officer and settled down to farm his estate at Kitley, near Plymouth. He died in 1960 at the age of seventy-nine.

After the war, Percy Chappell served again with the Somerset Light Infantry and then on intelligence duties in Ireland, and was awarded the M.B.E. for his work there, but by 1925 he was tired of army life and he retired with the rank of major.

Philip Howe was demobilized and returned to a law practice in Sheffield. In 1939, he went back into the army and served for five years as adjutant to the Army School of Physical Training in Aldershot. He described this as 'the best adjutant's job in the British Army'.

When Charles Matthews was discharged as disabled there was a fear that prohibition might be imposed in Britain and he was advised not to return to his old office job in the brewery at Northampton. He made a change and went into banking, a career which he followed for forty years.

Albert McMillan, who had spent over two years as a prisoner of war, was refused his old railway job back because he had joined up without permission. He wrote to one of the queen's ladies-in-waiting, who had served on a committee sending parcels to prisoners, and he was soon given employment as a parcels porter at King's Cross Station.

Bill Soar, too, came home from a prisoner-of-war camp. Although he was now a grown man, he completed his apprenticeship and, probably because of this, never had difficulty in getting work. For many years he was a joiner with Nottingham Corporation working on the maintenance of the city's schools. Unfortunately he died just before this book was published.

The poor health in which Paddy Kennedy found himself at the end of the war improved and he was able to resume his old office job in Manchester. Several times in the 1920s he visited the family in Rochdale to see the cat, Nigger, that he had taken at Montauban on 1 July. Few Rochdale people knew of this strange link between their town and the Battle of the Somme.*

The generals, too, had to face the post-war years.

Although Douglas Haig had brought the war to a successful conclusion, the heavy losses had tarnished his reputation and he was offered no worthwhile occupation after the war. He accepted this snub with dignity and spent his time co-ordinating the work of the various ex-servicemen's organizations. This reached its culmination when most of them combined to form the British Legion. Every Remembrance Day poppy sold by the Legion still bears Haig's name.

Henry Rawlinson and Edmund Allenby were both appointed to high positions: Rawlinson as C.-in-C. in India and Allenby as High Commissioner for Egypt. Hubert Gough, relieved of his command in 1918, was given nothing.

In 1919, some of the war generals were rewarded with titles and large sums of money from public funds. Of those who were on the Somme on 1 July, Haig received an earldom and £100,000, Allenby a viscountcy and £50,000, and Rawlinson and Horne became barons and were awarded £30,000 each. Again, Gough was passed over and received nothing.

At the same time, the king approved the award of campaign medals, hitherto only awarded to servicemen, to the two wartime prime ministers, Asquith and Lloyd George. These acts, especially the granting of such huge sums of money to the generals, were not well received by the men who had endured the horrors of war for 1*s*. a day and were now, as often as not, unemployed or underpaid.

One by one, the generals died, often unloved and unmourned by the men they had led in war. Rawlinson went first, in 1925, while still in India; Haig in 1928; Allenby in 1936.

* When this book was written (1969–71), Percy Chappell was living at Limpley Stoke near Bath; Philip Howe at Calver in North Derbyshire; Charles Matthews at Petersham, Surrey; Albert McMillan at Highgate, North London; Bill Soar near Trent Bridge in Nottingham and Paddy Kennedy at Levenshulme, Manchester.

In the same year, 1936, an unusual thing happened. It was recognized that Gough had been treated shabbily in 1918 and the immediate post-war years. Now he was created a Knight Grand Cross of the Bath as a public act of reparation for the injustices he had undergone. Gough survived all his contemporaries. The general who had been called, in turn, 'Thruster', 'Butcher' and 'Scapegoat' lived until 1963 when he died quietly at the ripe age of ninety-two.

The Somme was touched only very lightly by the Second World War. Twice, in 1940 and in 1944, mechanized armies swept over it in a few hours and war damage was, fortunately, very light. Most of the British gardeners had to leave when the Germans came and their cemeteries were abandoned. One gardener who did remain, a Mr Ben Leech, who had taken part in the capture of Montauban on 1 July with the Manchester Pals, was given permission by the local German commander to continue his work in one of the Serre cemeteries. Mr Leech joined the local Resistance group and, during the next four years, helped twenty-seven Allied airmen to escape after they had been shot down over the Somme. Mr Leech hid these airmen in the cemetery tool shed, and German soldiers often wandered around the cemetery, unaware that the escapers were only a few yards away.*

When the gardeners returned after the war, their beloved cemeteries presented a sorry sight. The fine lawns and flowers had grown wild and some of the trees had been cut down for fuel; it took over ten years of hard work to bring them back to their former glory.

The Somme, today, does not present the bustling scene of the 1920s.† From quiet Albert, the Virgin looks out over a landscape which, to the casual eye, shows no sign of what it suffered in 1916. Only the more diligent searcher will find signs that one of Western Europe's biggest battles was fought here.

The shattered woods have now completely re-grown but, between the trees, there is no level ground. The overlapping shell craters of 1916 may be grassed over, but are easily recognizable for what they are. In some of the woods, the lines

* After the war Mr Leech was honoured by the United States Government for his work. He died in 1965 but now his son works as a Commission gardener on the Somme.

† Readers may like to read Appendix 6, 'A Tour of the Somme Battlefield'.

of old trenches can be followed easily, bay by bay, but with the quiet, the grass and the mature trees, it is difficult to imagine the hell that these woods were in 1916.

Outside the woods, the fields have been ploughed and sown every year since the battle. The plough still brings up shells and, after heavy rain, unemployed still search for shrapnel balls, but otherwise there are few signs of the war, although if one can get a distant view of bare land, especially after the winter frosts, the distinct white lines in the earth show where the old trenches had been dug into the chalk beneath. But there is danger too; foolish Frenchmen are occasionally killed, trying to hammer off the valuable brass nose-caps of live shells. There are many of these, mostly British, evidence of the high proportion of duds in their artillery ammunition of 1916.

Sometimes, the remains of one of the many bodies that were never properly buried is found. The War Graves Commission only accepts the body if it is satisfied that it belonged to a British serviceman, but up to ten are recovered in this way on the Somme each year. If they can be identified, and this is sometimes possible, any relatives that can be found are informed.

There are other reminders of the battle, for the bigger mine craters were never filled in. Seven of these remain, great yawning holes in the ground, silent reminders of the violence that erupted on that sunny Saturday morning.

There are few visitors to the Somme now. Although Albert is as near to London as is York, Liverpool or Exeter, it is not on the popular holiday routes to the South. The more isolated cemeteries sometimes do not see an English visitor in a whole year. It does not matter to the gardeners, they keep them just as beautiful as the more popular ones.

The survivors of the Army of 1916 are growing old, but a few still make the journey to Albert, year after year. 'I first went back to the Somme on a motor-bike in 1935. I have been back twelve times since then and I intend to keep going as long as I can; I try to be there on 1 July. I go out and, at 7.30 A.M., I stand at the exact spot where we went over the top in 1916.' (Pte H. C. Bloor, Accrington Pals)

Even if the visitors stop coming, the cemeteries will always remain, for its Charter charges the War Graves Commission to maintain these 'in perpetuity'.

It is easy to read that 20,000 men were killed in one day, but only when one sees the cemeteries on the old battlefield with their rows and rows of white headstones does the figure begin to mean anything. It is a hard heart that is not moved by the beauty of these cemeteries and the sadness of the graves. 'Oh, the heartache, seeing all those thousands upon thousands of graves of young men in their prime, my eldest brother among them, who had come all the way from Australia. For what? Can anyone give the answer?' (Pte G. B. Gledhill, 1/5th West Yorks)

They will always be there, the men who fought and died on 1 July – Billy McFadzean and the other five dead V.C.'s; the gallant Brig.-Gen. Prowse; the thirty-one dead battalion C.O.'s; the company commanders – Maj. Gaffikin, the Orangeman, Capt. Nevill of the footballs and Capt. Martin, who knew where he would die; the subalterns – Sir Harry MacNaghten, the boy-baronet, William Hodgson, the poet, George Arthur, the unrecognized hero of Gommecourt; Matt Hamilton, the brave young sergeant-major.

Then there are the private soldiers, the Dick Kings, the unknown, humble men, who never had the chance to become famous. They died in their thousands, these fine men of 1916. They died for love of their country and 1*s*. a day.

The soldiers of 1916 were not supermen; they did not belong to a special generation. They were merely ordinary Britons, who believed that they had to fight to save their country. It turned out that theirs was to be an unlucky and ill-used generation. What do they think now, the men who survived the war and then fifty years of normal life? Their answers vary. The officer will give a different view from the private soldier; the extrovert from the sensitive man.

'My strongest recollection: all those grand looking cavalrymen, ready mounted to follow the breakthrough. What a hope!' (Pte E. T. Radband, 1/5th West Yorks)

'I made up my mind that, if ever I got out of it alive, there wasn't enough gold in the Bank of England to get me back again.' (L/Cpl J. A. Henderson, Belfast Young Citizens)

'One's revulsion to the ghastly horrors of war was submerged in the belief that this war was to end all wars and Utopia would arise. What an illusion!' (Cpl J. H. Tansley, 9th Yorks and Lancs)

'July 1st 1916 was the most interesting day of my life.' (Lieut P. Howe, M.C., 10th West Yorks)

'It was pure bloody murder. Douglas Haig should have been hung, drawn and quartered for what he did on the Somme. The cream of British manhood was shattered in less than six hours.' (Pte P. Smith, 1st Border)

'Even so, war is a daft game. Some say that they enjoyed every moment. Their comrades don't believe them.' (Sgt C. E. Linford, 466th Field Company R.E.)

'I might add that five minutes after the attack started, if the British public could have seen the wounded struggling to get out of the line, the war would have possibly been stopped by public opinion.' (Pte J. F. Pout, 55th Field Ambulance)

'I cursed, and still do, the generals who caused us to suffer such torture, living in filth, eating filth, and then, death or injury just to boost their ego.' (Pte W. H. Haigh, 1/5th Yorks and Lancs)

'From that moment all my religion died. All my teaching and beliefs in God had left me, never to return.' (Pte C. Bartram, 94th Trench Mortar Battery)

'We had "*Gott mit uns*" ("God with us") on our belt buckles, but we still lost the war.' (Gefreiter Hugo van Egeren, 55th Reserve Regiment)

'As I was one of the lucky ones, I still say I am glad I was there.' (L/Cpl C. F. T. Townsend, 12th Middlesex)

Appendix 1

Order of Battle of British Infantry Units, 1 July 1916

(Types of divisions are indicated as follows:
REG. – Regulars; T.F. – Territorial Force; N.A. – New Army.
Those battalions which were heavily involved in the fighting are shown in SMALL CAPITAL letters.)

FOURTH ARMY
(Gen. Sir H. Rawlinson)

III CORPS (Lieut-Gen. Sir W. P. Pulteney)

8th DIVISION (REG.) (Maj.-Gen. H. Hudson)

23rd Brigade
2nd DEVONS
2nd WEST YORKS
2nd MIDDLESEX
2nd Scottish Rifles

25th Brigade
2nd LINCOLNS
2nd ROYAL BERKS
1st ROYAL IRISH RIFLES
2nd Rifle Brigade

70th Brigade
11th SHERWOOD FORESTERS
8th KING'S OWN YORKSHIRE LIGHT INFANTRY
8th YORKS AND LANCS
9th YORKS AND LANCS

Pioneers
22nd Durham Light Infantry

34th DIVISION (N.A.) (Maj.-Gen. E. C. Ingouville-Williams)

101st Brigade
15th ROYAL SCOTS (1st EDINBURGH CITY)
16th ROYAL SCOTS (2nd EDINBURGH CITY)
10th LINCOLNS (GRIMSBY CHUMS)
11th SUFFOLKS (CAMBRIDGE)

102nd (Tyneside Scottish) Brigade
20th NORTHUMBERLAND FUSILIERS (1st TYNESIDE SCOTTISH)
21st NORTHUMBERLAND FUSILIERS (2nd TYNESIDE SCOTTISH)
22nd NORTHUMBERLAND FUSILIERS (3rd TYNESIDE SCOTTISH)
23rd NORTHUMBERLAND FUSILIERS (4th TYNESIDE SCOTTISH)

103rd (Tyneside Irish) Brigade

24th NORTHUMBERLAND FUSILIERS (1st TYNESIDE IRISH)
25th NORTHUMBERLAND FUSILIERS (2nd TYNESIDE IRISH)
26th NORTHUMBERLAND FUSILIERS (3rd TYNESIDE IRISH)
27th NORTHUMBERLAND FUSILIERS (4th TYNESIDE IRISH)

Pioneers

18th NORTHUMBERLAND FUSILIERS

19th (WESTERN) DIVISION (N.A.) (Maj.-Gen. G. T. M. Bridges)

56th Brigade

7th King's Own
7th East Lancs
7th South Lancs
7th Loyal North Lancs

57th Brigade

10th Royal Warwicks
8th Gloucesters
10th Worcesters
8th North Staffs

58th Brigade

9th CHESHIRES
9th Royal Welch Fusiliers
9th Welch
6th Wilts

Pioneers

5th South Wales Borderers

VIII CORPS (Lieut-Gen. Sir A. G. Hunter-Weston)

4th DIVISION (REG.) (Maj.-Gen. Hon. W. Lambton)

10th Brigade

1st ROYAL IRISH FUSILIERS
2nd ROYAL DUBLIN FUSILIERS
2nd SEAFORTH HIGHLANDERS
1st Royal Warwicks

11th Brigade

1st SOMERSET LIGHT INFANTRY
1st EAST LANCS
1st HAMPSHIRES
1st RIFLE BRIGADE

12th Brigade

1st KING'S OWN
2nd LANCS FUSILIERS
2nd DUKE OF WELLINGTON'S
2nd ESSEX

Pioneers

21st West Yorks

29th DIVISION (REG.) (Maj.-Gen. H. de B. de Lisle)

86th Brigade

2nd ROYAL FUSILIERS
1st LANCS FUSILIERS
16th MIDDLESEX (PUBLIC SCHOOLS BATTALION)
1st ROYAL DUBLIN FUSILIERS

87th Brigade

2nd SOUTH WALES BORDERERS
1st KING'S OWN SCOTTISH BORDERERS
1st ROYAL INNISKILLING FUSILIERS
1st BORDER

88th Brigade

1st ESSEX
1st NEWFOUNDLAND
4th Worcesters
2nd Hampshires

Pioneers

1/2nd MONMOUTHS

31st DIVISION (N.A.) (Maj.-Gen. R. Wanless O'Gowan)

92nd Brigade

10th EAST YORKS (HULL COMMERCIALS)
11th East Yorks (Hull Tradesmen)
12th East Yorks (Hull Sportsmen)
13th East Yorks (T'Others)

93rd Brigade

15th WEST YORKS (LEEDS PALS)
16th WEST YORKS (1st BRADFORD PALS)
18th WEST YORKS (2nd BRADFORD PALS)
18th DURHAM LIGHT INFANTRY (DURHAM PALS)

94th Brigade

11th EAST LANCS (ACCRINGTON PALS)
12th YORKS AND LANCS (SHEFFIELD CITY BATTALION)
13th YORKS AND LANCS (1st BARNSLEY PALS)
14th YORKS AND LANCS (2nd BARNSLEY PALS)

Pioneers

12th KING'S OWN YORKSHIRE LIGHT INFANTRY (HALIFAX PALS)

48th (SOUTH MIDLAND) DIVISION (T.F.) (Maj.-Gen. R. Fanshawe)

143rd Brigade

1/5th Royal Warwicks
1/6th ROYAL WARWICKS
1/7th Royal Warwicks
1/8th ROYAL WARWICKS

144th Brigade

1/4 Gloucesters
1/6th Gloucesters
1/7th Worcesters
1/8th Worcesters

145th Brigade

1/5th Gloucesters
1/4th Oxford and Bucks Light Infantry
1st Bucks
1/4th Royal Berks

Pioneers

1/5th Royal Sussex

X CORPS (Lieut-Gen. Sir T. L. N. Morland)

32nd DIVISION (N.A.) (Maj.-Gen. W. H. Rycroft)

14th Brigade

19th LANCS FUSILIERS (3rd SALFORD PALS)
1st DORSETS
2nd MANCHESTERS
15th Highland Light Infantry (Glasgow Tramways)

96th Brigade

16th NORTHUMBERLAND FUSILIERS (NEWCASTLE COMMERCIALS)
2nd ROYAL INNISKILLING FUSILIERS
15th LANCS FUSILIERS (1st SALFORD PALS)
16th LANCS FUSILIERS (2nd SALFORD PALS)

97th Brigade

11th BORDER (THE LONSDALES)
2nd KING'S OWN YORKSHIRE LIGHT INFANTRY
16th HIGHLAND LIGHT INFANTRY (GLASGOW BOYS' BRIGADE)
17th HIGHLAND LIGHT INFANTRY (GLASGOW COMMERCIALS)

Pioneers

17th NORTHUMBERLAND FUSILIERS (NEWCASTLE RAILWAY PALS)

36th (ULSTER) DIVISION (N.A.) (Maj.-Gen. O. S. W. Nugent)

107th Brigade

8th ROYAL IRISH RIFLES (EAST BELFAST)
9th ROYAL IRISH RIFLES (WEST BELFAST)
10th ROYAL IRISH RIFLES (SOUTH BELFAST)
15th ROYAL IRISH RIFLES (NORTH BELFAST)

108th Brigade

11th ROYAL IRISH RIFLES (SOUTH ANTRIM)
12th ROYAL IRISH RIFLES (CENTRAL ANTRIM)
13th ROYAL IRISH RIFLES (CO. DOWN)
9th ROYAL IRISH FUSILIERS (CO. ARMAGH, MONAGHAN AND CAVAN)

109th Brigade

9th ROYAL INNISKILLING FUSILIERS (CO. TYRONE)
10th ROYAL INNISKILLING FUSILIERS (CO. DERRY)
11th ROYAL INNISKILLING FUSILIERS (DONEGAL AND FERMANAGH)
14th ROYAL IRISH RIFLES (BELFAST YOUNG CITIZENS)

Pioneers
16th Royal Irish Rifles (2nd Co. Down)

49th (WEST RIDING) DIVISION (T.F.)
(Maj.-Gen. E. M. Perceval)

146th Brigade
1/5th WEST YORKS
1/6th WEST YORKS
1/7th WEST YORKS
1/8th WEST YORKS
147th Brigade
1/4th Duke of Wellington's
1/5th Duke of Wellington's
1/6th Duke of Wellington's
1/7th Duke of Wellington's
148th Brigade
1/4th Yorks and Lancs
1/5th YORKS AND LANCS
1/4th King's Own Yorkshire Light Infantry
1/5th King's Own Yorkshire Light Infantry

Pioneers
1/3rd Monmouths

XIII CORPS (Lieut-Gen. W. N. Congreve V.C.)

18th (EASTERN) DIVISION (N.A.) (Maj.-Gen. F. I. Maxse)

53rd Brigade
8th NORFOLKS
6th ROYAL BERKS
10th ESSEX
8th Suffolks
54th Brigade
11th ROYAL FUSILIERS
7th BEDFORDS
6th NORTHAMPTONS
12th MIDDLESEX
55th Brigade
7th QUEEN'S
7th BUFFS
8th EAST SURREYS
7th ROYAL WEST KENTS
Pioneers
8th ROYAL SUSSEX

30th DIVISION (N.A.) (Maj.-Gen. J. S. M. Shea)

21st Brigade
18th KING'S (2nd LIVERPOOL PALS)
19th MANCHESTERS (4th PALS)
2nd WILTS
2nd GREEN HOWARDS
89th Brigade
17th KING'S (1st LIVERPOOL PALS)
19th King's (3rd Liverpool Pals)
20th KING'S (4th LIVERPOOL PALS)
2nd BEDFORDS

90th Brigade

2nd ROYAL SCOTS FUSILIERS
16th MANCHESTERS (1st PALS)
17th MANCHESTERS (2nd PALS)
18th MANCHESTERS (3rd PALS)

Pioneers

11th SOUTH LANCS

The 9th (Scottish) Division was in reserve.

XV CORPS (Lieut-Gen. H. S. Horne)

7th DIVISION (REG.) (Maj.-Gen. H. E. Watts)

20th Brigade

8th DEVONS
9th DEVONS
2nd BORDER
2nd GORDON HIGHLANDERS

22nd Brigade

2nd ROYAL WARWICKS
20th MANCHESTERS (5th PALS)
1st Royal Welch Fusiliers
2nd Royal Irish

91st Brigade

2nd QUEENS
1st SOUTH STAFFS
21st MANCHESTERS (6th PALS)
22nd MANCHESTERS (7th PALS)

Pioneers

24th Manchesters (Oldham Pals)

17th (NORTHERN) DIVISION (N.A.) (Maj.-Gen. T. D. Pilcher)

50th Brigade

10th WEST YORKS
7th EAST YORKS
7th GREEN HOWARDS
6th Dorsets

51st Brigade

7th Lincolns
7th Border
8th South Staffs
10th Sherwood Foresters

52nd Brigade

9th Northumberland Fusiliers
10th Lancs Fusiliers
9th Duke of Wellington's
12th Manchesters

Pioneers

7th Yorks and Lancs

21st DIVISION (N.A.) (Maj.-Gen. D. G. M. Campbell)

62nd Brigade

12th NORTHUMBERLAND FUSILIERS
13th NORTHUMBERLAND FUSILIERS
1st LINCOLNS
10th GREEN HOWARDS

63rd Brigade
8th LINCOLNS
8th SOMERSET LIGHT INFANTRY
4th MIDDLESEX
10th YORKS AND LANCS
64th Brigade
9th KING'S OWN YORKSHIRE LIGHT INFANTRY
10th KING'S OWN YORKSHIRE LIGHT INFANTRY
1st EAST YORKS
15th DURHAM LIGHT INFANTRY
Pioneers
14th NORTHUMBERLAND FUSILIERS

THIRD ARMY
(Gen. Sir E. Allenby)

VII CORPS (Lieut-Gen. Sir T. D'O. Snow)

46th (NORTH MIDLAND) DIVISION (T.F.) (Maj.-Gen. Hon. E. J. Montagu-Stuart-Wortley)

137th Brigade
1/5th SOUTH STAFFS
1/6th SOUTH STAFFS
1/5th NORTH STAFFS
1/6th NORTH STAFFS
138th Brigade
1/4th LINCOLNS
1/5th LINCOLNS
1/4th Leicesters
1/5th Leicesters
139th Brigade
1/5th SHERWOOD FORESTERS
1/6th SHERWOOD FORESTERS
1/7th SHERWOOD FORESTERS
1/8th Sherwood Foresters
Pioneers
1/1st MONMOUTHS

56th (LONDON) DIVISION (T.F.) (Maj. Gen. C. P. A. Hull)

167th Brigade
1/1st London
1/3rd LONDON
1/7th Middlesex
1/8th Middlesex
168th Brigade
1/4th LONDON
1/12th LONDON (RANGERS)
1/13th LONDON (KENSINGTON)
1/14th LONDON (1st LONDON SCOTTISH)

169th Brigade

1/2nd LONDON

1/5th LONDON (1st LONDON RIFLE BRIGADE)

1/9th LONDON (QUEEN VICTORIA'S RIFLES)

1/16th LONDON (QUEEN'S WESTMINSTER RIFLES)

Pioneers

1/5th CHESHIRES

The 37th Division was in reserve.

Appendix 2

Order of Battle of German Divisions facing the British Attack, 1 July 1916

12th DIVISION

23rd Regiment (2nd Upper Silesian)
62nd Regiment (3rd Upper Silesian)
63rd Regiment (4th Upper Silesian)

52nd DIVISION

66th Regiment (3rd Magdeburg)
169th Regiment (8th Baden)
170th Regiment (9th Baden)

10th BAVARIAN DIVISION

16th Bavarian Regiment
6th Bavarian Reserve Regiment
8th Bavarian Reserve Regiment

2nd GUARDS RESERVE DIVISION

15th Reserve Regiment
55th Reserve Regiment
77th Reserve Regiment
91st Reserve Regiment

26th RESERVE DIVISION

180th Regiment (10th Württemberg)
99th Reserve Regiment
119th Reserve Regiment (1st Württemberg)
121st Reserve Regiment (3rd Württemberg)

28th RESERVE DIVISION

109th Reserve Regiment
110th Reserve Regiment
111th Reserve Regiment

Appendix 3

Senior Officer Casualties

(Including acting battalion commanders)

4th DIVISION

Brig.-Gen. C. B. Prowse, 11th Brigade	killed
Lieut-Col. D. Wood, 1st Rifle Brigade	killed
Lieut-Col. J. A. Thicknesse, 1st Somerset Light Infantry	killed
Maj. J. N. Bromilow, 1st King's Own	killed
Lieut-Col. Hon. L. C. W. Palk, 1st Hampshires	killed
Maj. L. P. Walsh, 2nd Royal Dublin Fusiliers	died of wounds
Lieut-Col. J. E. Green, 1st East Lancs	wounded
Lieut-Col. Sir G. Stirling, 2nd Essex	wounded

7th DIVISION

Lieut-Col. H. Lewis, 5th Manchester Pals	killed

8th DIVISION

Lieut-Col. B. L. Maddison, 8th Yorks and Lancs	killed
Lieut-Col. A. J. B. Addison, 9th Yorks and Lancs	killed
Lieut-Col. A. M. Holdsworth, 2nd Royal Berks	died of wounds
Lieut-Col. C. C. Macnamara, 1st Royal Irish Rifles	died of wounds
Capt. K. E. Poyser, 8th K.O.Y.L.I.	wounded
Lieut-Col. H. F. Watson, 11th Sherwood Foresters	wounded
Lieut-Col. E. T. F. Sandys, 2nd Middlesex	wounded

17th (NORTHERN) DIVISION

Lieut-Col. A. Dickson, 10th West Yorks	killed

21st DIVISION

Lieut-Col. C. W. D. Lynch, 9th K.O.Y.L.I.	killed
Lieut-Col. H. Allardice, 13th Northumberland Fusiliers	killed
Lieut-Col. M. B. Stow, 1st East Yorks	died of wounds
Lieut-Col. A. E. Fitzgerald, 15th Durham Light Infantry	died of wounds
Lieut-Col. H. J. King, 10th K.O.Y.L.I.	wounded
Lieut-Col. J. W. Scott, 8th Somerset Light Infantry	wounded

29th DIVISION

Lieut-Col. R. C. Pierce, 1st Royal Inniskilling Fusiliers	killed
Lieut-Col. A. V. Johnson, 2nd Royal Fusiliers	wounded
Lieut-Col. A. J. Ellis, 1st Border	wounded

30th DIVISION

Lieut-Col. H. A. Johnson, 2nd Manchester Pals	wounded

31st DIVISION

Maj. C. S. Guyon, 1st Bradford Pals	killed
Lieut-Col. M. N. Kennard, 2nd Bradford Pals	killed
Lieut-Col. A. W. Rickman, Accrington Pals	wounded
Maj. A. Plackett, Sheffield City Battalion	wounded
Maj. R. B. Neill, Leeds Pals	wounded

32nd DIVISION

Lieut-Col. P. W. Machell, 11th Border	killed
Lieut-Col. D. Laidlaw, Glasgow Boys' Brigade Battalion	wounded
Lieut-Col. J. V. Shute, 1st Dorset	wounded

34th DIVISION

Lieut-Col. C. C. A. Sillery, 1st Tyneside Scottish	killed
Lieut-Col. F. C. Heneker, 2nd Tyneside Scottish	killed
Lieut-Col. A. P. A. Elphinstone, 3rd Tyneside Scottish	killed
Lieut-Col. W. Lyle, 4th Tyneside Scottish	killed
Lieut-Col. L. M. Howard, 1st Tyneside Irish	killed
Brig.-Gen. N. J. G. Cameron, 103rd Brigade	wounded
Lieut-Col. J. H. M. Arden, 2nd Tyneside Irish	wounded
Lieut-Col. M. E. Richardson, 3rd Tyneside Irish	wounded

36th (ULSTER) DIVISION

Lieut-Col. H. C. Bernard, South Belfast Volunteers	killed

46th (NORTH MIDLAND) DIVISION

Lieut-Col. D. D. Wilson, 1/5th Sherwood Foresters	killed
Lieut-Col. L. A. Hind, 1/7th Sherwood Foresters	killed
Lieut-Col. C. E. Boote, 1/6th North Staffs	killed
Lieut-Col. W. Burnett, 1/5th North Staffs	died of wounds
Lieut-Col. R. R. Raymer, 1/5th South Staffs	wounded

48th (SOUTH MIDLAND) DIVISION

Lieut-Col. E. A. Innes, 1/8th Royal Warwicks	killed
Lieut-Col. H. Franklin, 1/6th Royal Warwicks	wounded
Lieut-Col. C. Howkins, R.A.M.C.	wounded

49th (WEST RIDING) DIVISION

Lieut-Col. H. O. Wade, 1/6th West Yorks	wounded

SUMMARY

Killed	25
Died of wounds	6
Wounded	22
Total	53

Appendix 4

Victoria Cross Winners of 1 July 1916

Capt. E. N. F. Bell, 9th Royal Inniskilling Fusiliers (attached 109th Trench Mortar Battery), killed 1 July, no known grave.

Lieut G. St G. S. Cather, 9th Royal Irish Fusiliers, killed 2 July, no known grave.

Capt. J. L. Green, Royal Army Medical Corps (attached 1/5th Sherwood Foresters), killed 1 July, buried Foncquevillers Military Cemetery.

Maj. S. W. Loudoun-Shand, 10th Green Howards, killed 1 July, buried Norfolk Military Cemetery, Bécordel-Bécourt.

Pte W. F. McFadzean, 14th Royal Irish Rifles, killed 1 July, no known grave.

Pte R. Quigg, 12th Royal Irish Rifles, died at Bushmills, Co. Antrim, 1955.

Drummer W. Ritchie, 2nd Seaforth Highlanders, died at Edinburgh, 1965.

Cpl G. Sanders, 1/7th West Yorks, died at Leeds, 1950.

Sgt J. Y. Turnbull, 17th Highland Light Infantry, killed 1 July, buried Lonsdale Cemetery, Authuille.

Appendix 5

Battalions Suffering More than 500 Casualties

Battalion	*Type*	*Casualties*		
		officers	*men*	*total*
10th West Yorks	N.A.	22	688	710
1st Newfoundland	EMPIRE	26	658	684
4th Tyneside Scottish	N.A.	19	610	629
1st Tyneside Irish	N.A.	18	602	620
8th Yorks and Lancs	N.A.	21	576	597
Co. Down Volunteers	N.A.	17	578	595
Donegal and Fermanagh Volunteers	N.A.	12	577	589
1/8th Royal Warwicks	T.F.	25	563	588
1st Hampshires	REG.	26	559	585
Accrington Pals	N.A.	21	564	585
1st Tyneside Scottish	N.A.	27	557	584
1st Border	REG.	16	559	575
1st London Rifle Brigade	T.F.	19	553	572
1st Royal Inniskilling Fusiliers	REG.	20	548	568
2nd Royal Fusiliers	REG.	23	538	561
1st London Scottish	T.F.	14	544	558
1st King's Own Scottish Borderers	REG.	19	533	552
2nd Middlesex	REG.	23	517	540
8th King's Own Yorkshire Light Infantry	N.A.	21	518	539
4th Tyneside Irish	N.A.	20	519	539
3rd Tyneside Scottish	N.A.	20	517	537
Armagh, Monaghan and Cavan Volunteers	N.A.	14	518	532
Leeds Pals	N.A.	24	504	528
The Cambridge Battalion	N.A.	15	512	527
Public Schools Battalion	N.A.	22	500	522
11th Border	N.A.	26	490	516
1st Bradford Pals	N.A.	22	493	515
1st Edinburgh City Battalion	N.A.	19	494	513
Sheffield City Battalion	N.A.	17	495	512
Glasgow Boys' Brigade Battalion	N.A.	19	492	511
Queen's Westminster Rifles	T.F.	28	475	503
1st East Lancs	REG.	17	485	502

There are many sources for the above figures: battalion war diaries; brigade and divisional records; battalion and regimental histories published after the war. Frequently there are conflicting casualty figures for the same battalion. Where this has happened, the *lowest* from those available have been used. The casualties quoted should, therefore, be regarded as the minimum losses suffered.

Appendix 6

A Tour of the Somme Battlefield

These notes have been prepared as a guide for the general visitor to that part of the Somme covered by the book, and features described are connected, if possible, to incidents in the text. Only easily recognizable features are included; these are marked on map 11 with a number which corresponds with the bold bracketed numbering in this appendix. It is unfortunate that many interesting positions have been obliterated with the passage of time. All places of interest and comments appertain to 1 July 1916, unless otherwise stated.

The tour is intended to be made by car and all features are directly accessible by road, track or short footpath. Those who wish to walk the battlefield are advised to do so in spring or early summer, when the trench lines can be clearly seen as lines of chalk in the fields, or in the autumn when the wheat has been harvested. Farmers are used to such visitors. Care should be taken in some woods, where there are animal traps, and all unexploded missiles should be regarded as dangerous.

There are many more cemeteries than those included in these notes. All have a visitors' book and a register; the introduction to the register always makes useful reading and tells the visitor what happened in that area. The Commonwealth War Graves Commission, 32 Grosvenor Gardens, London S.W.1, will give the exact location of any grave, but at least two weeks should be allowed for replies. A useful purchase from the Commission is the Michelin 1:200,000 map, overprinted with all Commonwealth war cemeteries in this area.

Albert is a natural centre for a tour. It has several modest hotels, a caravan park and the local War Graves Commission office (25 rue Jean-Guyon). Arras and Amiens, although some distance away, are much bigger than Albert and have better hotels and more amenities.

Foncquevillers. This village, just behind the British front line, was the 'home' of the 46th (North Midland) Division for nearly a year.

In the Foncquevillers Military Cemetery (**1**) are buried many of the men of the 46th Division who were killed while that division

held this sector, including some who were killed on 1 July and whose bodies were recovered from the German wire and No Man's Land when the Germans retired in 1917 (page 297). Among these is Capt. J. L. Green, V.C., R.A.M.C. (page 191).

Gommecourt. The Gommecourt Salient was the objective of the diversionary attack by 46th (North Midland) and 56th (London) Divisions. It was evacuated by the Germans in February 1917.

The Gommecourt Wood New Cemetery (**2**) was formed after the war from nine small battlefield cemeteries and lies in the middle of the old No Man's Land over which the Staffordshire Brigade attacked. Many of the graves are of North Midland Division men and the cemetery is dedicated to that division. 465 of the 749 graves are 'unknowns'.

The German front line ran along the edge of Gommecourt Park (**3**) and the remains of the trench can be easily seen near the Gommecourt–Hébuterne road. The London Rifle Brigade succeeded in getting into these trenches and it was along the road to Hébuterne that Rfmn Hollis took his message (page 215). Inside the park, the ground is still heavily cratered in contrast to the level fields outside.

Gommecourt British Cemetery No. 2 (**4**) is another that was made up from several smaller cemeteries. It lies in the middle of the No Man's Land over which the London Division attacked and contains mostly men from that division.

Serre. The objective of the 31st Division which was on the left flank of the main Fourth Army attack. Serre did not fall until the Germans retired in 1917. A memorial to the Sheffield City Battalion (**5**) stands in the village.

Railway Hollow Cemetery (**6**) (by footpath). This cemetery forms part of the Sheffield Park on the edge of which a portion of the old British front-line trench can be found (near the gate), although it was the Accrington Pals who actually attacked from this trench. A short walk across the field facing the park – that is, across the old No Man's Land – brings the visitor to a grass field. Here can be found, on the site of the German front line, the roof of a concrete machine-gun post.

The Serre Road Cemetery No. 1 (**7**) is a large cemetery on the No Man's Land over which the Leeds and Bradford Pals attacked. A French military cemetery nearby is a reminder that this was once a French sector.

The Serre Road Cemetery No. 2 (**8**) is another large cemetery, this time on the site of the German Quadrilateral Redoubt. It was in the tool shed of this cemetery that Mr Leech hid many Allied airmen from the Germans in 1940–44.

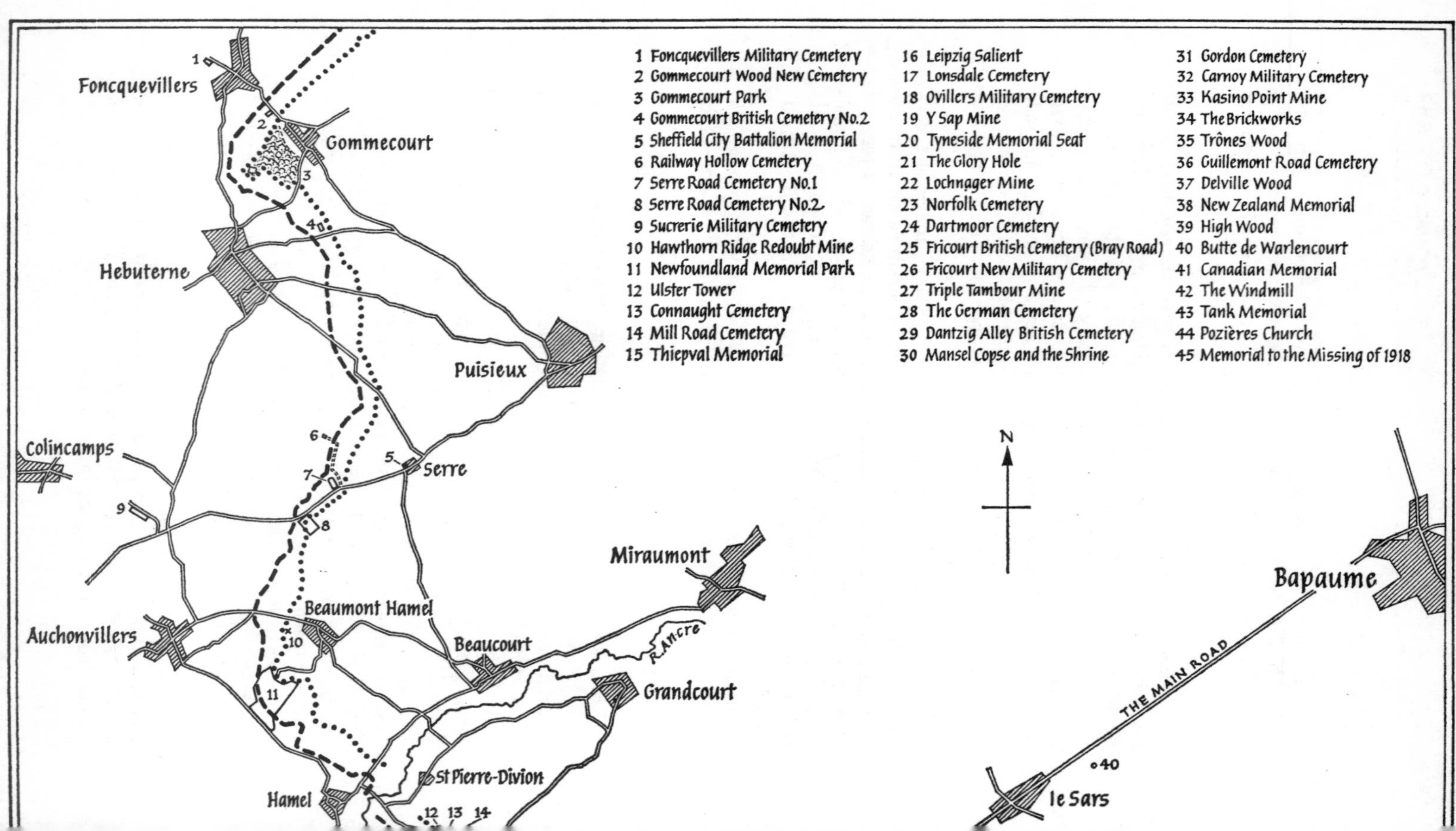
1 Foncquevillers Military Cemetery
2 Gommecourt Wood New Cemetery
3 Gommecourt Park
4 Gommecourt British Cemetery No.2
5 Sheffield City Battalion Memorial
6 Railway Hollow Cemetery
7 Serre Road Cemetery No.1
8 Serre Road Cemetery No.2
9 Sucrerie Military Cemetery
10 Hawthorn Ridge Redoubt Mine
11 Newfoundland Memorial Park
12 Ulster Tower
13 Connaught Cemetery
14 Mill Road Cemetery
15 Thiepval Memorial
16 Leipzig Salient
17 Lonsdale Cemetery
18 Ovillers Military Cemetery
19 Y Sap Mine
20 Tyneside Memorial Seat
21 The Glory Hole
22 Lochnager Mine
23 Norfolk Cemetery
24 Dartmoor Cemetery
25 Fricourt British Cemetery (Bray Road)
26 Fricourt New Military Cemetery
27 Triple Tambour Mine
28 The German Cemetery
29 Dantzig Alley British Cemetery
30 Mansel Copse and the Shrine
31 Gordon Cemetery
32 Carnoy Military Cemetery
33 Kasino Point Mine
34 The Brickworks
35 Trônes Wood
36 Guillemont Road Cemetery
37 Delville Wood
38 New Zealand Memorial
39 High Wood
40 Butte de Warlencourt
41 Canadian Memorial
42 The Windmill
43 Tank Memorial
44 Pozières Church
45 Memorial to the Missing of 1918
Foncquevillers
Gommecourt
Hebuterne
Puisieux
Colincamps
Serre
Miraumont
Bapaume
Beaumont Hamel
Auchonvillers
Beaucourt
R. Ancre
Grandcourt
THE MAIN ROAD
St Pierre-Divion
Hamel
le Sars
N

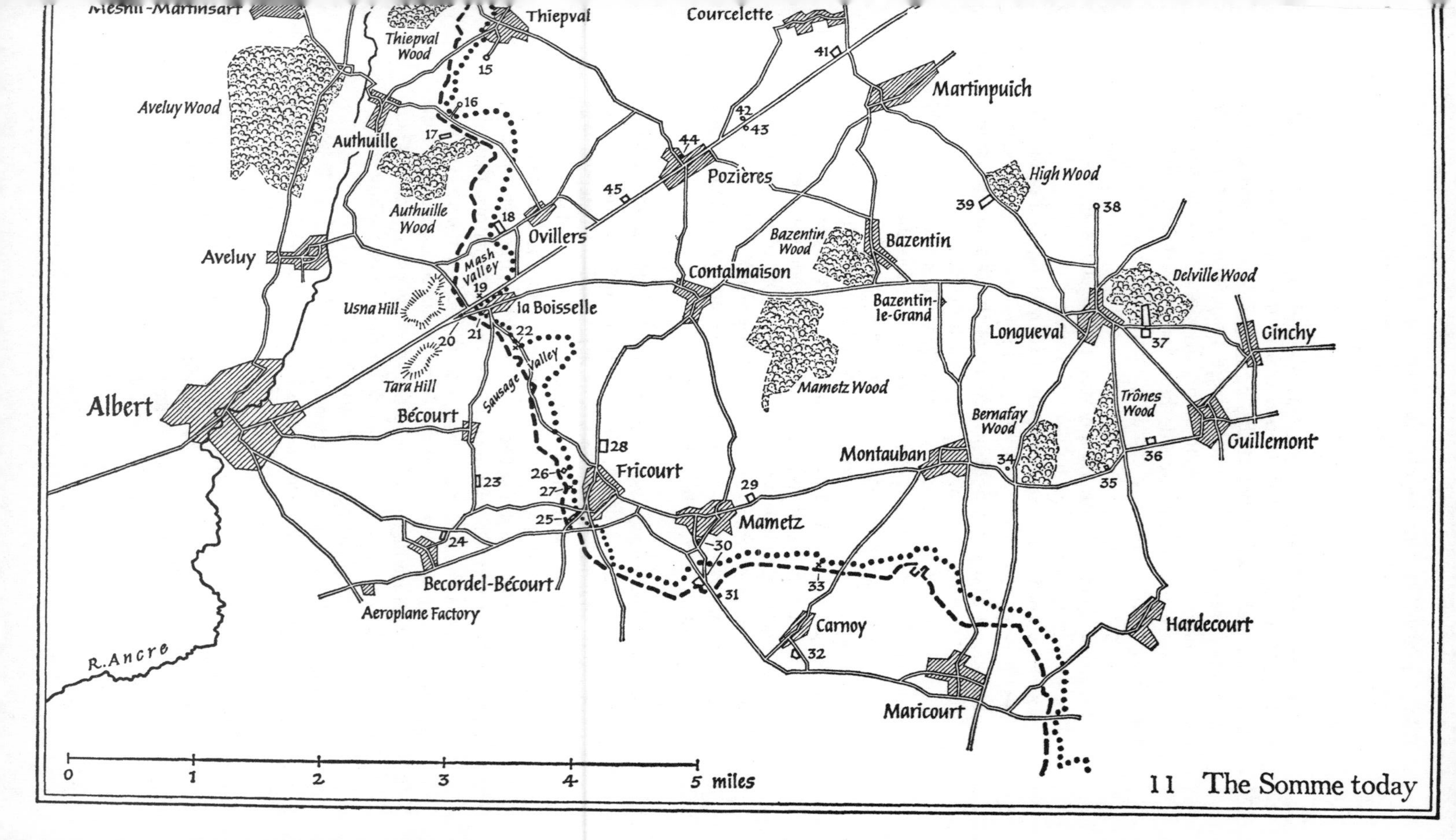

11 The Somme today

The Sucrerie Military Cemetery, Colincamps (**9**) (by rough track). Many battalions had to march past the ruined sugar beet factory on their way to the attack. Some passed the mass graves dug nearby, ready for the battle (page 109). The cemetery now contains many graves from the 4th Division. Four lieutenant-colonels were buried side-by-side here (page 249) but, after the war, the graves of only two could be identified.

Beaumont Hamel. This village was the objective of the 29th Division but was not taken until 13 November.

The Hawthorn Ridge Redoubt Mine (**10**) was the first of the big mines to be exploded on 1 July (page 119). The crater is on the highest point in a grass field just south of the Beaumont Hamel–Auchonvillers road and can only be reached by foot.

The Newfoundland Memorial Park (**11**). Here are preserved the trenches on the ground over which the Newfoundlanders made their disastrous attack (page 188). For many years the barbed-wire defences were also preserved but these had to be removed as too many sheep were trapped in the wire. The park is the property of the people of Newfoundland and a bronze caribou commemorates their battalion. A unique cemetery at the far end of the park contains the bodies of men from the 51st (Highland) Division which took Beaumont Hamel in November. Their dead were buried in a large shell hole, now Hunter's Cemetery.

Thiepval. The village was the objective of the 32nd Division, while the Schwaben Redoubt, north of the village, was the scene of the famous advance of the 36th (Ulster) Division. Thiepval was finally taken on 26 September by the 18th (Eastern) Division.

The Ulster Tower (**12**) stands on that part of the German front line taken by the Ulster Division. The tower is an exact replica of Helen's Tower at Clandeboyne, near Belfast; visitors may, by arrangement with the caretaker, go to the top of the tower from where they can see how easily the German machine-gunners in the ruins of Thiepval village enfiladed the advancing Ulstermen. There is a swastika cut into the stonework on the top of the tower by a German soldier of the Second World War.

Thiepval Wood and the Connaught Cemetery (**13**). (Thiepval Wood is marked on French maps as Bois d'Authuille.) It was from the edge of the wood that the Ulster Division attacked and the Connaught Cemetery, which contains many Ulster graves, lies in No Man's Land in the middle of their divisional front.

The Mill Road Cemetery (**14**) (by footpath). This is on the site of the Schwaben Redoubt and the headstones of the graves were laid flat, for fear of subsidence in the old tunnels and dug-outs in the redoubt.

The Thiepval Memorial (**15**). This huge memorial commemorates the 73,077 British soldiers missing on the Somme in 1916 and 1917, although the bodies or graves of 1,002 men have been found since erection. Of those soldiers mentioned in the book, the following are named on the memorial: the three Ulster v.c.'s – Pte Billy McFadzean, Capt. Bell and Lieut Cather; Pte Dick King of the 10th K.O.Y.L.I.s; 2nd Lieut Arthur, the Cheshire Pioneer officer; and C.S.M. 'Matt' Hamilton of the London Scottish.

The memorial stands on the site of the ruins of Thiepval Château, one of the strongest positions in the German line. A small cemetery, in front of the memorial, contains 300 British and 300 French graves, a symbol of the united effort of the two allies on the Somme in 1916. These graves are on the old German front line where men of their 99th Reserve Regiment stood on the parapet and taunted the Newcastle Commercials who were pinned down in No Man's Land.

A village lady in a cottage near the memorial sells genuine battle souvenirs.

Authuille. This village was just behind the British trenches on the 32nd Division's sector.

The Leipzig Salient (**16**). This German-held position was the scene of very fierce fighting (page 147) and was the only permanent gain of the 32nd Division. It was here that Sgt James Turnbull, v.c., of the Glasgow Commercials, was killed. It is now a disused chalk quarry, planted with rows of poplars, and can be reached by car along a track.

The Lonsdale Cemetery (**17**) (by footpath) is where the 11th Border (known as the Lonsdales) suffered heavy casualties as they advanced from the shelter of Authuille Wood (Bois de la Haie). One of the graves is that of Sgt Turnbull, v.c.

Ovillers. The objective of the unsuccessful 8th Division; it took two weeks of heavy fighting to capture the village.

Ovillers Military Cemetery (**18**) overlooks the notorious Mash Valley which lies between Ovillers and the main Albert–Bapaume road. It was in Mash Valley that so many of the 8th Division, including the 2nd Middlesex which had to cross 750 yards of the valley to reach the German trenches, were killed. Sir Harry Lauder's son, Capt. J. C. Lauder (killed December 1916), is buried in the cemetery. It was after his death that Sir Harry wrote the famous song 'Keep Right on to the End of the Road'.

La Boisselle. This village, on the spur between the valleys of Sausage and Mash, was the objective of the 34th Division, which suffered more casualties than any other division on 1 July. Many of these casualties were caused by the German machine-guns at La Boisselle. The village fell to the 19th (Western) Division on 4 July.

Y Sap Mine Crater (**19**) was one of the two large mines blown at La Boisselle (page 120). Its position shows how the German trenches, which ran alongside the main road at this point, overlooked the British troops attacking up Mash Valley. The crater is a few yards from the main road, in a grass field.

The Tyneside Memorial Seat (**20**), on the other side of the road, is on the site of the German front-line trench and commemorates the attack of the Tyneside Scottish and Tyneside Irish.

In a field, near the village, can be seen the numerous small craters of the Glory Hole sector (**21**), where the opposing trenches were so close.

The Lochnager Mine Crater (**22**) was the largest mine exploded on 1 July and, during that day, became a place of refuge for many men of the 34th Division (pages 135 and 218). From the raised lip of this crater the visitor can get a perfect view of two important features. To the south is Sausage Valley, not quite as spectacular as Mash Valley, but still a deadly place on 1 July, where the Grimsby Chums, the Cambridge Battalion and the two Edinburgh City Battalions suffered heavy casualties. To the west, in the direction of Albert, can be seen the long ridge of the Tara–Usna Line. The 3,000 men of the Tyneside Irish Brigade had to advance from the top of the ridge, down the open slope and across Avoca Valley (page 141). It can be seen how they presented a perfect target to the German machine-gunners in and around La Boisselle.

Albert. This was the only town immediately behind this part of the British front and thousands of British soldiers looked up at the leaning Virgin on their way to the trenches. The Basilica has been rebuilt and now appears exactly as it did before the war in 1914. On 1 July it was used as a Dressing Station (page 229). The River Ancre still flows beneath the church. The link between Albert and Birmingham has now been dropped. In 1962, the Communist town council of Albert made a new link, this time with the East German town of Niesky, near Dresden.

Bécordel-Bécourt. The village of Bécordel and nearby Bécourt Château were just behind the British lines.

The Norfolk Cemetery (**23**) contains the graves of many men of the 21st Division which successfully captured its objectives between Sausage Valley and Fricourt. One of these graves is that of Maj. S. W. Loudoun-Shand, V.C. (page 135).

The Dartmoor Cemetery (**24**) was next to a Dressing Station and was used for several weeks after the opening of the battle. Among those buried here are: Lieut-Col. H. Allardice, an Indian

Army officer commanding the 13th Northumberland Fusiliers and killed on 1 July; Lieut Henry Webber, the sixty-eight-year-old officer (page 293); Pte J. Miller, 7th King's Own, who won a v.c. and was killed at the end of July; Sgt G. Lee and Cpl R. F. Lee, a father and son serving in a London artillery unit who were killed on the same day in September 1916.

Fricourt. The objective of a brigade of the 17th (Northern) Division and evacuated by the Germans during the night of 1–2 July.

Fricourt British Cemetery (Bray Road) (**25**). Here, in the middle of the old No Man's Land, are buried the men of the 7th Green Howards, many of whom were killed when one company attacked in error in the morning (page 138).

Fricourt New Military Cemetery (**26**) (access by a track) is situated in the middle of the No Man's Land over which the 10th West Yorks attacked in the morning and the 7th East Yorks in the afternoon (page 206). The 10th West Yorks suffered more casualties than any other battalion during the day. The cemetery contains the graves of 159 men of the 10th West Yorks, including their c.o., and 38 men of the 7th East Yorks.

The Triple Tambour Mine Craters (**27**) are in a grass field approximately 100 yards south of the last cemetery and can only be reached by foot. There are three overlapping craters of mines which were blown under the German front line. Some accounts say that only two mines exploded at the time, the third failing because of damp. Possibly it was exploded later to dispose of the explosive.

The German Cemetery (**28**). This is the only cemetery for German dead in the area covered by this book. After 1918, the Germans, a vanquished nation, had no organization like the War Graves Commission and their dead were buried in one large, utilitarian cemetery which is a harsh contrast to over 100 more intimate British cemeteries in this area. There are approximately 5,000 German soldiers buried here, each wooden cross carrying at least two names. A high proportion of German dead were never recovered from the Somme battlefield.

Mametz. Captured by the 7th Division in the afternoon of 1 July.

Dantzig Alley British Cemetery (**29**). This large cemetery is sited on an important German trench that was captured by the right-hand battalions of the 7th Division. It contains many 1 July graves from the 7th, 18th and 30th Divisions.

Mansel Copse and the Shrine (**30**). This is the scene of the attack of the 9th Devons, where Capt. D. L. Martin predicted his men would be caught from the fire of a German machine-gun at the Shrine (pages 86 and 125). The Devonshire Cemetery, a beautiful cemetery on the top of Mansel Copse, contains the graves of 160 men of the 8th and 9th Devons who fell on 1 July. Among these are Capt. Martin and Lieut W. N. Hodgson, the poet.

In the civilian cemetery of Mametz, there is a large crucifix which is on the site of the old Shrine. It can be seen, from here, how the German machine-gunners had an easy target as the Devons came over and around Mansel Copse.

The Gordon Cemetery (**31**) is the burial place of six second-lieutenants and ninety-three men of the 2nd Gordon Highlanders who were killed on 1 July and were buried in one of their old trenches.

Carnoy. A village behind the British trenches held by the successful 18th (Eastern) Division. The village square was full of wounded on the afternoon of the battle and it was here that L/Cpl Charles Matthews had to wait, under fire, for evacuation (page 230).

The Carnoy Military Cemetery (**32**) contains the grave of Capt. W. P. Nevill, the 8th East Surreys company commander who gave his platoons footballs to kick across No Man's Land (pages 86 and 124). His headstone bears the badge of his old regiment, the East Yorks.

The Kasino Point Mine Crater (**33**) is difficult of access, being in a ploughed field north-west of the Carnoy–Montauban Road. This is the mine which was late being fired and then spread its debris so far that many British soldiers were hit (page 126).

Montauban. This village was captured by the 30th Division on the morning of 1 July. It was the first village to fall to the British in the Battle of the Somme.

A single brick chimney, built in the 1920s, is all that remains of the Brickworks (**34**) that were captured by the 4th Liverpool Pals (page 212). Although the original Briqueterie was a few yards south of this chimney, it can be seen how near was Bernafay Wood. No attempt was made to capture this wood until two days later.

This concludes the tour of the British battle front of 1 July 1916. The visitor may wish to see some of the main features connected with later stages of the Battle of the Somme.

Trônes Wood has a memorial to the 18th (Eastern) Division (**35**). Just inside the entrance of the Guillemont Road Cemetery (**36**) is the grave of Lieut Raymond Asquith, the prime minister's son, who was killed in September. There is the South African National Memorial and a large cemetery at Delville Wood (**37**) and, up a track due north of Longueval, is a New Zealand Memorial (**38**). At High Wood (**39**) (Bois des Forceaux) there is a cemetery named after another London Division.

Just off the main road to Bapaume is the Butte de Warlencourt (**40**), a small hill which marked the limit of the British advance during the Battle of the Somme.

Returning in the direction of Albert, one passes the Canadian Memorial (**41**) and arrives at the interesting village of Pozières which was an objective of the first day of the battle but was not taken until 26 July There are several interesting features in and around the village. The Windmill (**42**) was the highest part of the Pozières Ridge and is a simple, but effective, memorial to Australian troops. An interesting memorial (**43**) to the first tanks in action is on the other side of the road, although the tank attack was at Flers, three miles away. The village church (**44**) is where Herr Kircher was shelled out of his observation post (page 101); this is not the original church, of course.

The Pozières Memorial to the Missing of 1918 (**45**) is a reminder that this ground was fought over twice more before the war finished.

Acknowledgements

I would like to acknowledge the help of the following men who were all present on the Somme on 1 July 1916. (Ranks shown are those held on that date. Decorations are those awarded before then or won on the day of the battle.)

THE BRITISH ARMY

4th DIVISION

1st Royal Irish Fusiliers: Capt. W. Carden Roe, M.C., Foxrock, Co. Dublin, Eire; Pte J. Coyle, Cavan, Eire; Sgt G. Moore, Woodford Green, Essex (died 1970). *2nd Royal Dublin Fusiliers*: Pte W. Durham, Liverpool; Lieut A. Sainsbury, Hoylake, Cheshire. *2nd Seaforth Highlanders*: L/Cpl J. Arbuthnott, Springburn, Glasgow; Pte J. S. Reid, Cardonald, Glasgow. *1st Royal Warwicks*: Pte F. Dodgson, Thornaby-on-Tees, Yorks. *1st Somerset Light Infantry*: C.S.M. P. E. Chappell, D.S.M., Limpley Stoke, Somerset; Pte W. G. Crook, Faversham, Kent. *1st East Lancs*: Pte L. Westby, Great Harwood, Lancs. *1st Hants*: Pte F. C. Binstead, St Albans, Herts; Pte W. H. Chalmers, Christchurch, Hants; Capt C. D. Fawkes, M.C., Ropley, Hants. *1st Rifle Brigade*: Rfmn F. J. Conyer, Oakwood, London; Cpl G. Stone, Wolverhampton, Staffs; Rfmn A. Withers, Chessington, Surrey. *1st King's Own*: Pte T. Lowery, Great Yeldham, Essex; L/Cpl J. Riding, Debolt, Alberta, Canada. *2nd Lancs Fusiliers*: Pte W. Hall, Clay Cross, Derbys. *2nd Essex*: Pte G. T. Rudge, Aveley, Essex. *21st West Yorks (Pioneers)*: Pte J. W. Shearman, Moldgreen, Yorks; Pte J. Walton, Skipton, Yorks. *Z4 Heavy Trench Mortar Battery*: Lieut R. D. Jeune, Old Heathfield, Sussex.

7th DIVISION

8th Devons: Pte H. E. Bathurst, Sutton Scotney, Hants; Pte A. V. Conn, New Eltham, London; Pte J. E. Mitchelmore, Marley Head, Devon; Pte W. Tratt, Rayleigh, Essex. *9th Devons*: Pte W. T. Cotterill, Winson Green, Birmingham; Pte G. Kidd, Battersea, London; Pte E. W. Lee, Lapford, Devon; Pte J. E. Stone, Kingsbridge, Devon; Pte H. L. Wide, Clevedon, Somerset. *2nd Border*: Capt. W. Chetham-Strode, Playden, Sussex. *2nd Gordon Highlanders*: Sgt W. Phillips, Aberdeen; Pte V. Smith, Edinburgh. *1st Royal Welch Fusiliers*: Pte V. F. King, Redcar, Yorks. *2nd Queens*: 2nd Lieut H. B. Secretan, M.C., South Broom, Natal, South

Africa. *1st South Staffs*: Pte C. H. Talbot, Wednesbury, Staffs; Pte A. Wilson, Compton, Staffs. *5th Manchester Pals*: Pte A. Francis, Droylsden, Manchester; Pte J. Kirkham, West Didsbury, Manchester; Pte T. Leary, Fallowfield, Manchester; Pte W. Lloyd, Ashton-under-Lyne, Lancs. *6th Manchester Pals*: Pte F. Cloudsdale, Manchester; Lieut G. Langdon, Bournemouth, Hants; Pte W. Scott, Salford, Lancs. *7th Manchester Pals*: Pte W. Binns, Droylsden, Manchester; Pte J. Costello, Royton, Lancs. *22nd Brigade* H.Q.: Lieut A. W. Lee, M.C., Tisbury, Wilts. *91st Brigade Machine Gun Company*: Pte A. J. Butterfield, Bridlington, Yorks; Pte J. E. Holmes, Treeton, Yorks. *14th Brigade R.H.A.*: Sgt L. Cook, Cullompton, Devon (died 1970).

8th DIVISION

2nd Devons: Pte J. N. Arnold, South Oxhey, Herts; Pte W. Green, Tiverton, Devon; Pte J. R. Parkman, Tiverton, Devon; Pte A. D. Snell, Rackenford, Devon. *2nd Middlesex*: Capt. E. E. F. Baker, Amersham, Bucks; Pte W. Claydon, Southend, Essex; Pte A. E. Hollingshead, Hindley, Lancs; L/Cpl F. Lobel, M.M., Norwich. *2nd Scottish Rifles*: Rfmn R. C. Logue, Townhead, Glasgow. *2nd Lincolns*: Sgt A. Ingall, Branston, Lincs; Pte. J. Johnson, Accrington, Lancs; Pte F. Perry, Bulwell, Nottingham. *2nd Royal Berks*: Pte W. S. Gubbins, Ilford, Essex. *8th King's Own Yorkshire Light Infantry*: Pte J. Dobson, Wheatley Hills, Yorks; L/Cpl W. J. Evans, Worthing, Sussex. *8th Yorks and Lancs*: Pte J. Bodkin, Thrybergh, Yorks. *9th Yorks and Lancs*: Pte J. W. Bescoby, Orwell, Herts; Pte H. Johnson, High Green, Yorks; Pte T. A. Senior, Rotherham, Yorks; Cpl J. H. Tansley, Corby, Northants; Pte H. A. Winders, Rotherham, Yorks. *11th Sherwood Foresters*: Pte F. Davies, Chesterfield, Derbys; L/Cpl R. Cowley, Huthwaite, Notts; Pte F. W. A. Turner, Bilsthorpe, Notts. *23rd Brigade Machine Gun Company*: Pte E. Green, Tiverton, Devon. *33rd Brigade R.F.A.*: Bdr A. Harlow, Bedford; Lieut F. L. Lee, Kinoulton, Notts. *Y8 Heavy Trench Mortar Battery*: Sgt R. Payne, Kempston, Beds.

17th (NORTHERN) DIVISION

10th West Yorks: Pte G. T. Giles, Hull, Yorks; Lieut P. Howe, M.C., Calver, Derbys. *7th East Yorks*: Pte L. Blashker, Hull, Yorks; Pte F. Booth, Bradford, Yorks; Pte W. Stansfield, Huddersfield, Yorks. *7th Green Howards*: Pte A. W. Askew, Lowthorpe, Yorks; Pte J. A. Hooper, Hetton-le-Hole, Co. Durham; Pte F. S. Metcalfe, Middlesbrough, Yorks.

18th (EASTERN) DIVISION

8th Norfolks: Capt. C. F. Ashdown, Framingham Pigot, Norfolk; Pte W. C. Bennett, Hellesdon, Norfolk; Pte R. W. Gant, Tittleshall, Norfolk; L/Cpl E. J. Hubbard, Pulham St Mary, Norfolk; Pte R. G. Jarvis, Old Costessy, Norfolk; Cpl J. Norton, Frettenham,

Norfolk; Pte N. H. Norton, Taverham, Norfolk; Pte W. R. Rumbles, Burnham Overy, Norfolk; Pte C. E. Sandell, Sloley, Norfolk; Pte J. Savoury, Wighton, Norfolk; Pte J. W. Seely, Loddon, Norfolk. *6th Royal Berks*: Pte E. Gray, M.M., Bracknell, Berks; Pte J. H. Harwood, Binfield, Berks; Lieut N. B. Hudson, Maida Vale, London (died 1970); Pte J. L. Hunt, Tilehurst, Berks; Pte A. H. Williamson, Wells-next-the-Sea, Norfolk. *10th Essex*: Capt. R. A. Chell, Romford, Essex; L/Cpl E. J. Fisher, Orpington, Kent; L/Cpl W. G. Sanders, Holloway, London. *11th Royal Fusiliers*: Pte G. R. S. Mayne, Honor Oak, London. *7th Bedfords*: L/Cpl J. J. Cousins, Luton, Beds; Pte F. G. Foskett, Gravenhurst, Beds. *6th Northamptons*: Cpl H. Hunt, Leighton Buzzard, Beds; L/Cpl C. E. Matthews, Petersham, Surrey; Pte R. V. Moore, Burton Latimer, Northants; Pte W. R. Thompson, Kettering, Northants; Pte A. Young, Finedon, Northants. *12th Middlesex*: Cpl G. W. Allen, Woking, Surrey; Pte G. C. Baker, Croydon, Surrey; Pte W. B. Bird, East Acton, London; Pte J. Price, Lewisham, London; L/Cpl C. F. T. Townsend, Drayton, Norfolk. *7th Queens*: Pte R. A. Cole, Newhaw, Surrey; L/Cpl C. Dennison, Hull, Yorks; Pte G. C. Mills, Sidcup, Kent. *7th Buffs*: Pte H. J. Goddard, South Norwood, London; L/Cpl S. E. Marsh, Canterbury, Kent; Pte F. P. Weston, Shoeburyness, Essex. *8th East Surreys*: Pte C. E. Beckett, Croydon, Surrey; Pte R. J. Curtis, South Walsham, Norfolk; Lieut-Col. A. P. B. Irwin, Moyard, Co. Galway, Eire; L/Cpl J. Kenyon, M.M., Bury, Lancs; L/Cpl C. J. Richards, Isleworth, Middlesex. *7th Royal West Kents*: Pte A. R. French, Swanscombe, Kent. *8th Royal Sussex (Pioneers)*: Pte L. S. Price, Ruislip, Middlesex. *83rd Brigade R.F.A.*: Cpl H. R. Wise, Leyton, London (died 1969). *55th Field Ambulance*: Pte J. F. Pout, Ditton, Kent. *80th Field Company R.E.*: Spr F. Clark, Spital, Derbys; Spr J. W. Oakes, Lepton, Yorks.

19th (WESTERN) DIVISION

7th South Lancs: Capt. B. W. Ridley, Colmworth, Beds. *7th Loyal North Lancs*: Pte C. B. Mawbey, Almondbury, Yorks. *9th Welch*: Sgt D. J. Price, Nantyffyllon, Glamorgan. *58th Field Ambulance*: Pte A. Streets, Mattersey, Notts; Pte H. Streets, Bakestone Moor, Notts. *87th Brigade R.F.A.*: Dvr C. W. Garrard, Brixton, London.

21st DIVISION

12th Northumberland Fusiliers: L/Cpl A. T. Crosby, Middlesbrough, Yorks; L/Cpl H. Fellows, Beechdale Estate, Nottingham; Pte J. P. Turner, Long Eaton, Notts. *13th Northumberland Fusiliers*: Pte G. Brownbridge, Blyth, Northumberland. *1st Lincolns*: Pte W. Blackburn, Boston, Lincs; Pte G. H. Burgess, Deptford, London; Cpl M. McGuire, Middlesbrough, Yorks; Cpl W. Robinson, Stockton-on-Tees, Co. Durham. *8th Lincolns*: Sgt A. P. Britton, Leverton, Lincs. *10th Green Howards*: Pte M. M. Watkin, Weston Turville, Bucks; Pte G. Wilkinson, Redcar, Yorks.

4th Middlesex: Pte J. R. Brightman, St Pancras, London. *1st East Yorks*: Pte C. W. Smith, Hull, Yorks. *10th King's Own Yorkshire Light Infantry*: Pte F. King, Eastwood, Notts. *15th Durham Light Infantry*: Pte J. G. Crossley, Sunderland, Co. Durham. *14th Northumberland Fusiliers (Pioneers)*: Pte J. W. Malkinson, Skegness, Lincs; Pte B. Butterworth, Stacksteads, Lancs. *63rd Brigade Machine Gun Company*: Pte A. Warwicker, Dulwich, London; Sgt W. B. Dixon, Hagworthingham, Lincs.

29th DIVISION

2nd Royal Fusiliers: Pte W. A. Harris, Raynes Park, London; Pte G. S. Wyman, Hitchin, Herts. *1st Lancs Fusiliers*: Pte J. W. Burrill, Littleborough, Lancs. *16th Middlesex (Public Schools Battalion)*: Pte E. Houston, Southend-on-Sea, Essex; Pte W. A. Lane, Herne Bay, Kent (died 1969); Pte W. J. Leakey, Tulse Hill, London; Pte A. T. Liney, Morden, Surrey; Pte A. McMillan, Highgate, London. *1st Royal Dublin Fusiliers*: Pte F. McLaughlin, Dublin, Eire; Pte W. J. Parsons, Battersea, London. *1st King's Own Scottish Borderers*: Pte F. H. Cameron, Isle of Whithorn, Wigtownshire; Pte S. P. Riley, Shoeburyness, Essex. *1st Border*: Pte G. Henry, Fallowfield, Manchester; Pte P. Smith, Carlisle, Cumberland. *1st Essex*: Pte J. Anderson, Walthamstow, London; Pte J. Barrow, Kirkby Lonsdale, Lancs; Pte J. Jackson, Thurcroft, Yorks; Pte C. Mayes, Ridlington, Norfolk; Pte H. Parker, Lewisham, London; Pte C. W. Wells, Chesterfield, Derbys. *1st Newfoundland*: Pte B. Forsey, Vacaville, California, U.S.A.; 2nd Lieut C. S. Frost, Toronto, Ontario, Canada; Pte J. F. Hibbs, Codroy Valley, Newfoundland; 2nd Lieut G. Hicks, Grand Falls, Newfoundland; Cpl F. Moakler, Bellerose, New York, U.S.A.; Pte W. A. Pollett, Trinity Bay, Newfoundland. *15th Brigade R.H.A.*: Capt. C. J. P. Ball, Brown Candover, Hants. *147th Brigade R.F.A.*: Bdr F. C. Kench, Eydon, Northants.

30th DIVISION

1st Liverpool Pals: Pte W. L. P. Dunn, Eastham, Cheshire; Pte C. E. A. Parrott, Spital, Derbys. *2nd Liverpool Pals*: Pte J. A. Deary, Childwall, Liverpool; Pte G. E. Fowkes, Newcastle-under-Lyme, Staffs. *3rd Liverpool Pals*: Sgt T. P. Bennett, Ryde, Isle of Wight; Pte J. G. Hanaghan, Masterton, New Zealand; Pte F. Waterworth, Hoylake, Cheshire. *4th Liverpool Pals*: Pte R. G. Robertson, Heversham, Westmorland. *1st Manchester Pals*: 2nd Lieut G. Barr, Cowichan Station, British Columbia, Canada; Pte S. P. Dawson, M.M., Didsbury, Manchester; L/Cpl F. Gudgeon, Filey, Yorks. *2nd Manchester Pals*: Pte A. A. Bell, Gatley, Cheshire; Pte E. Conroy, South Dartmouth, Massachusetts, U.S.A.; Pte F. J. Day, Burnage, Manchester; Pte A. E. Hall, Bolton, Lancs; Sgt D. F. Hay, Whalley Range, Manchester; L/Cpl F. Heardman, Edale, Derbys; 2nd Lieut A. T. S. Holt, Hale, Cheshire; Pte W. Speakman, Leigh-on-Sea, Essex. *3rd Manchester Pals*: Pte P. J.

Kennedy, Levenshulme, Manchester; Pte J. Sudlow, Wallasey, Cheshire. *2nd Green Howards*: Pte T. S. Frank, Scarborough, Yorks; Pte W. E. Nelson, Sheffield; Pte J. T. Shutt, Yarm, Yorks. *2nd Bedfords*: L/Cpl H. J. Bennett, Ampthill, Beds; Sgt T. H. Bennett, Bedford. *2nd Royal Scots Fusiliers*: Pte A. Bryce, Girvan, Ayrshire; Capt. G. D. Fairley, R.A.M.C., Ferndown, Dorset; Pte J. Frier, Edinburgh; Pte J. Russell, Possilpark, Glasgow (died 1969 or 1970); Pte R. Sim, Hamilton, Lanarkshire. *21st Brigade Machine Gun Company*: Pte E. H. Furnell, Thrapston, Northants. *89th Brigade Machine Gun Company*: L/Cpl C. O. Law, Sale, Cheshire. *98th Field Ambulance*: Q.M.S. B. Benson, Hoylake, Cheshire. *200th Field Company R.E.*: Spr A. Turner, Audenshaw, Manchester.

31st DIVISION

Hull Commercials: Pte W. E. Aust, Kirk Ella, Yorks; Pte W. H. Dickinson, Hull, Yorks; Pte A. Jordan, Reading, Berks (died 1970). *Leeds Pals*: Pte J. W. Allsop, Bramley, Leeds; Pte R. N. Bell, Farnham, Surrey; Pte A. Howard, Burley-in-Wharfedale, Yorks; Pte A. V. Pearson, Saltburn-on-Sea, Yorks; L/Cpl T. H. Place, Leeds; Pte J. W. Taylor, Middlesborough, Yorks. *1st Bradford Pals*: Pte W. H. T. Carter, Worlaby, Lincs; Pte H. Licence, Bradford; Pte G. Monkman, Peterborough, Ontario, Canada; Pte G. Morgan, Bradford; L/Cpl E. Thackray, Bradford Moor, Bradford; Cpl A. Wood, Lidget Green, Bradford; Pte G. E. Woodhall, Bradford. *2nd Bradford Pals*: Pte E. Brook, Bradford; Cpl. P. W. Bunney, Barking, Essex; Drmr J. D. Currie, M.M., Great Horton, Bradford; Pte L. Frankland, Bradford; Pte L. G. Lincoln, Shipley, Yorks; Pte H. Mills, Bradford; Pte W. Slater, Baildon, Yorks. *Durham Pals*: Pte J. G. Bainbridge, Seaham, Co. Durham; L/Cpl F. W. Campbell, Hetton-le-Hole, Co. Durham; Sgt A. S. Durrant, Sunderland, Co. Durham; Pte G. E. Ramshaw, East Herrington, Co. Durham; L/Sgt H. Stanley, Hull, Yorks; Pte R. T. Tait, South Shields, Co. Durham; Pte F. W. Temple, Seaham, Co. Durham. *Accrington Pals*: Pte R. Barrow, Euxton, Lancs; Pte H. C. Bloor, Accrington, Lancs; L/Cpl H. Bury, Tilsworth, Beds; Pte C. Smith, Blackburn, Lancs. *Sheffield City Battalion*: Pte W. Brogan, Mosborough, Yorks; Cpl D. E. Cattell, Sheffield; Pte A. Fretwell, Aspley, Nottingham; Pte J. E. C. Goodrich, Sheffield; Pte W. C. Hartley, Sheffield; Pte A. H. Hastings, Curbar, Derbys; L/Cpl J. A. Linsley, Sheffield; L/Cpl T. Quinn, Thurcroft, Yorks; Pte J. W. Stevenson, Everton, Notts; Pte F. B. Vaughan, Sheffield; Pte W. J. Watson, Rotherham, Yorks; Sgt J. A. Willoughby, Rotherham, Yorks. *1st Barnsley Pals*: Lieut M. Asquith, Wentbridge, Yorks; 2nd Lieut P. Brocklesby, Tealby, Lincs; Pte R. W. Carr, Barnsley, Yorks; Lieut R. A. Heptonstall, Goole, Yorks (died 1969); Pte C. Tyas, Barnsley, Yorks; Sgt H. Wainwright, Barnsley, Yorks; Pte J. Wiper, Darton, Yorks. *2nd Barnsley Pals*: Pte T. W. Sabin, Hoyland, Yorks. *12th King's Own Yorkshire Light Infantry (Pioneers)*: Cpl A. Jaggar, Sandal, Yorks. *93rd Brigade Machine Gun Company*: Pte J. R. Thompson, Shipley, Yorks.

94th Trench Mortar Battery: Pte C. Bartram, New Rossington, Yorks. *170th Brigade R.F.A.*: Gnr H. W. Beaumont, Huddersfield, Yorks; 2nd Lieut T. Reilly, Bexhill, Sussex. *94th Field Ambulance*; Sgt F. F. Webber, Drumheller, Alberta, Canada.

32nd DIVISION

Glasgow Tramways Battalion: Cpl T. Renton-Gordon, South Shields, Co. Durham. *Glasgow Boys Brigade Battalion*: L/Cpl J. Blair, Girvan, Ayrshire; Pte D. M. Miller, Glasgow; Pte L. Ramage, Glasgow; Pte G. E. Waller, Glasgow. *Glasgow Commercials*: Sgt H. M. Abercrombie, Glasgow; Pte F. R. Carson, Dunblane, Perthshire; Pte G. Forrest, Ashburton, Devon; Pte R. Love, Glasgow; Pte J. MacDonald, Rutherglen, Glasgow; Pte A. W. MacKinlay, Bearsden, Dunbartonshire; Pte A. C. McInnes, Girvan, Ayrshire; L/Cpl L. C. Palmer, North Halling, Kent. *1st Salfords*: Pte J. Eastwood, Prestatyn, Flintshire. *3rd Salfords*: Cpl A. Newton, Urmston, Lancs. *Newcastle Commercials*: Pte J. Haining, High Heaton, Newcastle; L/Cpl S. Henderson, High Heaton, Newcastle; Pte A. Rutherford, High Heaton, Newcastle; Pte B. Richardson, North Shields, Northumberland. *11th Border* (*Lonsdales*): L/Cpl F. Allan, Carlisle, Cumberland; Pte F. Graves, Carlisle, Cumberland; L/Cpl J. Mounsey, Workington, Cumberland; Pte R. L. Walker, Carlisle, Cumberland. *2nd Royal Inniskilling Fusiliers*: R.S.M. T. Maguire, Omagh, Co. Tyrone. *2nd King's Own Yorkshire Light Infantry*: Lieut-Col. E. H. Rigg, D.S.O., Lymington, Hants. *Newcastle Railway Pals* (*Pioneers*): Pte J. Harris, Scotswood, Newcastle. *97th Brigade Machine Gun Company*: Pte C. A. Turner, Swindon, Wilts. *155th Brigade R.F.A.*: Dvr H. Clay, Crossgates, Leeds; Gnr H. Sykes, Holmfirth, Yorks (died 1969). *161st Brigade R.F.A.*: Sgt R. T. Oates, Cambridge, New Zealand. *32nd Signal Company*: L/Cpl E. G. Catley, Westcliff-on-Sea, Essex.

34th DIVISION

1st Edinburgh City Battalion: Cpl H. Beaumont, M.M., Combe Martin, Devon; Pte W. B. Corbett, Edinburgh; Pte J. S. Kidd, Edinburgh; Pte A. M. Leslie, Dundee, Angus; Pte W. McHardy, Altrincham, Cheshire; Pte M. Richardson, Edinburgh; Pte J. Sutherland, Brechin, Angus; Pte L. Welch, Withington, Manchester. *Grimsby Chums*: Sgt H. Benzing, Grimsby, Lincs; Pte R. D. Carter, Keelby, Lincs; L/Cpl H. E. Chapman, Cleethorpes, Lincs; Cpl F. Colebrook, Humberstone, Lincs; Cpl A. Dickinson, Boston, Lincs; Lieut C. H. Emmerson, Grimsby; Pte C. R. Frankish, Barnetby, Lincs; Pte H. Kemp, East Keal, Lincs; Pte G. Leeman, Grimsby; Pte G. T. Mason, Saughall, Cheshire; Pte F. R. Miller, Scarthoe, Grimsby; Pte W. T. Parkin, Scarthoe, Grimsby; Pte F. Perry, Cleethorpes, Lincs; L/Cpl A. Turner, Cleethorpes, Lincs. *11th Suffolks* (*Cambridge Battalion*): Pte R. W. Allen, Cambridge; L/Cpl W. B. Cousins, Histon, Cambs (died 1969 or 1970); L/Cpl A. W. Crawford, Cambridge; Pte H. Dockerill, Ely, Cambs;

Pte A. E. Fletcher, Longstanton, Cambs; Pte W. Gathercole, Prickwillow, Cambs; Pte W. H. Gillingham, Cambridge; Pte G. Gordon, Girton, Cambridge; Pte J. Page, West Wickham, Cambs; Pte A. W. Robinson, Papworth Everard, Cambs; Pte H. A. Rogers, Papworth Everard, Cambs; Pte W. J. Senescall, Needingworth, Hunts; Pte W. C. Sheldrick, Fowlmere, Cambs; Pte B. West, Soham, Cambs. *1st Tyneside Scottish*: Sgt J. Wilson, Backworth, Northumberland (died 1968). *2nd Tyneside Scottish*: Pte J. G. Barron, Dalton-le-Dale, Co. Durham; Pte C. W. Coulter, Gateshead, Co. Durham; Pte T. Easton, Stakeford, Northumberland. *4th Tyneside Scottish*: Pte L. Dodd, Clipstone, Notts; Sgt R. E. Jackson, Bayswater, London; Pte R. Peardon, Seaham, Co. Durham. *1st Tyneside Irish*: Pte N. Fitzpatrick, Jarrow, Co. Durham; Pte J. R. Fowler, Longframlington, Northumberland. *2nd Tyneside Irish*: Pte R. W. Flockton, Bedlington, Northumberland; Pte H. Monaghan, Byker, Newcastle. *3rd Tyneside Irish*: Sgt J. Galloway, Hull, Yorks; Lieut W. J. White, Sunderland, Co. Durham. *4th Tyneside Irish*: Lieut-Col. G. R. V. Steward, D.S.O. (died 1969). *18th Northumberland Fusiliers (Pioneers)*: Pte A. D. Grey, Jesmond, Newcastle; Pte A. Warren, Freckleton, Lancs; Capt. R. Wood, St Helier, Jersey. *175th Brigade R.F.A.*: Gnr J. D. Brew, Albrighton, Shropshire. *152nd Brigade R.F.A.*: Bdr H. Gates, Nottingham. *209th Field Company R.E.*: Spr G. H. Anderson, Reepham, Norfolk. *34th Signal Company*: Cpl S. F. Hill, Monkstown, Co. Dublin, Eire.

36th (ULSTER) DIVISION

East Belfast Volunteers: C.S.M. R. S. Drean, M.C., Belfast; Pte A. Morrison, Ballymena, Co. Antrim. *West Belfast Volunteers*: Pte J. Donaldson, Banbridge, Co. Down; Sgt G. Fleming, Donaghadee, Co. Down; Cpl G. A. Lloyd, Belfast; Pte A. V. Wilson, Larne, Co. Antrim. *South Belfast Volunteers*: Pte J. Quinn, Londonderry. *Central Antrim Volunteers*: Pte J. Kinnaird, Cloyfin, Co. Derry. *Co. Down Volunteers*: L/Cpl R. Johnston, Dromore, Co. Down. *Belfast Young Citizens*: 2nd Lieut L. S. Duncan, Belfast; Pte W. J. Ellis, Coventry, Warwicks; Pte J. Grange, Belfast; L/Cpl J. A. Henderson, Bangor, Co. Down; Sgt J. A. B. Maultsaid, Belfast; Pte S. Megaw, Moneymore, Co. Derry. *Armagh, Monaghan and Cavan Volunteers*: Cpl R. D. Meredith, Tanderagee, Co. Armagh; Pte W. A. Patterson, Belfast. *Co. Tyrone Volunteers*: Pte R. Irwin, Pomeroy, Co. Tyrone; Cpl T. McClay, M.M., Omagh, Co. Tyrone; Pte C. Shannon, Mullaghmore, Co. Tyrone (died 1970). *Co. Derry Volunteers*: Pte L. Bell, Moneymore, Co. Derry; Pte J. Devennie, Whiteabbey, Co. Antrim; Pte D. Jordan, Moneymore, Co. Derry; Capt. N. Strong, Tynan, Co. Armagh. *Donegal and Fermanagh Volunteers*: Pte R. J. Little, Ballinamallard, Co. Fermanagh; Pte A. McMullen, Magherafelt, Co. Derry. *108th Machine Gun Company*: Pte E. J. Brownlee, Larne, Co. Antrim. *109th Trench Mortar Battery*: Pte F. G. Gardner, South Shields, Co. Durham. *108th Field Ambulance*: Capt. S. B. B. Campbell, Ballycastle, Co. Antrim; Pte J. Savage, Oswaldtwistle, Lancs. *109th Field Ambulance*: Capt.

J. G. Johnston, Lisburn, Co. Antrim; Sgt W. Tozer, Belfast. *121st Field Company R.E.*: Cpl P. Nicholls, Cape, Warwicks; Spr M. H. Walker, Coatbridge, Lanarkshire.

46th (NORTH MIDLAND) DIVISION

1/5th South Staffs: Pte F. Birch, Wednesbury, Staffs; Cpl C. T. Edwards, Walsall, Staffs; Cpl A. C. Smith, Walsall, Staffs. *1/6th South Staffs*: Pte H. D. Bowdler, Wolverhampton, Staffs; Pte A. Crutchley, Wombourne, Staffs; Pte F. A. Griffiths, Wombourne, Staffs; Pte A. W. Jenkins, Southsea, Hants; Cpl D. Morton, Cannock, Staffs; Pte B. Tranter, Lower Gornal, Staffs; Pte J. E. Williams, Fremantle, W. Australia (died 1970). *1/6th North Staffs*: Pte J. Foster, Uttoxeter, Staffs; Pte G. S. Young, Kilburn, London. *1/4th Lincolns*: 2nd Lieut A. V. Coulson, Westcliff-on-Sea, Essex; Pte W. Miller, Dawsmere, Lincs; Cpl J. Ward, Boston, Lincs. *1/5th Lincolns*: Pte W. E. Martin, Boston, Lincs (died 1969); Pte A. Ward, Dunstable, Beds. *1/5th Sherwood Foresters (Derby)*: Pte J. T. Commons, Derby; L/Cpl W. Disney, Derby. *1/6th Sherwood Foresters (Derbyshire)*: Pte W. H. Riley, Derby; Capt. V. O. Robinson, M.C., Holymoorside, Derbys; Drmr W. Waterhouse, Chesterfield, Derbys. *1/7th Sherwood Foresters (Nottingham)*: L/Cpl N. J. Buckley, Bulwell, Nottingham; 2nd Lieut J. Garner, Tollerton, Notts; Pte J. E. Salt, M.M., Nottingham (died 1969); Pte J. Singleton, Aspley, Nottingham; Bglr W. H. Soar, Trent Bridge, Nottingham (died 1970); Pte A. H. Tomlinson, Skegness, Lincs; Bglr H. Waldram, Sheffield; Cpl C. Wooley, M.M., Old Basford, Nottingham. *1/8th Sherwood Foresters (Nottinghamshire)*: L/Cpl H. Hickman, Collingham, Notts. *232nd Brigade R.F.A.*: Gnr A. Clarke, Willenhall, Staffs. *1/3rd North Midlands Field Ambulance*: Pte H. Kendrick, Wolverhampton, Staffs. *466th Field Company R.E.*: Sgt C. E. Linford, Heath Hayes, Staffs. *46th Signals Company*: Spr R. M. Arnold, Tauranga, New Zealand. *46th Divisional Ammunition Column*: Capt. O. B. Giles, Boston, Lincs (died 1970).

48th (SOUTH MIDLAND) DIVISION

1/6th Royal Warwicks (Birmingham): Pte H. Jones, Wolverhampton, Staffs. *1/8th Royal Warwicks (Birmingham)*: Pte C. G. Barff (served as Dickens), Northolt, Middlesex; Pte J. Parkes, Erdington, Birmingham; Pte E. C. Stanley, Cheltenham, Glos. *1/6th Gloucesters*: Cpl J. T. Brewer, Ottershaw, Surrey. *48th Divisional Ammunition Column*: Bdr W. F. Spriggs, Duffield, Derbys (died 1970).

49th (WEST RIDING) DIVISION

1/5th West Yorks (York): Pte G. B. Gledhill, York; Pte E. T. Radband, Holgate, York. *1/6th West Yorks (Bradford)*: Pte J. G. Dooley, Bradford; L/Cpl J. B. Field, Wibsey, Bradford; Pte T. Firth, Bradford; Pte E. G. Hall, Godalming, Surrey; Pte G.

Scaife, Bradford; Sgt J. H. Thompson, Lidget Green, Bradford; Pte J. Wilson, Buttershaw, Bradford. *1/8th West Yorks (Leeds)*: Pte H. E. Allen, Colwyn Bay, Denbighshire. *1/5th Duke of Wellington's*: Pte H. Battye, Honley, Yorks; Pte C. Helliwell, Almondbury, Yorks; Pte N. Smith, Cowlersley, Yorks. *1/5th Yorks and Lancs*: Pte W. H. Haigh, Barnsley, Yorks. *1/5th King's Own Yorkshire Light Infantry*: Pte A. Eastwood, Oakville, Ontario, Canada. *246th Brigade R.F.A.*: Cpl H. Delves, Stockport, Cheshire.

56th (LONDON) DIVISION

1/2nd London: Sgt R. L. Mallett, Nordelph, Norfolk. *1/4th London*: Pte H. B. Barr, Southgate, London; Pte H. H. Conrad, Bookham, Surrey; Pte F. Dent, Leigh-on-Sea, Essex; L/Cpl H. C. Lancashire, Tiverton, Devon. *Rangers*: Pte F. S. Martin, Sawbridgeworth, Herts; Pte E. T. Salter, Harringay, London. *Kensingtons*: Pte G. L. Arnold, Hayling Island, Hants; Pte G. Tollman, Three Bridges, Sussex. Pte H. L. Witts, Hayling Island, Hants. *1st London Scottish*: Pte T. C. Clynes, Brixton Hill, London; Maj. C. J. Low, D.S.O., Reigate, Surrey. *1st London Rifle Brigade*: L/Sgt H. L. Bamford, Eastcote, Middlesex; Rfmn H. A. Barber, Surbiton, Surrey; Rfmn A. Hollis, Hove, Sussex; Rfmn A. E. Holmes, Ilford, Essex; L/Cpl E. R. Hughes, Great Missenden, Bucks; Cpl L. Jessop, Balcombe, Sussex; Rfmn N. H. Lockhart, Leigh-on-Sea, Essex; Rfmn S. G. Richardson, Herne Hill, London; L/Cpl T. R. Short, East Horsley, Surrey (died 1970); Rfmn W. G. Terrett, Merton Park, London. *Queen Victoria's Rifles*: Rfmn P. W. Harris, Poole, Dorset; L/Cpl F. Howell, Richmond, Surrey; Cpl C. R. Tennant, Leigh-on-Sea, Essex; Rfmn R. E. Walter, New Barnet, Herts; Rfmn F. J. Williams, Walton-on-Naze, Essex. *Queen's Westminster Rifles*: L/Cpl T. Flin, Epsom, Surrey; Rfmn A. F. Pays, Putney Hill, London; Bglr A. J. Price, South Benfleet, Essex; Rfmn A. H. Rose, Hove, Sussex. *1/5th Cheshires (Pioneers)*: Capt. P. H. Joliffe, Chester. *168th Brigade* H.Q.: Capt. P. Neame, V.C., Selling, Kent. *168th Brigade Machine Gun Company*: Cpl W. G. Martin, Elham, Kent. *169th Brigade Machine Gun Company*: Pte N. W. Nielsen, St Neot, Cornwall. *2/3rd London Field Ambulance*: Pte A. V. Atkinson, Swanage, Dorset. *56th Signals Company*: Spr H. C. Salter, Camden, London.

HEAVY ARTILLERY

12th Heavy Battery R.G.A.: Gnr F. W. J. Clark, Moulton, Suffolk. *13th Siege Battery R.G.A.*: Gnr L. Thomas, Highlane, Cheshire. *56th Siege Battery R.G.A.*: Gnr A. G. Bourne, Hamilton, New Zealand. *97th (Canadian) Siege Battery R.G.A.*: B.S.M. W. J. Jussup, Halifax, Nova Scotia, Canada; Gnr F. B. Ferguson, Goldborough, Nova Scotia, Canada. *110th Siege Battery R.G.A.*: Gnr J. Blackburn, New York, Lincs.

CAVALRY

2nd Dragoon Guards: L/Cpl E. A. Mahoney, Cambridge, New Zealand (died 1969). *3rd Dragoon Guards*: L/Cpl G. J. R. Wraight, Beckenham, Kent. *7th Dragoon Guards*: Tpr R. C. Cornforth, Southport, Lancs. *Royal Horse Guards*: Cpl F. Webber, Penryn, Cornwall. *1/1st North Somerset Yeomanry*: Capt. R. Marshall, R.A.M.C., Belfast. *6th Inniskilling Dragoons*: Tpr J. McKeown, Dungannon, Co. Tyrone. *South Irish Horse*: Sgt G. Tracey, Blackrock, Co. Dublin, Eire.

ROYAL FLYING CORPS

3rd Squadron R.F.C.: Lieut T. W. Stallibrass, Coddenham, Suffolk. *9th Squadron R.F.C.*: Lieut G. Chetwynd-Stapleton, Tilford, Surrey. *Wireless Section*: 2nd Air Mechanic S. H. Matts, New Malden, Surrey; 2nd Air Mechanic M. V. Pocock, Cannich, Inverness-shire.

OTHER UNITS

5th Battalion, Special Brigade R.E.: 2nd Lieut P. R. Koekkoek, Mapledurham, Berks; Cpl S. G. Tupman, Southall, Middlesex. *178th Tunnelling Company R.E.*: Spr C. Nixon, Woolsthorpe, Lincs. *11th Casualty Clearing Station*: Sgt G. B. Crooke, Gourock, Renfrewshire. *13th Corps Cyclist Battalion*: Pte H. W. C. Corbin, Waterloo, Liverpool. *British Liaison Officer at French Sixth Army* H.Q.: Capt. E. L. Spears, Warfield, Berks.

THE GERMAN ARMY

8th Bavarian Reserve Regiment: Soldat Lorenz Schneider, Penzing, Bavaria. *55th Reserve Regiment*: Gefreiter Hugo van Egeren, Kleve, Northrhine-Westphalia. *62nd Regiment*: Oberleutnant Heinrich Schneider, Bruckenau, Hesse. *66th Regiment*: Feldwebel Peter Collet, Trier, Rhineland-Pfalz. *99th Reserve Regiment*: Gefreiter Peter Kuster, Frankenberg, Hesse; Soldat Wilhelm Lange, Wemding, Bavaria. *109th Reserve Regiment*: Grenadier Emil Goebelbecker, New Jersey, U.S.A.; Unteroffizier Karl Goll, Karlsruhe, Baden-Württemberg; Grenadier Emil Kury, Waldkirch, Baden-Württemberg; Unteroffizier Gustav Luttgers, Karlsruhe; Unteroffizier Paul Scheytt, Ettlingen, Karlsruhe; Unteroffizier F. W. Thomas, Karlsruhe. *119th Reserve Regiment*: Hauptmann Karl Schall, Stuttgart, Baden-Württemberg. *169th Regiment*: Musketier Karl Blenk, Grotzingen, Karlsruhe; Feldwebel Karl Stumpf, Karlsruhe. *180th Regiment*: Oberleutnant Heinrich Vogler, Bad Oldesloe, Schleswig-Holstein.

ARTILLERY

16th Reserve Heavy Artillery Regiment: Leutnant August Bielefeld, Gelsenkirchen, Northrhine-Westphalia. *21st Field Artillery Regiment*: Kanonier Hermann Heinrich, Lenzfried, Bavaria. *26th Field*

Artillery Regiment: Feldwebel Felix Kircher, Lauingen, Bavaria.
60th Artillery Regiment: Gefreiter Helmuth Buchholz, Berlin.

An unknown number of the above men have died in addition to the deaths shown, which were mostly reported by relations. I failed to get replies to an increasing proportion of the letters written during the three years it took to prepare the book for publication.

PERSONAL ACKNOWLEDGEMENTS

As an inexperienced author tackling a complex subject, I have relied heavily upon the help of many people in the preparation of this book. These cheerfully performed a legion of duties without which it could never have been completed: research and technical advice, help in interviewing survivors of the battle, translation of German letters and documents, preparations of maps, reading and criticism of trial chapters and the correction of my very rusty grammar and punctuation. To all who helped I express my sincere thanks.

I have no hesitation in placing one name before all others. Patrick R. H. Mahoney of Chadwell Heath, Essex, offered himself as unpaid research assistant, mainly because of his own intense interest in the subject. His willingness to tackle any task, his diligence in inspecting a mass of documents and his uncanny flair for uncovering hidden stories lie behind nearly every page of the book. Over a period of two years, Patrick Mahoney gave up uncounted hours of his spare time to ensure that this book should be published.

Another stalwart has been John Howlett of Boston, who was involved in much of the early planning and research and would have gone on to be a co-author if circumstances had permitted. For his early help and encouragement, at a time when it would have been easy for me to give up, I am much indebted.

The following friends gave freely of their time in a multitude of ways; the order in which the names appear does not imply any order of merit: Miss Margaret Brocklebank, Mrs Margaret Howlett, Mrs Annemarie Lamb, Michael Harden, John Kilshaw, David Middlebrook, Ted Sylvester and Tom Wallace, all of Boston; Robert and Anne Clarkson of Irby near Skegness; Michael Parker of Hadlow, Kent; 'Lol' Spinks of Nottingham (died January 1970); Tom Steele of Exeter College, Oxford; Mr G. Cook, of the Commonwealth War Graves Commission, Albert, and Herr Heinrich Koch of Verden/Aller, West Germany.

I would like to thank my wife Mary and my daughters, Jane,

Anne and Catherine for their encouragement and help in many small tasks.

My thanks, also, to three typists, Mrs Molly Stevens, Mrs Sonia Hubbard and Mrs Janet Mountain, who coped with a massive correspondence and a complicated manuscript with much patience and skill.

I am grateful to Anthony Farrar-Hockley for finding, at the last moment, an interpreter for a visit to Germany.

I express my appreciation to the families of the late Reginald Bastard, Dick King, Billy MacFadzean and Henry Webber for allowing me to use the stories of these men. For help in piecing together the story of Henry Webber I am indebted to Mrs N. Copland, Mrs B. Martin and Rev. E. A. Noon of Horley, Surrey and Miss M. Gollancz, the Archivist of Surrey County Council.

Of the official organizations, two, the Imperial War Museum and the Commonwealth War Graves Commission, deserve special mention. The enthusiastic help given by their officials went far beyond the strict limits of their duties and I am very grateful to them, especially to Miss N. Bowden and Miss I. Doig of the War Graves Commission. Other bodies who provided willing help to less demanding requests were the Public Record Office (Chancery Lane and Portugal Street); the Public Record Office of Northern Ireland at Belfast; the National Army Museum, Camberley; the Stock Exchange; the military attaché of the West German Embassy; the City of Nottingham Publicity Department; the Glasgow Chamber of Commerce and the staffs of the Boston Borough Library and the Ilford Central Library (the latter for their help to Mr Mahoney).

To trace over 500 survivors of the battle, appeals were made through national and local newspapers and journals in many countries. Over ninety published these appeals; none made a charge for their services and I would like to express my gratitude for this generous help. These newspapers are identified in the 'Newspaper List' overleaf. My thanks also to Allan Eves of the Lincolnshire Standard Group for providing the information which enabled me to conduct this newspaper campaign.

I regret that I am unable to name the many regimental secretaries and old comrades associations who helped me and those people who kindly loaned battalion histories and other books which proved very useful. To those and to all those other people, whose names there is not space to mention, I give my thanks.

There is one group of people, above all others, who have made this book possible – the 526 British and twenty German ex-soldiers who fought on 1 July 1916 and who so willingly gave their personal accounts. Many enjoyed the opportunity to tell of their experiences; others were distressed to delve into the past but did so that a record of how their friends lived and died might be provided. I am pleased to be able to acknowledge each of these contributors, by name, elsewhere. My one regret is that some did not survive to see the book published.

OTHER ACKNOWLEDGEMENTS

Acknowledgements for permission to include quotations from books and documents are gratefully given as follows: *History of the 7th Battalion Green Howards*, to the Regimental Headquarters of the Green Howards; *History of the 16th, 17th, 18th and 19th Manchesters*, to John Sherratt and Sons of Altrincham; *The Old Front Line*, to the Society of Authors as the literary representative of the Estate of John Masefield; *Sagittarius Rising*, to the publishers, Peter Davies; *General Jack's Diary 1914–1918*, to John Terraine; *The Private Papers of Douglas Haig, 1914–1919*, to Earl Haig, Robert Blake and Eyre & Spottiswoode; and the Official War Histories to the Controller of H.M. Stationery Office.

For permission to quote from the original diaries of Baron Rawlinson, I am indebted to the members of the Rawlinson family and to Churchill College, Cambridge, who own the diaries. Similarly, I thank Mrs S. Clive of Nunnington Hall, York, for allowing me to quote from the diaries of her late father, Lieut-Col. R. Fife of the Green Howards. Quotations from Crown copyright records in the Public Record Office appear by permission of the Controller of H.M. Stationery Office.

Maps 1 to 10 were based on those appearing with the Official Histories and Map 11 on maps produced by the National Geographic Institute in Paris.

NEWSPAPER LIST

Guardian; Daily Telegraph; The Times Literary Supplement; Accrington Observer and Times; Barnsley Chronicle; Bedfordshire Times; Birmingham Evening Mail; Blyth News; Bournemouth Times; Bradford Telegraph and Argus; Bury Times; Cambridge News; Cheshire Observer; Cumberland Evening News; Cumberland News; Derby Evening Telegraph; Derbyshire Times; Devon and Somerset News; Doncaster Gazette; Dunstable Gazette; Eastern Daily Press; Grimsby Evening Telegraph; Hampshire Chronicle; Hampshire Herald; Horley Advertiser; Huddersfield Weekly Examiner; Hull and Yorkshire Times; Kent Messenger; Kentish Times; Kettering Evening Telegraph; Lancashire Evening Telegraph; Lancashire Life; Lincolnshire Echo; Lincolnshire Life; Lincolnshire Standard; Liverpool Weekly News; London Evening News; Luton News; Middlesborough Evening Gazette; Newcastle Evening Chronicle; Newcastle (Staffordshire) Times; Northumberland Gazette; Nottinghamshire Guardian Journal; Penrith Observer; Reading Mercury; Rotherham Advertiser; Salford

City Reporter; Sheffield Telegraph; Shields Gazette; Southend Standard; South Yorkshire Times; Staffordshire Advertiser and Chronicle; Stretford and Urmston Journal; Sunderland Echo; Surrey Comet; Wakefield Express; Warwickshire Advertiser; Western Morning News; Westmorland Gazette; Wolverhampton Express and Star; York Evening Press; Yorkshire Life; Ayr Advertiser; Edinburgh Evening News; Glasgow Daily Record; Glasgow Herald; Inverness Courier; Perthshire Peoples Journal; Belfast Telegraph; Ulster Star; Anglo-Celt, Cavan; *Cork Examiner; Dublin Evening Press; Irish Press,* Dublin; *Northern Standard,* Monaghan; *The People,* Wexford.

Allgauer Zeitung; Augsburger Algemeine; Berliner Morgenpost; Die Fackel; Kyffhauser; Memminger Zeitung; Minden Tageblatt; Neue Rhein Zeitung; Saarbrucker Zeitung; Newfoundland News; St John's Evening Telegraph, Newfoundland; *Royal Canadian Legion Magazine; Royal Gazette,* Hamilton, Bermuda; *Legion Magazine,* Melbourne, Australia; *New Zealand Returned Servicemen's Review.*

Army Medical Services Magazine; British Legion Journal; The Church Times; London Scottish Gazette; Nursing Mirror; Pulse Magazine; The Universe.

Bibliography

The Official Histories (published by HMSO):

Brig.-Gen. Sir J. E. Edmonds, *France and Belgium 1916*, vol. 5 (London, 1931)

Maj.-Gen. T. J. Mitchell and G. M. Smith, *Casualties and Medical Statistics* (London, 1931)

Maj.-Gen. Sir W. G. MacPherson, *Medical Services General History*, 4 vols. (London, 1921–4)

Col. A. M. Henniker, *Transportation on the Western Front 1914–1918* (London, 1937)

The Private Papers of Douglas Haig, 1914–1919, ed. Robert Blake (London, 1952)

Maj.-Gen. Sir F. Maurice, *The Life of General Lord Rawlinson*

Gen. Sir H. Gough, *Soldiering On* and *The Fifth Army*

B. Gardner, *Allenby* (London, 1965)

Sir Basil Liddell Hart, *A History of the World War*

A. H. Farrar-Hockley, *The Somme* (London, 1964)

General Jack's Diary, 1914–1918, ed. John Terraine

Capt. W. Grant Grieve and B. Newman, *Tunnellers*

A. Barrie, *War Underground*

E. G. D. Liveing, *Attack*

Siegfried Sassoon, *Memoirs of an Infantry Officer* (London, 1965)

John Masefield, *The Old Front Line*

H. A. Taylor, *Goodbye to the Battlefields*

P. Longworth, *The Unending Vigil* (London, 1967)

G. W. L. Nicholson, *The Fighting Newfoundlanders*

E. K. G. Sixsmith, *British Generalship in the Twentieth Century* (London, 1970)

A. E. Ashbolt, 'The Sociology of Trench Warfare 1914–1918', *British Journal of Sociology*, December 1968

John Harris, *Covenant with Death* (fiction) (London, 1969)

and many divisional, brigade, regimental and battalion histories

Index